Blazing the Neoliberal Trail

Blazing the Neoliberal Trail

Urban Political Development in the United States and the United Kingdom

Timothy P. R. Weaver

PENN

UNIVERSITY OF PENNSYLVANIA PRESS

PHILADELPHIA

Published by
University of Pennsylvania Press
Philadelphia, Pennsylvania 19104-4112
www.upenn.edu/pennpress

Printed in the United States of America
on acid-free paper

10 9 8 7 6 5 4 3 2 1

Library of Congress Cataloging-in-Publication Data
ISBN 978-0-8122-4782-4

Contents

Introduction

> The ideas of economists and political philosophers, both when they
> are right and when they are wrong, are more powerful than is
> commonly understood. Indeed the world is ruled by little else.
> Practical men, who believe themselves to be quite exempt from any
> intellectual influences, are usually the slaves of some defunct
> economist. Madmen in authority, who hear voices in the air, are
> distilling their frenzy from some academic scribbler of a few years
> back. I am sure that the power of vested interests is vastly exaggerated
> compared with the gradual encroachment of ideas.
>
> —John Maynard Keynes, *The General Theory of Employment,
> Interest, and Money,* 1936

As New Deal and Great Society liberalism and Keynesianism unraveled in
the 1970s amid a stagflationary malaise, a set of neoliberal ideas came to
dominate the political landscape in the United States and Britain. Those
who came to power at the turn of the 1980s looked to their favored academic scribblers whose ideas, they hoped, would provide solutions where
liberals informed by John Maynard Keynes and John Kenneth Galbraith
had ostensibly failed. Nowhere was this shift more sharply felt than in cities.
The most noted urban impact of the neoliberal turn was the reduction of
aid from central government.[1] But the incoming administrations of the
right under both Ronald Reagan and Margaret Thatcher also had ambitious
urban policy proposals that reflected their shared commitment to reconsti-
tuting the relationship between the state, the citizen, and the market. For
instance, they both offered the enterprise zone, a policy that symbolized
their commitment to market forces. In the United Kingdom, local institutions would be further transformed by the creation of urban development

corporations (UDCs). But while urban areas in the United Kingdom, such as London Docklands, were transformed along ideological lines from the top down, in American cities, such as Philadelphia, neoliberalization emerged as much from the quotidian practices of coalition politics as from the work of neoliberal ideologues.

By the mid-1990s, however, "new" Democrats and Labour Party politicians had taken control of the levers of power, heralding the prospect of a novel "third way."[2] On one hand, Bill Clinton and Tony Blair were keen to eschew the "big-government" image that had tarred previous Democratic administrations and Labour governments, while on the other, they claimed that their policies would provide an alternative to free-market individualism. Instead, rights would be balanced with responsibilities; hard-working people would be offered a hand up, not a "hand-out."[3] But while both Clinton and Blair were committed to significant investment in the public realm,[4] their respective urban policies had more in common with their Republican and Conservative predecessors than with previous generations from their own parties. As would be the case with Clinton's and Blair's economic and social policies, the New Democrats and New Labour developed urban policies that not only failed to reverse the significant cuts to cities of the 1980s but also characterized urban problems as primarily the result of moral failure and "social exclusion" rather than because of structural economic decline of a sort that might have been addressed through a reorientation of national economic policy, investment in infrastructure, and the promotion of advanced industry.[5] As such, their urban policies were far more closely aligned with neoliberal ideas than with those associated with Keynesian interventionism.[6] This is most striking in Clinton's Empowerment Zone/Enterprise Community program and with Blair's visions of an "urban renaissance." At worst, these policies did little more than consolidate their predecessors' policies; at best, they were inadequate attempts to ameliorate the deleterious effects of their macroeconomic policies, which accelerated deindustrialization, free trade, and growing inequality. Thus, while national urban policies of the 1980s were corollaries to neoliberal policy prescriptions in general, those of the mid-to-late 1990s reflected the partial accommodation of the putative center-left to those neoliberal ideas, which they clothed in progressive garb. In the realm of policy making, therefore, political development along neoliberal lines was ensured once the opportunity to forge an alternative course under Clinton and Blair was eschewed.

But ideas alone were not simply daubed onto a blank canvas.[7] Rather, to flourish, they had to take root in institutional settings from which political actors could fashion them into policy proposals and ultimately into concrete outcomes.[8] Hence, whatever their ideological commitments, politicians had to navigate their way through a thicket of institutional obstacles that shaped the degree to which policy change was possible.[9] This challenge is illuminated by viewing the American experience through a comparative lens. In the British context, centralized national political institutions, unitary government, and strong party discipline enabled policy makers to institute their ideas with relative ease as the rapid introduction of enterprise zones and urban development corporations reveals. However, in a story familiar to scholars of American political development, the institutional matrix in the United States proved impenetrable because those who opposed the scheme were able to use each bottleneck in the institutional structure to block change. Republican urban policy entrepreneurs were unable to construct the necessary political coalition to forge the political change they sought.[10] Over time, however, the enterprise zone coalition was steadily built, not least because federalism presented another avenue for enterprise zone proponents: the states. By the mid-1990s, more than 2,000 enterprise zone programs were in existence in forty states.

But the story told below is not simply a case of the top-down imposition of ideologically motivated neoliberal policies. Much work has already been done that examines the rise of the neoliberal project that either focuses purely on national or international politics or deals with the concept of neoliberalism abstractly.[11] In contrast, I provide a grounded account of how these policy innovations interacted with institutional structures and local trajectories of political-economic development to produce change in Philadelphia and London Docklands. Until recently, mainstream political scientists have neglected the city in political development. However, recent work, such as Richardson Dilworth's edited volume, *The City in American Political Development*, suggests that urban political analysis may be on the cusp of migrating from the margins of the discipline to resume a more prominent position.[12] This book contributes directly to this endeavor.

In Philadelphia, I argue that neoliberal ideas interacted with the slow-moving processes of deindustrialization, racial change, and the logic of coalition building. This produced a sometimes reluctant turn to pro-business techniques as the policy options open to Democratic mayors appeared to constrict during the 1980s. Meanwhile, in London Docklands, an activist state used the powers of government to dramatically reconfigure local political institutions in ways that local borough councils, activists, and ordinary residents were unable to resist. In both London and Philadelphia, the character of urban political development over the past four decades has limited significantly cities' ability to address the social and economic needs of their citizens.[13] Thus, while some scholars of American and British politics have argued that the retrenchment of the state under Thatcher and Reagan was limited,[14] I find that the cases of Philadelphia and London Docklands reveal that the neoliberal turn has resulted in a significant reduction in governing capacity and authority at the local level. Therefore, bringing the city into the analysis reveals locally occurring "durable shifts in governing authority"[15] that may not be evident at the national scale.

Thus, national urban policy in the United States and the United Kingdom, as well as urban political development in Philadelphia and London Docklands, provides political terrain for the three key contributions this book makes. First, it provides an account of the specific processes by which ideas take root among political elites and are rendered into policy proposals. Second, I show how the interaction of national and local institutional configurations and neoliberal ideas affects the pace and extent of change. Last, the urban-level cases illustrate how the battle to enhance the role of the market plays out in the urban trenches. There, the new political economy has produced enormous wealth for those in the financial and professional sectors while failing to provide adequate employment opportunities, living standards, or public services for the working class or the poor.

The remainder of this introductory chapter will lay out the logic of ideational political development and explain why, in certain circumstances, it offers a more compelling account of change than the principal alternative explanations. This leads to a brief discussion of neoliberalism and a preliminary assessment of the nature of the neoliberal turn. I will then discuss the implications of this study for the extant literature on urban politics. Finally, a short overview of the book will be provided.

The Logic of Ideational Political Development

Despite the recent growth of work on ideas and politics, there is little scholarly consensus as to the definition of ideas.[16] For Daniel Béland and Robert

Cox ideas are "causal beliefs," which involve a series of "discrete dimensions." They argue that ideas are products of cognition, which enable us to posit the relationship between people and material objects and provide "guides for action."[17] Clearly, Béland and Cox are correct that ideas, by necessity, are products of cognition. However, their notion that ideas are inherently about *causality* seems overly restrictive, for this would seem to rule out normative or categorical beliefs. Therefore, for me, ideas are normative, categorical, or causal beliefs. What is of greater concern than matters of definition, however, is the issue of how ideas become politically relevant.

In order for ideas to propel political development, the following four conditions must be met. The first is simply that a given policy idea needs to be present. The second necessary condition is that the policy idea needs to be clearly expressed by politically relevant actors so that it structures the debate surrounding the policy domain. Third, the policy needs to be adopted by key political officials who possess—or are likely to possess—the institutional tools of government. Fourth and finally, the ideationally induced policy needs to be introduced and institutionally embedded. An idea's "success" in terms of impact (although not necessarily the desired impact) would be achieved to the extent that policy changed *and* that it resisted rapid replacement. A central concern, however, is to consider the degree to which political institutions mediate ideationally defined policy innovations. In order to show convincingly that change is ideationally rather than materially driven, one must demonstrate that alternative explanations of a particular political development fail to explain the outcome in question or fail to capture as much of the shift as do ideational accounts.

Typically, social scientists consider the key drivers of change (or continuity) as falling into three categories: ideas, institutions, and interests.[18] Often, each of these categories is further subdivided, as Taylor and Hall do with respect to the "three new institutionalisms."[19] There are costs to separating these explanations given that they are all inextricably linked and may therefore be best studied in a single analytical frame.[20] However, for heuristic purposes, I will separate them out in order to clarify my argument, using various policy areas as examples.

Arguments that place interests at their heart assert that the neoliberal turn in urban policy, by which the burdens on business have eased, arose as a result of the demands of capital or because capital was able to coalesce with some other societal entity whose interests were mutually supportive.

Scholars such as William Goldsmith, for example, have argued that the enterprise zone idea "has been seized upon by some (sometimes consciously, to be sure) as a weapon for business in the struggle with labour over production costs."[21] Indeed, this is hardly an outlandish claim. In London Docklands, for example, the obvious beneficiary of enterprise zones and urban development corporations certainly has been capital (see Chapter 6).[22] However, as is shown in detail in Chapters 1 and 2, business in the United States and in the United Kingdom was at best split on the issue of enterprise zones and, at worst, opposed them outright as was the case (initially) with the National Federation of Independent Business in America and the Chamber of Commerce in Britain.

In light of these views, interest-based arguments that claim enterprise zone policy was created as a result of business-lobbying are not persuasive. Therefore, a more thorough investigation of the historical record is required. While it *became* the case that major business interests rallied around some neoliberal urban policy prescriptions after their introduction, capital was not the motive force. But while class-based interest group politics may not have been central to the creation of enterprise zones, the consequences of neoliberal urban policy have unquestionably been the restoration of class power and wealth in the hands of the extraordinarily wealthy.[23] What my research demonstrates, however, is that we cannot simply assume that these interests themselves determined the policy shift that occurred, nor that such a turn would have proved as robust as it did without a neoliberal ideological foundation. Thus, it was certainly the case that business eventually strengthened neoliberal policies over time, through a "positive feedback loop," a concept deployed by scholars who built on E. E. Schattschneider's insight that "new policies create a new politics."[24] However, even for this account to explain continuity and change, an institutional dimension is required.

The arrival of historical institutionalism represented a crucial development in the study of politics, as reflected in the creation of the subfield of American political development. A primary aim of this scholarship has been to "bring the state back in" to political analysis as a corrective to Marxist, rational-choice, and behavioralist tendencies in political science that often downplay the combined effects of institutions and ideational factors in shaping political continuity and change.[25] In the British context, Margaret Weir provides an institutional explanation of the acceptance of Keynesianism.[26] Meanwhile, numerous scholars of American political development have deployed historical institutionalist analysis to account for the growth of the American state,[27] the patchwork nature of the welfare state,[28] the emergence of the bureaucracy,[29] and institutional shifts in Congress.[30]

In respect of urban policy, the historical institutionalist tradition would predict that radical new policies such as enterprise zones are likely to encounter institutional friction as they permeate their way through granite-like political structures, especially in the British state with its permanent civil service packed with appointed representatives of the establishment. Indeed, Geoffrey Howe, the politician who introduced enterprise zones in the United Kingdom, harbored precisely these fears.[31] Moreover, some scholars have argued that "policy erosion" occurred precisely because of interdepartmental turf battles.[32] However, as Chapter 2 demonstrates, the Conservatives were able to radically reconstitute urban policy and institutions in a very short period of time. In the American context, it is clear that the separation of powers and divergent partisan control of the executive and legislative branches of government undermined urban policy change at the national level (see Chapter 1). Thus, institutional analysis is essential for explaining why the Thatcher government was able to achieve deeper policy change more quickly than its American counterpart. But what institutional accounts cannot explain is the emergence of neoliberal urban policy ideas in the first place or the process by which neoliberals persuaded others of their efficacy. As with other areas of political development, institutionalists tend to overpredict stability and underpredict change.[33] With interest-based arguments insufficient and institutionalist accounts necessary but not sufficient, an ideational lens is required to complete the picture.

Until recently, American political scientists have taken a dim view of ideational accounts of political phenomena. However, over the past two decades, we have witnessed a concerted effort to bring ideas "back in."[34] The profession's skepticism with respect to ideas is aptly captured in Paul Pierson's argument regarding welfare state retrenchment in the United States and the United Kingdom:

> Throughout this analysis, I have downplayed the independent role
> of ideas and learning processes in policy formation. In the politics
> of programmatic retrenchment, hostility toward public provision
> has been uniform among conservative policymakers and it has been

difficult to establish cases in which aspects of ideology or learning processes might explain why some programs survived and others did not. There were, however, considerable differences during the critical period in the assumptions guiding economic policy-making in the two countries.[35]

For Pierson, these differences are explained not by ideas but by "the particular context in which these governments operated."[36]

Along similar lines, Desmond King and Stewart Wood, in their work on the organizational basis for the neoliberal turn, maintain that even were one to establish a link between neoliberal ideas and the radical nature of the Thatcher government's agenda, one cannot simply "read off" the Tory policies "from the tenets of the ideology that underpins them." After all, to automatically jump to ideological explanations "ignores the ways in which policies *themselves* are informed by past policies, economic structures, and political expediency."[37]

In contrast to such skeptical views of ideas, Mark Blyth, in his persuasive account of the rise and fall of "embedded" liberalism in Sweden and the United States, avers that ideas can operate independently to structure interests, provide for institutional stability, and offer ways out of the uncertainty produced by major economic crises.[38] Rogers Smith's view of ideas is almost as radical. In his work on racial and political orders in American political development, Smith seeks to "place the analysis of 'ideas' and 'institutions' within a single analytical frame."[39] While Smith is loath to consider "ideational orders" as equivalent to "political orders," he does contend that "ideologies are constitutive elements of such orders."[40] Yet ideologies do not work on their own; rather, they "are always carried by organizations or sets of organizations within the coalition that constitutes a political order. . . . Ideas can produce political change only when particular identifiable political institutions, groups, and actors advance them."[41]

Finally, Peter Hall's analysis of British economic policy making between 1970 and 1989 suggests that an ideational account is required to explain the "radical shift from Keynesian to monetarist modes of economic regulation" by which "inflation replaced unemployment as the preeminent concern of policymakers."[42] For Hall, Margaret Thatcher's election in 1979 resulted in an intense break in economic policy through which the "settings of policy changed," and "the hierarchy of goals and sets of instruments employed to guide policy shifted radically."[43] These shifts were also accompanied by "substantial changes in the discourse employed by policymakers and in the analysis of the economy on which policy was based," that is, a "wholesale shift in policy paradigms."[44] While Hall acknowledges that Thatcher's election was crucial to this paradigmatic change, "the play of ideas was as important to the outcome as was the contest for power."[45]

The argument presented here is that urban policies such as enterprise zones represent paradigmatic change that cannot be understood without reference to ideas.[46] Their emergence in the United States and the United Kingdom cannot be readily explained by conventional interest-based arguments: they were not promoted by businesses, nor could they be said to have been a central part of the Republican or Conservative electoral strategy. Thus, while King and Wood are correct that it would be an inexcusable folly to ignore the "policies, economic structures, and political expediency," it may be appropriate to consider turning King and Wood on their heads to claim that it would be a mistake to try to read off the emergence of neoliberal policies by *only* considering these elements while assuming ideational explanations to be necessarily misleading.

In the United Kingdom, politicians motivated by neoliberal ideas, having gained control of the key institutions of the state, implemented enterprise zones and urban development corporations—themselves new neoliberal institutional forms. To be sure, without power (i.e., the control of state institutions), these ideas may not have come to fruition. But without these ideas, the changes documented below would not have occurred either. By way of contrast, the American institutional matrix presented roadblocks as well as avenues of opportunity. On one hand, the separation of powers among the three branches of government meant that Reagan encountered more veto points than did Thatcher, which ultimately undermined his repeated attempts to persuade Congress to pass his enterprise zone legislation. Yet, on the other hand, federalism enabled neoliberal policy entrepreneurs to pursue their urban policy goals at the state level of government. As in Britain, however, an ideational account is required in order to understand why these policies were considered desirable in the first instance, despite the ambivalence of business, and why Democrats became persuaded of their merits over time even though the evidence showed that they were not especially effective at reducing unemployment or generating growth.

This short discussion illustrates that Robert Lieberman's point, that ideas "give us motive but not opportunity," is correct.[47] Therefore, throughout the following chapters, ideas and institutions are seen as inter-linked, sometimes working in tandem, while at others pulling in opposite directions. In other moments and in other policy domains, material inter-ests undoubtedly advance political development. However, the striking fea-ture of the key urban policy shifts in the early 1980s is that ideas led the way.

But the focus on ideas is not pursued here simply to set the empirical record straight, although that is an important and worthwhile task. The additional reason for showing that the neoliberal turn had as much to do with ideology as with material forces is that such an understanding reveals the contingent nature of this shift. That it was not determined by the inevi-table demands of capital is crucial for the claim that there were alternatives then and that there are now. Historical institutionalists remind us that over time, the range of alternatives can become narrowed as new institutions and practices get "locked in" and interests become organized to defend changes they approve of, but this does not make change impossible. It does suggest, though, that change requires the construction of a new ideological worldview and a concomitant set of political strategies and institutional designs. This is not to say that change is easy or even likely; an ideological framework is neither quickly built nor easily dismantled. But it does suggest that the path taken was a path *chosen* from among many possibilities. The next section considers the key idea that launched the trajectory of urban political development since the 1970s: neoliberalism.

Neoliberalism as a Concept

Neoliberalism was the ideological dynamo that drove the most persuasive and consequential critiques of Keynesianism, the "postwar settlement," and New Deal liberalism and that provided the intellectual weapons that were deployed in the battles to secure major political and institutional change on both sides of the Atlantic. But although neoliberalism increasingly appears in social scientific and historical scholarship, neoliberalism "ap-pears to have become a rascal concept—promiscuously pervasive, yet inconsistently defined, empirically imprecise and frequently contested."[48] Moreover, the concept is all too often used pejoratively, which in turn has hampered scholarly efforts to contest definitions. Yet given the degree to which the term is used in scholarly and popular discourse, it is imperative to promote and propel debate surrounding its conceptualization. Moreover, since it captures more completely the current ideological climate and political economy than other terms such as *liberalism* and *conservatism*, *neoliberalism* must be demystified in order to make the concept tractable.

Therefore, I define *neoliberalism* as follows: a political-economic theory and rhetorical framework that rests on the notion that freedom, justice, and well-being are best guaranteed by a political-economic system, undergirded by the state, which promotes private property (including via privatization of state assets), open markets, and free trade and which privileges the interests of financial capital above all.[49] In practice, neoliberalization entails lowering tax rates on individual income, capital gains, and corporate profit; deregulation of property and financial markets; privatization or marketization of public services; cuts to downwardly redistributive transfers; and attacks on union power. As such, neoliberals rejected the ideas and institutions associated with New Deal and Great Society liberalism in the United States, the "postwar settlement" in the United Kingdom, and continental European social democracy and were determined to dismantle them.[50] As I will show below, while neoliberal ideas failed to make their mark on institutions such as Social Security or promote the elimination of the National Health Service, they did significantly shape urban political development, which reflected a genuine ideational and practical shift in respect to economic policy and governance.

The Nature of the Neoliberal Turn

There is considerable debate about the extent to which the political-economic policy shifts that occurred in the late 1970s and early 1980s represented a clean break with the past. In other words, did the neoliberal turn result in consequential political development? Scholars such as Paul Pierson think not, while others like Stephen Skowronek are ambivalent.[51] Yet compared with their respective parties' governing priorities, prime ministers in Britain and presidents in the United States have followed very different goals in economic, social, and urban policy than their pre-1980s predecessors. As Judith Stein shows, both Presidents Nixon *and* Johnson operated in a political context in which high unemployment was viewed unacceptable to both parties.[52] Meanwhile, both Labour *and* Conservative governments of the 1970s used Keynesian techniques to try to control inflation and promote growth. One should not overemphasize the degree of agreement, however. Indeed, as Margaret Weir's work illustrates, the American commitment to full employment was never sufficiently institutionalized, and the version of Keynesianism the United States pursued fell far short of fulfilling the social democratic goals of some of its advocates.[53] Nevertheless, Weir notes that "although pronouncements of a 'Reagan Revolution' were certainly overblown, policymaking during the two Reagan administrations did manifest a clear shift in the role of government."[54] Therefore, as the urban political innovations showed, if the 1970s was the pivotal decade and the 1980s the age of fracture,[55] the 1990s and 2000s were the decades of neoliberal consolidation.[56]

In each period, the parties behaved like planets in two different solar systems. In the immediate postwar period, they orbited a Keynesian sun, with the Democratic planet's orbit passing closer than the Republican one. The 1970s and 1980s represented a period of relative chaos while the Keynesian sun spluttered into extinction and a neoliberal star began to pull the Republican orb into its force field. Over time, the Democratic planet moved into the outer reaches of the neoliberal solar system and was gradually dragged in closer. In both periods, although each party's paths were different, each party's trajectory overlapped—this is the area of consensus. Thus, while it is obvious that the Clinton and Blair eras were not merely the 1980s repackaged, it is clear that the policies of the New Democrats and New Labour were different in a number of regards from the policies of both parties between the 1940s and 1970s and had much in common with the Reagan and Thatcher administrations of the 1980s.

Thus, the 1980s did indeed herald a key break with the past, although the pressure for such a shift had been building for decades.[57] But did this necessarily entail a shift in a neoliberal direction? Scholars such as Pierson and Skocpol argue that American politics has indeed been transformed, but they see this as reflecting the rise of *conservative* administrations that engage in ever more "activist" government, which they consider a contradiction.[58] Similar points have been made specifically with respect to urban policy innovation, which also involved significant state intervention. Efforts by supposedly "conservative" or neoliberal governments to radically reconfigure state institutions seem to present a paradox.[59] After all, radical change and state intervention seem antithetical to Burkean conservatism and to Hayekian neoliberalism. For the former, change should be gradual while the latter argues that the state's role in the economy ought to be reduced.

The argument presented here is that the nature of governance ushered in by Reagan and Thatcher is indeed incompatible with Burkean conservatism but does not necessarily contradict the central aim of neoliberalism, which is to promote markets and private ownership. Thus, for neoliberals, there is no contradiction in state intervention per se. Rather, the key is the behavior of the state. Here the goal is not the destruction of the state but rather its *reorientation*. To the extent that the state intervenes to promote markets, privilege capital, and resist claims on private property, it is a most welcome weapon in the neoliberal armory.[60] As Jamie Peck points out, both F. A. Hayek and Milton Friedman were clear that the state played a key role in neoliberal ideology.[61] Indeed, Friedman was at pains to show how neoliberalism was far more pragmatic than the "naïve ideology" that characterized nineteenth-century liberalism: "In place of the understanding that laissez-faire is the means to achieve [the goal of individual freedom], neoliberalism proposes that it is *competition* that will lead the way. . . . The state will police the system, it will establish the conditions favorable to competition and prevent monopoly, it will provide a stable monetary framework, and relieve acute poverty and distress. Citizens will be protected against the state, since there exists a free private market, and the competition will protect them from one another."[62] In a similar vein, Hayek argued in *The Road to Serfdom* that "it is important not to confuse opposition to . . . . planning with a dogmatic *laissez-faire* attitude. . . . Planning and competition can be combined only by planning *for* competition, not by planning *against* competition. . . . The planning against which all our criticism is directed is solely the planning against competition."[63] One could not imagine a more apt description of neoliberal urban policy since the 1980s.

These quotations bring into sharp relief the degree to which neoliberalism is in tension with both classical liberalism and what became known as "New Deal liberalism" in the United States. At its most expansive, this latter view was articulated by Franklin Delano Roosevelt in his "second bill of rights," delivered as part of the 1944 State of the Union address. In his speech, Roosevelt outlined his vision of social citizenship, which involved a contract between the state and the citizen by which governmental authority would be deployed to guarantee, as a matter of right, protection from the vagaries of the market.[64]

Among the rights enumerated were the right to work and have decent pay and standards of living for industrial and agricultural workers; the right to protection from "unfair competition"; the right "of every family to a decent home"; the right to "adequate medical care"; "the right to adequate protection from the economic fears of old age, sickness, accident, and unemployment"; and the "right to a good education." These ideals were fulfilled only in part in the United States, but the principle that government should intervene to ensure some level of employment and social protection did become institutionalized and became broadly accepted by all presidents until Reagan and by governing majorities in Congress, certainly until the mid-1970s. As such, it is relatively straightforward to identify how, in theory and often, but not always, in practice, neoliberalism departs from New Deal liberalism.

Finally, the shift in urban, social, and economic policy in the United States that began in the late 1970s is not simply an American phenomenon. The transatlantic comparisons of urban policy and between Philadelphia and London Docklands reveal the degree to which, although the paths of change have differed, the ultimate destination is remarkably similar. Thus, we should think of the past four decades less as the "Age of Reagan"[65] and more as an international political transformation inspired by neoliberal ideas and propelled by the interests of capital.

The Implications of the Neoliberal Turn for Urban Politics

The urban policies that emerged since the late 1970s, their concrete institutional manifestations, and their ramifications for citizens' well-being are rooted in this set of neoliberal ideas, which came to form the "common-sense" understanding of the urban crisis. Many scholars of urban politics have illustrated the degree to which "developmental," pro-market elites have come to dominate urban regimes in recent decades. Those working in the neo-Marxist vein find the locus of these changes in the material, macroeconomic shift from a Fordist economic mode to an "entrepreneurial" or neoliberal one.[66] According to this view, elected politicians are either unwilling or unable to resist the material demands for the creation of "business-friendly" climates. As Jonathan Davies puts it, "The force unifying the capitalist class is the imperative to accumulate in order to compete."[67] For these scholars, ideas play no more than the secondary role of providing a post hoc justification for material interests.[68]

John Logan and Harvey Molotch's powerful analysis of growth machines pays less attention to ideological and macroeconomic trends and instead focuses on the contingent alliances formed between business and political elites.[69] The dynamo in their estimation, however, is the materialist demand for profit via growth. For them, it is crucial for local publics to "favor growth and support the ideology of value free development."[70] Yet, they see pro-growth arguments as *merely legitimating ideology*, not accurate descriptions of reality."[71] Similarly, Clarence Stone argues that "upper-strata" interests have structural advantages afforded to them by the fact that urban elites require their support in order to effect change.[72]

In another major contribution to urban neoliberalization, Jason Hackworth offers more sustained discussion of ideology vis-à-vis neoliberalism, rightly pointing out that *both* structural constraints and ideological shifts have moved the "boundaries of urban governance"[73] and that "neoliberalism has become naturalized as the 'only' choice available to cities in the United States and elsewhere."[74] Ultimately, however, Hackworth seems to pull back from his initial commitment to the independent role of ideas. For example, when exploring why cities hew to a neoliberal path, he ultimately roots his explanation in institutional and material terms: "I argue that the shift to entrepreneurial or neoliberal urban governance is less the result of an organic shift to the right made in the face of capital flight than it is the result of an institutionally regulated (and policed) disciplining of localities. That is, the central justifications of Keynesian managerialism have disappeared . . . because of an institutionally rigid set of ideological constraints *imposed by finance capital*."[75] Meanwhile, urban theorists working in the public choice tradition, such as Paul Peterson, suggest that a city's economic policies are conditioned by its position in an inherently competitive system where the city, without the sovereignty that national states enjoy, is forced to pursue a business-friendly strategy in a bid to generate a competitive advantage over its rivals and bolster its tax revenues.

By contrast, Jamie Peck's recent work does afford ideas a more central role. However, for him, neoliberalism as an ideology "has only ever existed in its 'impure' form, indeed *can* only exist in messy hybrids."[76] Nevertheless, he demonstrates persuasively the crucial function of think tanks in promoting policy innovation and institutional change. Yet his account does not go far enough in tracing out concretely how the production of ideas in think tanks results in policy outcomes in practice. In this sense, political development is "black boxed," with think tanks providing the ideational inputs and neoliberal policies the outputs. Following Peck's recommendation that "concretely grounded accounts of the process must be chiseled out of the interstices of state/market configurations,"[77] this book aims to show how neoliberal ideology provides the necessary glue to bind electoral coalitions and to hold them together for the task of governing, paying special attention to the processes by which ideas are used to frame problems, shape policy solutions, and bring about institutional transformation and political development.

As the case of Philadelphia highlights, the neoliberalization of urban politics is rarely a local affair. Rather, it is also profoundly shaped by national- and international-level material forces, some of which may be ideologically inspired, others not. This insight suggests that it is crucial to avoid the temptation to reduce urban politics simply to what occurs in cities.[78] The most direct of these influences were the cuts to federal urban spending that began under Jimmy Carter but were accelerated by the Reagan administration.[79] As federal aid receded, many state governments failed to step into the breach, not least because the proportion of state legislators from urban areas has fallen since the 1960s.[80] While the specific effect on local urban politics varies among cities depending on local circumstances, the overall impact of such massive reductions of federal aid has been the adoption of "entrepreneurial" activities, which are directed toward expanding the revenue base. These include those very policies aimed at generating a "business-friendly" environment, the privatization of city services, and the erosion of the local welfare state. This has two important implications for our understanding of the urban politics literature. First, it suggests that Peterson's "city limits" thesis is most relevant only under a *specific* set of historically contingent circumstances, which often result from such policies as cuts to federal urban spending. As such, it cannot be simply taken as read that cities in a market system will "naturally" follow this logic. As the example of Philadelphia shows, there has been significant variation over time as to the degree to which the city has assumed an entrepreneurial stance. Therefore, the following chapters examine when, how, and why this variation occurs, paying particular attention to the interaction between national political and economic trends and local coalition building.

Second, such historical variation in turn suggests that a city's ability to bargain with business is determined in part by the prevailing economic and urban policies from higher levels of government.[81] Therefore, the particular political-economic *order*, bounded in time and articulated in place, is likely to be crucial. The neoliberal order is especially inimical to the urban working class and poor and even to the middle classes who depend on public services because it tolerates high levels of unemployment, pushes responsibility for the poor down to lower levels of government, and seeks to erode the local (and national) welfare state. In contrast, the neoliberal pattern of development is a boon to corporations and real estate interests, since property-led development becomes one of the few tools available for enhancing revenues. As such, it is crucial to pay attention to the interplay between macroeconomic policy and urban policy at the federal level, on one hand, and local urban politics, on the other, since the former can profoundly shape the capacity and authority of cities to address the needs and demands of their citizens. National trends can also shape the degree to which business enjoys a privileged position vis-à-vis the local state. The evidence below suggests that our understanding of urban politics will be greatly enhanced through focusing on the influence of such political-economic orders.[82]

But since the character of urban politics is fundamentally rooted in local-level coalition building, any satisfactory account of urban political development must, of course, devote significant attention to local factors as well. The Philadelphia story highlights the racial politics involved in the emergence of the alliance between African Americans and business to promote neoliberalism in the 1980s. As such, this book charts explicitly the interplay between the local and national forces and argues that only by doing so can we arrive at a compelling account of urban political development. My emphasis on historical analysis chimes with the emerging trend among urban scholars in the United States to locate city politics in the broader temporal and spatial context of American political development.[83]

Furthermore, the case of London Docklands helps to clarify the role cities play in advancing the national project of neoliberalization. As the site of the first enterprise zone and UDC, Docklands helped to blaze a trail for the comprehensive assault on the postwar settlement that was to come later in the 1980s and in the 1990s. Consistent with the work of David Harvey,[84] Susan Fainstein,[85] and Neil Smith,[86] I argue that places like Docklands stand at the cutting edge of the neoliberal project, their transformation being central to the emergence of the neoliberal order, as the state continues to "roll out" neoliberal institutions.[87] In contrast to the work of Sue Brownill and Mike Raco, I maintain that New Labour did not fundamentally depart from this trajectory.[88] While there are elements of "hybridity"—that is, a combination of urban policies that reflect both Labour's social democratic roots and the Conservatives' neoliberal priorities—this view underestimates the degree to which New Labour has advanced neoliberalism programmatically and naturalized it ideologically through institutions such as urban regeneration companies and policies that promote "urban renaissance" via state-led gentrification.[89]

Finally, the cases of London Docklands and Philadelphia are used to sketch out two distinct processes of the neoliberalization of urban policy and governance. The first, *neoliberalism by design*, describes a process by which national and local elites (political and/or business) harness the power of central state institutions to impose a neoliberal blueprint. Under such conditions, elites, relatively unencumbered by the need to bargain with adversaries, are able to construct institutions that bear a strong resemblance to the original ideological vision. The rapid and radical transformation of Docklands reflects this pattern of political development. By contrast, *neoliberalism by default* emerges when the logic of coalition building, financial collapse, and ideological constriction propels urban policy and local political economies in a pro-market direction, even when the principal political actors may not set out as ardent neoliberals. Philadelphia's political development from the late 1970s is illustrative of this process.

Therefore, the extent to which *neoliberalism by design* or *default* is likely to emerge is conditioned by a number of factors, of which the configuration and relationship of national and subnational institutions is central. This conceptual distinction therefore helps to explain why and how neoliberalism assumes the kind of variegated character highlighted by Brenner, Peck, and Theodore.[90] The comparisons both of the United Kingdom with the United States and of London Docklands with Philadelphia provide maximal variation along two important dimensions: with respect to executive control of policy (high in the United Kingdom, low in the United States) and as regards the relationship between central government and local authorities (strong in the United Kingdom, weak in the United States). Thus, we can chart how the pace, extent, and character of neoliberalization are shaped by the ways in which these different institutional contexts shape the channels through which almost identically articulated neoliberal ideas flowed.

Thus, the analysis offered below grounds the neoliberalization of urban policy and politics in its historical political-economic context, examining closely the ways in which ideas, interests, and institutions—at both the national and local levels—combine to propel this project through time and across space.

Overview

This book is divided into two parts. Part I explores national urban policy development in the United States and the United Kingdom. Chapter 1 focuses on enterprise zones, the signature urban policy of the Reagan administration. While enterprise zones failed to receive federal approval, they proliferated through the states in the 1980s and attracted the support of Democrats. This chapter argues that these developments reveal the first stage of neoliberal realignment of American politics. Chapter 2 details how, in contrast to the U.S. experience, enterprise zones were introduced in Britain almost immediately after the Conservative Party came to power in 1979. In the United Kingdom, lawmakers pursued the policy because they thought it would help persuade friends and foes alike that their ideas worked. Chapter 2 further examines how ideologically informed policy entrepreneurs used the institutions of state to effect a radical change in urban policy during the 1980s. Both chapters argue that policies such as the enterprise zone were articulations of neoliberal ideas that informed the broader political agenda and governing philosophy of the Reagan and Thatcher governments, which shaped their efforts to transform the relationship between citizens, the state, and the market. Particularly in the United Kingdom, these policy ideas were seen as a way of demonstrating the efficacy of pro-market approaches to economic development.

Chapter 3, the final chapter of Part I, also uses the lens of urban policy to examine the contribution of the center-left to the transatlantic neoliberalization of the state as the Democrats and the Labour Party came to power in the mid-1990s. It maintains that policies such as the Clinton administration's empowerment zones reflected the degree to which neoliberal ideology came to constrict the range of policy options that were considered politically feasible. But Bill Clinton and Tony Blair were not simply trapped in the neoliberal cage; they actively reinforced and promoted further neoliberalization.

Part II moves from the university campuses and corridors of power, where neoliberal ideas germinated, took root, and bloomed into policy, into the neoliberal trenches: the cities in which these ideas came to life and became concrete. As a result, I complement the contributions of scholars of neoliberalism whose work considers neoliberalism in abstract terms or in national-level settings. Chapters 4 and 5 are devoted to a careful analysis of Philadelphia's political development since the early 1950s.

In order to understand the pro-business bias in Philadelphia's local urban policy, which emerged in the 1980s, we must place Philadelphia's development in political, economic, and ideological context and chart the interplay between national urban policies and local urban politics over time while acknowledging the independent and interactive elements of both. In this rendering, the demands of capital are necessary but not sufficient conditions for the neoliberal transformation.

Chapter 4 charts the processes by which a particular sequence of slow-moving phenomena—deindustrialization and the influx of working-class African Americans—intertwine with rapid, ideologically informed cuts to federal aid during the 1980s. These national shifts in turn interact with local political strategies to produce Philadelphia's pro-developmental governing apparatus. This regime rested on a coalition between African Americans and business who backed locally based enterprise zones. However, the benefits of political incorporation did not improve conditions for blacks as the city's governing capacity was eroded. As such, I argue that it is impossible to discuss the political-economic transformation of urban areas wrought by neoliberalism without discussing the impact of race. As Adolph Reed Jr. points out, often "the black regime comes to power within a local system already organized around a pro-growth framework."[91] This was certainly true of Philadelphia, where the alliance between African Americans and business, undergirded by shared ideology and mutual hostility toward the established Philadelphia machine, played a central role in creating the city's pro-growth policies.

Chapter 5 explores Philadelphia's adjustment to the wrenching changes of the 1990s under the city's New Democrat mayor, Ed Rendell, who helped secure the city's business-friendly reputation. Services were privatized, unions defeated, and deficits reduced. Meanwhile, the city bifurcated along racial, class, and ethnic lines. Empowerment zones—adopted with great fanfare—did little to address rising inequality, a hallmark of neoliberalism. Philadelphia's experience during this period reflects the transformation of the American political economy more broadly, as the shift from manufacturing to services was completed.

The result of these processes has been a city deeply divided along class and racial lines. The benefits from the bursts of economic growth in the 1980s and the long expansion of the 1990s did not merely trickle down but were filtered through a series of political institutions at the federal, state, and local scales that exacerbated existing inequalities between the city and the suburbs and created new inequalities within urban places. In short, neoliberal policies have distinct urban characteristics that need to be studied in order to understand the full significance of the neoliberal turn.

Finally, Chapter 6 examines the emergence of neoliberal institutions, such as enterprise zones and the unelected London Docklands Development Corporation (LDDC), which transformed London Docklands. The creation of the LDDC, a nondemocratic institution that assumed the land and planning powers of elected and accountable local authorities, shows how durable shifts in governing authority can occur at lower levels of government with consequential effects. The glittering skyscrapers that house major financial institutions are testament to the extent of change that has occurred. In a recurrent theme, however, New Labour made little progress in addressing the pockets of deprivation that stand cheek-by-jowl with these monuments to neoliberal transformation.

In both Philadelphia and London Docklands, the explosion of wealth at the top of the income distribution, alongside stagnating median incomes, high levels of unemployment, rising inequality, and endemic poverty, all signify this shift. National-level data, however, obscure the degree of these trends. For example, during the 1990s, in both the United Kingdom and the United States, national rates of unemployment and poverty fell while median incomes rose. As illustrated below, however, in Philadelphia and Docklands, median household income fell while unemployment and poverty increased. Indeed, Philadelphia is not unique in this regard.[92] Thus, the study of cities is necessary to fully comprehend the ramifications of the neoliberal turn for citizens' well-being. While recent work on inequality alerts us to the incredible concentration of wealth in the top 1 percent of the population, a disaggregated, urban-level view reveals the flipside to this discovery and thus completes the picture.[93]

In the late 1970s, the left and center-left struggled to articulate a coherent response to the transatlantic malaise. National economies were sagging under the weight of stagflation while deindustrialization and population loss ravaged the cities. The Democratic and Labour Parties were thrown out of office as the public looked for alternatives. Both the incoming Reagan and Thatcher governments arrived already well schooled in neoliberal ideas. They used these ideas to fashion policies for the inner cities that would, at different speeds and in various forms, fundamentally alter urban institutions and capacities. This is a story of how these ideas worked their way through governing institutions to radically reconfigure the relationship between the state, citizen, and the market.

The Neoliberalization
of National Urban Policy

Chapter 1

Losing the Battle but Winning the War: The Story of the Federal Enterprise Zone Program That Never Was: 1980–1992

> It is time for us to find out if two of the most dynamic and
> constructive forces known to man—free enterprise and the profit
> motive—can be brought into play where government bureaucracy
> and social programs have failed.
>   —Ronald Reagan, Message to Congress, March 1982

As the Reagan administration's flagship urban policy, enterprise zones deserve scrutiny. Informed by the ideas of neoliberal economists and political philosophers, enterprise zones appeared in five State of the Union addresses and in presidential debates, were adopted by President George H. W. Bush, and were promoted by all three candidates in the 1992 presidential election. Yet, they were not enacted by Congress in any substantial form. The story of the abortive struggle to pass federal legislation to create enterprise zones during the Reagan and Bush years is one that distills many of the arguments, battles, and paradoxes of the neoliberal remaking of American social and economic policy. Most important, it charts the gradual shift in thinking toward neoliberal urban policy on the part of politicians, the press, and political parties and interest groups, on the right and the left, which in many ways reflects the ideological reorientation of American politics more generally. In particular, the battle of ideas regarding America's urban woes mirrored broader debates about the appropriate role of the state and the market across an array of policy domains.

Given that the only federal enterprise zone legislation enacted merely gave the Department of Housing and Urban Development (HUD) the power to designate zones but offered little in the way of deregulation or tax incentives, one might be tempted to conclude that this is an example that supports the argument that the Reagan Revolution achieved far less than is often stated,[1] another example of successful Democratic congressional action to proscribe Republican efforts to reduce the size of government. However, to stop the clock at 1988 or even 1992 would be to miss the ultimate effect of the enterprise zone story: the passage of the Empower-ment Zone/Enterprise Communities Act of 1993. Moreover, to conclude that the failure to enact full-blooded enterprise zones indicates the absence of consequential shifts in elite thinking would be too glib. This chapter will show how, despite this failure, the battle over enterprise zones in the 1980s and early 1990s resulted in a number of key victories on the part of neolib-erals disguised in part by President George H. W. Bush's veto of legislation in 1992 that would have established enterprise zones. Indeed, fine-grained analysis of archival materials, congressional hearings, co-sponsorships of bills, and personal interviews with key players, reveals that support for enterprise zones, which initially was almost totally dominated by Republi-cans, became increasingly widespread and bipartisan in character between 1980 and 1983, then waned in the mid-1980s, before resurfacing with stronger support than ever. The culmination of this effort was passage of the 1992 Enterprise Zone Tax Incentives Act.[2]

The central argument of this chapter is that the growing popularity of enterprise zones presents two paradoxes: support for the policy broadened and deepened over the course of the 1980s and early 1990s despite a burgeon-ing body of empirical evidence that cast doubt on its effectiveness and, sec-ond, business—the ostensible beneficiaries of enterprise zones—did not initially promote them. Institutional and interest-based arguments alone (or even in combination) are insufficient to the task of solving this puzzle. Rather, these paradoxes are resolved through a focus on the role of ideas, without which these apparent inconsistencies cannot be rendered intelligible. Indeed, in order to understand why enterprise zone legislation was intro-duced at all, an ideational dimension is required. In the case of enterprise zones, neoliberal ideas, promoted by political entrepreneurs and ideologically driven institutions, provided an ideational "blueprint" for urban policy.[3]

This chapter will identify the sources of the enterprise zone idea itself and situate them in their institutional context. I will then explicate briefly the central features of the enterprise zone concept before discussing the legislative history and sketching the coalitions that formed around the enterprise zone issue. Finally, I will summarize the key scholarly evaluations of various state-level enterprise zone experiments, which serve as a launching pad to address the question as to why enterprise legislation ultimately received passage in the face of empirical evidence that cast doubt on its effectiveness. Before an explicit examination of the enterprise zone's policy trajectory, it is necessary to place it in historical and political-economic context and to consider where the enterprise zones fitted into the Reagan administration's most consequential urban policy: reductions in federal aid to cities.

Urban Policy in the "Age of Fracture"

Amid the upheavals of the 1970s, the American economy lurched from one stagflationary crisis to the next. During this period, political elites groped for solutions to the country's apparent malaise. This "pivotal decade"[4] heralded an "age of fracture" in which shared notions of social solidarity, collective institutions, and cultural commitments gave way as a new set of ideas arose that stressed the primacy of markets, cut adrift from their institutional moorings, and wherein individuals were cast as rational, utility-maximizing egoists.[5] The dissemination of these ideas, which had been in existence for decades, was greatly enhanced by the mobilization of big business, which took significant steps in the 1970s especially to underwrite the production of neoliberal ideas that chimed with their interests.[6] As both Daniel Rodgers and Judith Stein agree, this shift is most obviously detected in the realm of economic policy.

While it would be wrong to suggest that there was full-fledged bipartisan consensus around intervention in the economy along Keynesian lines in the three decades following the end of the Second World War, there was considerable support for government intervention in the economy to promote economic growth and to pursue full employment.[7] Perhaps most famously, Republican president Richard Nixon declared in January 1971 that "I am now a Keynesian in economics."[8] Indeed, this posture was reflected in his 1972 budget, which called for expansionary fiscal and monetary policy to promote full employment. Indeed, as part of his plan, Nixon proposed to boost federal revenue sharing for states and cities and to increase spending on the administration's Family Assistance Plan.

But by the time Nixon's successor, Gerald Ford, entered office, inflation had begun to replace unemployment as the preeminent economic challenge. In an address to Congress, Ford described inflation as "public enemy number one" and declared that "we must whip inflation right now."[9] Yet, like his British counterparts of the mid-1970s, Ford's proposed remedies bore the hallmarks of Keynesianism rather than monetarism. He announced that controls would be imposed by his Council on Wage and Price Stability in the public sector and requested wage restraint in the private sector. While Ford argued that "prudent monetary restraint is essential," he had secured assurances from the Federal Reserve that "the supply of money and credit will expand sufficiently to meet the needs of our economy and that in no event will a credit crunch occur."[10]

As in the United Kingdom, which grappled with very similar problems in the 1970s (see Chapter 2), it was an administration of the center-left that first drifted in a neoliberal direction. Although inflation had fallen following Ford's "Whip Inflation Now" speech from 12.3 percent in December 1974 to 4.9 percent in 1976, by the end of 1978, inflation stood at 9 percent and was rising fast. Thus, President Carter came to office in 1977 as the economic consensus reached a breaking point. Ultimately, Carter set the stage for the embrace of monetarism through the appointment of Paul Volcker as chairman of the Federal Reserve in August 1979. Shortly thereafter, Volcker established targets for monetary growth and raised interest from 11 percent to a peak of 21 percent in 1981. Volcker's monetarist techniques to lance the inflationary boil worked but did so at the price of recession and mass unemployment.

Similar trends were evident regarding urban policy. While federal spending from the New Deal to Great Society had delivered massive increases in federal support for cities, by the mid-1970s, urban aid had reached its zenith.[11] As with his economic policy, President Carter's urban policy reflects his presidency's fragmented and contradictory posture.[12] Although Carter introduced the Urban Development Action Grants (UDAG) and generated increased aid for cities via the Comprehensive Employment Training Act (CETA) programs and the Community Development Block Grant (CDBG), "by the time Carter left office he seemed to be abandoning urban policy altogether."[13] Indeed, his 1979 and 1980 budgets significantly reduced aid to cities in real terms.[14] Moreover, Carter's Presidential Commission on the

National Agenda for the 1980s, which reported shortly before Ronald Reagan took office in 1981, suggested that many older industrial cities were outmoded and increasingly irrelevant as the global economy was transformed. The most responsible course of action, the report maintained, was to facilitate rather than resist this process of change.[15]

But while the tide had turned under Carter, the Reagan administration articulated a direct repudiation of liberalism and offered a more coherent reorientation of urban policy along neoliberal lines. As Reagan acknowledged, his critique of government and his commitment to market forces were grounded in the ideas of neoliberal intellectuals: "There are so many people and institutions who come to mind for their role in the success we celebrate tonight. Intellectual leaders like Russell Kirk, Friedrich Hayek, Henry Hazlitt, Milton Friedman, James Burnham, Ludwig von Mises—they shaped so much of our thoughts."[16] Moreover, correspondence between President Reagan and Milton Friedman not only reflected his admiration for Friedman but also signaled his role in influencing policy and executive personnel. Reagan thanked Friedman for his help in "developing policy recommendations, proposing appropriate personnel." He went on to remark that "we realize that we have only begun our program, and that its success depends on the continued support and energy of those who, like you, have done so much to ensure the success of our first steps."[17]

The influence of Reagan's "intellectual leaders" was immediately apparent. His administration's macroeconomic policies, grounded in neoliberal interpretations of America's economic and social differences, focused on monetarism, deregulation, and tax cuts. The material impact of the drastic increases in interest rates caused by monetarism was recession and unemployment, which rose above 10 percent in 1982. This pattern almost precisely corresponds to the political-economic shift in the United Kingdom under Margaret Thatcher's Conservative government.

In respect of urban policy, neoliberal ideas were applied in the starkest terms. Eschewing all responsibility for unemployment in America's great cities, Reagan told a press conference in 1981 that residents "should vote with their feet" and leave to look for work.[18] Moreover, the Reagan administration's cuts to urban aid were justified on the basis that "the private market is more efficient than federal program administrators in allocating dollars."[19] Therefore, cities would have to compete to attract private investment while the costs associated with poverty and unemployment grew. To be sure, when Reagan entered office, he inherited high rates of urban poverty and unemployment that were grounded in long-run difficulties produced by deindustrialization and declining productivity. Still, since the 1930s, the deleterious effects of these processes had been blunted by countercyclical Keynesian urban spending and through the creation of categorical urban grants from the 1960s onward.[20] However, Reagan's macroeconomic stance aggravated these trends significantly, and his withdrawal of federal aid to cities exacerbated urban hardship still further. While not all of Reagan's intended cuts to urban areas were secured, between 1980 and 1990, federal grants to cities were cut by 42 percent, the equivalent of $46 billion in constant 2012 dollars.[21]

Buttressing these cuts were arguments that government spending on cities was the *cause* of urban problems. As Reagan's treasury secretary, William Simon, wrote in a foreword to Robert Poole's *Cutting Back City Hall*, "People have been bamboozled for too long into believing the myths that government holds the keys to the economic kingdom and that government alone serves the public interest."[22] The insight of Poole's study, argued Simon, was that through tax cuts and private provision of "so-called public goods," a city could actually "*improve* service and make it much more *responsive* to citizen desires."[23] Thus, he claimed that the lives of urban populations would be improved if their local governments had less money to spend on services since cities would be forced to harness the potential of the private sector to provide for citizen well-being. But the potential for a private-sector initiative to revive cities was also central to a more ambitious urban policy innovation of the 1980s: the enterprise zone.

The British Are Coming

Like many neoliberal ideas, the enterprise zone idea enjoyed initial support from a limited number of political elites from across the political spectrum, although it was primarily associated with the right. This provided the policy with the hue of bipartisan approval. Moreover, the heritage of the enterprise zone has a geographical dimension whose pathways lead as much to the United Kingdom as to the United States. The central cast of characters who promoted the enterprise zone idea on the transatlantic stage included British geographer and erstwhile socialist Sir Peter Hall, Conservative Chancellor of the Exchequer Sir Geoffrey Howe, and Heritage Foundation policy analyst

Stuart Butler, another Briton. Taken together, this triumvirate is largely responsible for the idea's introduction to the Anglo-American scene.

The idea is commonly identified as the brainchild of the British urban planner Sir Peter Hall. As a socialist and former chairman of the Fabian Society, Hall's advocacy of "free zones" received much attention following his 1977 address to the Royal Town Planning Institute. Hall argued that such zones, based on "fairly shameless free enterprise," were required to arrest the decline of inner-city areas in the manufacturing towns and cities of the United States and the United Kingdom.[24] These zones would be "free of . . . taxation, social services, industrial and other regulations. Bureaucracy would also be kept to an absolute minimum; so would personal and corporate taxation."[25] This environment, Hall averred, would promote "a new kind of enterprise in our countries: a low-skill, low-wage, but highly innovative kind of economy that competes successfully with the newly industrializing countries on their own terms."[26] Hall suggested that "we look to the model provided by the real economic success stories of the 1960s and 1970s—Taiwan, Hong Kong and Singapore. We would try to recreate, in selected areas of British cities, the same spirit of unbridled enterprise that has characterized those economies."[27]

Hall's radical departure from the cross-party consensus, which rested on various forms of state intervention rather than withdrawal, was inextricably linked to his growing anxiety about the state of the British economy under the Labour Party and the rise of trade union militancy: "I was beginning to have rather serious doubts, you could say quasi-religious doubts, in the late 70s about the way we were going, in particular in terms of Labour politics. . . . There was a feeling that the Labour Party in particular was totally in the hands of the trade union barons. . . . Many, many people felt that the country was coming to a literal standstill. This caused me to go very blue sky. And it was in a way anticipating Thatcherite policies."[28] Given the extensive influence of Hall's ideas, it is ironic that his "blue sky" thinking was something of a flight of fancy: "I wrote this paper slightly tongue in cheek, but slightly seriously, to say this was a model which seemed to work there [in Hong Kong]."[29] Moreover, he "did not expect anyone to take this seriously in policy terms," so he was "surprised when Geoffrey Howe called to have lunch!"[30]

At the time, Geoffrey Howe was the shadow chancellor of Margaret Thatcher's official opposition to Harold Wilson's embattled Labour government. Howe would later go on to become Chancellor of the Exchequer when Thatcher's Conservative Party won office in 1979. Just days after Howe became aware of Sir Peter's speech, he wrote to Thatcher, enclosing a copy. He noted that Hall, "who is or was a socialist . . . [is] clearly mindful of the importance of markets, and of services, in addition to the manufacturing industry, and arrives . . . at an approach very similar to the one I suggested in my recent paper 'Liberating Free Enterprise.'"[31] As her frequent underlinings on the document reveal, Mrs. Thatcher clearly paid close attention, although she was yet to be persuaded that the Conservative Party should adopt the idea.

A year later, Howe again urged Thatcher to include enterprise zone proposals in the party's manifesto for the upcoming general election: "I hope very much that we may be able to give the Party's blessing during the run-up to the election. It could, if we wished, be incorporated into the manifesto in a very short sentence, declaring our intention to make possible, in our worst afflicted areas, the establishment of zones of this kind, as a means of starting the revival to which we all look forward and of demonstrating the way in which our policies are likely to deliver economic success."[32] Thatcher, however, was reluctant to officially endorse the idea, noting that while considering it an "imaginative proposal," she did "not think we can commit ourselves in the manifesto."[33] This would not be the final word, however.

In March 1979, Howe, still undeterred, pressed Thatcher a final time on the issue. This letter is significant to the American story because it appears to be the first time that the connection between the enterprise zone idea and the Heritage Foundation, a right-wing think tank in the United States, is established. Howe's sheer commitment to the idea is reflected in the tone of the letter's opening statement: "Can I have another go at persuading you to endorse my 'enterprise zone' proposal as something we should put forward at the general election?"[34] In this last-ditch effort, Howe deployed a report written by Stuart Butler[35]: "I am encouraged to press the point again by a copy which I enclose of a report produced by the Heritage Foundation . . . which describes the proposal as 'arguably the most important proposal on urban problems to be put forward for many years.'"[36]

As I will show in Chapter 2, the enterprise zone proposal did eventually receive Margaret Thatcher's backing and became government policy in 1980. In the United States, meanwhile, Stuart Butler, who authored the report, took up a permanent position at the Heritage Foundation in Washington, D.C. and became the leading advocate of the enterprise zone idea.

Butler Did It

Butler's report, which introduced the idea to a U.S. audience, was written at the behest of Heritage Foundation director Ed Feulner following a trip to Hong Kong.[37] Although still at the Adam Smith Foundation in London when the paper was published in 1979, Butler soon thereafter became a full-time policy analyst at Heritage. Citing Hall and Howe as progenitors of the idea, Butler introduced it in its purest form: "The essence of the proposal . . . is for the most decayed segments of major cities to be classified as 'Enterprise Zones,' and for virtually all zoning, employment protection, and other controls within them to be suspended—and perhaps even for property taxes to be abolished."[38] Thus, the enterprise zone idea distilled the central tenets of neoliberalism: deregulation and tax cuts.

In light of his training in American history and political culture, Butler was persuaded that the enterprise zone concept "should strike a chord in the United States."[39] After all, "the philosophy of experimentation and individual initiative is well rooted in the American way of life."[40] Furthermore, Butler saw the causes of urban decay in the United Kingdom and the United States to be "sufficiently similar to allow possible solutions voiced in Britain to be given serious consideration in the United States."[41]

But although the British version of the enterprise zone idea focused almost exclusively on industrial and commercial redevelopment of often sparsely populated areas of cities, Butler's vision blended classically neoliberal goals of deregulation and tax cuts with the communitarianism of Jane Jacobs.[42] In her influential bestseller, *The Death and Life of Great American Cities*, Jacobs launched an assault on city planning, particularly in its most destructive form in the 1950s and 1960s, referred to as "urban renewal." The attack on urban renewal was extended most famously by future Reagan appointee Martin Anderson's *The Federal Bulldozer*.[43] For Butler, Jacobs's work "was a key factor in the erosion of the consensus that had led to many of the urban planning disasters of the 1950s and the 1960s."[44] She also advocated for cities as places of diversity and community. In Butler's view, this meant "the mixed use of buildings, leading to a variety of economic activity, making the area better able to adapt to changing economic conditions, and to a flourishing street life throughout the city, reducing the incidence of crime. It also means recognizing that neighborhood organizations are crucial to the development process."[45] One can read Butler's appeal to Jacobs's communitarian impulse as a way to link the neoclassical liberalism reflected in Hall and Howe's approach to the republican themes present throughout American political culture. Hence, Butler's key contribution in the American context was to add a Jacobsian twist to the British idea:

> My value added to this was to blend that with the Jane Jacobs' vision of communities, and saying well ok we won't use this to get the bulldozers in or to have massive physical redevelopment. But we'll use the essence of the enterprise zone to get latent activity coming into fruition and then combine with that the idea that the route forward for new development, economic development, was more likely through small business activity, than through large business activity. I think both of those are very important in terms of the distinction of the enterprise zone philosophy, if you like, that it was going to be non-planning, in a sense, and based more on small enterprise.[46]

As such, "intellectually, it has Hayekian roots and American roots."[47] Butler's emphasis on small enterprises reflected the influence of MIT economist David Birch,[48] whose work suggested that between 60 and 80 percent of new jobs were produced by small business, which in "poor urban neighborhoods . . . turn out to be the only net producers of jobs."[49] Indeed, "advocates hoped that zone incentives would engender the proper business environment for the conception and incubation of new, small businesses."[50] Thus, in addition to deregulation and tax cuts, the promotion of small business forms the third prong of the enterprise zone approach.

At this embryonic stage of the enterprise zone idea's development, Stuart Butler, informed by Hall and Howe in the United Kingdom, as well as Jacobs and Birch in the United States, harnessed the institutional support of the Heritage Foundation to promote the idea, which was readily picked up by the media. A prime example is "Heritage in the News: Special Enterprise Zone Issue," a newsletter that featured a collection of articles on the enterprise zones from a series of national and local newspapers ranging from February 1979 to July 1980.[51] The publication includes sixteen stories printed in thirty-one newspapers. Thirteen link the enterprise zone idea specifically with Hall, Howe, and/or Margaret Thatcher's Conservative government in the United Kingdom. Moreover, fourteen mention the Heritage Foundation and/or Butler specifically.[52]

Thus, the media coverage of enterprise zones reflects the fact that Stuart Butler, with the institutional support of the Heritage Foundation, was largely responsible for the introduction of the idea to the United States. Having sparked the idea in the United Kingdom, Peter Hall, having immigrated to the United States in the early 1980s, then helped Butler promote the idea in the United States.[53]

EZ Ideas

In many respects, the enterprise zone is a neoliberal policy prescription par excellence. As Butler argued, it was "in effect a supply-side program to save the inner cities: It was the urban complement to the general conservative strategy of cutting taxes and regulation to stimulate economic growth."[54] While it is true that various enterprise zones, particularly at the state level, differ in practice from the original vision,[55] there are a number of unifying themes around which virtually all enterprise zones coalesce. These are a specific understanding of urban distress, the purposes of enterprise zones, eligibility requirements, deregulation, and tax incentives, credits, and cuts. I will deal with each of these in turn.

Causes of Urban Distress

Butler's framing and diagnosis of the urban ills circa 1980 are given their most extensive treatment in his book, *Enterprise Zones: Greenlining the Inner Cities*. Butler posits a conspicuously apolitical explanation for the decline of inner cities. He identifies population loss, industrial decline, and the deterioration of city finances as the key factors of urban distress. While it is undoubtedly true that these processes were important, Butler errs by not connecting these factors to their political-economic context.

Butler sees population loss, for example, as a function of shifting demographics and preferences for suburban living[56] but fails to note the political sources of this phenomenon, such as the role of federal agencies in promoting the building and purchasing of suburban homes.[57] Furthermore, Butler views industrial decline as the result of a "general population movement, which has in turn induced a movement of business."[58] Again, Butler ignores the politically constructed patterns of federal regulation and spending that encouraged shifts in population and industry away from the frostbelt to the suburbs and to the South and West, which were neither accidental nor inevitable but shaped significantly by government policy.[59] As political scientists Dennis Judd and Todd Swanstrom argue, since the 1950s, "accelerated depreciation allowances deducted from corporate income taxes provided tax breaks for constructing new commercial and industrial structures but not for rehabilitating old buildings [which] speeded up the flow of capital out of older industrial cities to suburban and Sunbelt locations."[60]

Butler also saw cities' fiscal problems as rooted in apolitical factors. For him, cities' coffers were strained by increased costs associated with population loss, such as increased policing in abandoned areas coupled with reduced tax receipts and because of the "ratchet effect" of snowballing service provision and costs arising from trade unionism.[61] While it is undoubtedly so that the combination of rising costs and declining tax revenues is a central part of the story, cuts in federal aid to cities, the role of credit rating agencies, or the politically determined basis for the flight of capital and labor are all glossed over.

Perhaps the most crucial explanation of urban distress, also one with clear links to neoliberal critiques of the state more generally, is the stifling effect of regulation and excessive taxation on economic growth. Butler avers, "What we must do . . . [is to] remove the obstacles that have transformed the inner cities from centers of opportunity into blighted sinks of hopelessness."[62] Like Hall, Butler's examples include the minimum wage laws whose "only effect has been to make young unskilled workers less attractive to employers leading to an increase in unemployment among young blacks and hence to a worsening of the economic and social structure within poorer areas of major cities."[63]

Thus, for early enterprise zone advocates, the "urban crisis" emerged from a combination of naturally functioning markets; rational, although short-sighted, responses by local governments (e.g., increased taxes); and the entrenched interests of labor.[64] This account flowed from the general critique of "big government," with its attendant regulations and high levels of taxation, popularized by those such as William Simon whose 1978 polemic *A Time for Truth* bemoaned the "monstrous growth of government."[65] Butler echoes this rhetoric of crisis to describe 1970s urban America: "The social problems produced by this vicious cycle have now produced a situation where in the minds of many people abroad American cities are synonymous with squalor, chaos, and crime."[66] This partial definition and interpretation of crisis, which drew from neoliberal critiques increasingly prevalent in American and British political discourse, was central to the justification of a set of ideas that found expression in policies proposed by political entrepreneurs embedded in key institutions such as the Heritage Foundation.

The Purposes of Enterprise Zones

For most enterprise zone advocates, particularly in the United States, job creation was seen "as the principal goal of the concept."[67] On the basis of Birch's arguments about the employment potential of small business, Butler argued that jobs would best be created in an environment in which the budding entrepreneur would thrive. Moreover, he stressed that enterprise zones would "*add* to the national economy by removing obstacles that stifle creative activity, not reallocate the fruits of the economy."[68]

In addition to their economic purposes, Butler's paternalistic vision also saw enterprise zones as part of an "empowerment strategy" by which "social improvement" and "self-worth" could be achieved through the growth of neighborhood organizations, which would provide services themselves as opposed to the state "coming in and assuming that people are too stupid to understand how to run their own lives."[69] Furthermore, Butler combined his materialist account of unemployment with now familiar "culture of poverty" shibboleths[70]: "In many ways, the most important element of all would be the psychological benefit: enterprise zones would help to break the spiral of defeatism in inner cities—the feeling that the way ahead consists only of handouts and subsidies. Instead, they offer a future with real jobs that provide new skills and new opportunities."[71] These themes would be taken up in earnest both rhetorically and legislatively by the Reagan, Bush, and Clinton administrations, as housing vouchers, school choice, and welfare reform attest, and even more strongly under Tony Blair's Labour government.

Eligibility Requirements

Early enterprise zone advocates only reluctantly addressed eligibility requirements for the zones. Stuart Butler's initial proposals simply noted that "the most decayed segments of major cities" should be designated enterprise zones. He conceded that the federal government would have to "lay down broad guidelines regarding the degrees of distress that must occur in an area for it to be considered"[72] but provided little further detail regarding how to measure "the degree of distress," except to say that "unemployment and poverty would have to be substantially higher than the national average."[73] In respect of zone size, Butler suggested that they should "be small—say a square mile or so" in "highly distressed sections of the city, where tax rates can be cut with little or no cost to the government."[74]

As the enterprise zone idea moved from mere aspiration to concrete policy proposals and congressional bills, sharper eligibility criteria emerged. In the first iteration, an area would be eligible for zone designation if either (1) they had double the national average of unemployed persons *and* had 30 percent of families below the poverty level or (2) the unemployment rate was three times the national average or where at least 50 percent of families lived below the poverty line. Furthermore, a minimum population of 4,000 people would be required.[75] Throughout the 1980s and early 1990s, eligibility criteria usually focused on a small geographical area where a certain percentage of residents were unemployed and living in poverty.[76]

Deregulation

Reflecting its neoliberal roots, deregulation was a central part of the enterprise zone vision in which the laceration of red tape would unleash the potential of free enterprise, the ostensible lifeblood of the city. Peter Hall's proposals are archetypal in this regard. His "free zones" would be "outside the limits of the parent country's legislation," free from taxes and regulations and where "bureaucracy would be kept to an absolute minimum."[77] Butler envisaged enterprise zones that would "experiment with a reduction or elimination of the minimum wage in some zones" and "eliminate rent control" as part of a plan to introduce housing vouchers.[78] When it came to developing concrete legislative proposals, however, this swashbuckling vision quickly fell off the table.

For example, one of the earliest enterprise zone bills famously promoted by renowned supply-sider U.S. Rep. Jack Kemp (R-NY) and Latino Democrat Robert Garcia (D-NY) did not seek substantial deregulation. Even diehard Kemp recognized the political reality that "the very thought of streamlining regulation, or of cutting the minimum wage and other supposed protections, sends shock waves through the enterprise zone coalition."[79] The same was true of the administration's 1982 Enterprise Zone Tax Act.

While the act envisaged employing the 1980 Regulatory Flexibility Act to enable agencies to relax nonstatutory regulations, this would require the consent of all three levels of government, which reduced the prospect of agreement and in turn weakened the act's deregulatory punch. Moreover, the 1982 bill omitted a proposal for subminimum youth wages in the zones.

This trend would characterize most future federal proposals. As the Urban Institute's Marc Bendick noted, the deregulatory measures in the administration's 1983 enterprise zone plan were "surprisingly meager": "Left intact are the minimum wage, equal employment opportunity, OSHA [Office of Health and Safety Administration] and environmental restrictions, and all other regulations mandated by federal law."[80] Moreover, the 1992 enterprise zone legislation, passed by Congress but pocket vetoed by President Bush, contained no provisions for deregulation. As such, the key feature of the enterprise zone proposals of the 1980s and early 1990s, beyond its place-based approach that targeted distressed neighborhoods, was tax cuts.

Tax Incentives, Credits, and Cuts

The ideological claim that lies at the heart of the enterprise zone idea is that high business costs, largely arising from taxation, bear significant responsibility for high levels of urban poverty, unemployment, and dereliction and that the solution to these ills can be found in lowering these costs. Therefore, tax cuts are the sine qua non of the enterprise zone idea. This harkens back to Hall's argument that "the real economic success stories of the 1960s and 1970s—Taiwan and Korea, Hong Kong and Singapore"— achieved their success due to the "spirit of unbridled enterprise that has characterized their economies."[81] Jack Kemp, the superlative enterprise zone champion in U.S. politics, echoed this sentiment: "Look at Hong Kong. . . . It's a free-trade zone, a free-banking zone and a free-enterprise zone."[82] The way of "creating a Taiwan in the Bronx," as Butler put it, would be through "creating a climate of opportunity in depressed neighborhoods through the reduction of regulation, taxes, and other government-imposed costs."[83] The tax that enterprise zone advocates saw as especially deleterious to the kind of entrepreneurial risk taking necessary to revive the urban areas was capital gains tax. The conservative development consultant Paul Pryde argued that the surest way to make enterprise zones attractive to potential investors would be to allow "a loss reserve of

20 percent of the invested capital"[84] and defer all taxes on capital gains made on investments in zone firms so long as the proceeds are reinvested in other eligible zone companies. Even as early as the 1980 presidential campaign, Ronald Reagan saw the zones as a key institutional solution to the problem of the dearth of investment in poor urban areas and to reducing the welfare rolls.[85]

As such, a variety of tax incentives was designed to create the kind of environment that neoliberals considered necessary for urban revitalization. Cutting the capital gains tax became one of the principal preoccupations of the Reagan administration and was especially important to enterprise zone advocates. As Butler explained, "The capital tax argument which is what Kemp and [Joe] Lieberman [D-CT] and myself were arguing, is the 'risk-taking' argument. In order to help small businesses get access to capital, you have to make it worthwhile for venture capitalists to say, 'I'm prepared to gamble on this and I want my reward from success.' "[86] As such, virtually all enterprise zone bills contain measures to reduce or defer capital gains tax. Other related features of enterprise zone proposals are property tax cuts, depreciation on fixed items, tax credits to employers, and tax credits to employees.

No EZ Victory: In Congress and the White House

If Peter Hall and Geoffrey Howe are largely responsible for the enterprise zone idea itself, and if Stuart Butler is to be credited with introducing the idea to the American scene, then Jack Kemp was the key figure who transformed the idea into concrete legislative proposals.[87] Moreover, in a sign of the growing momentum behind enterprise zones, the idea was given additional support from Ronald Reagan as a candidate and as president. As will be shown below, the legislative history of the enterprise zones falls into three periods. The first, 1980–1983, saw the concept shift from mere idea, promoted by a few institutions and political entrepreneurs, into a series of legislative proposals. While enterprise zone bills were mainly Republican creatures in Congress, supported intermittently by Reagan, the idea attracted some Democrats but was ultimately stymied by the Democratic leadership. The second period, 1984–1988, represents an interregnum in which support for enterprise zones waned in Congress but was increasingly backed publicly by the White House and featured in the 1988 Republican platform. Ironically, it was during this period that enterprise zone legislation was actually passed. However, the bill that emerged was largely symbolic and toothless and thus represented a Pyrrhic victory for enterprise zone proponents. Between 1989 and 1992, enterprise zones came into their own. During this third period, strong levels of bipartisan support can be found in each year except 1990. Consensus around enterprise zones reached its zenith in 1992, when the House and Senate passed a bill that would have created a federal program of fifty urban zones but for President Bush's veto. For each of these periods, I will map out the national coalitions and levels of congressional support that developed around the various enterprise zone proposals.

From Ideas to Proposals: 1980–1983

During this period, support for enterprise zones propelled numerous bills, hearings, and presidential messages as the contours of the ideological and political debate were solidified. What is most striking is the fact that enterprise zones were clearly a political project promoted by intellectuals, think tanks, and Republicans. While a smattering of Democrats offered support, most opposed the idea. Notably, business interests represented by organizations such as the Chamber of Commerce, the National Association of Manufacturers (NAM), and the National Federation of Independent Business (NFIB) either opposed enterprise zones or came to support them *after* they had been promoted by politicians. Indeed, Stuart Butler recalls deep frustration with the struggle to get big business associations on board with the enterprise zone idea: "We were desperately trying to find large interest groups that would support this . . . but to get some of the really large business organizations was just an uphill battle. The Chamber and the NAM and so on, they were in with the old philosophy. If you wanted a large manufacturing approach, the last thing you wanted was to have an approach that said 'sorry we don't want to send the bulldozers in; you are not the answer.' They didn't want to hear this. So we could never get much support in the large very active business organizations."[88] This suggests that ideas rather than economic interests were driving the policy forward. While it was certainly the case that big business mobilized in the 1970s to underwrite organizations such as Heritage to promote neoliberal ideas and policy proposals,[89] the enterprise zone example demonstrates that

this did not mean that the emergent proposals would automatically correspond with the interests of those organizations. This case also shows how
business interests themselves were subject to change from "the old philosophy" to a new one. A second significant development during this period
was the broadening and deepening of a pro–enterprise zone coalition. This
was especially striking given the slew of theoretical and empirical evidence
presented in Congress and the media suggesting that enterprise zones were
not likely to work.

Even before Ronald Reagan won the 1980 presidential election, plans
were afoot to mold urban policy in the neoliberal image. That Kemp was
at the forefront of this effort should come as no surprise. After all, according to Reagan adviser Martin Anderson, he was "the earliest and strongest
political leader for tax cuts."[90] Indeed, Kemp is often credited with popular-
izing the Laffer curve, which formed part of the intellectual justification for
massive tax cuts.[91] In June 1977, the indefatigable congressman joined
forces with Senator William Roth (R-DE) to introduce the first version of
the monumental Kemp-Roth tax bill, which was ultimately enacted in 1981.
Kemp's neoliberal interpretation of the nation's economic difficulties was
also extended to the city: "Only individuals can restore economic growth
to our inner cities. Government will not—cannot—create enough jobs for
city residents."[92]

In addition to his ideological commitment to supply-side economics,
Kemp also had presidential ambitions; he had even been suggested as a
potential challenger to Reagan for the 1980 Republican presidential nomination.[93] Ultimately, he decided against the idea, campaigned for Reagan,
and used money raised by his political action committee—the Committee
to Rebuild American Incentive—to support candidates who backed the
neoliberal agenda reflected in Kemp-Roth.[94] Given these ambitions, Kemp's
promotion of the zones should be seen as part of his overall strategy to
strengthen Republican appeal in cities, particularly among African Americans, whom Kemp courted assiduously as a congressman and then as secretary of HUD from 1989 to 1993. Indeed, enterprise zones were seen by
Republicans such as Kemp as central to building Republican support
among black voters. In a memo to the White House, Kemp's implication
in this regard is clear: "I obviously believe that enterprise zones are good
public policy. But they are also good politics. The GOP and the President
could send a powerful signal to urban communities that we do not break
our promises, and that we are a Party with an agenda that includes all of

the people, even those who have not voted for us. . . . Enterprise Zones can be a symbol—Ronald Reagan's symbol—of hope that the Republican Party will not concede our nation's poorest communities in its attempt to become the majority party."[95] In May 1980, Kemp sponsored H.R. 7240, the first of two enterprise zone bills introduced that year. The central features of the bill correspond with the main elements of the enterprise zone vision outlined above—that is, poor urban areas would be targeted with tax cuts for individuals and corporations.[96] H.R. 7240 garnered only moderate levels of support from House Republicans, with thirty-one co-sponsoring the bill, and managed to attract the co-signature of just one Democrat: Henry Nowak of Buffalo, New York, Kemp's neighboring district. Of far greater symbolic value, however, was the introduction of the Kemp-Garcia Enterprise Zone bill (H.R. 7563), sponsored by Robert Garcia, who represented the South Bronx. Garcia brought with him ten other Democrats. His view of the zones was a harbinger of the neoliberal synthesis of conservatism and liberalism, which would eventually hold strong bipartisan appeal: "When you look around my district, the liberals failed, the conservatives failed. I thought just maybe if I can get a coalition of groups together, maybe it will work."[97]

The Kemp-Garcia bill was virtually identical to H.R. 7240. It enjoyed the support of conservative Republicans in the House, such as Newt Gingrich, and of Stuart Butler, who saw it as "a major step forward for the Enterprise Zone idea in America."[98] Moreover, Butler saw "liberal Democrat" Robert Garcia's backing as "a clear demonstration that the underlying theme of the Enterprise Zone spanned the political spectrum."[99] While prescient of future levels of bipartisan support, Butler's claim in respect of Democratic support circa 1980–1981 was overstated. After all, only eleven Democrats had sponsored the bill, and more important, key gatekeepers able to set the legislative agenda, such as Ways and Means Committee Chairman Dan Rostenkowski (D-IL), opposed it. In contrast, thirty-six Republicans co-sponsored the legislation.[100]

Although the enterprise zone bills of late spring and early summer of 1980 were thwarted in Congress, candidate Ronald Reagan promoted the idea readily. At a speech before the National Urban League, Reagan argued that "enterprise zones would remove many of the barriers to investment and job creation. . . . Thus entrepreneurs would be encouraged to start new enterprises and put people back to work."[101] Moreover, his attack on the Carter administration's social and economic policy was framed in starkly ideological terms. For Reagan, Carter himself was not "the major problem" but instead "the philosophy he believes in and the policies he promotes."[102] In a 1980 presidential debate, Reagan expressed his support for enterprise zones, which was presented in terms almost identical to Butler's and Kemp's:

> I've talked of having zones in those cities that are run down, where there is a high percentage of people on welfare, and offer tax incentives. The government isn't getting a tax now from business there because they aren't there, or from individuals who are on welfare rather than working. Why don't we offer incentives for business and industry to start up in these zones? Give them a tax moratorium for a period if they build and develop there. The individuals that would then get jobs; give them a break that encourages them to leave social welfare programs and go to work.[103]

Thus, as 1980 drew to a close, the enterprise zone idea had been translated into legislative proposals supported by a small but not insignificant number of Republicans in the House and Senate, the Republican presidential nominee, and a few Democrats. Support also came from conservative and neoliberal institutions, such as the Heritage Foundation, the Cato Institute, and the American Legislative Exchange Council (ALEC). As Karen Mossberger notes, ALEC comprised conservative state legislators and members of Congress. Its "1980 Source Book of American State Legislation" included a draft enterprise zone bill that was widely disseminated.[104] These coalitions would broaden and solidify during the early 1980s.

However, conservative and business elites were not unanimously in favor. For example, the National Federation of Independent Business (NFIB), a lobbying organization for small business, and the Chamber of Commerce were cool toward the idea. John J. Motley, NFIB deputy director of federal legislation, expressed concern that providing tax relief to zone businesses could put undue pressure on firms outside the zone that would be placed at a competitive disadvantage.[105] Moreover, the pro-market *Economist* doubted "whether the tax incentives will be big enough to lure industry, especially since business everywhere has done well out of the Reagan tax-cut plan."[106]

Meanwhile, liberals were similarly split on the issue. Zone advocates included the U.S. Conference of Mayors (USCM), the National Association for the Advancement of Colored People (NAACP), and, to a lesser extent, Lawrence B. Simons, Carter's assistant secretary at HUD, who thought "a version of it is worth giving a try," although he believed that some kind of "training element" would be necessary.[107] Organizations such as the National League of Cities (NLC) offered more qualified support. An internal report by analyst William Barnes reflects the NLC's tempered view. He concluded that while the bill had "many problems . . . it is an important idea, well worth trying on an experimental basis."[108] However, Barnes also argued that "as the centerpiece or sole component of federal urban policy, it is unacceptable; in fact, if the foregone revenues it envisions could be converted into direct expenditures, several alternative programs would be more desirable than the zones proposal."[109] However, given the lack of any serious alternatives, the NLC was inclined to see how the legislation might be shaped to yield the most positive results.[110]

In contrast, the American Federation of Labor and Congress of Industrial Organizations (AFL-CIO) rejected the proposal outright on the basis that it represented "little more than a localized version of 'trickle-down' economics . . . based exclusively on the false notion that local economic problems will disappear if government would spend less, tax less, and protect less."[111] Labor would remain opposed to the enterprise zone idea throughout the 1980s and early 1990s. In addition, the *New York Times* was decidedly skeptical: "Large cities keep losing residents. Left behind, in every respect, are the poor who are becoming an ever larger proportion of the urban population. They can qualify for the low-skilled manufacturing jobs that used to proliferate in cities. But these have also moved out. Enterprise zones might slow down the shift, but they are unlikely to reverse it. What are increasing in the cities are white-collar jobs—for which unskilled poor people rarely qualify."[112] Despite their failure in 1980, enterprise zone bills were reintroduced in the House and Senate in 1981. In June, Kemp introduced the Urban Jobs and Enterprise Zone Act of 1981 (H.R. 3824). While congressional support had nearly doubled compared with the 1980 Kemp-Garcia bill, Republicans made up the lion's share of the co-sponsors. Of the eighty-three legislators who signed on to the bill, just seventeen were Democrats. Similarly, in the Senate, only two Democrats backed Rudolph Boschwitz's (R-MN) bill (S. 1310). Ultimately, the 1981 proposals died in committee, although during the summer of 1981, hearings were held in the House and Senate. Although the content of congressional hearings often reflects the agenda of those who called them, they nevertheless provide an insight into the public stance of those individuals and institutions that comprise the coalitions on either side of the enterprise zone issue. They show that although some Republicans and even fewer Democrats doggedly promoted the proposals, most witnesses gave qualified support, while a few opposed enterprise zones outright. Moreover, these hearings were the first of many occasions that Congress was warned that tax incentives were inefficient means by which to reduce urban unemployment and stimulate economic growth in cities.

Those who spoke in favor of the zones included a smorgasbord of legislators, think tankers, and mayors. Stuart Butler and the Sabre Foundation's Mark Frazier testified in favor of the program, as did David Birch. Senator John Chafee (R-RI) was particularly enamored of the concept. He argued that job creation would best be delivered by reducing the burdens on business: "Given the limited resources of our federal government, it is imperative that the energy and creativity of private enterprise can be harnessed for this monumental task."[113] Further, Boschwitz claimed that the enterprise zone "isn't going to cost any money" and even suggested that the idea was axiomatically sound: "quite clearly the government would benefit from it in any number of ways that don't even require explanation."[114]

As noted above, the work of David Birch provided one of the key empirical planks on which the rationale for enterprise zones stood. Kemp readily referred to Birch to justify his approach: "The point is that the most labor intensive industry is the small start-up company." Furthermore, following other advocates, Kemp hailed Hong Kong as an example of how deregulation and low taxation create robust economic growth. In an apparent attempt to assuage liberals' concern, Rep. Garcia argued that the legislation was consistent with the vision of both John F. Kennedy and Jimmy Carter. Moreover, he claimed that "at the heart of the proposal is not the package of tax incentives, but rather . . . a method in which community investment and support can be organized to solve a community's real problems."[115] However, the enterprise zone idea was widely understood at the time as being a right-wing idea, anathema to the programs of Presidents Kennedy, Johnson, and Carter, with the exception of UDAG.[116] Moreover, few observers saw community involvement as central to the proposals; it was neither mentioned in press reports nor in the Congressional Research Service's summaries.

In addition to the zones' steadfast supporters were those who offered more qualified support. These included the National Urban League, the

National Urban Coalition, and the National Congress for Community Economic Development. Also in this category were mayors such as Ed Koch of New York and Donald Fraser of Minneapolis, who testified on behalf of the U.S. Conference of Mayors. While Fraser declared the USCM to be "supportive of the concept," he noted concern about the "unproven efficacy of tax incentives in revitalizing distressed neighborhoods."[117] When pressed, Fraser conceded that enterprise zones were not the USCM's priority: "if I were asked to make a choice between a continuation of manpower training programs and this [enterprise zones] I would pick manpower training programs."[118] Thus, while the official position was one of "support for the concept," a more thorough probing reveals ambivalence for the plan and a clear preference for an alternative.

Others, including labor representatives, experts on tax policy, academics, and think tank types, voiced firmer skepticism. The AFL-CIO objected that the legislation would enable "existing business to reap a windfall," which would mean "shifting unemployment from one area to another rather than a net increase in jobs."[119] Additionally, tax expert Jacques Schlenger maintained that "small business people don't think it does much in the way of tax incentives. They don't help them."[120] Dr. Douglas Johnson, of Atlanta University's Institute for Urban Affairs, echoed Schlenger's point: "What is clear is that tax incentives are not very effective instruments for attracting industry and commerce to poor areas. Enterprise zones, as proposed, will not generate significant investment in poor communities."[121]

Thus, the hearings held by the House and Senate during 1981 revealed that while a large majority of witnesses supported the proposals, a significant number were firmly against and, in most cases, presented empirical evidence that gave credence to their position. The tone of the hearings shows that most members of Congress who attended were yet to be convinced. Between 1982 and 1983, however, support steadily rose, as reflected by the co-sponsorships of bills introduced in the House and in the Senate.

In his 1982 State of the Union address, President Reagan reasserted his commitment to enterprise zones. His remarks reflect the degree to which the idea corresponded with the administration's distinctly neoliberal vision for America: "A broad range of special economic incentives in the zones will help attract new business, new jobs, new opportunity to America's inner cities and rural towns. Some will say our mission is to save free enterprise. Well, I say we must free enterprise so that, together, we can save America."[122] In March, Reagan again pressed Congress. He argued it was time "for us to find out if two of the most dynamic and constructive forces known to man—free enterprise and the profit motive—can be brought to play where government bureaucracy and social programs have failed."[123] Congress duly responded: enterprise zone bills were then introduced by John Chafee in the Senate (S. 2998) and by Rep. Barber Conable (R-NY) in the House (H.R. 6009).[124]

Shortly before enterprise zone hearings were held in April, the Committee for Economic Development released a report forecasting that enterprise zones "will not significantly affect corporate decisions on where to locate."[125] Committee members were particularly concerned that tax breaks could "drain off revenues needed to repair roads and bridges and improve schools, police and fire protection and other public services, and build resentments among homeowners who do not get tax breaks." Similar concerns were also expressed by Senator Bob Dole (R-KS). In a letter to President Reagan's chief of staff, James Baker, Dole noted that "there is strong evidence that incremental tax advantages are not a significant factor in locational decisions for most businesses." Moreover, Dole also expressed concern that the zones might act as tax shelters and thus constitute "just another boon to big business."[126]

The 1982 Senate and House committee hearings further reveal the paradoxical character of the enterprise zone coalition. Although numerous arguments cast doubt on the assumptions and expectations of zone proponents, the pro–enterprise zone coalition broadened markedly. The key criticisms leveled against the zones focused on cost, the effectiveness of small business in creating employment, and the inherent contradictions evident in Reagan's urban policy.

In contrast to claims that enterprise zones would cost very little, John Chapton, assistant treasury secretary for tax policy, predicted substantial tax receipt losses: $100 million for 1983, $400 million in 1984, and $1.3 billion in 1987.[127] Chapton's comments also reveal that the administration had the real estate industry in mind when assessing the zones' viability: "Capital gains will be accorded a favorable tax treatment in enterprise zones to stimulate investment in the zone by *real estate developers* and by entrepreneurs and venture capitalists."[128] Yet, there is no evidence that the real estate developers were driving the process.

In addition, Bendick and Rasmussen challenged Birch's claim that small businesses accounted for two-thirds of job growth. They argued that "researchers at the Brookings Institution, reanalyzing data used in Birch's earlier studies, have concluded that in fact small businesses . . . generate only about 40 percent of all job openings in the economy."[129] Moreover, they noted that the kinds of jobs produced by small businesses are likely to be low paying and short term and therefore inadequate to the task of reviving the nation's most depressed neighborhoods. Fearing a critical stance could endanger future federal funding, leaders at the Urban Institute had urged Bendick to moderate his opposition to enterprise zones,[130] which had been expressed in a 1982 article.[131] Bendick refused, arguing he was ethically obligated to testify honestly before the committee.[132]

A final note of criticism was struck by Rep. Shirley Chisholm (D-NY), who delivered a comprehensive and sustained critique of enterprise zones: "It is difficult for me—as it is for many tax, business, and urban experts—to believe that merely the lure of lower tax rates will set off an eruption of business development in depressed urban areas."[133] After all, taxes "pale to insignificance in comparison to the cost, quality, and availability of labor, energy, material, transportation and markets." Moreover, her critique highlighted the fact that the Reagan administration had institutionalized, via the tax code, an incentive structure that undermined cities' economic prosperity by providing "incentives such as relocation credits and accelerated depreciation for business to move out of depressed areas."[134]

Despite mounting empirical and rhetorical criticism, influential politicians and institutions were wooed by enterprise zone advocates. Senator Charles Schumer (D-NY), for example, while concerned that the zones might simply be a smokescreen for significant cuts in federal aid to cities, nevertheless concluded that "it is an intelligent idea, an idea that should be encouraged, as long as it is not regarded as a substitute for other programs."[135] Furthermore, the National League of Cities appeared to drop its reservations.[136] Moreover, previously skeptical voices, like the *New York Times*, warmed to the idea. Despite highlighting potential pitfalls, it argued that "these misgivings should not discourage the experiment. Unlike former urban renewal programs, these zones would not indiscriminately level poor neighborhoods. If the administration would relent on further cuts in complementary programs and add incentives for lenders and investors, the zones might well prove the skeptics wrong."[137]

Moreover, in Senate hearings, the Chamber of Commerce registered its "support for the concept of enterprise zones." It invoked Birch's work to reiterate the standard neoliberal claim that the economic potential of depressed neighborhoods "is being blocked by high marginal tax rates that deny entrepreneurs of the rewards needed to compensate for the higher risks of operating in a depressed area and by excessive regulation that suffocates initiative."[138] However, the chamber saw tax cuts as secondary to other forms of spending: "It is infrastructure repair and restoration that is most important for enterprise zones to succeed."[139] It failed, however, to explain how increased spending on infrastructure would be achieved while cutting taxes and reducing aid to cities.

A final striking feature of the 1982 hearings is Jack Kemp's concern about the negative coverage of the British enterprise zones, given the unpopularity of the Thatcher government. He felt compelled to reassure the House that his vision of enterprise zones is "quite separate and distinct from what Britain did" and, with characteristic hyperbole, that "while the British just abolished the government . . . we intend quite the opposite."[140]

Despite increased support in favor of enterprise zones from the White House, in Congress, and among key institutions, the House and Senate bills ultimately died in committee because many Democrats, including Ways and Means Committee Chairman Dan Rostenkowski (D-IL), "staunchly opposed the plan."[141] Furthermore, relations between the White House and urban interest groups soured in the summer of 1982 following the leak of a HUD draft urban policy report, *Privatizing the Public Sector—How to Shrink Government*, which characterized local officials as "wily stalkers of Federal funds."[142] It lamented that spending on welfare and social services "has created a crippling dependency rather than initiative and independence" and concluded that the "Federal Government cannot develop the flexible, broad range of policies and partnerships needed to rebuild and revitalize urban life. Neither can it guarantee a city's long-term prosperity." Rather, "cities can learn to become masters of their own destinies— regardless of the level of Federal support."[143]

In a further blow, a 1982 General Accounting Office (GAO) report concluded that enterprise zone tax incentives would not be "sufficiently attractive to many businesses with limited liabilities, such as small businesses."[144] Furthermore, it averred that "even if enterprise zone incentives were sufficient to attract business into a depressed area, they could have adverse effects," such as placing "businesses operating outside the zone in a weaker competitive position," "merely shifting economic activity and jobs from one area to another without creating any new net activity and jobs," and "residential displacement . . . [of] low-income residents."[145]

Despite these setbacks, the Reagan administration, members of Congress, and various lobbying groups made a final effort to pass enterprise zone legislation in 1983. In the shadow of crippling unemployment, which in November 1982 hit a thirty-eight-year high of 10.8 percent, Reagan again used the State of the Union address to argue that "passage of enterprise zone legislation will also create new incentives for jobs and opportunity."[146] Soon after, Barber Conable (R-NY) introduced H.R. 1955, by far the most broadly supported enterprise zone bill introduced in Congress during the 1980s.[147] On Reagan's behalf, Boschwitz introduced the Enterprise Zone Employment and Development Act (S. 863), supported by nearly half of the Senate, although still heavily along Republican lines: of the forty-four senators co-sponsoring the bill, five were Democrats. In May, the Senate Finance Committee voted 14 to 2 in favor of the bill, and in November, Rostenkowski finally relented and scheduled hearings before the full Ways and Means Committee.

That the hearings were held at all is remarkable given Rostenkowski's opposition to the zones. One explanation might be the growing support for the plans among some Democratic constituencies. George Voinovich, mayor of Cleveland representing the NLC, argued that although the league wanted existing programs to continue, it "supports the use of targeted tax incentives to encourage job creation and capital investment in enterprise zones."[148] Moreover, John Smith, mayor of Prichard, Alabama, told the committee that "the National Conference of Black Mayors . . . are in total support of H.R. 1955." He linked their support to popular neoliberal tropes on "self-reliance": "The technical emphasis is on municipal self-reliance through economic recovery investment techniques—we believe that this particular emphasis within EZs allows the local government to begin to imagine itself as a self-reliant vehicle."[149]

The hearings also provided the opportunity for critical voices to be heard. Bendick, the most outspoken, argued that "the enterprise zone approach . . . is not likely to work because it is based upon erroneous assumptions about how government can most usefully aid business."[150] Neither deregulation nor tax incentives are "cost-effective ways to provide assistance to local governments," he averred. Following scholars such as Paul Peterson,[151] Bendick noted that the enterprise zone approach failed to recognize that cities operate in a fundamentally competitive environment whereby "spatially targeted local development activities are primarily a means of making the target area attractive for economic activity, which would exist somewhere else, rather than generating jobs and incomes which would not otherwise exist." Moreover, "the experience of past tax credit programs is that such incentives engender only modest changes in business behavior, particularly with respect to hiring disadvantaged workers."[152] Bendick stressed that in the rare cases that tax credits get utilized, they are "often largely claimed for hires which would have been made even in the absence of the credit." Thus, the corresponding revenue loss "represents a windfall to firms with little new employment generated."[153] Bendick's opposition to the plan is significant not only in light of his substantive criticisms but also because of the coverage it received.[154] Representative Charles Rangel (D-NY), who hitherto opposed the proposal, pointed out that while 3,000 areas in U.S. cities met the enterprise zone poverty and unemployment criteria, no more than seventy-five communities would benefit under the proposals. He concluded, "I am thinking about the other communities that will see this little parade, this experiment, passing them by."[155]

Despite the hearings, the Byzantine institutional structures of Congress had again stymied passage of the enterprise zone. But the tide had certainly turned. Increasingly, Democrats signed up for enterprise zone bills, even in the absence of significant concessions, in an apparent acknowledgment of the new political "reality," which meant that enterprise zones were the best that could be hoped for. Moreover, groups such as the NLC, whose positions reflected a rough aggregation of the preferences of many city mayors, gave up the fight and adjusted their positions to reduce friction with the prevailing political winds. As the *Washington Post* reported, leading mayors abandoned calls for new federal programs and "frankly admitted that they weren't sure how to help cities such as Cleveland, Gary, Detroit, Buffalo and Newark, where unemployment still ranges between 14 and 20 percent."[156] Thus, as the sun set on 1983, enterprise zone proposals languished in Congress, failing yet again to negotiate the institutional hurdles in their way. On the basis of congressional hearings, newspaper reports, primary documents, the academic literature, and interviews, Table 1 depicts the coalitions on either side of the enterprise zone issue in 1983.

The Lull: 1984–1988

At the beginning of 1984, the prospects for enterprise zone legislation looked bright. Over time, though, this outlook dimmed considerably, albeit

Table 1. Enterprise Zone Coalition c. 1983

Supportive	Indifferent/Mixed Position	Opposed
Institutions	*Institutions*	*Institutions*
➤ Heritage Foundation	➤ National Federation of	➤ AFL-CIO
➤ Sabre Foundation	Independent Business	➤ AFSCME
➤ American Legislative	➤ National League of	➤ Urban Institute
Exchange Council	Cities	➤ *Washington Post*
(ALEC)	➤ National Conference of	➤ *The Economist*
➤ Cato Institute	Mayors	➤ Democratic Party
➤ Chamber of	➤ General Accounting	leadership
Commerce[a]	Office	
➤ Real estate	➤ U.S. Treasury	*Key Individuals*
➤ NAACP	➤ Democratic caucus	
➤ National Conference of		Dan Rostenkowski
Black Mayors	*Key Individuals*	Arnold Cantor (AFL-CIO)
➤ *New York Times*[a]		Marc Bendick
➤ Republican caucus	Charles Rangel	
➤ Some of the	Bob Dole	
Democratic caucus		
➤ HUD		
➤ Reagan presidency		
Key Individuals		
Stuart Butler (Heritage)		
Jack Kemp		
Robert Garcia		
Barber Conable		
Rudy Boschwitz		
John Chaffee		

[a] Denotes a switch of position in favor during the 1980–1983 period.

with a few important flickers. Most noteworthy is the Housing and Community Development Act of 1987, the only legislation that established enterprise zones in the 1980s. Regrettably for its advocates, the bill did little more than provide HUD the authority to designate zones. It would not be until the late 1980s, with Kemp at the helm as HUD secretary, that enterprise zones would once again enjoy sustained support. This period thus stands as a lull, an interregnum, during which it appeared the enterprise zone idea would die a slow death. However, its tireless advocates were patient and organized. And while federal enterprise zone legislation stumbled in Congress, enterprise zones proliferated through the states. Moreover, during this period, the enterprise zone coalition beyond Congress continued to strengthen, propelled by institutions with the resources, influence, and ideas necessary to continue the campaign.

For a third year in succession, President Reagan called for enterprise zone legislation in the State of the Union address. Once again, he invoked that putative power of the free market: "I ask your help in assisting more communities to break the bondage of dependency. Help us to free enterprise by permitting debate and voting 'yes' on our proposal for enterprise zones in America."[157] Congress, however, showed little appetite to grant the president's wishes. Although two bills were introduced in the House (H.R 6182 and H.R. 6373) and one in the Senate (S. 2914), only the Senate bill drew significant support in the form of co-sponsorships. No major congressional actions were taken on these bills, and no hearings were held. Once again, the administration identified obstruction by Rostenkowski as the chief cause of the legislative failure.

In June 1984, during an acrimonious U.S. Conference of Mayors, HUD Secretary Samuel Pierce directly attacked Rostenkowski for blocking the administration's proposals: "To be blunt about it, the only thing that stands between an eligible community and this . . . initiative is one man: Congressman Dan Rostenkowski." Pierce further averred that Rostenkowski opposed the scheme "because he just can't stand the idea of a Republican president getting credit for a bold, new economic development initiative."[158] However, the failure of the bills to make it out of committee also resulted from opposition from elements within the executive branch, in particular from the Treasury Department, and at the Office of Management and Budget, within which private concerns were raised about the arbitrary nature of the policy.[159] More damaging still, the Congressional Research Service released a July 1984 report that stated, "There is no empirical evidence that the administration's enterprise zone proposal would create economic activity, without the added stimulus of public investment."[160] Nevertheless, the president remained fiercely committed to the project.

In his renomination speech to the Republican National Convention, President Reagan castigated Democrats for killing the scheme: "When we talk of the plight of our cities, what would help more than our enterprise zones bill, which provides tax incentives for private industry to help rebuild and restore decayed areas in seventy-five sites all across America? If they really wanted a future of boundless new opportunities for our citizens, why have they buried enterprise zones over the years in committee?"[161] Moreover, despite congressional Democrats' skepticism about the scheme, Democratic presidential candidate Walter Mondale signaled that he was open to the idea. In the first 1984 presidential debate, Mondale remarked, "I don't mind those enterprise zones—let's try them, but not as a substitute for the others."[162] Yet, the institutional and political resistance to the idea from within the executive and legislative branches, as well as a splintered enterprise zone coalition, prevented any serious advances for the plan.

The 1985 State of the Union address fell on the president's birthday. Reagan used the opportunity to ask for a special gift from Speaker of the House Tip O'Neill: "We have repeatedly sought passage of enterprise zones to help those in the abandoned corners of our land find jobs, learn skills and build better lives. . . . Let us place new dreams in a million hearts and create a new generation of entrepreneurs by passing enterprise zones this year. And Tip, you could make that a birthday present."[163] Congress responded by introducing three urban enterprise zone bills. Of these, the most significant was H.R. 1 (which passed as the Housing Act of 1986), which created enterprise zones under title VII. But while title VII empowered the HUD secretary to designate enterprise zones and to waive certain departmental regulations within zones, it did not provide for any tax incentives or other forms of spending on the zones. Although H.R. 1 eventually passed in the House on June 12, 1986 (340–36), it failed to get through the Senate, largely due to the threat of a presidential veto arising from concerns about its estimated $15 billion to $19 billion cost.[164]

Also of interest is the Enterprise Zone Job Creation Act (H.R. 3232) introduced in September 1985 by Robert Garcia. Although introduced by a Democrat, Garcia was only able to garner the co-sponsorship of sixteen fellow Democrats, while seventy-one Republicans signed up. The dearth of Democratic support indicates that many Democrats circa 1985 were still reluctant to endorse a neoliberal urban policy.

The picture for enterprise zones looked similarly mixed throughout 1987. On one hand, 1987 represents another year in which efforts to institute a federal program failed. On the other, the year did witness the only enterprise zone legislation to reach Reagan's desk. Unfortunately for the president, the enterprise zone legislation, without tax incentives or significant deregulation, was largely symbolic. The bill itself, the Housing and Community Development Act (H.R. 4), introduced by Rep. Gonzalez

(D-TX), largely duplicated H.R. 1. It authorized seventy-five urban enterprise zones at an estimated cost of up to $1 million a year.[165] The bill passed with heavy backing in the House, and its companion bill in the Senate (S. 825) passed with bipartisan support, and the bill was sent to the president in the last days of 1987. Reagan signed the legislation on February 5, 1988, the first and only piece of legislation that included enterprise zones. Dissatisfied with the extremely limited enterprise zone provisions contained in H.R. 4, on May 25, Jack Kemp introduced what would be the final enterprise zone bill of the Reagan era: the Enterprise Zone Development and Employment Act (H.R. 4690). With its blend of tax cuts and credits, "regulatory flexibility," and free trade provisions, Kemp's bill was a faithful incarnation of the original concept. However, like so many others, this enterprise zone bill died in committee.

Thus, the legislative history of enterprise zones during Reagan's second term contrasts in two key ways with the first term of his presidency. While Reagan did have the opportunity to sign legislation that included provisions for enterprise zones, albeit in a rather neutered form, support for enterprise zones waned. It appeared, therefore, that the prospects for substantive enterprise zone legislation under the next president would be bleak. Yet, if one peers beyond the congressional arena, important changes in the landscape favorable to enterprise zones are evident. For instance, by 1988, enterprise zone programs had been initiated in thirty-five states.[166] Not only were they increasingly prevalent among the states, but some key liberal groups and institutions supported them, such as the National Conference of Black Mayors, the NAACP, and the recently formed Democratic Leadership Council. Moreover, groups such as the National League of Cities were increasingly equivocal in their opposition. The spread of state enterprise zones led to the creation of the American Association of Enterprise Zones (AAEZ), an institution that in turn promoted spread of additional state zones and the creation of federal zones.[167] Thus, the institutional entrenchment of state zones reverberated back to Washington, D.C., where conservatives and liberals began to develop an ideologically informed institutional blueprint for the cities.

Back in Business: 1989–1992

The 1988 GOP platform, on which George H. W. Bush ran and won, both embodied the philosophy of Reaganism and served as a clear precursor to Bill Clinton's presidency. In respect of urban policy, the platform reasserted its conviction that the best way to achieve economic growth in cities as in the nation as a whole was to cut taxes. In urban areas, this meant enterprise zones "where tax incentives and regulatory reforms open the way for creating jobs and rebuilding neighborhoods from the ground up."[168]

As with much of the GOP platform, its vision for urban policy closely resembled much of the "third way" philosophy espoused by Bill Clinton and Tony Blair. For example, the platform claimed that "local control is the best form of administration," that "citizen choice is the key to successful government," and stated that "options in public housing transform slums into real communities, bustling with enterprise and hope."[169] Once again, there was support for enterprise zones at the heart of government, not least due to Jack Kemp's appointment as secretary of HUD. Indeed, it was suggested that Kemp only accepted the job after having secured a commitment to enterprise zones from President-Elect Bush.[170] However, just weeks before Bush took office, the efficacy of the enterprise zone approach was once again called into question by a GAO report.

The report was conducted at the behest of Kemp and Garcia, who sought an assessment of the state zones in order to inform federal legislation. The comptroller general chose to focus solely on the state of Maryland's zone because of its similarity to the provisions in the Enterprise Zone Development and Employment Act of 1985.[171] In addition to measuring the effect of zone designation on levels of employment, the study surveyed approximately 500 zone employers to ascertain which factors influenced their business decisions. The report made four key findings. First, any increases in employment that were identified in the Maryland zones "could not be attributed to the enterprise zone program."[172] Second, "employers who responded . . . were less likely to cite enterprise zone incentives as important to business location decisions than to cite as important other factors that are not part of an enterprise zone program."[173] Third, the Maryland enterprise zone program "yielded neither local nor federal program cost offsets." Fourth, it found "that the program did not achieve reductions in welfare dependence among workers employed by program participants."[174] Ultimately, the GAO concluded as follows:

> Although we do not claim the ability to fully generalize from this
> one state program to a federal program, these findings increase

doubt that a similar federal program implemented in similar conditions could stimulate local employment growth, produce local program cost offsets, or reduce welfare dependence among workers. This apparent weak performance of the EZ program may be caused, in part, by a mismatch between EZ program features and the factors that employers claim are most important in their business location decisions.[175]

The effect of the GAO report on elite journalistic opinion is difficult to discern. Although the *New York Times* editorial page cited the GAO's finding that the enterprise zones "failed to stimulate the economy or reduce unemployment and welfare rolls," in a signal of the ideological power of neoliberal ideas, it nevertheless renewed calls for a limited number of zones to be established.[176] While examples from elsewhere made for "mixed reviews based on too little experience," the *Times* thought the experiment would be worthwhile, since there is "good reason for government to take risks on behalf of the urban poor."[177] In contrast, *The Economist*, hardly unsympathetic to free-market approaches, argued that the enterprise zone idea was misguided because it would likely generate "wasteful tax subsidies." Moreover, it further argued that the kind of businesses most likely to be attracted are those that "would have opened up there anyway" and would not generate "truly new businesses."[178] These were exactly the same arguments made against the zones by those on the left, such as the AFL-CIO. Given the opposition of papers like *The Economist*, organizations such as the NFIB, and politicians such as Bob Dole, it is hard to dismiss criticism of the plan as a product of left-wing ideology. Nevertheless, the administration, with Kemp now at the helm as HUD secretary, continued to pursue the project.

President Bush used his first State of the Union address to continue his predecessor's tradition of calling for enterprise zones: "This is the year we should finally enact urban enterprise zones, and bring hope to the inner cities."[179] This sparked a battle between HUD and the Treasury over the net cost of the zones. While Kemp insisted that they would ultimately raise money for the Treasury, since the new businesses produced would pay taxes over the long term, Treasury Secretary Nicholas F. Brady argued that the tax incentives central to the idea would result in a net loss to the Treasury, which would increase the deficit.[180] As a compromise, Richard Darman,

Bush's budget director, agreed to a plan that would create seventy zones at a cost of $1 billion, far fewer than Kemp had wanted.[181]

Meanwhile, Congress took up enterprise zone legislation with renewed vigor. Of particular interest is the position of Charles Rangel, who switched from enterprise zone critic to sponsor of the Enterprise Zone Improvement Act of 1989 (H.R. 6). With the support of 118 Republicans and 103 Democrats, H.R. 6 proved remarkably popular. In addition to Rangel's bill, Kemp also submitted a proposal to Congress. Throughout the year, Kemp launched a charm offensive, which included meetings with the editorial boards of national newspapers to promote the idea and suggested it would be "absolutely crucial to reinvigorate this nation's anti-poverty agenda."[182] However, Kemp's efforts to rally support for the proposal were hampered by the GAO report, which had received a great deal of attention in the media and among skeptical Democratic legislators.

Advocates of the enterprise zone legislation attempted to confront this by challenging the validity of the GAO's claim that one could draw generalizable conclusions about enterprise zones on the basis of the Maryland study. Kemp's first line of attack was to argue that its findings were suspect because the Maryland zone did not feature significant tax incentives. At a March 1989 House subcommittee hearing, Kemp complained, "I just don't want to go through another eight years of getting these studies of some zone someplace that show that nobody started a business because there was no incentive. We've got to put some incentives, some teeth, some carrots, out there."[183] In summarizing enterprise zones, Kemp maintained that "in some states, they work; in other states, they don't particularly work because, frankly, as the GAO found out, where the incentives at the margin do nothing to attract the entrepreneur into that area, they don't work very well."[184] With a rhetorical flourish, he summed up, "Well, you don't need any study by the GAO to tell you that you are not going to get any empirical evidence of success if there are no incentives."[185]

Thus, the essential argument was that the Maryland zones failed because their incentives were too modest. However, a close look suggests that Kemp seriously underplayed the significance of the Maryland tax incentives, which were in fact substantial.[186] While the plan did not include relief from capital gains tax, a major component of the federal plan, it is unjustified to claim the incentives were minimal. The second move was to question the case selection.[187] The implication was that the Maryland zone differed substantially from other potential sites of investigation. However, the rationale was crystal clear: the Maryland program was "chosen because of its similarity to H.R. 3232."[188] Moreover, when considered alongside the Housing and Community Development Act of 1987, H.R. 6 was "substantially identical."[189]

A last line of attack cast doubt on the overall quality of the report. Congressman Schulze (R-PA) led the charge, arguing that the GAO report was "irrelevant" because it "compared apples with oranges. It was similar to comparing fine wine and cinder block." Schulze castigated the report for being "based on an incomplete, 2-year old report and fail[ing] to live up to the standards our committee deserves." Yet, even a cursory reading shows that the report was neither incomplete nor sloppily done. Indeed, the GAO made serious efforts to explore the key questions at hand systematically and to develop a methodology by which to make valid conclusions. Moreover, the report did not rule out the possibility of future success and even recommended that Congress institute demonstration zones to "experiment with incentives that can influence important factors in employers' business decisions (such as market access and property taxes) and [explore] arrangements that might reduce the possibility of employers' receiving incentives for behavior that was incidental to the program."[190]

The October 1989 hearings also involved the testimony of witnesses who presented evidence that both supported and opposed the plans. On the positive side were reports by those such as Marilyn Rubin, a professor of public policy at City University of New York, which showed that enterprise zones were successful in improving the relative position of designated areas within New York state. Rubin surveyed businesspeople to establish the effect of zone designation on their decisions to move or set up in a zone. According to her worst-case scenario, the total number of jobs created was 3,984 at a cost of $13,070 per job. She argued that the multiplier effect would account for an additional 12,322 jobs.[191]

In contrast, Brett Birdsong of the Urban Institute testified that the weight of evidence failed to bear out the advocates' claims. On the basis of a relatively exhaustive review of the literature, Birdsong concluded that enterprise zones were a "costly way" to achieve what "appear to be uncertain benefits for a very limited number of people and areas." He pointed out that few had found the zones "to have been effective at increasing investment and employment; and where growth has been observed in designated zones, it has not been directly attributable to enterprise zone incentives."[192]

The 1989 hearings also reveal a post hoc repositioning of the enterprise zone idea away from its roots in Conservative Britain. Jack Kemp claimed the enterprise zone idea came from the "Operation Bootstrap" Plan by the erstwhile Puerto Rico governor, Luis Munoz Marin: "Mrs. Thatcher used them in Britain. The difference between our policy under President Bush and Mrs. Thatcher's proposal is that they wanted to get people to move into areas rather than trying to target the incentive into the most depressed areas. Incidentally, the area of Britain, or London, that has been targeted for zone renewal is the docklands area of the Thames, and you will see probably one of the most magnificent rebuilding and renaissance in the docklands area. But, basically, it was taken from the free trade zone, and the Luis Munoz Marin idea."[193] However, as the evidence presented here and in Chapter 2 shows, the role of Operation Bootstrap in the development of the enterprise zone idea was minimal. As Cornell Professor William Goldsmith argued, the analogy with Operation Bootstrap is "very inapt" since it "hinged upon the eagerness of tens of thousands of Puerto Ricans to work at very low wages . . . and on a Federal waiver of all corporate income taxes." [194]

Also noteworthy is the ongoing reluctance of the Chamber of Commerce to endorse the concept. It urged Congress to "proceed with caution" because enterprise zones "are inherently discriminatory." Nevertheless, the chamber stated that the idea "should be tried but monitored carefully."[195] Furthermore, as Kemp accepted, it was clear that ongoing division within the administration continued to undermine the plan: "The president and Dick Darman looked at this as to how it would fit the needs of the Gramm-Rudman and the Budget Committee, and so it got pared back a little bit . . . Darman isn't honored by my testimony here."[196]

Thus, a combination of reluctant support within the administration, tentative commitment from key interest groups, and the GAO report helps to explain why Congress failed to pass enterprise zone legislation in 1989. Still unclear, though, is why H.R. 6 secured the co-sponsorship of over 200 members of Congress and why Congress would again consider enterprise zone legislation in 1990 and 1991.

After receiving a passing mention in the 1990 State of the Union address, in a key victory, Kemp secured $100 million for enterprise zones in the budget for fiscal year 1992, although it would create just twenty-five zones. Perhaps more important, in June 1990, Ways and Means Chairman Rostenkowski dropped his opposition to the plan and even proposed his

own bill (H.R. 5190). An aide to the chairman suggested that Rostenkowski's switch was born of concern to do *something* for cities that got little out
of budget negotiations: "Even though the chairman is not philosophically
supportive . . . it's not an absolute position. We don't have any money to
give the cities. Appropriating money for cities is just not popular up
here."[197] Rangel, who supported H.R. 5190, also proposed a bill (H.R.
4990), but ultimately, neither bill had sufficient support to go beyond the
committee stage and were dropped during budget negotiations. While Rostenkowski's bill was co-sponsored by just two Republicans and ten Democrats, seven Republicans and eighteen Democrats signed on to Rangel's.

One other noteworthy feature of the 1990 enterprise zone debate was
the rise of "empowerment" discourse by Kemp and those such as James
Pinkerton, who, along with a number of future Clinton aides, developed the
"New Paradigm Society," which focused on five principles: free markets,
individual choice, empowerment, decentralization, and a focus on "what
works."[198] Kemp sought to wrest the term *empowerment* from the left during the late 1980s. He began to call for a new "war on poverty" through
which enterprise zones would unleash the potential of the market, which
in turn would empower people.[199] *The Economist* also latched onto Kemp's
"empowerment" theme, explaining "he does not want to cut the government out, but to use it to empower the poor with choices."[200] This theme
of empowerment was woven into President Bush's discussion of enterprise
zones in the 1991 State of the Union address, in which he argued that such
initiatives would "put power and opportunity in the hands of the individual. . . . Freedom and the power to choose should not be the privilege of
wealth. They are the birthright of every American."[201]

Shortly afterward, Kemp used an article in the *Washington Post* to assert
that the achievements of the Great Society and other government programs
have been "meager" and that America's "socialist-like welfare and tax systems undermine the poor and perpetuate poverty."[202] True to form, Kemp
argued that eliminating the capital gains tax—"the tax on the American
Dream"—in "ghettos and barrios," through the creation of enterprise
zones, would be "the greatest affirmative action strategy of entrepreneurial
capitalism since the Steiger Amendment in 1978 and the Reagan tax cuts of
1981."[203] Here, empowerment rhetoric is the logical complement to the
neoliberal critique of embedded liberalism, which argued that the size of
the state was inversely related to individual freedom. Given this stance,

"empowerment" required and justified the rollback of the welfare state and the rollout of state institutions that promoted markets.[204] These themes, however, were no longer the preserve of the right. As Chapter 3 shows, they were further propelled by Bill Clinton and Tony Blair in the 1990s.

In the summer of 1991, two enterprise zone bills were introduced in the House, this time by Democrats: Rostenkowski's Enterprise Zone Tax Incentives Act (H.R. 11) and Rangel's Enterprise Zone Jobs Creation Act (H.R. 23). Rangel's bill, submitted on behalf of the administration, drew praise from the Heritage Foundation that claimed it "embodies much of the original vision of the enterprise zone concept" and went further than Rostenkowski's bill on capital gains tax relief.[205] The Rangel/administration bill received significant Republican support (ninety-four co-sponsors) and moderate Democratic backing (forty-three co-sponsors) but did not get out of committee. By contrast, Rostenkowski's bill, although it received ostensibly less support (nine Republicans to twenty-three Democrats), eventually made it to the president's desk. Like so many bills that contained enterprise zone proposals, H.R. 11 was initially ensnared by the committee system for a year. But in late April, riots in Los Angeles, sparked by the acquittal of the police officers implicated in the gratuitous beating of Rodney King, jolted the political establishment into action. With fifty-eight people dead and thousands injured, the political class accepted the need to address the urban crisis. Thus, talk of federal enterprise zones reemerged: H.R. 11 was back.[206]

While Los Angeles burned, commentators groped for explanations for the riots themselves and for what they revealed about the state of racial and class inequality in American cities. For Kemp, the events of spring 1992 only underscored the need for his favored prescriptions: "eliminating the tax on capital gains in enterprise zones" and empowering the poor through Earned Income Tax Credits, getting people off welfare into work, and expanding Home Ownership Opportunities for People Everywhere (HOPE)—all themes promoted by Clinton.[207] Sensing an opportunity, the American Legislative Exchange Council pressed for enterprise zones. Executive Director Samuel Brunelli argued the link between enterprise zones and empowerment was clear: "Job creation promotes dignity and self-sufficiency; government handouts promote dependency and despair. Enterprise zones create jobs. Government regulations and over taxation destroy entrepreneurship."[208]

On July 2, 1992, Congress restarted work on H.R. 11. Within just a week, 198 Democrats and 158 Republicans voted in favor, while 48 Democrats and 6 Republicans voted against. Democrats, led by Dick Gephardt, accepted a 50 percent cut in capital gains taxes—from 28 to 14 percent—for zone businesses as part of a compromise that secured the bill's passage.[209] But in a signal of the growing chasm between congressional Democrats and urban America, the plan was greeted with "disappointment and derision from the nation's mayors," who saw enterprise zones as "far too limited to answer the serious needs of the cities."[210] J. Thomas Cochran, U.S. Conference of Mayors executive director, argued, "We should really not call it an urban aid package, it's not worthy of the name."[211] Many of the nation's mayors called for direct spending through grants to fund infrastructure projects and other forms of job creation.

Having secured a compromise bill in the House, the Senate Finance Committee considered the enterprise zone proposals as part of a larger tax bill.[212] On July 29, the committee approved a $31 billion tax bill that contained just $2.5 billion for urban areas, despite calls for massive federal aid following the riots.[213] The incentives included a 40 percent credit against the first $20,000 of wages paid to each employee living within the zones, expansion of a targeted jobs tax credit for those employing zone residents, an increased expense allowance and accelerated depreciation of property. However, the bill removed the reduction in capital gains taxes that Kemp and Bush had sought. The Senate bill provided for 25 (15 in cities) enterprise zones, half the number in the House bill and far fewer than the 300 that Kemp had originally hoped for.

Massively disappointed with these revisions, Kemp suggested that the bill would draw a presidential veto. He argued that the plan "will not address the problems of L.A.; it will not address the problems of Detroit, of Newark, of the cities of this nation."[214] Kemp's shrill denunciations—"It's hollow; it's a hoax; it's a sham"—set off a spat with an "outraged" Lloyd Bentsen (D-TX), Senate Finance Committee chairman.[215] However, the White House described its view of the bill as "generally positive."[216] *The Washington Post* disagreed, describing it as the "worst bill of the year" in which urban aid had "been turned into a minor pumpkin of some enterprise zones that hardly anyone believes in, plus a little bit of social spending."[217]

In a bid to avert a Republican-sponsored bill[218] that would include the complete elimination of capital gains taxes in the zones, Bentsen doubled the amount of money proposed for the enterprise zones to $5.3 billion and increased the number of zones planned to 125 (75 in urban areas).[219] Ultimately, the Senate voted to pass the $34 billion urban aid and tax relief bill that included plans to create 125 enterprise zones.[220] In conference, legislators reached agreement on a five-year, $28 billion urban aid and tax relief bill. It included creation of fifty enterprise zones, had provisions for capital gains tax relief, and dropped the two tax-raising measures that President Bush vowed to veto. However, all the costs associated with the bill were matched by revenue-raising measures, which could have been construed as tax increases, although the bill was revenue neutral. On October 6, the House narrowly passed the final bill 235 to 201. This time, Democrats comprised the overwhelming majority, voting 196 to 79 in favor of the bill. Meanwhile 122 Republicans voted against the bill, while 39 remained in favor. Two days later, after a sixteen-hour filibuster, the bill passed the Senate on a bipartisan basis.[221]

With President Bush fearing that the minor tax increases in the bill would be used as a stick with which to beat him in the campaign, a veto looked likely. Bush had committed himself to raising "no new taxes" and lambasted Clinton for raising minor taxes while governor of Arkansas. Thus, Clinton threatened to exploit Bush's signing of the bill: "There is no question that if he signs it, it's inconsistent with his position, which is that he is not going to sign any tax increases, even though we all know he's raised a slew of them."[222] However, Clinton signaled his support for provisions of the bill itself: "There are a lot of good things in this bill."[223]

Realizing that the enterprise zone bill placed Bush in an invidious position, given the November 3 election, Democrats held it back to enable the president to sign it on November 4, 1992.[224] Nevertheless, Bush pocket vetoed the bill, even though his electoral fate was sealed. While he remained committed to enterprise zones, he railed against the pork contained in H.R. 11: "The original focus of the bill—to help revitalize America's inner cities—has been lost in a blizzard of special-interest pleadings."[225] Had the bill not succumbed to pork barrel politics, federal enterprise zones would have undoubtedly been created in 1992.

One may argue that the Los Angeles riots presented an opportunity for Democrats to propose a more radical alternative to enterprise zones. Yet the enterprise zone idea became seen as the only blueprint available. Increasingly, Democrats and organizations that ostensibly promoted urban interests, such as the NLC, refused to call for the restoration of aid to cities.

In a reflection of the Democrats' conversion to many of the neoliberal ideas that just a few years prior were primarily supported by the Republican right, the Democratic National Committee's 1992 platform pledged to "encourage the flow of investment to inner-city development and housing through targeted enterprise zones."[226] Moreover, its candidate reiterated his commitment to the concept. In August 1992, Clinton argued that "we need to bring free enterprise to south central Los Angeles and the inner cities of America and the rural communities of America."[227] One of the ways he envisaged doing that was through the creation of 75 to 125 enterprise zones, at a cost of an estimated $4.8 billion. Given that Clinton promoted enterprise zones as Arkansas governor, it is hardly surprising that he promoted them as a presidential candidate and would sign a bill creating a version of enterprise zones once in the White House.[228]

The political development of the enterprise zone shows how an idea initially promoted by a minority of Republican neoliberals, a few Democrats, and a couple of conservative and liberal institutions became the flagship urban policy of all three presidential candidates in 1992. The key effect of the enterprise zone debate was the creation of a ready-made coalition for incoming President Clinton, reflected in Table 2. This is surprising given the overall balance of evidence generated by empirical inquiry, which suggested enterprise zones would have little overall effect, and the indifference of those interest groups that stood to gain most materially from the proposals. A key part of the answer lies in the triumph and institutionalization of neoliberal ideas. Before concluding, I will sketch out the scholarly assessments of enterprise zones.

Scholarly Assessments of Enterprise Zones

The success of the final enterprise zone bill in Congress demonstrated that pivotal Democrats either supported enterprise zones or did not wish to spend their political capital to block them. With a new Congress and a new administration set to enter the political arena, one could argue that 1992–1993 represented a window of opportunity for the approach to be shelved. It is therefore worth considering briefly what conclusions the scholarly literature had reached about the state enterprise zones by the end of 1992.

Table 2. Enterprise Zone Coalition c. 1992

Supportive	Indifferent/Mixed Position	Opposed
Institutions	*Institutions*	*Institutions*
➤ Heritage Foundation	➤ National Federation of	➤ AFL-CIO
➤ Sabre Foundation	Independent Business	➤ AFSCME
➤ American Legislative	➤ National League of	Urban Institute
Exchange Council	Cities	➤ *Washington Post*
(ALEC)	➤ General Accounting	➤ *The Economist*
➤ Real estate	Office	➤ Some rank-and-file
➤ AAEZ	➤ U.S. Treasury	Democrats
➤ NAACP	➤ Chamber of Commerce	
➤ National Conference of	➤ Office of Management	*Key Individuals*
Black Mayors	and Budget	Arnold Cantor (AFL-CIO)
➤ National Conference of	➤ *New York Times*[a]	Marc Bendick
Mayors[a]		
➤ Republican Party		
➤ Democratic Party		
leadership[a]		
➤ DLC		
➤ HUD		
➤ G. H. W. Bush		
presidency		
Key Individuals		
Stuart Butler (Heritage)		
Jack Kemp		
Barber Conable		
John Chaffee		
Charles Rangel[a]		
Dan Rostenkowski[a]		

[a] Denotes a switch of position in favor between 1984 and 1992.

The most prominent scholar whose work supports the enterprise zone concept is Marilyn Rubin.[229] In short, she finds that of 500 companies that she interviewed, 70 percent said the enterprise zone incentives had no effect on their location and/or expansion decisions, while 30 percent said the incentives did. In 1992, Rubin appeared before a House committee to summarize her work on New Jersey: "My study concluded that . . . the impact of the program on New Jersey's economic and on its fiscal base has been positive. . . . [But] Zone incentives, if significant, could so enhance the competitiveness of zone establishments as to hurt business competitiveness of establishments outside the zones. The results may thus overstate the impact of New Jersey's program to the extent that they do not reflect displacement of economic activity from non-zone areas in the State."[230] Professor Michael Wolf also testified on behalf of enterprise zones. His main contribution to the scholarship regards his insight into how the political process has shaped intergovernmental and public-private relationships. Although Wolf cited some studies that show a somewhat positive effect of enterprise zones on job creation, he noted that "too often these and other analyses fall short when it comes to tracing employment and investment figures directly to the attributes of the program."[231]

Thus, even the two most supportive scholars, who were called to Congress to testify in favor of enterprise zones, only provide limited empirical evidence and equivocal support for the concept. By far, the arguments on which enterprise proponents relied upon most were based on a theoretical commitment to a loose version of supply-side economics or, to put it differently, to neoliberal ideology. The balance of scholarly evaluation as a whole, however, shows that state enterprise zones have enjoyed little success in significantly reducing urban unemployment or promoting economic growth.

Many studies that appear to show a positive impact of enterprise zones often fail to demonstrate that zone designation primarily accounts for the changes observed, as Erickson and Friedman's findings and the 1986 HUD study of ten enterprise zones illustrate.[232] Moreover, while Erickson and Friedman find a positive relationship between enterprise zones and employment growth, they show that the zones in which this occurred were "characterized as having basic labor skills, public infrastructure, and transportation access that can make areas attractive for investment with marginal but catalytic contributions that EZ designation, incentives, and visibility can provide."[233] Moreover, while they detect a mean *gross* gain in employment of 232 jobs per year, based upon surveys from zone administrators, they do not identify the *net* employment change. Rubin and Wilder's analysis, which does take these factors into account, concludes that while "there is a clear temporal relationship between the establishment of an enterprise zone program and increased economic activity . . . the evidence is equally clear that in certain urban areas, enterprise zones have failed to generate significant economic growth. Every study that examined data from multiple cases revealed variable outcomes."[234]

The GAO finding that tax incentives had little or no effect on job creation in Maryland's enterprise zone has been discussed above, as have Marc Bendick's critiques. In addition to these studies, Sar Levitan analyzed the experiences of Michigan, Virginia, Maryland, Indiana, and New Jersey. He found that while the zones in Michigan, Virginia, and Maryland were largely ineffective, the Indiana and New Jersey zones did see increases in both employment and tax revenue. However, the apparent successes in Indiana and New Jersey, as Rubin acknowledged, may be a function of the selection process that "favored areas with a strong potential for becoming economically viable."[235] Levitan draws the following conclusions: "The ability of small businesses to utilize investment-oriented tax incentives is questionable"; "in the absence of an education and basic skills training program, the deficiently educated and the unskilled . . . will not benefit from the program"; and, "from a macroeconomic view, enterprise zones policies created few new jobs or businesses."[236] Finally, Levitan points out the limits to the "empowerment" rhetoric promoted by Bush and Kemp: "Empowering zone residents requires that they be economically self-sufficient. For this to happen, residents need to be able to compete effectively in the labor market. Tax expenditures offered by the pending federal enterprise zone bills will not accomplish this nor will they provide the mechanisms needed to 'empower' zone residents."[237] A number of scholars have echoed Levitan's conclusions. Dabney has argued that "financial incentives, such as tax refunds, credits, and abatements that are offered to new businesses through enterprise zone programs, only marginally affect the firm's location decision and are not a major location factor."[238] Furthermore, Greenbaum and Engberg found that enterprise zone "programs did not lead to increased housing prices nor occupancy rates in zone areas, nor did they have any positive impacts on employment measures."[239]

Peters and Fisher provide the most exhaustive evaluation of enterprise zones, based on analysis of 75 zones in thirteen states. They note that "the vast majority of the recent literature suggest[s] that enterprise zones have little or no positive impact on growth." Their own statistical work reinforces this finding because "in distressed places [incentives] are not likely to be large enough to make a huge difference," although they contend that "enterprise zones could be effective if they were targeted appropriately, were managed correctly, and were large."[240] In respect of creating jobs for residents, Peters and Fisher argue that "it is a mistake to believe that the location of enterprise zones in older inner-city neighborhoods will improve the employment opportunities available to inner-city residents."²⁴¹ Indeed, they estimate only about one-quarter of jobs in enterprise zones go to residents. On the fiscal impact of enterprise zones, they conclude that "the direct revenue effects of enterprise zone incentives on state and local governments combined are very likely to be negative, and very strongly so."²⁴² Thus, the balance of evidence suggests that while a few enterprise zones have modest positive effects on business and employment growth, the vast majority have little or no net effect. These include those identified by Kemp as the most successful.²⁴³

Conclusion

So why were enterprise zones promoted? It is clear that pure interest-based explanations are inadequate. After all, the interest groups outside of Congress whose members stood to gain the most—the Chamber of Commerce and the NFIB—at best lent tepid support. Furthermore, the empirical evidence certainly did not provide a basis for legislators to promote or be convinced of the need for enterprise zones; the evidence was mixed at best. Instead, enterprise zones were promoted by conservatives because doing so dovetailed with their overarching ideology and provided cover while they cut federal funding to cities. However, that conservatives supported tax cuts to businesses is not especially surprising.

More puzzling is why Democrats supported enterprise zones. Two explanations stand out. The first is the "no alternatives" argument, which claims that while Democrats ideally would have proposed increased direct expenditures, they knew that doing so would draw a presidential veto, so did not propose any. But doing nothing for cities was not politically acceptable, and so voting for enterprise was the least-worst option.²⁴⁴ This explanation appears to hold up fairly well but fails to explain why they wrote the idea into their 1992 party platform. Nor does it explain why they passed very similar legislation in 1993. Second, it could be argued that Democrats were responding to urban constituencies that demanded enterprise zone legislation. This is closer to the mark, but those constituencies could have been equally satisfied with a range of policies, not all of which would have been infeasible. My argument is that ideas played an independent role. Enterprise zones represented a neoliberal blueprint to which Democrats increasingly turned in a context of uncertainty about what do about chronic urban poverty and unemployment.[245] Even while Congress stalled, this blueprint became embedded in the states and was promoted nationally by key institutions with time, resources, and influence to promote their agenda. The sense of urban crisis was heightened in the face of the Los Angeles riots, during which time the window of opportunity for change opened. But enterprise zones obscured the view. As such, Clinton's urban policy would be a small variation on a neoliberal theme. Thus, while Butler, Kemp, Garcia, and Rangel lost the battle to institute enterprise zones, they won the war of ideas and built a coalition able to support Clinton's empowerment zones.

Chapter 2

Dealing with Those Inner Cities: The Neoliberal Turn in British Urban Policy

We have a big job to do in those inner cities, a really big job . . .
because we want them too next time.
—Margaret Thatcher, Conservative Party Central Office, June 1987

As I am one of your keenest supporters, I am determined that we
should succeed. If we do so, your contribution to our ultimate victory
will be immense.
—Margaret Thatcher to F. A. Hayek, May 5, 1979

As Margaret Thatcher stood on the steps of Conservative Party Central Office in the aftermath of her historic third general election victory in June 1987, she declared "we have a big job to do in some of those inner cities, a really big job . . . because we want them too next time." Implicit in her statement was the notion that urban voters had punished the Conservatives for their neglect of cities. Yet it could hardly be argued that her party's lackluster performance in Britain's urban areas was the result of inaction on her government's part. To the contrary, the urban policies instituted by Margaret Thatcher's government in the early 1980s were at the heart of the Conservative Party's neoliberal ambitions. Indeed, enterprise zones and the urban development corporations (UDCs), both established in 1980, were among the government's first forays into the clear blue waters of tax cuts and deregulation. They not only preceded the more famous examples of neoliberalization—privatization, the full embrace of monetarism, the wholesale transformation of the tax system, the sale of public housing, and the defeat of the trade unions—they were also at the crest of the neoliberal wave.

The Conservatives' radical agenda was also reflected in the institutional revolution of urban government by which an entire level of local government—the metropolitan county councils, including the Greater London Council—was abolished. Such activism stands in marked contrast to the virtual absence of a federal urban policy in the United States, notwithstanding the Reagan administration's abortive attempts to pass federal enterprise zones, as detailed in the previous chapter.

But while the Conservatives' urban initiatives valorized isolated pockets of Britain's inner cities, all too often these gilded ghettoes were surrounded by vast urban tracts of dereliction characterized by widespread unemployment, escalating inequality, and weakened public services. No wonder, then, that in 1987, few city dwellers turned out to vote for the Iron Lady.[1] Yet the government's response to these election returns was not a change in the substance or tenor of policy but rather more of the same. Within months, more UDCs were created and, by 1991, competitive bidding and public-private partnerships were institutionalized via City Challenge and the Single Regeneration Budget.

Neoliberalism was the ideological lynchpin that gave these urban policies coherence, just as it did for the Conservatives' economic policies more broadly. It both provided a diagnosis of the urban condition and offered an ostensible set of solutions to arrest cities' decline. These analyses and prescriptions bore a striking resemblance to the critique of the institutions and policies often associated with the "postwar consensus" and to the neoliberal celebration of the virtues of individualism, free markets, and deregulation. But beyond providing a theoretical framework to understand and correct the British political economy, neoliberalism also served to justify the measures whose benefits clearly served the interests of property and service-led capital at the expense of the manufacturing sector, the working class, and the poor.

This chapter traces the evolution of urban policy under the Conservative Party in the context of the political and economic development of Britain from the late 1970s to the early 1980s. In doing so, I link the neoliberal ideas, electoral and economic interests, and the institutional constraints that shaped the Conservative Party's economic policies more broadly to its approach to urban policy by focusing on enterprise zones, urban development corporations, and the rise of public-private partner-ships. Contrary to the claims made by a number of scholars,[2] that Thatch-er's government neither represented a radical break with the past nor was propelled by a commitment to neoliberal ideas, my analysis shows that her government was clearly motivated by neoliberal ideological goals that had profound effects for urban areas. This ideational mission was quickly institutionalized in the form of enterprise zones and the UDCs. However, I do not argue that ideas alone explain the outcomes observed below. I will show how neoliberal ideas interacted with key interests and institu-tions to refashion urban policy in a neoliberal mold. Throughout, I reflect upon the ideational and institutional similarities and differences between the United States and United Kingdom to provide an account as to why neoliberal urban policy came to fruition rapidly in the United Kingdom but was stymied at the federal level in the United States while proliferat-ing in the states. This chapter details the overarching argument that Con-servative rule resulted in a clear break with the past in both principle and practice and that this shift turned on the ideological commitment to building neoliberal institutions rather than the dominance of pro-business interests.

The Neoliberal Breakthrough: Economic Crisis, Ideological Splits, and Policy Change

Out of the ruins of the Second World War emerged a British political accord best described as the "postwar settlement."[3] Like its American cousin, "embedded liberalism," the postwar settlement amounted to a bipartisan commitment to full employment driven by Keynesian demand-management and to the maintenance of the welfare state. These goals were realized amid a period of sustained economic growth from the late 1940s to the early 1970s. Yet even during this relatively prosperous period, con-cerns about the relative decline of the British economy were beginning to surface.[4] These anxieties mushroomed when a series of global economic shocks in the 1970s raised the specter of absolute decline and even eco-nomic catastrophe. The perception of crisis shattered the postwar settle-ment, creating an intellectual lacuna into which neoliberal ideas poured. This chapter argues that the Conservative Party's urban policies that sprang up from this tumult not only reflected these ideas but were intended to blaze a trail for some of the archetypal neoliberal policy developments of the Thatcher era. In order to substantiate this claim, I sketch the key economic, political, and ideological developments that gave rise to Margaret Thatcher's election victory in 1979.

While the prime targets of the neoliberal critique are often considered to be the Labour governments of Harold Wilson (1974–1976) and James Callaghan (1976–1979), Thatcherism was "as much a repudiation of the record of the [Conservative] Heath government" (1970–1974).[5] As Thatcher recalled in her memoirs, "Ted Heath's government . . . proposed and almost implemented the most radical reform of socialism ever contemplated by an elected British government. It offered state control of prices and dividends and the joint oversight of economic policy by a tripartite body representing the Trades Union Congress, the Confederation of British Industry and the Government in acquiescence in an economic policy."[6] What Thatcher describes are the institutional arrangements very similar to those followed by both Labour and Conservative governments in the 1960s and 1970s in their bid to contain inflation while maintaining (almost) full employment, as a series of both Republican and Democratic presidents had done in the United States. In respect of unemployment, the postwar settlement had been relatively successful: the average rate of unemployment between 1948 and 1971 was just 2.1 percent.[7] Despite governing during a period of low unemployment (or perhaps because of this), Heath was engaged in protracted battles with the trade unions, in part sparked by his attempt at comprehensive labor reform through the Industrial Relations Act of 1971, which made unions responsible for the costs of broken contracts during strikes. Heath had entered office in 1970 on the promise to "change the course of history of the nation," which meant, in part, abandoning Labour's incomes policies and turning in a more pro-market direction. However, in the face of rising unemployment and the 1972 miners' strike, Heath made his famous U-turn and, like Nixon in the United States, pursued a Keynesian approach of statutory incomes and prices policies and a loose monetary policy as part of his "dash for growth."

It is important to note in this regard that unlike Thatcher, who was willing to let unemployment rise above three million, Heath's U-turn occurred after he made the calculation that one million people out of work would be too high a price to pay. In stark contrast, in 1980, when unemployment was over two million and still rising, Margaret Thatcher told her enraptured party conference that this time there would be no such reversal:

"We shall not be diverted from our course. To those of you waiting with bated breath for that favorite media catchphrase, the 'U' turn, I have only one thing to say. 'You turn if you want to. The lady's not for turning.'"[8]

Although inflation and unemployment were already creeping up by 1972, in part fueled by the collapse of the Bretton Woods system, it was the surge in world oil prices, triggered by the Yom Kippur War in November 1973, that plunged Britain and the world into a period of economic instability that fostered a series of political crises. The price of oil quadrupled in the space of a year and U.K. inflation leapt from 9.2 percent to 16 percent. In late 1973, with energy prices soaring, the miners began industrial action, which led Heath to declare a state of emergency and impose a three-day working week to conserve energy. In December, the prime minister called a general election to determine "who runs Britain." The electorate decided twice in 1974 that it would be Labour, led by Harold Wilson.[9]

Once in power, the Labour Party attempted to control inflation while keeping unemployment down via the "social contract" with the trade unions.[10] Across the Atlantic, President Ford attempted to deal with inflation using similar techniques. In the United Kingdom, efforts by Wilson and his chancellor, Denis Healey, appeared to come to naught, however, as inflation, unemployment, and the government debt levels—measured by the Public Sector Borrowing Requirement (PSBR)—continued to rise. By 1976, Britain's economic woes were compounded by a run on the pound, which forced the government, now led by James Callaghan,[11] to go to the International Monetary Fund to secure a $3.5 billion loan. In return, the Fund demanded drastic cuts in public spending to ease the budget deficit, maintenance of high interest rates, and the sale of £500 million of government shares in British Petroleum.[12] After fierce debates within the cabinet, the government acceded, and with that the commitment to full employment was abandoned and the acceptance of monetary targeting began. The postwar settlement lay in ruins. While in 1971, Richard Nixon had declared that he was now a Keynesian in economics, five years later, the irony was now reversed as a Labour government imposed monetarist measures.[13] Labour's reluctant turn away from Keynesianism and toward monetarism was reflected in a famous passage from Prime Minister James Callaghan's speech to the Labour Party Conference in 1976: "We used to think that you could spend your way out of a recession and increase employment by cutting taxes and boosting government spending. I tell you in all candour that that option no longer exists, and insofar as it ever did exist, it only worked on each occasion since the war by injecting a bigger dose of inflation into the economy, followed by a higher level of unemployment as the next step."[14] While Labour had adopted monetarist techniques to try to control inflation, it was not the case that "all were neoliberals now." After all, Labour remained committed to keeping unemployment from skyrocketing and certainly did not accept the Hayekian view that state intervention in the economy was by necessity antithetical to personal freedom. As such, this shift in policy making should be considered what Peter A. Hall refers to as a "second-order change" by which policy makers "altered the instruments of macroeconomic policy without radically altering the hierarchy of goals behind policy."[15] The paradigmatic, third-order change would come later.

For a brief period, it appeared that Callaghan and Healey were successful. After the trade unions had been persuaded to accept a pay settlement around a 4.5 percent norm in June 1976, inflation, having peaked at 24.2 percent in 1976, fell to 8.3 percent by 1978;[16] GDP growth in 1978 ran at 3.2 percent;[17] unemployment held steady at around 5.5 percent; and the Labour Party was ahead in the polls. This confluence of factors led commentators and even members of the cabinet to anticipate that Callaghan would call a snap general election in October 1978. However, he opted to wait and, as a result, led the country into the "Winter of Discontent" of 1978–1979, during which a wave of strikes swept across Britain. Labour was doomed. During this torrid time, most infamously, industrial action left rubbish piled high in the streets and, as a result of striking gravediggers in Liverpool, left the dead unburied. Thus, it was in this context, with these images seared into the public mind, with unemployment again creeping up and inflation back on the rise, that the last rites of the Labour government and of the postwar settlement were read.

The immediate political beneficiaries of these events were of course the Conservatives. Under Margaret Thatcher's leadership, they went on to win the general election in May 1979 with an overall majority of forty-three.[18] In contrast to Callaghan's reluctant turn toward monetarism, the neoliberal shift in the Conservative Party was ultimately far more comprehensive and enthusiastic. But this only occurred after the victory of the neoliberal "economic evangelicals" over the old guard represented by Ted Heath.[19] As noted above, Margaret Thatcher viewed Heath's economic and industrial policies as politically disastrous and ideologically bankrupt. However, initially she was not as vocal or as fervent in her view as the radical Conservative MP Keith Joseph, who in many respects was the chief intellectual architect of the neoliberal turn in the Conservative Party after 1974.[20]

Although Joseph is now regarded as one of the most outspoken neoliberals of the Thatcher era, he only became so after a Damascene moment. Joseph describes his ideological transformation into a full-fledged free marketeer in almost religious terms. In the run-up to Ted Heath's general election loss, his neoliberal views suddenly crystallized: "It was only in April 1974 that I was converted to conservatism. I had thought I was a Conservative but now I see that I was not really one at all."[21] His "conversion" took place through contact with the ideas, pamphlets, and books emanating from the pro-market Institute of Economic Affairs (IEA), where, upon leaving government, he went for intellectual sustenance and guidance. Joseph received it in droves. The IEA had provided a platform for the work of F. A. Hayek and Milton Friedman, the intellectual fathers of neoliberalism.[22] The ideas of Hayek and Friedman, who received the Nobel Prize in economics in 1974 and 1976, respectively, influenced profoundly the understanding of the nature of the "crisis" in which Britain found itself and shaped the Thatcher-led Conservative Party's strategy for resolving it.

There have been a number of excellent books and articles by scholars who have drawn attention to the personal and intellectual influence of key neoliberals such as Hayek and Friedman on Conservative Party policy in the 1970s, so I will not go into detail here beyond a couple of illuminating examples.[23] First, Yergin and Stanislaw, on the basis of numerous interviews with the key personnel, claim that Thatcher demonstrated her unequivocal commitment to neoliberal ideas in the most dramatic fashion:

> In the mid-1970s, not long after becoming leader, she visited the Conservative Party's research department. One of the staff was partway through his paper advocating that the Tories adopt a middle way between left and right when she brusquely interrupted him. She was not interested in refurbishing Harold Macmillan. Instead, she reached into her briefcase and pulled out a book. It was Hayek's *The Constitution of Liberty*. She held it up for all to see. "This," she said sternly, "is what we believe." She slammed it down on the table and then proceeded to deliver a monologue on the ills of the British economy.[24]

A more concrete example of the connection between Hayek and Thatcher exists in the archives. Upon receiving the news that Thatcher had been elected prime minister, Hayek sent a congratulatory telegram thanking her for "the best present on my eightieth birthday anyone could have given me."[25] Her response makes clear the link between his ideas, her thinking, and the Conservative government's agenda: "I was very touched by your kind telegram. It has given me great pleasure and I am very proud to have learnt so much from you over the past few years. I hope that some of those ideas will be put into practice by my government in the next few months. As I am one of your keenest supporters, I am determined that we should succeed. If we do so, your contribution to our ultimate victory will be immense."[26] Finally, it was indeed clear as early as 1976 that leading members of the Conservative shadow cabinet saw Hayek and Friedman's ideas as consistent with their own. This is made plain in an exchange between Keith Joseph, Willie Whitelaw,[27] and Geoffrey Howe, who had become extremely concerned about an upcoming BBC series in which the Keynesian economist John Kenneth Galbraith would deliver a series of lectures. Joseph saw Galbraith as "the most dangerous intellectual that we have on the economic front."[28] As such, he feared that "the series could be immensely damaging to the country, and to us" and could not go without a weighty rebuttal.[29] This sparked a debate as to who might respond. Howe suggested "the proper balance to Galbraith might be provided by a series of talks from Hayek or Friedman."[30]

Joseph understood that in order to translate into concrete policy proposals the ideas that were generated and promoted by the IEA, an alternative institution was required. In June 1974, Joseph managed to persuade Ted Heath to allow him to found the Centre for Policy Studies (CPS), whose central task, Joseph argued, would be to "convert the Tory Party" to neoliberal ideas.[31] He recruited Thatcher to be his vice-chairman. The CPS would promote radical ideas and would expose the alleged contradictions of the mixed economy through the dissemination of key books and pamphlets and in speeches, which Joseph delivered in droves. At the top of the reading lists handed out by Joseph was Hayek's 1944 *The Road to Serfdom*, "the bible of Joseph and his coterie."[32] In September, just a month before Ted Heath lost his second election of 1974, Joseph delivered his famous "Preston Speech," described by some as the " 'seminal text' of the Conservative intellectual rethink."[33] Joseph issued a stinging repudiation of Heath's policies, arguing along the lines of Hayek and Friedman that inflation and unemployment had been caused by government and that Keynesianism should be abandoned in favor of monetarism. "To us, as to all post-war governments, sound money may have seemed out of date: we were all dominated by the fear of unemployment. It was this which made us turn our back against our own better judgment and try and spend our way out of unemployment."[34] The speech was a major political event, evidenced by its verbatim publication in the *Times* newspaper.[35] But persuasive speeches and well-funded think tanks would do little in themselves to foster the desired shift in the climate of opinion; ideas alone would not be sufficient. Although neoliberal breakthrough would be greatly aided by the IEA and the CPS, what was required was the capture of the political institutions of the Conservative Party and then, of course, the country.

Having lost the general election and having been publicly undermined by his erstwhile cabinet colleagues, Ted Heath might have resigned. Instead, the stubborn Heath limped on, which prompted an election contest for the party leadership in January 1975. Initially, Joseph considered standing and enjoyed the support of Thatcher and Howe. However, a highly controversial speech in October 1974 damaged him greatly, and he soon withdrew his name from potential consideration.[36] Nevertheless, he "had blazed the trail" for Margaret Thatcher, who soon stepped into the breach.[37] Given her commitment to Joseph's neoliberal policy preferences, she inherited his would-be supporters. After two rounds of elections, Thatcher was duly elected Conservative leader. When it came to building her shadow cabinet, she left Joseph in charge of policy matters and made Howe her shadow chancellor on the basis that "we're the ones who have the same idea of where we need to go."[38]

The idea of where, in Thatcher and Howe's view, the country "needed to go" was reflected in two key documents on economic policy, both of which were published in 1977: *The Right Approach to the Economy* and *Stepping Stones: The Right Approach*, coauthored by Geoffrey Howe, Keith Joseph, Jim Prior, and David Howell, set out the Conservative Party's economic strategy for the next government.[39] The document represented a somewhat tamer version of what was to come, due to an effort to achieve compromise between Howe and Joseph's neoliberal approach and Howell and Prior's more moderate views. Nevertheless, it highlighted many of the future Thatcher government's key themes: a monetarist prescription for tackling inflation, reductions in government spending, tax cuts for individuals and business, and an end to Labour's social contract.[40] Underpinning *The Right Approach* was the idea that Britain's economy was undermined by excessive "obstacles to enterprise," which must be overcome through an "enterprise tax package" and the deregulation of planning and employment laws. In an especially ideological passage from *The Right Approach*, the logic that would inform the Conservative assessment of Britain's urban condition was showcased in stark terms: "It is the small business sector that has been throttled, first by the war on profits, then by personal taxation, and finally by a crudely destructive chaos of capital taxes. Small businesses depend for their existence and prosperity on the accumulation of capital in private hands; such an accumulation is anathema to the socialist, so deeply resented that he often hardly realises when his anti-capitalist policies end up by knocking away his own job from under him."[41] Just as an "enterprise package" would be required to revive the economy as a whole, enterprise zones—areas in which taxes and regulations would be reduced to a minimum—would breathe new life into urban areas that had long been suffocated by the *dirigiste* state.[42] It would also help to foster a new cultural mode—the "enterprise culture" that the neoliberals were so committed to inculcating among the British people. For Thatcher, the policies themselves were a means to that end: "Economics are the method; the object is to change the soul."[43]

The Embrace of Monetarism

The paradigmatic economic shift of the late 1970s was the change by which "inflation replaced unemployment as the preeminent concern of policy-makers."[44] The ostensible method for doing this would be the application of monetarism. My purpose here is not to provide an account of Thatcher's economic policy through the 1980s but rather to offer an example of the shift in economic policy that reflects the commitment to the same type of neoliberal thinking that informed the urban policy changes that occurred concurrently and were extended throughout the 1980s. Long before entering office, Thatcher, Joseph, and Howe were all determined to use monetarist techniques to squeeze inflation out of the system. As we have seen, Callaghan introduced cash limits in public spending in 1976, but his approach would pale in comparison to what occurred under the Conservatives.

As Hall notes, replacing unemployment with inflation as the overarching concern of policy makers meant that "monetary policy replaced fiscal policy as the principal macroeconomic instrument, and it was reoriented toward fixed targets for the rate of monetary growth."[45] Meanwhile, incomes policies, exchange controls, and other regulatory methods were abandoned. For reasons that need not detain us here, the Treasury was instructed to focus on M3, the broadest measure of money supply in the economy, which includes currency in circulation, bank deposits, and other nonbank savings deposits, which was strongly influenced by the PSBR.

The major assault on M3 was launched in Geoffrey Howe's March 1980 budget, which he describes in his memoir in a chapter entitled "The Apex of Monetarism."[46] Howe had clearly been inspired by the embrace of monetarist techniques in the United States. He described Paul Volcker as "America's sheet-anchor of economic sanity."[47] The basis for Howe's actions was laid out in the Medium Term Financial Strategy, which called for firm target ranges for monetary growth and high interest rates. Moreover, it took no action to reduce the rising exchange rate. The result of this strategy was massive deflation, which undermined industry and triggered a rise in unemployment unprecedented since the 1940s. As Lord Kaldor wrote in 1983, "These [policies] together have reduced the national output by nearly 20 percent and increased the level of unemployment by 2 million or more."[48] In Keegan's view, what propelled the Conservatives, despite opposition from the Treasury, the Bank of England, and the Confederation of British Industry, was a "monetarist ideology . . . [which] meant that the warning signals in the economy were not heeded and sensible reactions were delayed."[49] Eventually, the government did change course, and inflation did abate, but not before the livelihood of millions was sacrificed at the altar of ideological consistency.

The Neoliberal Prescription for Cities in the Early 1980s

Geoffrey Howe argued in a 1978 speech to the conservative Bow Group[50] that, like the general malaise in the British economy, the decline of the inner cities resulted from the exorbitant levels of taxation and burdensome regulations that stifled small business activity: "The consequent lack of success is breeding social tension and threatening to destroy the framework of civilized existence. And in many areas, the burgeoning of State activity now positively frustrates healthy private initiative, widely dispersed and properly rewarded. Over-regulation is a major part of the British disease."[51] For

Howe, the solution was to be found in the application of one of neoliberalism's key tenets: supply-side economics, which proposes that high marginal tax rates are fetters on the willingness of investors to take risks in the marketplace. According to this view, since levels of investment in a given area are determined by the prospective rate of return, lower tax rates would provide incentives for entrepreneurial risk taking, which ultimately would create jobs. As Howe argued for the inner cities and for the country as a whole, the "return to economic vitality crucially depends upon the fundamental reform of our tax system. . . . We must restore the legitimacy of becoming rich by taking risks: *that* is the way to promote the creation of real jobs."[52] The other "almost equally urgent need is to set about the sensible deregulation of our economy."[53] Although the Conservatives had comprehensive national plans for both tax relief and deregulation, Howe understood the Conservatives "would have to wait to get support." While his primary aim was to use the enterprise zones "to encourage investment, enterprise and, above all, job creation," he also saw enterprise zones as a "kind of trial run intended to foster support for the other possible changes, which we sought to introduce more broadly in the British economy."[54] "An 'enterprise-zone' initiative would be designated to go further and more swiftly than the general policy changes that we have been proposing to liberate enterprise throughout the country. It would *not* be based upon considerations of regional policy. . . . Rather it would be set up to test market areas or laboratories in which to enable fresh policies to prime the pump of prosperity, and to establish their potential for doing so elsewhere."[55] Howe later stated that "enterprise zones were meant to offer proof of what could be achieved in the very worst parts of our economy by sudden, concentrated bursts of capitalism. They were a product, to a large degree of our wish to show quickly that our overall economic policy of supply-side incentives would work."[56] Thus, in Howe's estimation, enterprise zones themselves were the shining example of policy that would reignite the entrepreneurial flame that had been snuffed out by the state. Moreover, through convincing others as to the efficacy of such ideas and techniques, enterprise zones would play a central role in the neoliberal persuasion.

In this inchoate rendering, Howe proposed the following: the suspension of all detailed planning controls, the forced sale of public land by auction, exemption from Development Land tax "and perhaps exemption from rates," a guarantee to new businesses in the zones that tax law would not be changed in ways that disadvantaged them, the suspension of price controls and pay policies, and a commitment that "all these conditions would be guaranteed for a stated and substantial number of years."[57]

As Chapter 1 detailed, Howe's enterprise zone concept built upon the idea presented almost a year earlier by Sir Peter Hall, a planner, Fabian, and erstwhile socialist. In June 1977, while *The Right Approach to the Economy* was being drafted, Hall delivered a speech to the Royal Town Planning Institute Conference that soon caught Sir Geoffrey's eye. The biggest challenge, as Hall saw it, was to provide the conditions to "get innovation going again." This, he argued, would require something rather different from the conventional strategies of attracting industry given the "general sense . . . of decay and apprehension" in many of Britain's inner cities.[58] Inspired by the remarkable innovative strides made in parts of the Far East, Hall suggested a more radical solution that dovetailed nicely with the neoliberal principles espoused by Hayek, Friedman, Howe, and Thatcher:

> If we really want to help inner cities, and cities generally, we may have to use a final possible remedy, which I would call the Freeport solution. This is essentially an essay in Non-Plan. Small, selected areas of inner cities would be thrown open to all kinds of initiative, with minimal control. In other words, we would aim to recreate the Hong Kong of the 1950s and 1960s inside inner Liverpool or inner Glasgow. The area would be based on fairly shameless free enterprise. It would be free of United Kingdom taxes, social services, industrial and other regulations. Bureaucracy would be kept to an absolute minimum. So would personal and corporate taxation. Trades unions would be allowed, as in Hong Kong, but there would be no closed shops. Wages would find their own level.[59]

Despite Hall's caveat that his idea "would represent an extremely last ditch solution to urban problems," one could scarcely have imagined a concrete policy proposal that chimes more harmoniously with the ideal-typical neoliberal urban policy. Small wonder, then, that it so enamored Howe and many neoliberals in the United States. But while the idea struck Thatcher as an "imaginative proposal," she decided not to include it in the 1979 Conservative Party manifesto.[60]

The manifesto did preview some—although by no means all—of the key policies of the government: monetarism to control inflation, reduction in the deficit, the sale of council houses, trade union reform, cutting income tax, and a hint at privatization. With Labour in disarray in the aftermath of the Winter of Discontent, the Conservatives were swept to power. Not only was the chancellor able to implement key neoliberal economic reforms, but he could also promote his self-professed "pet project," enterprise zones.

Howe included enterprise zone proposals in his 1980 budget, as part of his "enterprise package," which included raising the threshold on the capital transfer tax and cutting the development land tax and the corporation tax for small businesses. Whereas before the election, pleas for enterprise zones came from an opposition spokesman, Howe's requests now came with institutional backing. As a result, "Margaret [Thatcher] was not disposed to resist the idea, now that it came from a Chancellor in office—and when unemployment, above all in areas of urban dereliction was a growing problem."[61] Thus, Howe announced that enterprise zones would be created in the upcoming Finance Bill. Companies in the zones would enjoy 100 percent capital allowances for both industrial and commercial buildings (meaning the total costs of new buildings could be deducted from taxable profits); complete relief from development land tax, rating, industrial training certificates, and levies; and a drastically simplified planning scheme.[62]

Eventually, through the Local Government Planning and Land Act of 1980 and the Finance Act of 1980, eleven ten-year zones were designated during the first round: Salford/Trafford, Swansea, Wakefield, Clydebank, Dudley, Hartlepool, Corby, Tyneside, Speke (Liverpool), Isle of Dogs (London's Docklands), and Belfast.[63] The zones were selected because they contained high levels of unemployment caused by the flight of heavy industry.

Besides enterprise zones, the other major urban policy innovation of the early Thatcher period was the introduction of UDCs by Michael Heseltine, the secretary of state for the environment. UDCs were created at the same time as the enterprise zones under the Local Government Planning and Land Act (LGPLA) of 1980. In contrast to enterprise zones, UDCs were to become quasi-autonomous governing institutions, run by unelected boards, which would coordinate economic development in a given area. Although fully committed to the Thatcherite agenda, Michael Heseltine viewed (and still views) himself as a practical politician, with little interest in the neoliberal canon. Moreover, his ideas about the appropriate role for government are far less radical than those of some of his neoliberal colleagues. In marked contrast to Thatcher, Howe, and Joseph, Heseltine bristles at the very notion of his ideas being informed by Hayek or Friedman:

"I wasn't in the business of carrying out other people's thoughts. I was in the business of solving problems as I saw them."[64] Indeed, Heseltine's biographer suggests that he "often expressed skepticism of the harsher aspects of monetarism" and questioned whether the government should be making cuts in public spending "during a recession."[65] Moreover, he took a dim view of the classical liberal philosophy espoused by some fellow Tories: "The laissez faire idealists may hold that all government action, to the extent that it inhibits the free exercise of the citizen's will must threaten his liberty and weaken his spirit. This is too romantic and impractical a view for men and women who hold public office, and it has nothing to do with the Tory party."[66] This line of thinking led Heseltine to think that the hands-off enterprise zone method was likely to be insufficient. For him, the state needed to play an active role in making public lands attractive for private investors:

> The underlying problem of deprivation, in philosophical terms, is that the areas are uncompetitive . . . the task of the public sector is to get rid of the negative value and if you get rid of the negative value, the capitalist system will flow in. So if you have large areas of toxic land, don't think that the private sector are going to invest there, because they're not . . . [if] all around is deprivation and toxicity, then they won't [invest] because they'll be a sore thumb sitting out in this derelict area. So you have to take a comprehensive view and the enterprise zone would not have done that.[67]

Yet, he was firmly committed to a "Tory philosophy" that was consistent with a neoliberal approach insofar as it consists of promoting markets and market mechanisms, using state power to do so if necessary. In reflecting on his work on urban policy, he argued, "Slowly but steadily the culture of the enterprise system was being forcibly injected into the attitudes of local government towards the spending of public money. These policies were right, the philosophy essentially Tory."[68]

According to the Local Government Planning and Land Act, "the object of an urban development corporation shall be to secure the regeneration of its area" by "bringing land and buildings into effective use, encouraging the development of existing and new industry and commerce, creating an attractive environment and ensuring that housing and social facilities are available to encourage people to live and work in the area."[69] The act empowered the secretary of state to vest land in the UDCs and provided them with development control, which in practice meant that the corporations could grant themselves planning permission by resolution.[70] Moreover, it also enabled the secretary of state to declare a UDC if he or she "is of the opinion that it is expedient in the national interest to do so."[71]

Given the scale and sweeping powers of the corporations, Imrie and Thomas have some justification of the description of UDCs as the "flagship, the jewel in the crown, of Conservative government urban policy."[72] In the initial round, only two were created: the London Docklands Development Corporation (LDDC) and the Merseyside Development Corporation (MDC). However, between 1987 and 1992, the government considered it to be "expedient in the national interest" to add ten more.[73] In both the LDDC and the MDC, the boards were appointed directly by the secretary of state and assumed the planning powers of the local authorities. In Chapter 6, I investigate the enterprise zones and the LDDC in detail through my London Docklands case study, so for the present, I will focus briefly on the national picture.

UDCs share a number of themes with enterprise zones, not the least of which is to provide for a business-friendly environment. As Minister for Local Government Tom King noted, "Urban Development Areas, like much of the rest of inner urban areas, need the private sector's energy and resources." King asserted that "we must enlist the flair, drive and initiative of the private sector as the only possible way of restoring lasting prosperity to the decaying areas of some of our towns and cities."[74]

The Conservatives were not shy in enlisting the help of the private sector; in fact, they celebrated it. In a reflection of the pro-market goals of the Thatcher government's centralizing tendencies, the Department of the Environment directly appointed pro-business chairpersons and members of the UDC boards. In 1981, Heseltine named Nigel Broackes as chairman of the London Docklands Development Corporation and Basil Bean as chief executive officer of the Merseyside Development Corporation. Tellingly, Broackes, described by the *Times* as "Britain's most elegant tycoon," was the chairman of Trafalgar House, a property, shipping, and engineering conglomerate.[75] Given that both Broackes and Bean were "well known within the City and market institutions," it is unsurprising that "under this kind of control the UDCs have tended to pursue market-oriented strategies within their designated areas."[76] Both in Docklands and Merseyside, the primary strategy was to sell off land to private developers with minimal input from local communities.[77]

While an ideational account of Conservative urban policy is central to my analysis, it is plain that the UDCs cannot simply be seen as the institutional manifestation of neoliberal ideas. Unlike enterprise zones, UDCs also chimed perfectly with the Conservative Party's political agenda of eliminating or at least side-stepping Labour-controlled local authorities who impeded their transformation of the British state.[78] This also occurred with the abolition of the metropolitan county councils through the Local Government Act of 1985. Yet this brazenly political dimension was laced with ideological calculation. After all, the Labour-controlled authorities whose powers were abolished had "self-consciously adopted alternative [arguably socialist] models to the more conventional policies of the Conservative government, although the differences were sometimes more rhetorical than substantive."[79] Indeed, Heseltine apparently convinced Thatcher to acquiesce to his decision to abolish the metropolitan county councils on the basis that they were socialist.[80]

Thus, the objective was to enhance the central state's power *for the purpose* of achieving ideologically determined goals; that is, the preference for an increased role for business, private property, and markets in urban areas. As such, the UDCs represent an interesting manifestation of neoliberal urban policy, which points to the ostensible contradiction between neoliberalism in theory and what David Harvey and Brenner and Theodore call "actually existing neoliberalism."[81] The apparent tension arises from the centralization reflected in the government-appointed UDC boards, which assumed the powers hitherto enjoyed by the local authorities, which were subject to democratic control. This seems to conflict with the theoretical preference among neoliberals for reducing the size and scope of the state. I argue, however, that usurping the power of "socialist" local authorities and placing it in the hands of state-sponsored capitalists is consistent with the broader neoliberal goal of reducing the influence of those interests and institutions hostile to the pro-market agenda. Hence it is a prime example of *neoliberalism by design*. For purists, the creation of quasi-autonomous nongovernmental organizations (QUANGOs) clearly will not do. But for politicians who hold a neoliberal agenda, there is no contradiction whatsoever in using their authority to promote market mechanisms and to empower those who "know what they're doing," that is, businesspeople.

The final notable innovation of Conservative urban policy was the creation of public-private partnerships (PPPs). As we saw in Chapter 1, the enterprise zone idea is a case of urban policy crossing the Atlantic from Britain to America. In the case of PPPs, the winds of policy change blew in the opposite direction. As Barnekov et al. point out, advocates of PPPs were inspired by the entrepreneurialism at the heart of the apparent revival of America's inner cities as a result of policies such as the Urban Development Action Grant: "Debates in the House of Commons, government reports, technical documents, professional conferences, and academic publications all promoted the benefits of the US style public-private partnership."[82] In an explicit example of transatlantic policy learning and transfer, Donna Shalala, assistant secretary for policy development at the U.S. Department for Housing and Urban Development, met with British officials in 1979 to advise them on PPPs and ways to use public funds to "leverage" private capital.[83] Moreover, in April 1981—in the aftermath of a series of riots in British cities—an Anglo-American conference was held in which officials exchanged ideas as to how to enhance the role of the private sector. One result of this conference was the creation of "Business in the Community" (BIC), an umbrella organization of large corporations, which enjoyed the "support of staff from central government and the private sector, government grants and tax exemptions for company contributions."[84] BIC's primary purpose was to produce ideas for small business development in urban areas and present recommendations to the secretary of state. At roughly the same time, Heseltine also created the Financial Institutions Group (FIG), comprising senior managers drawn from leading banks, building societies, and pension funds. According to the House of Commons Environment Committee, the purpose of the group was "'to develop approaches and ideas for securing urban regeneration,' and to increase 'private sector involvement in urban questions.'"[85] Heseltine dispatched this group to the United States to explore how incentives could be used to lure business into the cities.[86] Thus, in a sign of things to come, the government outsourced its own policy making to the private sector, which unsurprisingly delivered a series of proposals for reducing the role of local and national government in urban development.

A telling outcome of these transatlantic transmissions was the Urban Development Grant (UDG), which Heseltine "modeled on the Urban Development Action Grant developed in the USA."[87] For Heseltine, the UDG was "arguably the most important thing [he] did in the whole of this process."[88] This was because it made grants to local authorities contingent upon the inclusion of the private sector in their plans. For Heseltine, what "was revolutionary in 1979" worked over time to foster the enterprise culture that Thatcher, Joseph, Howe, and Heseltine felt so passionately about:

> The public and private sectors did not talk; no relationship; deep suspicion. [But] instead of shouting at each other, they became friends. Councilors talked to businesspeople. They were competing for government grants and there's nothing more incentivising for local government than to find that the only way to get money is to comply with certain conditions—i.e. partnership with the private sector—then they get the money. The whole climate changed and personal relationships changed.
>
> The Labour Party resisted it at every turn. But money has its own eloquence. In the end money prevailed. There was cash on the table. . . . But if you want it, these are the terms. So of course the resistance crumbled. . . . But instead of shouting at each other . . . they became Bill and Ben. But it worked. . . . That was the fundamental thing that changed and of course the Labour Party had to pack in their resistance to these ideas.[89]

The melding of the public and private spheres that these policy developments represent suggests a consequential shift from government to governance in which corporate interests are entwined with the development and delivery of public policy.[90] This change, in which the state itself becomes neoliberalized, was likely to create consequential structural advantages to business interests. As Harvey argues, "The neoliberal state will tend to side with a good business climate as opposed to either the collective rights (and quality of life) of labor or the capacity of the environment to regenerate itself."[91] As shown in Chapter 3, Tony Blair's urban policy continued in much the same vein, which highlights the degree to which the neoliberalization of the British state, like its American counterpart, has become consolidated by the very political parties that once opposed this process.

Having established the key elements of the Conservative Party's early urban policies, we now turn to focus more directly on the scholarly debate.

Controversies and Assessments

The academic debate about urban policy in many respects echoes broader controversies about the nature and impact of Thatcherism. In the upcoming sections, I will focus primarily on the debates surrounding enterprise zones. I will pay more attention to UDCs in my case study of London Docklands in Chapter 6.

Success or Failure?

Not surprisingly, much of the literature on enterprise zones is concerned with the empirical question of whether they "worked." In short, while there is not complete consensus, the general view is that the enterprise zone experiment did relatively little to create new jobs but did encourage new investment, albeit at significant cost to the taxpayer.[92]

As one might expect, Geoffrey Howe offers a sanguine appraisal of the experiment that he initiated. In a 1988 speech to the Bow Group, Howe focused on the effect of the zones in the Isle of Dogs. Given the estimated £1 billion of private investment, 85 percent of the land developed, and with the promise of the Canary Wharf, Howe argued that "the development effect has been spectacular."[93] He further noted of the zones in general that "by the beginning of last year [1987], a total of 63,000 people were employed in enterprise zones, compared with 30,000 in 1982."[94] Unlike some of the enterprise zone boosters in the United States, however, Howe avoids the error of assuming that all new development and employment within the zones can be attributed to the zone characteristics themselves: "It is impossible to tell precisely how many jobs might have occurred somewhere else in the economy without enterprise zones." However, he does argue that "there are indeed encouraging pointers which suggest that many real new jobs (that wouldn't have been created elsewhere) have come about."[95] Sir Geoffrey further noted that the enterprise zone had been successfully exported to the United States. While "few bear any resemblance to what we have seen here in Britain . . . [a]ll bear witness to the British Conservative belief that 'setting the people free' is the best route to prosperity for all." With uncharacteristic bravado, Howe concluded that the "spirit of enterprise" that the zones represent "is a symbol of the new Britain emerging under the most radical, the most innovative, the most successful and the most exciting government of this century."[96]

A series of more dispassionate analyses as to the effectiveness of enterprise zones have been conducted by the Department of the Environment (DOE).[97] They present a decidedly mixed picture. In an extremely comprehensive 1987 study, commissioned by the DOE and completed by PA Cambridge Economic Consultants, researchers considered the costs of the zones, the impact of zone designation upon net additional economic activity and employment, and the physical regeneration of their local areas.[98] As the report points out, two types of costs were involved. First, there were costs to the Treasury that accrued from (a) foregone proceeds from rate relief (local taxes), which were reimbursed to the local authority, and (b) receipts foregone as a result of capital allowances. Second, there were the costs of public expenditure associated with infrastructure that would not have occurred in the absence of the enterprise zone policy. Between 1981–1982 and 1985–1986, the total public cost directly attributable to the EZ policy was £297 million (in 1985–1986 prices). Of this amount, 27 percent represented rate relief, 22 percent infrastructure and land acquisition, and 51 percent capital allowances.[99]

Despite Howe's claim that it is "impossible" to know precisely the net effects of the enterprise zone incentives, the report tried to do exactly that. It shows that the effect of the enterprise zone expenditure on employment was a gain of 63,000 jobs, of which around 35,000 could be directly attributed to the zone. However, if one takes into account the job losses to areas immediately adjacent to the zones, "the total number of additional jobs supported directly and indirectly to the local area by the Enterprise Zone experiment is estimated to be 12,800," at a cost of between £23,000 and £30,000 per job.[100] These statistics led Peter Hall—the progenitor of the scheme—to an equivocal and somewhat unenthusiastic conclusion: "The experiment in practice produced relatively small numbers of really new jobs, and at appreciable—but perhaps not excessive—cost."[101]

In 1995, the DOE commissioned another study that considered the effect of the zone incentives upon levels of employment and physical regeneration.[102] The report's findings were based upon interviews with companies that sought to establish whether investment and location decisions were influenced by the incentives. Of the companies asked, 30 percent reported that their additional activity was wholly due to the enterprise zone, while 9 percent responded that it was partially due to the zones.[103] Therefore, 61 percent of businesses responded that "new" business activity was neither wholly nor partially attributable to the zone benefits. When weighted in terms of employment, 40 percent thought they would have located outside the local area but still in the United Kingdom, about 6 percent would have delayed or canceled startup, and 4 percent would have been smaller. Only 1 percent thought they would have located abroad. It is estimated that 48 percent of employment would have been based in the enterprise zone or in the local areas in the absence of zone subsidies.[104]

In respect of jobs created, the report shows that total employment in the nine first-round zones that were de-designated in 1991 was 74,600. However, the "total displacement" of jobs from the local area that was induced by the enterprise zone incentives was 48,000, "indicating that 28,100 permanent jobs were additional to the local area as result of the designation of the round one Enterprise Zones."[105] When one also takes into account the extra economic activity attributable to zone activity generated in the local area "through market linkage effects," the net additional permanent jobs amounted to 34,900.[106] The same pattern holds true for the second-round zones that were de-designated in 1993–1994. While the gross number of permanent jobs in the zones was measured at 51,100, the total net additional number of jobs, including local linkage and short-term multiplier effects, was estimated at 23,150.[107] The total cost to the taxpayer for these effects, as well as the infrastructural investments made, was between £798 million and £968 million (in 1994–1995 prices). Table 3 summarizes these findings.

In respect of jobs, then, the impact on enterprise zones might be deemed unimpressive compared to the promises made by their promoters, the vast scale of urban unemployment in the 1980s, and given the costs per job. Moreover, 72 percent of businesses within the zones were either already there (11 percent) or had moved in or set up new branches in the zones (61 percent). Thus, the overall effect of the zones did not generate substantial *net* increases in employment or in new businesses. The muted impact of enterprise zones is one of the reasons the government decided to end the experiment.[108] Yet, as will be discussed in the conclusion, the Conservative-led government (2010–2015) reintroduced enterprise zones in 2011. Interestingly, in the United States, where the results were similarly unimpressive, enterprise zones continued to be popular: by the mid-1990s, forty states of the union had established enterprise zones. As Chapter 1 illustrates, this is for institutional and ideological reasons.

How Radical Was the Conservatives' Urban Policy in Practice?

As has been established above, the enterprise zone *agenda* was radically neoliberal and, in this sense, was consistent with the Thatcherite approach

Table 3. Enterprise Zone Statistics

		Cost to the Exchequer	Gross Jobs Created	Net Jobs Created	Percentage of Firms on Site	Percentage of New Firms Transplanted/New Branches	Percentage of Firms Newly Created
DOE 1987 report		£297 million (1985–1986 prices)	63,000	12,800	23	37/14	25
DOE 1995 report	First-round zones	£632 million (1994–1995 prices)	74,600	28,100	N/A[a]	N/A	N/A
	Second-round zones	£336 million (1994–1995 prices)	51,100	18,624	N/A	N/A	N/A
	Total	£798–968 million in 1994–1995 prices	125,700	46,724 58,050 (includes multipliers)	11	38/23	28

[a] Not available.

to economic policy. However, some argue that *in practice*, enterprise zones are "a particularly poignant example of the way that, especially in Britain, radical ideas are taken on board by the establishment, only to be sanitized into something completely harmless."[109] In a similar vein, Stuart Butler—who, as Chapter 1 notes, was the person who introduced the idea to America—laments the dearth of radicalism apparent in the British enterprise zone experiment: "The British Enterprise Zones are not places in the inner city where the door has been thrown open to unfettered free enterprise. In truth, the door has only been partially opened to one segment of free enterprise and it is far from clear that it is the right segment to achieve an economic rebirth of the inner cities. The door still appears to be firmly closed to small entrepreneurs who offer the best hope for the innovative ideas and jobs that are needed.[110] James Anderson makes a similar point. He argues that, given the considerable state intervention involved in enterprise zones, in practice Conservative urban policy has been "markedly different from the rhetoric of laissez faire" associated with Geoffrey Howe's original pronouncement.[111] Similarly, Grant Jordan asserts that the bill introduced to parliament "represents a considerable retreat from the 1978 proposals."[112]

Even a cursory glance at the literature on Thatcherism reveals a similar line of reasoning among some scholars who attempt to correct what they consider an undue emphasis on radical change. Peter Jenkins implies that Thatcher's agenda, although somewhat radical in tone, had very little to do with the ideas of Hayek and Friedman. "She did not need to read books by Milton Friedman or Friedrich von Hayek to learn the importance of sound money or that the power of the State was the enemy of freedom. She had learnt these self-evident truths at her father's knee."[113] This "folksy" view of Margaret Thatcher's thinking is reflected in Gamble's point that she "was seen by some as comparable to a mid-West American politician, strong on principles, weak on understanding the modern economy."[114] Furthermore, Gamble, who does argue that Thatcherism represented a radical break from the past, nevertheless asserts that the Thatcher government had "no detailed blueprint for policy."[115] He cites privatization policy, which was not fully envisioned prior to 1979, as evidence for this view. Peter Kerr argues along similar lines that "Thatcherism emerged after 1979 as an ill-defined and often incoherent (except at a discursive level) strategy."[116] Thus, he maintains that the early Thatcher period, far from representing a radical break from the past, was ad hoc and experimental and only gained coherence over time. Yet, the archival evidence presented above and elsewhere suggests that the Conservatives did indeed have a radical agenda, informed by neoliberal thinkers, which was in many respects largely fleshed out in advance of taking office, as reflected in *The Right Approach to the Economy*, *Stepping Stones*, and their plans for urban enterprise zones and urban development corporations.

More frequently, though, skeptics have argued that while Margaret Thatcher and her supporters may indeed have harbored neoliberal ambitions, once in office, they fell short of their aim of radically transforming the British political institutions. Marsh and Rhodes and Peter Riddell all aver that, rhetoric aside, the first two Thatcher governments were far more pragmatic than ideological or radical in character.[117] Moreover, Paul Pierson, in his important book—*Dismantling the Welfare State?*—argues that Conservative efforts at retrenchment were limited and in fact reduced the chances for radical change later on:

> If the British Conservatives had only modest success in pursuing programmatic retrenchment, their record in achieving systematic retrenchment was if anything less impressive. Several changes in the political context in Britain have probably weakened the prospects for radical change in the welfare state. Shifts in public opinion, modifications of political institutions, and the restructuring of government finances have all tended to diminish rather than enhance prospects for further retrenchment. The Thatcher government did have some success in reducing the political influence of welfare state supporters—and of unions in particular—but its overall record could not be regarded as one of notable systematic retrenchment.[118]

Pierson's claims with respect to the Thatcher government echo his argument that the Reagan administration's reforms failed to deliver the transformation of the welfare state that its neoliberal supporters championed.

On economic policy specifically, some have argued—given the Labour government's turn toward monetarism in 1976—that the breakdown of the post-war settlement and the onset of neoliberalism occurred before the Conservatives even took office and that, therefore, the radical turn was not Thatcherite per se.[119] But while these claims rightly alert us to the limits of the Conservative Party's neoliberal project, the evidence presented here suggests that on economic and urban policy, the Tory achievements were indeed transformational, as the enterprise zones, UDCs, and the prioritization of tackling inflation over unemployment illustrate. While many have noted that the overall tax burden and levels of social expenditure *rose* during the 1980s and the early 1990s,[120] the tax system, through cuts to the top rates of income tax and the rise in value-added tax (a sales tax), was reformulated in a regressive direction, and part of the rise in social expenditure was a function of increased payments to the unemployed. Moreover, the Conservative Party's willingness to allow unemployment to rise to unprecedented levels contrasts sharply not only to previous Labour governments but also to Ted Heath's Conservative government, which abandoned its flirtation with monetarism when unemployment breached the 1 million mark. Conversely, under Margaret Thatcher's government, unemployment not only rose above 3 million but remained there for fifteen consecutive quarters (from 1983 Q3 to 1987 Q1) and only barely dipped below 2 million for three quarters in 1989–1990 before rising again until 1997.[121] Although some Conservatives expressed concern for the plight of the unemployed, Norman Lamont, the Conservative chancellor between 1990 and 1993 under both Thatcher and her successor, John Major, summed up the party's position and the neoliberal logic on which it was based when he remarked that "rising unemployment and the recession have been the price that we have had to pay to get inflation down. That price is well worth paying."[122] This view represents a radical shift away from the bipartisan consensus that government ought to (and did) intervene to assuage elevated levels of unemployment.

With respect to enterprise zones, while it is certainly the case that Howe's program did not correspond precisely to Hall's (or even Howe's) initial vision of total suspension of all regulations and taxes, Hall goes too far to suggest that they were "sanitized into something completely harmless."[123] As stated above, they included 100 percent capital allowances, complete relief from development land tax, rating, industrial training certificates and levies, and a drastically simplified planning scheme. Moreover, as illustrated in Chapter 6, the Conservatives radically reconfigured London Docklands' political institutions in ways that undermined greatly the capacity and authority of local democratic government. As noted above, such institutions were often headed by business interests, alienated elected officials, and gave local people little say. Moreover, Heseltine's innovations—such as the BIDs, the FIG, and the conditions for local government financing—increased the role of business and market forces at the expense of the local state. But Tory radicalism did not end there. Rate capping (i.e., a limit on local property taxes) and the abolition of the metropolitan authorities both represent a dramatic shift. Finally, as Chapter 3 illustrates, Pierson's prediction that changes in Britain's political context in the 1990s were likely to be fetters of retrenchment is not borne out with respect to urban policy or welfare reform. As such, the urban landscape both ideologically and institutionally was fundamentally neoliberalized during the 1980s, which challenges the narrative of Thatcherism as a limited and incomplete project.

What 1980s Urban Policy Tells Us About the Role of Ideas, Institutions, and Interests

As Christopher Hood points out, social scientists have often sought to explain economic policy changes with reference to interests, institutions, or ideas.[124] For the remainder of this chapter, the case of urban policy in the 1980s will be deployed to help advance our understanding in this regard by providing a grounded account of the ways in which interests, institutions, and ideas combine at certain moments in time *and in space* to shape concretely the trajectory of political development. As the introduction indicates, the argument advanced here is that while ideas are crucial to understanding urban policy, this does not render interests and institutions irrelevant; quite the contrary. The key is to identify those occasions when ideas interact with interests and institutions to produce durable political change. Moreover, while efforts to isolate the effect of each of these variables are unlikely to be convincing in the final analysis, there is value in considering the relative impact of ideas, institutions, and interests at various points on the arc of political change.

One of the most surprising findings of this study is that the role of business interests in shaping urban policy during this period was extremely limited in both the American and British contexts. This is contrary to expectations because small businesses and corporations (capital) stood, in principle, to benefit from a lightened regulatory load and reduced or eliminated tax burden. Furthermore, firms would surely benefit from the infrastructural investments made in enterprise zones by the UDCs. This has led some scholars and commentators, such as William Goldsmith, to argue that the enterprise zone idea "has been seized upon by some . . . as a weapon for business in the struggle with labour over production costs."[125] However, there is very little evidence to support both this view and the claim that business groups had a significant influence on the emergence of the enterprise zone idea.

Indeed, a close reading of the historical record shows that in both the United Kingdom and the United States, business was at best split on the issue of enterprise zones and, at worst, opposed them outright. While the Confederation of British Industry came out in favor of the zones in 1981, it noted that "the ironic part of the whole scheme is that businesses outside zone boundaries not only lose out completely but have to foot the bill for the £20 million capital allowances and the £50 million rates reduction."[126]

Many other business groups opposed the zones because of the comparative disadvantage that accrued to firms on the "wrong" side of the enterprise zone border. As Walter Goldsmith, director-general of the Institute of Directors, asserted, "The arbitrary manner in which the enterprise zone boundaries are being drawn up can mean the difference between life and death for those firms that find themselves outside the zone."[127] The director-general of the British Chamber of Commerce, Sir Terrence Beckett, also cast doubt on the efficacy of enterprise zones, although he did endorse the logic of deregulation and tax reductions for businesses across the board: "If the whole country were made an enterprise zone and removed from the crippling burden of business rates and planning restrictions, then we might really be talking."[128] Moreover, in the early 1980s, a number of businesspeople, including Bernard Tennant of the National Chamber of Trade, wrote to the *Times* to protest against the enterprise zone plans.[129] When in July 1982, Geoffrey Howe announced plans to create eleven new enterprise zones, the *Financial Times* reported that "many developers and estate agents [were] already concerned that the benefits provided by the existing zones have not been worth the disruption caused to some local markets."[130] In fact, as Doreen Massey points out, some business groups even lobbied for the reintroduction of planning controls, which resulted in automatic permission for retail outlets being limited only to developments below a certain size.[131]

In light of these views, interest-based arguments that claim enterprise zone policy was created as a result of business-lobbying are not persuasive. While Massey joins many others to argue that "enterprise zones will be just another addition to that collection of spatially discriminatory policies which . . . play one area, one group of workers, against another, to the net benefit of capital," it does not follow that these interests played a decisive role in shaping or lobbying for the policy.[132] Although it is certainly the case that enterprise zones served the interests of private property and resulted in the strengthening of class power in capitalists' hands,[133] it does not necessarily follow that enterprise zones were introduced *because* of these interests. This reasoning seeks to derive cause from outcome and rests on an unrealistically reductionist view of political actors as purely tools of certain interests with no agency, agenda, or independence of their own. Moreover, it assumes that there is no need to look at the empirical evidence in order to trace out the processes by which a particular idea evolved into policy.

Having established that the influence of business interests in the development and implementation of the enterprise zone policy was limited at best, the question of whether organized interests played a key role in propelling the policy once it was implemented remains. A range of scholars have shown how certain policies, once implemented, are likely to be reinforced or undermined through a policy feedback mechanism.[134] In Pierson's view, "policy feedback was a crucial determinant of retrenchment results in Great Britain and the United States. In both countries, policy choices generated resources and incentives that helped structure the development of relevant interest groups."[135] Thus, the Thatcher government was able to radically alter the pension system because its fragmented nature undermined interest group formation. In contrast, the neoliberal ambition to privatize Britain's National Health Service was stymied because the policy itself was not only universal but almost universally popular, so that it became self-reinforcing. As such, the Labour Party was easily able to "mobilize the electorate in favor of public health care for all, free at the point of delivery."[136]

In respect of enterprise zones, the relative absence of interest group lobbying for their continuation, in light of their limits and potentially disruptive impact, helps to explain why they were wound down.[137] The failure of the policy to create and nurture a coalition of business and local authority interests in favor of the policy meant that, unlike in the United States, the enterprise zone idea lost momentum.[138] But this is only part of the answer. Institutional and ideational explanations are required to complete the picture.

Efforts to "bring the state back in" to political analysis have resulted in the return of institutional analysis to political science research.[139] Of most relevance in the British context is Margaret Weir's argument that the timing and the manner of the adoption of Keynesian ideas were shaped by the character of Britain's governing institutions, most important, the Treasury.[140] Weir explains that the Treasury's "strategic position within the bureaucracy" interacted with the "hierarchical character of the British administration" to prevent policy innovation along Keynesian lines in the interwar years.[141] However, the exigencies of the Second World War "provided the shock to the economic orthodoxy that the Depression had been unable to produce," which opened up the Treasury to new personnel with new ideas, sources of information, and expertise. "These changes paved the way for the eventual acceptance of Keynesianism as the cornerstone of British economic policy."[142] After this critical juncture, Keynesian thinking became embedded in the Treasury, which reverted to type, but this time with a new economic orthodoxy that held sway until the mid-1970s.

With respect to the post-1979 Thatcher government, a number of scholars have argued that the constellation of institutional barriers faced by Conservatives blunted their ideological designs. For instance, Marie Gottschalk has shown that British carceral policy in the 1980s and 1990s was determined by the interaction between the Thatcherite agenda and the state's bureaucratic institutions.[143] Gottschalk illuminates a central tension within Thatcherism between an emphasis on law and order, on one hand, and neoliberal economic policy, on the other.[144] For Gottschalk, the vacillation between the growth of the carceral state during the early 1980s and moderation later on is partially explained by the tensions between the authoritarian and neoliberal strands of New Right ideology. But Gottschalk finds that "institutional factors also prodded the Conservatives to make some important retreats in the battle for law and order."[145] In an account that chimes with Weir's, Gottschalk notes that "because Britain has a more unitary coherent state, economic and social policy making is more centralized in London."[146] As a result, the law and order rhetoric of the Thatcher movement was blunted by the resistance both of the Treasury—which applied "constant pressure . . . to cut expenditures for prisons, law enforcement, and criminal justice"[147]—and enlightened Home Office career civil servants, who played a "pivotal role and exercised an important check on the penal population."[148]

Thus, those working in the historical institutionalist tradition would predict that radical new policies such as enterprise zones are likely to encounter institutional friction as they permeate their way through granite-like political structures, especially in the British state with its permanent civil service packed with appointed representatives of the establishment. Indeed, Geoffrey Howe harbored precisely these fears. In 1978, he predicted institutional resistance from "the grey men whose job it is to consider the 'administrative difficulties' of any new idea [who] would be ready enough to start manufacturing the small print that could stop the initiative in its tracks."[149] Grant Jordan suggests that interdepartmental struggles over enterprise zones led to "policy erosion resulting from lack of political agreement" among the key government departments.[150] As such, Jordan concludes that "in the evolution of British policy the radical concept of government-free zones was replaced by characteristics that added up to a traditional industrial location policy."[151]

In contrast to the emphasis of many historical institutionalist accounts, which highlight the blunting effect of institutional matrices on radical change, however, it would appear that for both enterprise zones and UDCs, institutions assisted rather than inhibited the neoliberal turn in British urban policy. Not least, this is because the primary champion of the enterprise zone—Sir Geoffrey Howe—became chancellor in 1979 and was thus in charge of the Treasury, arguably the most influential political institution within the British state. Looking back, Howe recalls very little resistance from within the Treasury.[152] Moreover, enterprise zones enjoyed the support of the prime minister personally, and there is no evidence that officials at 10 Downing Street opposed the scheme. Thus, while institutions, *given certain interests and ideas*, potentially afford a series of roadblocks to opponents of change, in the case of enterprise zones, I find that Howe's institutional setting gave him distinct advantages vis-à-vis other cabinet colleagues and their respective departments. Thus, unlike other areas of policy—for example, law and order, the National Health Service, and overall levels of taxation—where state institutions were able to stem the tide of Conservative radicalism, the promoters of urban policy were ultimately able to harness government institutions to their advantage and in some cases abolished those, such as the Greater London Council, which stood in their way.

Archival evidence also shows that the decision to retain certain regulations casts doubt on Jordan's hypothesis that institutional friction deradicalized the policy. What appears at first blush to be evidence in favor of the notion that enterprise zones were not radically neoliberal turns out to be evidence to the contrary. In a draft memo to Tom King, minister of state at the Department of the Environment, Nigel Dorling writes that "ministers decided that there should be no relaxation of rent controls; or of standards needed to control health or safety or to control pollution; or of employment protection relations. Such relaxations might deter larger scale developers and employers."[153] Thus, the *presence* of regulations resulted not from bureaucratic policy erosion but rather from the wishes of government to shape policy in ways that would nurture capitalist development (i.e., the project of neoliberalization).[154]

A final variation of the institutional approach to be considered is Gurr and King's view of the central role played by the national state and its interaction with the local state. In their critique of the neo-Marxist and pluralist interest-based accounts, Gurr and King argue "that it is absurd to think of the state as subordinate in theory or practice to any class or constellation of interest groups."[155] For them, the national state has interests of its own. In respect of urban affairs, those interests center on "maintaining public order and authority . . . securing public revenues, and the interest of the officials in the pursuit of *their* programmatic goals."[156] The local state also has institutionally derived interests in autonomy, both from the national state and from local interests who seek to shape the local state in their image. With the onset of economic restructuring, however, urban areas suffered decline, which, according to Gurr and King, undermined both types of their autonomy.

While Gurr and King find some empirical support for their claims that the state has an interest in urban stability, they find that "while the Government has wished to appear responsive to the 1981 and 1985 urban riots, the urban spending allocated has not been substantial in either period."[157] The other key feature of state-centric urban policy has been the tendency toward centralization during the Thatcher years, through increased central fiscal control over cities (via cuts and rate capping) and the abolition of the Greater London Council and the metropolitan borough councils.

Gurr and King's argument that the central state has certain interests in cities as sources of revenue and in urban order is well supported by the case of the urban policy in the United Kingdom. However, that they point to variation among Labour and Conservative governments vis-à-vis funding and devolution of power to cities suggests that the policies of the central state are not pure artifacts of "given" state interests but are contingent upon the political calculations and ideological preferences of government officials. Moreover, while it may be axiomatic that local authorities would like autonomy of action, the goals that they wish to use that autonomy to pursue are not necessarily institutionally given but are also determined by ideological and political preferences. As Gurr and King acknowledge, "In the case of British local authorities in the 1970s and 1980s, this interaction [between local and central state autonomy] has intensified because of the policy objectives and ideology of the central state."[158]

The case of urban policy has two important implications for the institutionalist literature on the Thatcher years. First, in contrast to the standard finding that state institutions tend to blunt the Conservatives' ideological ambitions, the cases of enterprise zones and UDCs illustrate how centralized state institutions worked with the grain to promote radical change. The second conclusion to be drawn, however, is that institutional explanations alone are insufficient to explain why radical policies were adopted in the first place. To reverse Robert Lieberman's formulation, an institutional perspective reveals the opportunity but not the motive.[159] As such, a satisfactory account can only be constructed with the addition of an ideological dimension.

As noted in the Introduction, political scientists have tended, until recently, to downplay the role of ideational explanations.[160] In regard to the rise of neoliberalism, for example, Monica Prasad has argued that "the 'ideas' explanation by itself cannot take us very far, because we must still explain why ideas that very few people actually believed became so politically powerful."[161] Prasad maintains that Thatcher and others adopted neoliberal policy positions as a means to wrest control of the Conservative Party from the "moderates" such as Ted Heath, whose policies had become "discredited."[162] However, she does not recognize the degree to which the central cleavage in the Conservative Party at the time was itself ideological. While Prasad is correct that ideational arguments *alone* cannot explain the full extent of neoliberalization, it is overly glib to dismiss ideational arguments entirely.

For instance, in her bid to reject the "folk theory of the neoliberal revolution that places academic economists at the center," Prasad cites the famous letter signed by 364 economists protesting the Thatcherite agenda.[163] However, while the letter illustrates that this agenda cut against the prevailing wisdom of the time, it does not follow that key personnel within and close to the Conservative Party were not convinced by the idea that (a) the state should intervene to promote market forces at the national and urban scales and (b) that monetarism was the best means by which to squeeze inflation out of the system.[164] These ideas, as we have seen, were central to neoliberal economists, philosophers, and leading political figures whose ideas were promoted in the decades following the Second World War and took root during the late 1970s and 1980s. Moreover, the evidence I have presented above demonstrates that many Thatcherites, like their neoliberal American counterparts, were very much motivated and convinced by neoliberal ideas and that these ideas provided a framework for a series of social, economic, and urban policies, of which enterprise zones were a flagship case. Moreover, policies such as the enterprise zone were used as a means to spread the efficacy of these ideas. That they used these ideas to build political coalitions to produce political change is crucial, but such methods should not be used to suggest that the content of the ideas themselves was secondary.

Therefore, any convincing account of the neoliberal turn in urban policy, as with economic policy more generally, requires an ideational dimension in order to complement, though not to preclude, institutional and interest-based accounts. Fortunately, scholars such as Mark Blyth provide useful frameworks for thinking about the role of ideas. For example, Blyth shows how ideas were important in the "great transformations" by which the institutions of liberalism were "embedded" and later "disembedded" in the United States and Sweden. For him, ideas operated independently to structure interests, provide for institutional stability, and offer ways out of uncertainty produced by the major economic crises of the Great Depression of the 1930s and the stagflation of the 1970s.[165]

Furthermore, of direct relevance to this chapter's argument, Peter Hall's analysis of British economic policy making between 1970 and 1989 suggests that an ideational account is required to explain the "radical shift from Keynesian to monetarist modes of economic regulation" by which "inflation replaced unemployment as the preeminent concern of policymakers."[166] While tinkering with economic policy aimed at tackling stagflation did occur during the 1970s, Hall argues that Margaret Thatcher's election in 1979 resulted in an intense break in economic policy. Crucially, Hall maintains that "the play of ideas was as important to the outcome as was the contest for power."[167] Thus, in contrast to Pierson, who takes the Conservative Party's neoliberal commitments as read, Hall reminds us that the ideas of its relatively new leaders, as well as their backers in industry and the financial press, were decisive.

The example of urban policy in the United Kingdom during the 1980s extends Hall's and Blyth's analysis by showing how ideas were central not only in radical shifts in policy but also to the transformation of local political institutions, which in turn resulted in the political remaking of places (see Chapters 5 and 6). The interplay between ideas and institutions, which improved the position of capitalist interests, illustrates why this chapter follows Rogers Smith by "plac[ing] the analysis of 'ideas' and 'institutions' within a single analytical frame."[168] As Smith notes, ideologies do not work on their own; rather, they "are always carried by organizations or sets of organizations within the coalition that constitutes a political order. . . . Ideas can produce political change only when particular identifiable political institutions, groups, and actors advance them."[169]

In particular, I have shown how enterprise zones, like monetarism, represent a paradigmatic change that cannot be understood without reference to ideas.[170] They cannot be readily explained by conventional interest-based arguments: they were not promoted by businesses, nor could they be said to have been a central part of the Conservatives' electoral strategy. After all, unlike the pledge to rein in the unions or lance the inflationary boil, urban policy was not a salient issue in 1979. Moreover, Margaret Thatcher decided against putting enterprise zones or UDCs in the Conservative manifesto. Hence, while it is essential to pay close attention, as King and Wood recommend, to "policies, economic structures, and political expedience," equally, the empirical evidence demonstrates that it would be a mistake to rule ideational explanations out of the analysis entirely.[171] After all, as Gurr and King note, "the Conservatives' efforts to increase their revenue base by intervening in local economies clash with central state policies which reflect an ideological commitment to market principles and contraction of the public sector; the advent of enterprise zones and urban development corporations represents a success for central policy in this regard."[172]

But clearly, the neoliberal ideas held by key members of the Thatcher cabinet could only be realized once these political figures gained control of the institutions of state. As such, Geoffrey Howe's position in the Treasury afforded him great institutional advantages that help to explain why a national enterprise zone policy was not stymied in the United Kingdom as it was in the United States. But it was not Howe's mere presence that guaranteed enterprise zones; they were determined by the neoliberal convictions to which he was committed. Thus, politicians motivated by neoliberal ideas, having gained control of the key institutions of state, implemented enterprise zones and urban development corporations—themselves new neoliberal institutional forms. To be sure, without power (i.e., the control of state institutions), these ideas may not have come to fruition. But without these ideas, the paradigmatic shift would not have occurred either.

Yet, it is important to note that the cases of the UDCs and public-private partnerships undoubtedly complicate an ideational account. They suggest that both political expediency and interest-based politics were of central importance in policy formation. Moreover, the abolition of the metropolitan county councils supports Prasad's argument that neoliberalization in the United Kingdom can be understood as a reaction to adversarial political institutions.[173] This stands to illustrate the key point that ideational accounts in certain cases are essential, such as the enterprise zone, while in other examples, such as UDCs and PPPs, ideas are more usefully seen in the background, while institutional configurations, electoral considerations, and organized interests take center stage.

Finally, while class-based interest group politics may not have been central to the creation of enterprise zones, the consequences of neoliberal urban policy have unquestionably resulted in the restoration of class power and wealth in the hands of the extraordinarily wealthy.[174] Thus, the significance of the transformation in urban policy has an unequivocal class dimension, which illustrates where "interests" are most important. What my research demonstrates, however, is that we cannot simply assume that these interests themselves determined the policy shift that occurred, nor that such a turn would have proved as robust as it did without a neoliberal ideological foundation.

Conclusion

Stagflation, industrial unrest, and rising unemployment in the 1970s created a transatlantic political crisis that not only brought down Callaghan's Labour government but also signaled the end of the Keynesian postwar settlement. The election of the Thatcher government in 1979 heralded a paradigmatic shift in a neoliberal direction in Britain. In that same year, President Carter's contradictory presidency eventually turned to monetarism to try to resolve spiraling inflation. Within a year, he was beaten by Ronald Reagan. As we have seen, enterprise zones were to be a flagship of what this brave new world had to offer. Their creation cannot be explained by past policy legacies, institutional design, or interest group politics.

Rather, they should be understood as place-based articulations of neoliberalism, the lynchpin of Thatcher's and Reagan's governing philosophies.

Moreover, their example helped blaze the trail for the slew of neoliberal innovations that were to follow. The UDCs and the public-private partnerships would not only represent the new institutionalized forms of "actually existing neoliberalism" but also reveal the shift from government to governance that brought private interests and market mechanisms into multiple areas of social and economic life with the effect of shifting the balance of wealth and power away from labor and toward capital. The true significance of this neoliberal period, however, is to be seen in the response of those who initially opposed these developments—the Democrats and the Labour Party. The impact of the neoliberal era on their urban agenda is the subject of the next chapter.

Chapter 3

Blair and Clinton: A Third Way?

> I believe in business. I believe in the marketplace. I believe that the best jobs program this country will ever have is economic growth. Most new jobs in this country are created by small businesses and entrepreneurs who get little help from the government.
> —Bill Clinton, "A New Covenant for Economic Change," November 20, 1991

> Of course you could make a perfectly good case for wealthy people paying more . . . but I wanted to preserve, in terms of competitive tax rates, the essential Thatcher/Howe/Lawson legacy. I wanted wealthy people to feel at home and welcomed in the UK so that they could bring more business, create jobs, and spread some wealth about.[1]
> —Tony Blair, *A Journey*, 2010

> Tony Blair is a man who won't let Britain down.
> —Margaret Thatcher, Speech at the Reform Club, 1997

If the 1970s provided the opening for neoliberal ideas to enter the political mainstream, and the 1980s enabled politicians of the right to etch their designs onto the American and British political landscape, the battles over the political trajectory of the 1990s would determine the extent to which neoliberalism was a passing trend or a political development of historic significance. The true test of the power of a political project lies in whether its detractors are able to fashion an alternative and propel politics in a different direction when the opportunity of elected office presents itself. The Democratic administration of Bill Clinton and the "New" Labour government of Tony Blair promised to do just that. Having suffered extended periods of time in the national political wasteland—twelve and eighteen years out of executive office for the Democrats and Labour, respectively— both Clinton and Blair were determined to deny their opponents the opportunity of defining them as outmoded left-wingers. But neither would they accept the laissez-faire approach to the economy that seemed to leave people, including the millions unemployed, to fend for themselves and that left their national infrastructures creaking. Instead, they would offer a "third way."

In respect of their political philosophies, electoral strategies, and programmatic commitments, the similarities between Clinton and Blair are as striking as those between Thatcher and Reagan. Both leaders sought to build political coalitions around the notion that there need not be a trade-off between economic efficiency and a fair society, between low inflation and high rates of employment, and between rights and responsibilities. Both argued that government had a clear role to play in promoting growth and addressing poverty. More abstractly, neither saw labor and capital as fundamentally in conflict. For them, unleashing the power of capital across national boundaries had been a welcome (if temporarily painful) development, which would ultimately benefit workers, rich and poor alike. In this regard at least, the similarities between their third way ideas and those associated with neoliberalism are considerable.

Clinton and Blair's common electoral strategy was to assuage the concerns of the market and the middle classes that the fundamental structure of the new neoliberal settlement would be dismantled: the significant reductions in personal or corporate taxes would not be reversed, except at the margins; their governments would do a better job of maintaining low inflation than their predecessors; labor would be kept on a tight leash; no new systems of downward redistribution would be introduced; and "globalization" would be embraced and advanced. On the other hand, they wanted to reassure their working-class supporters that they understood that the restructuring of American and British economies of the 1980s was wrenching and that they would take steps to ensure that investments in people and places would be made in order that those left behind hitherto would be better able to compete in the global marketplace. Moreover, they maintained that the government could play a key role in using the proceeds from economic growth to tackle poverty and provide for high-quality public services.

Yet, despite the remarkable ideological and programmatic similarities shared by Clinton and Blair, significant differences in their respective political environments merit close attention. First, like Reagan in the 1980s, Clinton had to contend with the same fragmented array of American political institutions characterized by the separation of powers, a bicameral legislature, and weak party discipline. Unlike Reagan, however, Clinton did "enjoy" two years of unified party government, although, with only fifty-seven senators, the Democrats were three seats short of a filibuster-proof majority during the 103rd Congress (1993–1995). Moreover, with just 43 percent of the vote, the lowest level of support that any president secured since Lincoln's election in 1860, Clinton could not easily claim a strong mandate. Thus, the inherent structural barriers to transformative presidential leadership, combined with the historically specific circumstances of the 1992 election, constrained considerably Clinton's ability to fashion a major challenge to the existing order if he so chose.

The contrasts in this regard with Tony Blair's circumstances are remarkable. Like Margaret Thatcher, Blair had the good fortune of governing in a parliamentary system of unified government, an upper chamber with limited powers, and with strong party discipline, all of which conferred a great deal of power and authority to the prime minister. Moreover, Blair's 1997 landslide victory gave him a parliamentary majority of 179, even greater than Margaret Thatcher's Conservative Party achieved at the pinnacle of its power in 1983. Hence, while Clinton was hampered by the inherently fragmented nature of American political institutions and limited by the equivocal nature of his mandate, Blair reigned supreme.

Given these differences, it is curious that Blair's priorities and first-term achievements are so similar to Clinton's. Although Clinton's agenda was highly constrained by his relatively weak bargaining position, Blair's reluctance to diverge fundamentally from the immediate neoliberal past cannot be said to have been induced by a precarious grip on political authority. Rather, it reflects Blair's determination to stick to the New Labour position, which casts considerable doubt upon claims that the third-way/neoliberal character of New Labour was purely an electoral gimmick. This apparent confusion is further resolved by political scientist Stephen Skowronek's observations about the inherently ambivalent nature of third-way politics, which involves playing "against type" in a

bid to preempt their opponents' efforts to associate them with a discredited political tradition.[2]

Clinton and Blair were also constrained by ideology: their own and
that held by the political, economic, and journalistic elites around them. In
particular, they both believed that changes in the global economy ruled out
the option of significant redistribution of wealth through fiscal means. They
also believed that their electoral fortunes depended on shedding the political clothes of the predecessors from their own parties who governed in the
1960s and 1970s. As such, they used their authority to ensure that the era
of "big government" was over. There would be no going back to the bad
old days of the past when the state was held hostage by the unions and the
work-shy lived the life of Reilly on welfare. People would be helped, but
they would be given "a hand up, not a hand out."[3]

Hence, programmatically, the Anglo-Saxon mode of the third way
would be geared toward promoting growth and "supply-side" investments
in education and skills. It would also maintain a safety net for those willing
to participate in low-wage, flexible labor markets. There was a philosophical
and strategic conviction, however, that a sizable chunk of the unemployed
were out of work as a result of individual choice rather than because of the
shortcomings of the neoliberal political economy. In a clear echo of their
neoliberal predecessors, these individuals who "lived a life on welfare" were
encouraged to do so by the welfare state's skewed incentive structure. Thus,
the incentives would be changed to force those unwilling, but physically
able, to enter the workplace irrespective of the wage rate they would receive;
that is, they would be compelled to work or lose their benefits.[4] In this light,
the distinctiveness of the third-way approach from the neoliberal worldview
becomes even more difficult to discern.

While much has been written about third-way economic and social policy,[5] less attention has been paid to urban policy. This is regrettable, for, as
we saw in Chapters 1 and 2, urban policy is often aimed at places that both
bear the scars of economic and social failure and harbor the potential for
the next frontier of economic dynamism or, in Marxist parlance, "capital
accumulation." Moreover, as the enterprise zone idea illustrates, urban policy can distill the political philosophy and governing priorities of a government, as it uses cities as laboratories to roll out its ideas, rendering concrete
its vision for society. Indeed, as 1980s urban policy showed, ideological
battles to reshape national political institutions are often waged in the first
instance in the city trenches. The same is true for the 1990s and 2000s.

The urban policy of both the Clinton administration and the Blair government is revealing in four important regards: first, it reflects a considerable degree of accommodation to neoliberal ideas; second, it simultaneously illustrates the significant shift in emphasis toward a genuine concern for the social fabric that was not stressed by their right-wing predecessors; third, it highlights the communitarian twist central to the third way; and fourth, it illustrates the contradictory and ultimately flawed nature of the third-way posture itself.

This chapter will focus on the Clinton administration's empowerment zone/enterprise community policy and Blair's "urban renaissance" and "Social Exclusion Unit." However, since a key argument of this book is that urban policy must be seen as an artifact of broader ideas and political strategies regarding economic and social policy more generally, it is first necessary to detail the rise of Clinton's New Democrats and Blair's New Labour and to examine their broader positions on economic and labor market policy. This chapter will conclude by providing a reassessment of the scholarly interpretations of Clinton and Blair's roles in propelling political development in light of the insights gleaned from their urban policies. I argue that both Clinton's and Blair's urban policies bore the hallmarks of a Janus-like political project, which on one hand flew close to the neoliberal flame, at times throwing fuel on the fire, while on the other hand attempted imperfectly to attend to some of the human casualties caught in the neoliberal blaze. In the end, the third way's urban policy captures the project's contradictory nature, which ultimately reinforced neoliberal trends alternating between the politics of *neoliberalism by default* and *neoliberalism by design*.

The Rise of the New Democrats and New Labour:
A Transatlantic Phenomenon

Both the Labour Party and the Democrats were ejected from office at the turn of the 1980s, having been painted successfully by those on the right as being responsible for the economic woes associated with stagflation and as being dominated by entrenched interests, such as unions, liberals, socialists, and other radicals, at odds with the mainstream. But the 1979 British general election and the American presidential election a year later were framed by the right and eventually by neoliberals from the "left" not simply as referenda on Prime Minister James Callaghan and President Jimmy Carter but as delivering negative judgments about the Keynesian settlement and New Deal/Great Society liberalism in general. Hence, those elections were historic in that they rejected not simply a party or leader but rather because they were seen as an indictment of the governing philosophies and institutions that had dominated the agenda of both countries' major political parties since the Second World War.

While this was not understood by all at the time—as the internecine battles within both political parties underscore—the power of the neoliberal critique of the bloated welfare state, vested union interests, and overbearing government intervention in the economy is reflected in the fact that during the 1980s and early 1990s, the Democrats and Labour were ultimately controlled by those who reinvented their message, style, and policy priorities in ways that echoed this critique, although the timbre of that echo was far more muffled on the left than it was on the right. In both countries, this was reflected in the emphasis on "novelty"—the New Democrat identity and rhetoric of the late 1980s was soon followed by the creation of "New" Labour after Tony Blair became party leader in 1994.

The rise of the New Democrats resulted from the growing influence and institutional capacity of the Democratic Leadership Council (DLC), which was formed in 1985 to push the party to the center (i.e., in a rightward or neoliberal direction) in the aftermath of Walter Mondale's crushing loss to Ronald Reagan in the 1984 presidential election and out of frustration with the dominance of labor and liberal interests in Democratic National Committee (DNC).[6] It is ironic in light of Mondale's positively Hoover-like support for increased taxes and spending cuts as the means to reduce the deficit in a downturn that his defeat is seen as a ringing rejection of postwar liberalism.[7] Indeed, that Democrats recognized and positively endorsed the right-wing mischaracterization of Mondale's position speaks volumes to the dominance of neoliberal ideas. As such, "moderates" in the Democratic Party, led by Al From, then-Representative Dick Gephardt (D-MO), Representative James R. Jones (D-OK), Governors Bruce Babbitt (D-AZ) and Chuck Robb (D-VA), and Senators Sam Nunn (D-GA) and Lawton Chiles (C-FL), sought in Nunn's words to "move the party—both in substance and perception—back into the mainstream of American political life."[8]

While the DLC initially provided a platform for Democrats of varying ideological stripes, after the third consecutive presidential defeat in 1988 and the failure of the DLC's innovation of a southern-dominated "Super

Tuesday" to deliver a "moderate" candidate, the organization became more deliberately "an ideas-based movement focused on shaping a specific main-stream alternative identity for the party."[9] The effort to generate new ideas was undertaken by the Progressive Policy Institute (PPI). After the PPI's founding, the DLC's task was to focus on fundraising and publicizing its vision, which it did through conferences, courtship of the media, and the publication of a magazine called *The New Democrat*.

While the PPI came, over time, to develop a positive message, its initial efforts were geared toward launching an assault on the liberal left of the Democratic Party.[10] In a notable monograph entitled "The Politics of Eva-sion," political scientists and DLC operatives, William Galston and Elaine Kamarck, argued that the Democrats' electoral failures arose because "Americans have now come to see the party as inattentive to their economic interests, indifferent if not hostile to their moral sentiments and ineffective in the defense of their national security."[11] Yet, according to Galston and Kamarck, Democrats had ignored these concerns and "embraced the poli-tics of evasion,"[12] which was based on the conviction that they could return to office without a revision to the party's "established orthodoxies" on race, poverty, and crime that rejected "liberal fundamentalism" in favor of ideas that communicated a shared commitment to "middle class values—individual responsibility, hard work, equal opportunity—rather than the language of compensation."[13] In short, they claimed that Democrats had moved to the left and, by the 1980s, were beholden to labor and "extreme" liberals, which was wrong on the substance and electorally disastrous.

Over time, the New Democrats sought to use the DLC and the PPI to alter the ideological essence of the Democratic Party. As Al From and PPI president Will Marshall put it, their aim was to "develop an intellectual counterforce that can fashion progressive alternatives to special interest politics."[14] In thinking about how to launch such a counterforce, the DLC sought to follow the lead of the Heritage Foundation, the highly influential think tank, described in Chapter 1, that played a central role in promoting neoliberal ideas within the Republican Party, such as enterprise zones. Impressed by Heritage's ability to reshape the ideological contours of the political landscape, From and Marshall met with Ed Fuelner, president of Heritage, to garner his advice on fundraising and the dissemination of new ideas.[15]

Given the scale of the DLC's ambitions, it was clear that substantial sums of money would have to be raised. Much of its initial funding came from hedge fund manager, Michael Steinhardt, who made three annual donations of $250,000. Steinhardt soon became chairman of the PPI's Board of Trustees, joined by Kenneth Brody and Barrie Wigmore, both partners at Goldman Sachs.[16] By the 1990s, funding for the DLC and PPI came almost exclusively from major *Fortune* 500 corporations and financial services firms, which would include AT&T, Philip Morris, and Goldman Sachs. Over time, the DLC offered seats on its executive council to companies in return for a donation of $25,000. These included Aetna, AT&T, American Airlines, AIG, BellSouth, Chevron, DuPont, Enron, IBM, Merck and Company, Microsoft, Philip Morris, Texaco, and Verizon Communications.[17]

This attraction of corporate and financial interests is a clear echo of the pattern established by right-wing think tanks in the 1970s and 1980s. Not surprisingly, the DLC and PPI also advocated policies that often corresponded closely to the policy preferences of those interests. Yet, it does not follow that they promoted such policies *because* of this financial connection. Indeed, as the enterprise zone idea illustrated, business groups had to be persuaded of the merits of the policy by think tankers who developed the concept. In the case of the DLC, it would appear that it was the policy positions that led to corporate and financial support, not the other way around. Over time, of course, the two became mutually reinforcing, as the DLC integrated corporate interests into its institutional structure. This underscores the importance of paying close attention to the sequencing of political change, which illuminates and clarifies the relationship between ideas and interests in shaping the transformation of political institutions, such as the DLC and, by extension, the Democratic Party and the American political economy.

This financial footing enabled the DLC to develop the institutional capacity to launch an ideological assault on New Deal/Great Society liberalism and transform the prevailing governing philosophy and programmatic agenda of the Democratic Party by assisting candidates for the House, Senate, and the White House that reflected its agenda. Indeed, when it came to replace Sam Nunn as chairman in 1990, the DLC leadership was keen to identify someone who would also serve as a potential presidential candidate. Having identified Bill Clinton as an exceptionally gifted speaker, with clear New Democrat *bona fides*, Al From traveled to Arkansas to present Clinton with an ambitious proposal. According to Kenneth Baer's account, From suggested to Clinton, "If you take the DLC chairmanship, we will give you a national platform, and I think you will be President of the United States. And you will do a lot of good for us because it will make us a national organization."[18] Indeed, in his courtship of Clinton, From explicitly highlighted the promise of access to fundraising networks in Washington, D.C. and New York. With the prospect of a higher national profile and fast-track access to elite political and financial networks, Clinton accepted the offer and became DLC chairman in March 1990.

Clinton's chairmanship coincided with the DLC's increasingly neoliberal stance. This was reflected in the New Orleans Declaration, which sought to draw sharp contrasts between the "old" and "new" Democratic outlooks.[19] It articulated a faith in the "free market, regulated in the public interest"; claimed the "Democratic Party's fundamental mission is to expand opportunity, not government"; and, in a not so subtle rejection of Great Society liberalism, asserted that "we believe that all claims on government are not equal. Our leaders must reject demands that are less worthy, and hold to clear governing priorities." The other themes mentioned in the declaration—free trade, a tough stance on crime, and a robust approach to foreign policy—also correspond either to a neoliberal or a neoconservative worldview. In perhaps the only echo of liberalism, the declaration states clearly that "we believe a progressive tax system is the only fair way to pay for government." However, beyond ruling out a flat tax, this statement gives one no indication as to whether the DLC thought that taxes should be increased or decreased.

Perhaps the most striking element of the New Orleans Declaration is that it takes its rhetorical cues from the neoliberal right in the sense that it relies on a caricature of Great Society liberalism, for example: "We believe in preventing crime and punishing criminals, not in explaining away their behavior."[20] In a similar vein, in his keynote address to the DLC's inaugural convention in Cleveland, Clinton averred that "governments do not raise children, people do, and it is time they were asked to assume their responsibilities and forced to do it if they refuse."[21] As if to confirm the extent of the DLC's political cross-dressing, the convention was in part funded by James Biggar, Ohio Republican and CEO of Nestle USA, who donated $50,000 to help underwrite the costs.

The Cleveland convention adopted a series of policy positions framed as "The New American Choice Resolutions."[22] These included commitments to free trade, welfare reform, deficit reduction, public spending cuts, employee stock ownership, school choice, and infrastructure investment, all of which, with the exception of the last, were wholly in line with neoliberal policy priorities of the GOP. The DLC also developed its ideas for urban policy that included public-private partnerships, not only the penchant of Republican and British Conservative Party neoliberals but also a policy tool firmly established by the Carter administration's Urban Development Action Grant (UDAG) program. Under a subtitle that read "Bolster poor people's efforts to enter the mainstream," the document argues the Democrats "must now adopt new strategies to break the cycles of discrimination and welfare dependency, and give poor people the means to win their own war on poverty."[23] The DLC also recommended that the government should "promote entrepreneurship in the inner cities" by helping to "underwrite public-private partnerships that provide credit and business advice to poor, budding entrepreneurs." The Cleveland conference also resolved to press Congress to "undertake a 'microenterprise' initiative for enterprising poor people, in which the federal government would subsidize local programs providing modest business loans to business people eager to start their own businesses. The program would also relax the regulatory hurdles facing welfare recipients who want to start their own enterprises."[24] This passage reveals key linkages with the neoliberal ideas of the 1980s that inspired Geoffrey Howe in the United Kingdom and Jack Kemp in the United States to promote enterprise zones. Urban poverty and unemployment are assumed to be functions of over-burdensome regulations, inadequate access to credit, or because of government-induced welfare dependency. The solution, therefore, is found in deregulation and support for small business. There is no indication that any help ought to be offered to the inner cities beyond cutting welfare, in order to deliver people from the perils of dependency, and providing credit funneled through public-private partnerships to "enterprising poor people." Neither is there any sense that the condition of the inner cities had a basis in the neoliberalization of the American political economy. Rather, the unit of analysis is the individual who, it is assumed, can resolve the problem of unemployment and poverty through a combination of welfare support withdrawal and access to credit supplied for entrepreneurship. In short, the government's role is to engage business and the "third" sector in helping nudge people into more productive habits.

With the financial support and the institutional capacity of the DLC at his back, Clinton announced his run for the presidency on October, 3, 1991. That fall, Clinton delivered three high-profile speeches at Georgetown

University, known as the New Covenant speeches, which detailed his political philosophy and outlined his domestic and foreign policy program.
These speeches bear all the hallmarks of his New Democrat identity. Written with the aid of the DLC's policy director, Bruce Reed, whom Clinton
had recruited to his campaign, the speeches were also shaped by William
Galston's ideas.[25]

These speeches underscore the challenge of both recognizing the emergence of a new order (in this case a neoliberal order) while running as a
candidate associated with the old order (in this case New Deal/Great Society
liberalism). As presidential scholar Stephen Skowronek puts it, as a third-
way leader, Clinton's aim "was to acknowledge the Democrats' three consecutive losses to liberal-bashing Republicans and to attempt to adjust the
Democratic alternative to the new political realities that had been created
by the Reagan Revolution."[26] Hence, on one hand, Clinton was sure to
signal to his political base that he rejected elements of the neoliberal transformation in the American political economy, attacking the "greed and the
selfishness" of the Reagan-Bush years and lamenting the struggles of
"middle-class families" whose wages fell while "taxes were lowered on the
wealthiest people whose incomes were rising."[27] On the other hand, Clinton
affirmed the neoliberal critique of his own party: "Democrats forgot about
real people too," he suggested.[28] Skowronek's characterization of Clinton's
"unabashedly mongrel politics" is perhaps best captured by Clinton's own
description of his vision: "The New Covenant isn't liberal or conservative.
It's both and different. The American people don't care about the idle rhetoric of left and right. They're real people, with real problems, and they
think no one in Washington wants to solve their problems or stand up for
them."[29] In applying this theme to economic policy, Clinton argued that
"stale theories produce nothing but stalemate. The old economic answers
are obsolete. We've seen the limits of Keynesian economics. We've seen the
worst of supply-side economics. We need a new approach."[30] But if this
implied equidistance between the two, there are clues in these speeches as
to the degree to which Clinton's agenda—even before having to deal with
the inevitable political compromises produced by the exigencies of the fragmented institutions that characterize the American political system—
tended substantively toward a reaffirmation of the neoliberal economic
order, albeit laced with largely symbolic language that excoriated corporate
greed and Republican neglect. Clinton's commitment to reform health care,
expand the Earned Income Tax Credit (EITC), and increase investment

spending are the only examples of major deviations from the neoliberal worldview.

While Clinton presents the notion of "reinventing government" as a radical new idea, few neoliberals would quibble with Clinton's proposed application of the concept: "I want to make government more efficient and effective by following the lead of our best companies: eliminating unnecessary layers of bureaucracy, reducing administrative costs and most important, giving the American citizens more choices in the services they get."[31] Moreover, Clinton's arbitrary pledge to insist on "3% across-the-board cuts in the administrative costs of the federal bureaucracy every year" could just have easily come from Thatcher or Reagan.

Finally, Clinton's understanding of poverty tends to favor conservative moralizing over any insights into the structural failures of the economy. While Clinton calls for responsibility for all—including for the private sector—the only sanctions for alleged irresponsibility are targeted toward the poor. The "hard-working" members of the middle class are portrayed as helpless victims, but the urban poor are considered responsible for their predicament: "Many inner-city streets were taken over by crime and drugs, welfare and despair. Family responsibility became an oxymoron for many deadbeat fathers who were more likely to make their car payments than to pay their child support."[32] Clinton further states that while those in "America's most troubled neighborhoods" need help, "they can't be let off the responsibility hook either. All society can ever offer them is a chance to develop their God-given capacities. They have to do the rest." He underscores that while "people who work shouldn't be poor," "in my administration we're going to put an end to welfare as we have come to know it. . . . No more permanent dependence on welfare as a way of life."[33] While the New Covenant speeches did not deal explicitly with Clinton's urban policy proposals, his support for enterprise zones had been well publicized (see below).

Thus, the New Covenant speeches laid out Clinton's themes for his campaign and for his presidency. The ideas and interests of the DLC were in full view, whose institutional capacity, which originally attracted Clinton, was developed further by Clinton once he became its chairman. The DLC's strategy of promoting its interests in Congress, throughout the states, and finally through a presidential candidate reached its zenith by the 1992 Democratic Convention, which approved the party platform, whose themes were almost entirely consistent with the DLC's New American Choice Resolutions and Clinton's New Covenant speeches.[34]

As political scientist Stephen Borrelli demonstrates, neoliberals and "moderates" in the Democratic Party were determined to exercise far tighter control over the drafting of the platform than was the case in the 1980s when "red-flag" left-wing ideas were given an airing.[35] Crucially, Clinton himself played a more deliberate role in this process than had previous presidential candidates Jimmy Carter, Walter Mondale, or Michael Dukakis because the membership of the drafting committee was not named until after Clinton had enough delegates to secure the nomination. As such, DLC members were prominently represented, with Al From joined by nine others, which meant that DLC members composed 40 percent (ten of twenty-five) of the participants involved in the drafting.[36]

But the nominating committee was not exclusively sympathetic to the DLC vision. For instance, it also included liberals such as Mary Frances Berry; labor representatives Kenneth Young (American Federation of Labor and Congress of Industrial Organizations [AFL-CIO]), Jack Joyce (International Union of Bricklayers and Allied Craftsmen), and Rachelle Horowitz (American Federation of Teachers); Nancy Pelosi; Jerry Brown; and David Dinkins, mayor of New York City. They were all able to offer amendments to the original draft. However, as Borrelli points out, in no case when DLC members "expressed disapproval did an amendment pass in its original form. At the same time, all but one of the amendments that were approved had received explicit endorsement from the Clinton campaign."[37]

A telling example of Clinton's dominance of the process occurred with respect to urban policy. The drafting committee met one month after the U.S. Conference of Mayors presented Congress with a seven-point plan for rebuilding urban America, which requested $35 billion dedicated to public works, transportation projects, job training, and support for small businesses.[38] However, when Mayor Dinkins proposed that the platform endorse the plan, Clinton's supporters resisted, including Sandra Freedman, mayor of Tampa, who wanted to prioritize deficit reduction and business-led growth over urban spending. Ultimately, Clinton's aides agreed to a compromise whereby the platform would give "consideration" to the plan, although Dinkins conceded that the inclusion of this language was a hollow victory.[39]

Clinton's resolve to eschew the liberal past of his Democratic predecessors was reflected not only in his reluctance to give credence to the U.S. Conference of Mayors' seven-point plan but also in his reaction to the Los Angeles riots, which was to recommend the creation of new enterprise zones. Therefore, far from trying to forge a third way in urban policy, the Democratic Party's 1992 platform included a pledge to "encourage the flow of investment to inner-city development and housing through targeted enterprise zones."[40]

As a result of Clinton's control over the process, the standard DLC priorities were showcased in the platform: deficit reduction, welfare reform, free trade, and investment in education and skills.[41] On this basis, Clinton was elected in November 1992, although with just 43 percent of the vote against George W. Bush's 37.5 percent and Ross Perot's 18.9 percent, the strongest showing of a third-party candidate since Theodore Roosevelt's run as a Progressive in 1912. Clinton's electoral success and the content of his program reflected the degree to which the range of plausible policy alternatives to neoliberalism had been constricted. The New Democrats' rise reflects the fracturing of liberal and progressive forces in the United States, in part due to the waning of labor power. Into this chasm flowed the ideas and policy priorities promoted by the DLC. This reflected the triumph of the view that New Deal/Great Society liberalism was neither electorally viable nor inherently attractive as a political project.

That said, one would not want to draw an unrealistically sharp contrast with the past. After all, within the New Deal coalition existed free traders and deficit hawks. Indeed, both Harry Truman and Lyndon Johnson saw balanced budgets as desirable and wanted to reduce trade barriers.[42] Moreover, even as he launched an "unconditional war on poverty" in 1964, Johnson did not set his sights on restructuring the American political economy. Instead, poverty was conceived as resulting from a dearth of opportunity. Nevertheless, these policy commitments came alongside the use of macroeconomic policy to promote full employment, significant expansions of the welfare state, and major increases in urban aid—all of which distinguish the New Deal/Great Society era from the Clinton presidency. Notably, the vast expansion of federal spending on social welfare was sustained under Presidents Nixon and Ford.[43] Thus, the War on Poverty, much like the New Deal, therefore reflected both the limits and contradictions of liberalism. When pushed to the extreme, liberal policy making could be effective in extending opportunity and reducing poverty but would fall short of creating an equal society.

Clinton's victory and policy priorities arose from the nexus between the DLC's ideas and institutional capacity; the interests of big business, keen to promote neoliberalism within the Democratic Party; and Clinton's assumption that "globalization" made accommodations to neoliberalism necessary. The character of Clinton's electoral victory would have consequential ramifications for the British Labour Party's transformation in both electoral and programmatic terms. Philip Gould, Tony Blair's pollster and strategist,[44] was an adviser to Clinton during the final weeks of the presidential campaign, an experience Gould describes as formative:

> Those Little Rock days . . . changed me, and I like to think they changed—in part through me—the subsequent course of progressive politics. Nothing would ever be the same again. Progressive parties would stop being victims and start being aggressive; they would regain contact with the values and hopes of middle-class and working-class people; they would develop campaigning techniques that meant the left started to win elections far more often than they would lose. Above all, they would regain the confidence and self-belief which had drained away in two decades of defeat.[45]

Gould's visit to Little Rock preceded Tony Blair's emergence as Labour leader in 1994. Indeed, like the Democrats, the Labour Party had been undergoing the process of transformation since its initial loss of power in 1979 was compounded by Margaret Thatcher's second general election victory in 1983, when Labour ran on a manifesto described by former Labour minister and MP Gerald Kaufman as "the longest suicide note in history."[46] Labour at the time was seen as being beholden to the hard left rather than the Keynesian social democrats and revisionist socialists that had dominated Labour's governing priorities during their stints in office in the 1960s and 1970s. The emergence of Thatcherism in Britain split the left irreparably. The hard left's policy positions and tactics so alienated moderate and "right-wing" Labour members that some bolted from the party to form the Social Democratic Party (SDP). Indeed, it may be argued that the acrimony that characterized this period gave rise to a perception of incompetence and division that alienated the public far more than the content of the 1983 manifesto.[47]

   In the aftermath of the 1983 defeat, Neil Kinnock, himself initially seen as a radical, was elected as leader alongside deputy leader Roy Hattersley, who was seen as being on the right of the party, although by no means a neoliberal. Faced with a formidable opponent in Thatcher and the competition from the SDP, Kinnock considered that internal control of Labour

Party policy would be necessary to quash the hard left, squeeze the SDP, and enhance the party's electoral credibility. Most scholars mark the origins of New Labour not to Tony Blair's election as leader but to Kinnock's famous attack on the Trotskyist "Militant" group in 1985 and to the party's policy review launched in the wake of Labour's third successive defeat to Margaret Thatcher in 1987, which aimed at a root-and-branch reconsideration of Labour's platform.[48]

The process of the policy review strengthened the role of the shadow cabinet and the center-left Institute for Public Policy Research (IPPR), founded in 1988, at the expense of the Trades Union Congress, whose influence on economic policy making was curtailed henceforth.[49] The effect was to revise Labour's positions on industrial relations, the welfare state, and foreign (and defense) policy, but the central debate in the policy review was over economic policy.[50] The antagonists were the neo-Keynesians, who favored strategic intervention in the economy to regulate market cycles and encourage long-term investment via a "Medium Term Industrial Strategy," and supply-siders who believed that Keynesian policies encouraged inflation, preferring instead to focus on supply-side public goods such as education, training, and research. Both groups differed from those on the Labour left in that they did not share antipathy to the market in general; in fact, they considered that markets promoted economic efficiency, allocation of scarce resources, and innovation. However, the neo-Keynesians were more apt to recognize the destabilizing effects of untrammeled markets than the supply-siders who were mainly concerned to ensure that the provision of public goods was such that it provided equal opportunity to all.[51] Moreover, they both rejected renationalization of the industries privatized by the Conservatives.

Both groups also seemed to accept that Labour's historic commitment to full employment would have to be abandoned given the perceived connection between demand-management and inflation. Concern about inflation further implied that the weakening of the trade unions by the Conservatives would not be substantially reversed. However, the policy review did conclude that more investment in the welfare state should be funded through higher taxation on the wealthy, although economic growth would be the central means to increase state spending.

While balance between the neo-Keynesian and the supply-side interpretations was maintained initially, the fact that Neil Kinnock and Gordon Brown (who would become chancellor in 1997) advocated the supply-side position ensured that it would ultimately prevail. As such, the policy review marks a clear turning point in the neoliberalization of Labour Party policy. However, as Hill puts it, Labour's position at this point did not amount to a wholesale "acceptance of market liberalism."[52] After all, Labour's 1992 election manifesto, *Time to Get Britain Working Again*, still contained elements that rooted it in the social democratic tradition, such as the introduction of a minimum wage, a major house-building program, a work program for the unemployed, new investment in the National Health Service and education, increased child benefit and state pensions, and the introduction of a 50 percent top rate of income tax for those on £40,000 a year (approximately $98,000 in 2012 constant dollars).[53]

While vestiges of Labour's social democratic past were apparent in 1992, the election of Tony Blair as leader resulted in a sharper break with that historical link. Keen to emulate the success of the New Democrats, Blair rebranded the party as New Labour. But this was not simply a question of a new marketing strategy. In a direct comparison to Bill Clinton, Blair makes this point forcefully:

> We were political soulmates. We shared pretty much the same analysis of the weaknesses of progressive politics. We were both quintessential modernizers. . . . The third-way philosophy that we both espoused was not a clever splitting of the difference between left and right. Neither was it lowest-common-denominator populism. It was a genuine, coherent and actually successful attempt to redefine progressive politics: to liberate it from outdated ideology; to apply its values anew in a new world; to reform the role of government and the state; and to create a modern relationship between the responsibilities of the citizen and those of society—a hand up not a handout on welfare, opportunity and responsibility as the basis of a strong society. It was a way of moving beyond the small-state, 'no role for society' ideology of the Republicans; and the big-state, anti-enterprise ideology of much of the traditional Democratic base.[54]

Thus, while Kinnock's policy review, as well as its consolidation by his successor John Smith,[55] was viewed by modernizers as a step in the right direction, those such as Blair thought Labour had to go far further in its accommodation to the economic "reality" of globalization and the political reality of the Conservatives' electoral dominance.

Blair summarized the challenges facing Labour in 1994 thus: "I assessed that there were three types of Labour: old-fashioned Labour, which could never win; modernized Labour, which could win and keep winning; and plain Labour, which could win once, but essentially as a reaction to an unpopular Conservative government."[56] Hence the need for *New* Labour. Symbolically, this change was embodied in the rewriting of Clause IV of the Labour Party constitution to replace its commitment to "common ownership of the means of production, distribution, and exchange" with a vague "statement of aims and values."[57]

While some suggest that Blair's policy program was not substantially different from Kinnock's,[58] key areas of Blair's policy indicate a decisive step change in a neoliberal direction. Most notably, Blair accepted the "globalization thesis," which suggests that social democratic parties cannot pursue Keynesian demand management, expansion of the welfare state, or redistribution because footloose capital, freed up by the neoliberal reforms of the 1980s, will not tolerate the kinds of tax regimes that would be required to pay for it or the inflation that it would inevitably create.[59] Moreover, industrial relations needed to be arranged in such a way as to make the country competitive.[60]

These themes were laid out by Blair as early as 1995 in his keynote Mais lecture, which set out New Labour's economic policy and which echoes the tone and content of Clinton's New Covenant speeches delivered four years earlier. It also reveals that New Labour's macroeconomic policy "fundamentally agreed" with that of Thatcher's second chancellor, Nigel Lawson.[61] In an effort to advance a third-way approach, Blair argued that "the right often promises to cut both taxes and spending irrespective of circumstance. The old Left was perceived as believing that higher taxation and spending are a good thing [*sic*] in themselves. Neither side is right, as the recent experience of both Labour and Conservative governments has shown."[62] As to the imperatives of globalization, Blair argued that the state's role should not be to reengineer the institutions that governed the international exchange of goods, services, and capital but rather to become entrepreneurial: "The growing integration of the world economy—in which capital, and to a lesser extent labour, moves freely—means that it is not possible for Britain to sustain budget deficits or a tax regime that are wildly out of line with the other major industrial countries. One of the requirements for our tax structure is to attract enterprise into the U.K. from overseas."[63]

Moreover, Blair adopted the classic argument that there is no alternative but to embrace globalization: "Since it is inconceivable that the U.K. would want to withdraw unilaterally from this global marketplace, we must instead adjust our policies to its existence." Blair does argue for the need to tackle unemployment, but this is justified as a means of reducing spending on "the dependency on welfare." Moreover, whereas previous Labour governments had put the goal of reducing unemployment ahead of tackling inflation, Blair argues there ought to be no trade-off between the two. Indeed, his speech devotes far more time to establishing his *bona fides* as an inflation hawk than to the question of unemployment. Claiming that "inflation is an evil which must be controlled," Blair went on to suggest that relatively low rates of inflation would not be tolerated under Labour: "The idea that inflation can be stabilized at around 5–10 percent, with permanent benefits to growth, is pure and dangerous fantasy."[64] Furthermore, like Clinton, Blair promised to outperform the right on deficit reduction and make strategic investments to improve the supply side.

As Blair hinted at in his Mais lecture, New Labour's position on welfare was a further example of the step change in Labour Party policy after he became leader. Informed by Clinton's approach to welfare reform, Blair, in conjunction with Gordon Brown and his advisers, introduced a "welfare to work" policy, later enacted, that introduced the principle of compulsion into Britain's welfare policy. As part of the "New Deal for the Unemployed," those who did not sign up for work placement or training schemes would lose part or all of their benefit. This signaled a rejection of Labour's 1988 *Charter Against Workfare* that unequivocally rejected the principle of compulsion. As King and Wickham-Jones point out, "The ambitious nature of the programme stands in contrast to the more limited schemes of the previous Conservative administration. At the same time, welfare to work presents a recasting of the Labour party's notion of social citizenship . . . this universalistic approach has given way to a market-based one. Individuals must accept responsibility for their own well-being in terms of entering labour markets and contributing to society through paid work."[65] Furthermore, just as Clinton went further than the right managed to on welfare reform and deficit reduction, Blair sought to reassure prospective international investors that Labour would go further than Thatcher and Major in deregulation. In a 1996 speech to business leaders in Bonn, Blair maintained that Labour was "prepared to rethink the whole philosophy in relation to the labour market."[66] Indeed, in a foreword to his government's

Fairness at Work white paper, he wrote that even after the introduction of the minimum wage and enhanced family-friendly employment rights, Britain would be "the most lightly regulated labour market of any leading economy in the world."[67]

In a postscript to his Mais lecture, written in 2000, Blair summed up Labour's approach: "Our task in government has been to preserve those things that the previous government got right, for example, a more flexible labour market, or an open economy, but to remedy the failings" regarding a lack of investment and neglect toward the unemployed.[68] What is most striking is that Blair appeared to rule out the connection between unemployment and flexible labor markets.

The Third Way in Power

The argument advanced here is that the modifier "New" for the Democrats and Labour did indeed indicate something novel. That is, contrary to those who claimed that this was just branding—"all style and no substance"—it is evident that there was a great deal more to it than that. It was a sincere attempt to craft a third way but one that endorsed much of the neoliberal project that had been more enthusiastically promoted by the Republican and the Conservative Parties. The key difference was that New Labour and the New Democrats saw a clear role for the state in investing in the supply side, through investment in education and skills, and in tackling unemployment and poverty. However, it was the continuities in respect of macroeconomic policy and the even "purer" version of neoliberalism in the form of deficit reduction, free trade, welfare reform, and financial deregulation that undermined efforts to live up to their liberal (in the American context) and social democratic (in the British context) traditions. Urban policy falls at the locus of this dilemma.

It seems that Clinton himself realized this very early in his presidency with respect to deficit reduction. According to Bob Woodward's account, Clinton bristled at the advice that dramatic deficit reduction was required to assuage the bond market: "You mean to tell me that the success of the program and my reelection hinges on the Federal Reserve and a bunch of fucking bond traders?"[69] Clinton's frustrations with the relentless focus on the deficit and the corresponding gutting of his program for investments—inflicted by his own decision to prioritize deficit reduction and by a bipartisan coalition of neoliberals in Congress—led him to lament the degree to which his policies would fulfill the Republican agenda: "We're Eisenhower Republicans here, and we are fighting the Reagan Republicans. We stand for lower deficits and free trade and the bond market. Isn't that great?"[70]

But despite his regret that his investments and "middle-class" tax cuts were abandoned, Clinton came to embrace not only the apparent political necessity of deficit reduction but the neoliberal logic behind the policy as well. As Taylor Branch explains, on the basis of private and secret conversations with Clinton at the time, the president "said the budget package was everything he hoped to achieve in both politics and the economy. Chronic deficits not only drove up interest rates, sucking investment money out of the private economy, but they also fostered cynicism. Public discourse was stunted by the belief that government was inherently bankrupt. Beyond labels of liberal and conservative, a resignation to deficits corroded democracy's core proposition that people can govern themselves."[71] This position is telling since it shows that Clinton had accepted the standard but highly contested neoclassical "crowding-out" and rational expectations theories.[72] Joseph Stiglitz, chairman of Clinton's Council of Economic Advisers, confirms that "market fundamentalism" had come to shape the administration's agenda from the outset: "Too many in the administration seemed to accept the notion that the bond market, or financial markets more generally, knew the best way forward. The financial markets, it seemed, represented America's best interests as well as their own."[73] This ideological constraint can also be identified through Clinton's selection of "the most aggressive of five options his advisors assembled for addressing the deficit."[74]

Clinton's acceptance, initially through gritted teeth, of neoliberal macroeconomic logic suggests that not only was Clinton operating in a fiscally and politically constrained environment, but he was also imprisoned by his own ideological fortress buttressed by his Wall Street advisers and the hagiography surrounding the chairman of the Federal Reserve, Alan Greenspan, whose collective vision was dimmed by the long shadow of the "successes" of the Reagan years. The area in which these influences were most sharply and consequentially felt was in financial market deregulation. Most notably, the Clinton administration supported repeal of the Glass-Steagall Act, which had separated the activities of commercial and investment banks, without proposing any updated safeguards against the creation of banks that would become "too-big-to-fail."[75]

Clinton's trade policy also bore all the hallmarks of the neoliberal agenda. Far from being forced into the North American Free Trade Agreement (NAFTA) by Republicans in Congress, Clinton had to garner their support in 1993 because he could not rely on his own caucus to deliver the votes. Furthermore, as economist Robert Pollin notes, the degree of compensatory support American workers received from the anticipated short-term loss of jobs and wages was largely symbolic.[76] Moreover, Clinton's labor market policies reflected his lukewarm relations with the labor movement. But since "the AFL-CIO is a permanent electoral prop of any Democratic candidate to the Presidency, its concerns cannot be completely disregarded in the Republican manner."[77] As such, it is important to note that Clinton did effect a modest increase in the minimum wage from $4.25 to $5.15 (which would have pushed someone working a 40-hour week to $206 or roughly $10,000 per year), but its 2001 value still remained at 35 percent below the real value of the minimum wage in 1968. More encouragingly, the Family and Medical Leave Act of 1993 was a victory that provided for twelve weeks of unpaid leave per year for workers with families. In comparison to other industrialized countries, this benefit looks meager indeed, but it improved lives for American families who risked losing a job through having a child or providing care to a family member.

Working families were also assisted by the significant expansion of the EITC, a bipartisan instrument created under the Ford administration that lifted the income of low earners. Between 1992 and 2000, overall spending on the EITC rose by $17.5 billion from $9.3 billion to $26.8 billion; the number of people eligible for the EITC was expanded from 14.1 million to 19.2 million, whose income supplements rose by 2001 on average $550 or approximately 33 percent.[78] However, the transformation of Aid to Families with Dependent Children (AFDC) into Temporary Assistance for Needy Families (TANF) resulted in a significant loss in effective income for poor families. In particular, expenditure on food stamps and other nutritional assistance dropped by $2.9 billion from $32.7 billion to $29.8 billion between 1992 and 2000. Undoubtedly, some of the decline in spending on food stamps is a reflection of the fall in the poverty rate from 14.8 percent in 1992 to 11.3 percent in 2000. However, as Pollin notes, "The decline in the number of people receiving food stamps . . . was 17 percent greater than the decline in the number of people officially defined as impoverished."[79] Put simply, as a result of the 1996 welfare bill, millions of poor people became ineligible for food stamps. This was reflected in a significant rise in requests for sustenance at soup kitchens and food banks. According to the U.S. Department of Agriculture, in 1999, 31 million Americans (10.1 percent of households) were "food insecure."[80] Furthermore, since the creation of TANF, the proportion of poor families that received cash aid dropped markedly from 68 percent in 1996 to 27 percent in 2010, despite an increase in family poverty rates in the late 2000s.[81]

Although the expansion of the EITC demonstrated more concern for the working poor than during the Reagan-Bush years, the need for such a policy underscores the fundamental failures of the neoliberal political economy, which the Clinton administration did not seek to alter. Moreover, given its abandonment of full employment as a goal, alongside its embrace of open markets, those without work were undoubtedly left in a weaker position. To add insult to injury, they were demonized for "their" failure to find gainful employment.

Overall, the pattern of expenditures under Clinton illustrates the degree to which his investment agenda was chastened. As a percentage of gross domestic product (GDP), federal expenditures were 17 percent lower in 2000 than in 1992. While much of this reduction came from cuts to military spending (36.7 percent) and debt interest servicing (28.2 percent), significant cuts were also apparent in education (23.9 percent), science (19.1 percent), income security (17.6 percent), and transportation (10 percent).[82]

In respect of taxation, Clinton's presidency is also Janus-like. His Omnibus Budget Reconciliation Act of 1993 raised taxes on those earning over $140,000 from 30 to 36 percent and included an annual surcharge of 10 percent on those earning over $250,000. Thus, a measure of progressivity was restored to the American tax code, which represents a clear departure from the neoliberal agenda. However, some of these progressive changes were undone by the Taxpayer Relief Act of 1997 that reduced the top rate of the capital gains tax from 28 to 20 percent and the lower rate from 15 to 10 percent. It also raised the inheritance tax threshold from $600,000 to $1 million. The effect of the act was to reduce overall taxation by 1 percent. Economist Flavio Romano estimates that 68 percent of the total tax cut went to the top 1 percent, who gained an average of $7,135, while those earning under $59,000 received an average tax cut of just $6.[83] Still, the tax changes that occurred during the 1990s reduced taxes for the bottom four-fifths of the population by 0.9 percent, while the top fifth saw their taxes rise by 2.6 percent.[84]

Much like Clinton, Blair's government, particularly in its first term, held back on public investments to such an extent that it "effectively abandoned them in favor of fiscal discipline."[85] Despite the chronic underinvestment in public services under the Thatcher-Major governments (1979–1997), which was one of the key motivating factors behind Labour's victory, Blair's government stuck to Conservative spending plans for the first two years of the parliament. Indeed, "total managed expenditure," which had ranged between a high of 48.1 percent of GDP (in 1983–1984) and a low of 38.9 percent of GDP (1989–1990) under the Conservatives, ranged under Tony Blair's Labour governments from a low of 36.3 percent of GDP (in 1999–2000) to a high of only 41.3 percent of GDP (in 2005–2006).[86] Therefore, Blair did not offer a third way in respect of investment—expenditure under his government was at similar or even lower levels than under the Conservatives. Even on public sector net investment, the median amount spent by Blair's Labour government between 1997 and 2007 was 1.25 percent of GDP, slightly lower than the median of 1.4 percent of GDP under the Tories.[87] Finally, even as spending began to rise after 1999–2000, real terms investment in Labour's first term averaged $6.6 billion, lower than every year since 1989.

In respect of revenues, Blair exhibited the classically neoliberal position that taxes should be low because "the presumption should be that economic activity is best left to the private sector."[88] This helps to explain why he and his chancellor, Gordon Brown, reduced corporation tax from 33 to 30 percent, the world's lowest at the time. Brown also introduced a lower rate of corporate tax of 20 percent for companies with annual profits less than £300,000. Most symbolically of all, Labour by 1997 had abandoned its pledge to raise taxes on the wealthiest and stuck to that commitment until 2008. To set this in historical context, Margaret Thatcher had reduced the top rate of personal tax from 83 to 60 percent in Geoffrey Howe's first budget of 1979 and reduced it to 40 percent in 1988. Once again, Labour had come to accept this fundamental shift, which in part set the stage for the spiraling inequalities of the 2000s.

Labour's key innovation with respect to monetary policy was the decision to grant independence to the Bank of England through the Monetary Policy Committee, which was charged with targeting an inflation rate of 2.5 percent per year. Hitherto, decisions about interest rates had been in the hands of politicians. The removal of such power was intended to eliminate political manipulation of interest rates in order to enhance the credibility of Labour's economic policy in the eyes of the financial markets.[89] However, to the extent that a trade-off between unemployment and inflation is likely to occur, this shift clearly enhanced the relative power and interests of capital over labor by removing the democratic mechanism by which labor can influence the setting of interest rates.

Labour also expanded the neoliberal program of privatization to air traffic control, student loans, and defense research. It also extended significantly the Conservatives' Private Finance Initiative (PFI), whereby private-sector finance was used in the construction, maintenance, and delivery of public services in return for a guaranteed income stream from the government.[90] A similar trajectory is evident with respect to Labour's "welfare to work," whereby the social democratic concept of income support as a right of social citizenship was replaced with the principle of time limits and compulsion.[91] Through its New Deal for the Unemployed, Labour's welfare-to-work program, more people would be pushed into the labor market, with the hope that competition for employment would lower wages and thereby expand the total labor pool, which would in turn lower unemployment without inflation.[92]

In addition to the New Deal, Labour hoped to promote more flexible labor markets, which were considered necessary in light of enhanced capital mobility. Key to this would be to ensure that union power was kept in check. Therefore, in the 1997 election manifesto, Labour was clear that "the key elements of the trade union legislation of the 1980s would stay—on ballots, picketing and industrial action." As such, there would be "no return to flying pickets, secondary action, strikes with no ballots or the trade union law of the 1980s."[93]

But as with the Clinton administration, it would be wrong to characterize New Labour as an exclusively neoliberal organ, indistinguishable from its predecessors. Indeed, Labour understood that workers had suffered greatly in the 1980s and 1990s and professed serious concern about perceived social injustices. As such, Labour introduced a minimum wage at £3.60 per hour and the Working Families Tax Credit (WFTC)—which was explicitly based upon the EITC—that provided for a minimum income for those in work. Moreover, the Labour Party took significant steps to address child poverty and what it termed "social exclusion." The Child Tax Credit worked alongside the WFTC to provide cash support for families with children. Studies have shown that the substantial reduction in child poverty, from 4.1 million in 1998–1999 to 3.4 million in 2004–2005, arose in large part because of the government's tax credit policies.[94] Such deliberate intervention in family incomes is clearly at odds with neoliberalism and has helped to reverse some of the deleterious effects of the neoliberal political economy.

However, as Glyn and Wood point out, the effectiveness of Labour's approach to the long-term unemployed in industrial areas where the impact of economic restructuring has been most keenly felt falls far short. Pushing the low-skilled into the labor market in places where demand is weak was never likely to generate the desired expansion on jobs:

> For the policy to work, either the less well qualified would have to be encouraged to move to the high-employment southern parts of the UK or jobs would have to be created deliberately in the areas where labour supply is expanded, reversing the process of job destruction which caused their unemployment and labour-force non-participation rates to be so high in the first place. . . . Ensuring work is available for such people without further substantial increases in pay dispersion, requires much more deliberate action to target increases in demand for labour on the areas and skill groups most affected by joblessness.[95]

It was precisely this kind of "deliberate action" that could have been part of Labour's urban policy. However, as the next section shows, Labour's urban policy proved largely inadequate to the task.

Hence, in the arenas of economic and social policy, Blair, like Clinton, had transformed his party's stance in ways that were far more consistent with neoliberalism than ever before. Nevertheless, both Clinton and Blair had not abandoned their respective liberal and social democratic roots entirely. They both believed that the state had a role to play, not simply in promoting markets, as the neoliberals believed, but also in supply-side investment (which some neoliberals like Michael Heseltine endorsed) and in addressing aggressively the problem of chronic unemployment and what Blair referred to as "social exclusion," which they both regarded as a market failure and a moral outrage. However, their critique of the 1980s and early 1990s was not fundamentally grounded in a view of political economy. Broadly, they thought the economic reforms were roughly right and should therefore be left alone but that action could be taken to help people who had been left behind. The notion that the economic framework itself was at fault was not seriously entertained in principle or practice. The respective urban policies reflect the contradictions of this equivocal stance.

Empowerment Zones, the "Urban Renaissance," and Tackling Social Exclusion: Third-Way Urban Policy Compared

The neoliberalization of the Democratic Party's urban policy was not simply a function of the rise of the New Democrats, since the roots of this process lie in the turn in urban policy during Carter's presidency. Initially, he had targeted the Community Development Block Grant (CDBG) funds exclusively to cities with high unemployment and had legislated for the Comprehensive Employment Training Act (CETA), which directed money to job training centers and to local governments to upgrade public facilities. However, despite these achievements, "by the time Carter left office he seemed to be abandoning urban policy all together."[96] Indeed, Carter's Presidential Commission on the National Agenda for the 1980s, which reported shortly after Reagan took office, recommended that the national government should withdraw its support for declining cities: "It may be in the best interests of the nation to commit itself to the promotion of locationally neutral economic and social policies rather than spatially sensitive urban policies that either explicitly or inadvertently seek to preserve cities in their historical roles."[97]

Moreover, in 1978, Carter introduced the UDAG program that aimed to encourage cities to become entrepreneurial.[98] Rather than funding public works or public services, UDAG was targeted at "severely distressed cities and urban counties" and was intended to "provide the necessary financing to close the gap in planned developments and stimulate private investment which otherwise would not occur in the distressed communities."[99] As such, approximately $1 billion ($3.2 billion in 2012 dollars) was funneled to 521 private-sector projects in 382 cities in the first two years of the program. While public subsidy of private development had long been at the heart of postwar growth politics,[100] the late 1970s witnessed a sea change in which the character of urban policy became focused on neoliberal policy mechanisms to a far greater extent. The introduction of enterprise zones at the state level throughout the 1980s, alongside cuts in federal aid (see Chapter 1), reinforced and accelerated this change. The ultimate result was to undermine the capacity of city governments precisely at the time when the pressure on them to address unemployment and poverty had reached its zenith.

Therefore, Clinton entered office after urban and economic policy had drastically undermined the condition of urban America, especially in rust-belt cities, but also in places such as Los Angeles, which erupted in the aftermath of the Rodney King beating in spring 1992.[101] Initially, it seemed that Clinton might use this episode to build a coalition of support in favor of rebuilding cities, which he recognized had suffered "twelve years of denial and neglect" during the Reagan-Bush years.[102] However, as Republicans blamed the riots on the Great Society programs, Clinton demurred. Meanwhile, in Congress, the momentum behind enterprise zones continued unabated. Indeed, Democrats had gradually come to endorse the concept and even sponsored an enterprise zone bill that was passed in Congress but ultimately vetoed by President Bush because it was contained in a bill that included tax increases that he was not willing to endorse. As a result, Clinton had a ready-made enterprise coalition in Congress that could easily be mobilized if he so chose.

As noted above, Clinton himself rejected the U.S. Conference of Mayors' seven-point plan for major investment in America's cities and supported the enterprise zone approach as a presidential candidate and as governor of Arkansas, which enacted its own enterprise program in 1983.[103] While urban scholar John Mollenkopf rightly notes that Clinton was "in a substantive as well as a political bind" in light of the scandals and financial difficulties at the Department of Housing and Urban Development (HUD),[104] it is also clear that the president was reluctant on an ideological level to try to build the necessary coalitions to effect a major change in federal urban policy. In a speech to the U.S. Conference of Mayors in June 1992, Clinton reiterated his support for "new incentives for the private sector, an investment tax credit, urban enterprise zones, new business tax incentives, research and development incentives and others." But given the fact that Clinton's core vote came from the cities, it was clear that his administration would have to provide this key constituency with some kind of reward. This would come, he told the conference, in the form of an expanded CDBG and "$50 billion in new investments over the next four years."[105]

On the campaign trail and in office, however, as a New Democrat, Clinton was careful to distance himself from the Democratic programs associated with liberalism. Given the hollowing out of his investment plan, the

only major urban policy initiative that the Clinton administration introduced was the Empowerment Zones/Enterprise Communities (EZ/EC)
program, which passed as Title XIII of the omnibus Budget Reconciliation
Act of 1993. Characteristically, in framing its new policy, the administration
sought to blend the rhetoric of the left with the ideas of the right. It claimed
that the empowerment zone concept "moves beyond the old debate that
the answer to every problem is top-down bureaucracy on the one hand
or trickle-down economics on the other."[106] In a 1993 speech to the U.S.
Conference of Mayors, Clinton further articulated his core message: "We
can't do everything for the cities or the people of America, but we can't
turn our backs on you either . . . I want a new spirit of empowerment that
offers you a hand up not a hand out . . . I want to offer more opportunity
and demand more responsibility."[107] Thus, he claimed to eschew the puta-
tively ideologically driven programs of his Democratic predecessors. Keen
to reassure observers that the empowerment EZ/EC program was "not the
Great Society,"[108] Clinton stressed that the zones were "not about imposing
federal formulas; they're about giving communities the right to define a
future for themselves and the resources to succeed." Yet, the legislation was
also developed "with business people in mind," that is, to make run-down
areas "attractive for new investment so that people [i.e., businesspeople]
can . . . fulfill their dreams."[109]

These themes indicate another strand of New Democrat thought, shared
by many on the right and not altogether inconsistent with neoliberalism,
that the government's role in addressing market failure should be reinvented. Informed in part by the rise of "entrepreneurial government" at
the local level, David Osborne and Ted Gaebler released their influential
book, *Reinventing Government* in 1991, which chimed perfectly with and
helped to refine the ideas promoted by the DLC and the PPI.[110] Osborne
and Gaebler maintained that while government has a vital role to play,
they embraced public choice theory, which claims that bureaucracies have
a tendency to become bloated and inefficient unless they are subject to
incentive structures that force individual bureaucrats to change their inevitably self-serving behavior. Because we live in "an era of breathtaking
change . . . an information society . . . [and] an age of niche markets,"
bureaucratic institutions must become "responsive to their customers,
offering choices of nonstandardized services."[111]

Osborne and Gaebler note, with apparent approval, that "the first governments to respond to these new realities were local government—in large

part because they hit the wall first" as Proposition 13, the monetarist-induced 1981–1982 recession, and Reagan's cuts to urban budgets exacerbated cities' fiscal difficulties.[112] As a result, "state and local leaders had no choice but to change the way they did business."[113] Examples from cities in Arizona, Michigan, Minnesota, and Ohio are cited to illustrate how municipalities "reinvented government" by adopting public-private partnerships, competition for and privatization of public service delivery, performance-related pay for teachers, and the sale of public housing. While the rise of entrepreneurial government is presented as an illustration of third-way politics, all of these activities are wholly in line with neoliberal thinking and emerged as a result of a deliberate effort to "starve the beast" of money.

However, Osborne and Gaebler do not advocate the privatization of all state functions, not least because markets will not be incentivized to provide public goods, such as free education for all. However, they do maintain that government will inevitably be inefficient unless radically reinvented. This requires the introduction of mechanisms such as competitive bidding for service delivery, which will drive officials "to embrace innovation and strive for excellence."[114] Notably, this view, much like public choice theory and neoclassical economics, rests on the notion that individuals are self-regarding utility maximizers. The idea that people enter public service for its own sake or that people might be motivated to excellence out of concern for others is disregarded according to this theory. Curiously, this view of human nature, which applies to bureaucrats, does not refer to members of the "community." For another key mechanism by which government can be made more effective, responsive, and efficient is if it "empowers" rather than "serves" the public.

This notion of reinventing government was adopted and promoted by key Clinton officials, such as Bruce Reed, William Galston, and Elaine Kamarck, and informed the creation of Clinton's own reinventing government initiative, headed by Vice President Al Gore. As Clinton remarked when announcing the plan, "Our goal is to make the entire federal government less expensive and more efficient, and to change the culture of our national bureaucracy away from complacency and entitlement toward initiative and empowerment. We intend to redesign, to reinvent, to reinvigorate the entire national government."[115] To ensure that these goals were achieved, shortly after entering office, Robert Rubin, a partner at Goldman Sachs, whom Clinton appointed as director of his National Economic Council (NEC), and Carol Rasco, assistant to the president for domestic policy, asked Bruce Reed and Gene Sperling to set up an interagency working group on "community development and empowerment."

In spring 1993, the NEC made a series of "enterprise proposals," including the creation of "economic empowerment zones." In a memo to the president, the group cited the Los Angeles riots as an "action forging event."[116] It suggested that "we cannot hope to succeed in the world economy or come together as a nation unless we empower these communities to join the economic mainstream." True to the third-way vernacular, the memo suggests that its solution "moves beyond the old left-right debate that the answer to every problem is more federal spending on the one hand and more tax breaks on the other." But despite efforts to show how the memo's proposals represent a major deviation from the previous administration, it uses the terms *empowerment* and *enterprise* interchangeably. Moreover, the primary aim of the group was to use the enterprise zone bill that passed in Congress in 1992 (H.R. 11) as their basis and make improvements on it there.

Clinton was presented with a "consensus proposal" that recommended the creation of ten economic empowerment zones, which would receive "the full array of tax incentives" and block grant funding and would participate in "community policing, community development banking, and reinventing government/deregulation initiatives."[117] These zones would be complemented by 100 enterprise communities, which would operate on a smaller scale. Despite the small scale of the envisaged program in relation to the extreme levels of poverty, unemployment, and economic collapse in America's cities, the group recommended that the areas be designated on the basis not of need but rather through competition. This was justified on the basis that "efforts to spur economic empowerment in distressed areas cannot be successful unless government at all levels invents a new way of doing business." These new arrangements would include strategic planning and reducing "complex regulations, duplication and lack of coordination that discourage private initiative." They suggest that all the zones would enjoy "significant deregulation" not only regarding the empowerment zone resources but that would also be applied to all "existing funds and existing programs."

With respect to expenditure, the group proposed a $6 billion program, with about half of that money dedicated to tax incentives (including property expensing, accelerated depreciation, employer tax credits) and the other half slated for community development banks, community policing, and various block grants that would be deployed in ways set out in each applicant's strategic plan. In line with the enterprise zone proposals of the 1980s, the group recommended that tax incentives be a key part of the legislation despite the Office of Management and Budget's (OMB's) advice, circulated to group participants, which raised major doubts about the effectiveness and costs of tax incentives. After conducting several weeks of careful analysis, the memo stated in boldface: "The use of tax incentives to stimulate new business investment and jobs, if successful in a few places, is too costly to replicate widely in hundreds of other distressed areas."[118] The OMB's reasoning is almost identical to that advanced by enterprise zone critics whose arguments were rehearsed in Chapter 1. It noted that "tax incentives are inherently inefficient" since "most of the benefits of the tax package will flow to those already employed and to established businesses. . . . The long-term unemployed and welfare-dependent populations are least likely to benefit." Moreover, the memo points out that the Treasury's estimate of the revenue loss associated with the tax incentives would mean that the cost per new job of $50,000 would make the program three times more costly than UDAG. With the extra direct spending included in the proposals, the cost would be four times higher. Furthermore, the OMB memo reported that "experience with enterprise zones in Britain and at the state level suggests that many of the new jobs will simply be shifted from other, nearby distressed communities." In conclusion, the OMB memo suggested that the administration eliminate or drastically scale back tax incentives and focus on a more comprehensive plan for addressing urban and rural economic distress.

Ultimately, the administration chose to ignore this advice and largely embraced the plan presented by the NEC. This casts serious doubt on the claim often made by American and British third wayers that they are only really interested in the pragmatic question of "what works," which sets them apart from ideologues on the right and left whose policy selection arises from doctrinal commitments to laissez-faire on one hand or "big government" on the other. The OMB memo provided officials with independent, empirically based arguments as to why the neoliberal tax incentive was not likely to work efficiently. So why include them? The most obvious answer could be that important constituencies in the Democratic coalition were campaigning for the inclusion of these measures. Yet, there is very little evidence of lobbying from business, and even the institution built to promote enterprise zones, the American Association of Enterprise Zones

(AAEZ), stressed to administration officials that "the coordination and leveraging of resources were more important than tax incentives."[119] Moreover, as shown above, the U.S. Conference of Mayors lobbied for a far more expansive plan that did not have tax incentives at its heart. This suggests that the same ideological forces that informed the Clinton administration's policies on the economy, trade, and welfare reform were also at work with respect to urban policy. Alternatives were rejected in favor of a solution for which the evidence of success was not readily apparent.

It may be that a more comprehensive urban spending bill would not have passed in Congress.[120] However, this has as much to do with the ideological constriction of the Democratic Party as with anything else. As Chapter 1 shows, the enterprise zone coalition in Congress and beyond broadened and deepened despite the welter of evidence that suggested the approach was of limited value. Moreover, since Clinton ruled out an ambitious urban program as a candidate and immediately after his election victory, there is no indication that he had any commitment to such a program because, as Bill Barnes of the National League of Cities remarked, "he was just not that kind of a Democrat."[121] This implies that even with a more agreeable Congress, Clinton would not have pushed a liberal urban agenda.

The reluctance to learn the principal lesson from the enterprise zone experience further suggests that political scientist Karen Mossberger's conclusion in respect of empowerment zones that "although learning occurred, it can best be characterized as limited" needs to be revised.[122] It was not simply that policy learning was "limited" but rather that the policy makers involved had a set of ideological commitments that seemed to trump the evidence. They appeared to have no interest in learning anything that would not correspond to their preestablished blueprint. As such, an ideological dimension to the learning process (or lack thereof) is required to bolster Mossberger's analysis.

As advised, Clinton created a cabinet-level "Community Enterprise Board," whose name was later changed to the Community Empowerment Board as part of a linguistic attempt to differentiate the administration from Reagan's. Headed by Al Gore, the board developed the bill that was passed as part of the Omnibus Budget Reconciliation Act of 1993. The empowerment zone legislation very nearly failed to be included in the final bill because it had been removed by the Senate Finance Committee during the markup. However, Charles Rangel (D-NY), once a firm opponent of enterprise zones, fought to reintroduce it in the House-Senate conference committee.[123] Rangel succeeded in this, but initially, the $3.5 billion that had been slated for empowerment zones was exclusively dedicated to tax incentives. With Rangel's help, however, $1 billion was channeled through a Title XX Social Service Block Grant for direct spending on the zones.[124] After Rangel's intervention, $2.5 billion would be spent on tax incentives and $1 billion on direct investment.

Over the course of three rounds—1994, 1998, and 2001—the federal government selected 122 cities to participate in the EZ/EC program. Each of the EZs (30 out of the total 122) received a Social Services Block Grant (SSBG) of $100 million for community programs. While this element of the plan represents a clear departure from the neoliberal enterprise zone vision, the range of tax incentives offered directly to businesses operating in or moving into the zones suggests a key continuity. These included Employment Credits (20 percent tax credit on the first $15,000 in wages paid to employees who live within the zone), Welfare-to-Work Tax Credit, Work Opportunity Credit, Brownfield Tax Incentives (full deduction of environmental cleanup costs for properties located within the zones and that meet particular land use and contamination requirements), and Section 179 Deduction (deduction of up to $38,500 for properties purchased or renovated within the zone). When Clinton announced the final tranche of new empowerment zones in 1999, he also announced his "New Markets Initiative" that created forty "renewal communities," which would operate similarly to empowerment zones. The new element that these zones and renewal communities would receive was the elimination of capital gains taxes, the key goal of Jack Kemp, who, along with fellow neoliberals, had been campaigning for such a policy since the late 1970s.[125]

In another example of continuity, Vice President Al Gore was keen to stress the private-public nature of the program: "With the community, the private and nonprofit sectors and governmental entities working together under our community empowerment program, we can help many of our decaying urban areas and poverty-stricken heartlands to become a part of America's future."[126] The Community Empowerment Board oversaw the competition for designation as an EZ/EC. Seventy-four urban areas submitted proposals for just ten empowerment zones slots. Ultimately, the Philadelphia-Camden bid was selected alongside Atlanta, Chicago, New York (Upper Manhattan), New York (Lower Bronx), Cleveland, Baltimore, Detroit, and Los Angeles. Of the winners, it was no coincidence that the majority were run by Democratic mayors. Moreover, the inclusion of the

Lower Bronx, New York's second empowerment zone area, is clearly connected to Rangel's role in promoting the program.[127]

Thus, certainly, the empowerment zone concept was not identical to the enterprise zone idea. The most obvious differences are the block grants of $100 million and the requirement that local residents participate in decisions regarding the use of these funds. However, it is equally clear that the faith in tax incentives as the route to economic development was consistent with the neoliberal thinking behind the enterprise zone. Furthermore, this approach reflects the sanguine view that a relatively small amount of money and a more "business-friendly" environment would be sufficient to combat structurally and historically rooted poverty, unemployment, and economic stagnation.

Unsurprisingly, in light of the evidence with respect to enterprise zones, this faith was misguided. A number of attempts to identify the independent effects of the empowerment zone have been made by comparing the trends of EZ census tracts with trends within "comparison" census tracts that share similar demographic characteristics.[128] On the whole, these assessments are strikingly similar to the evaluations of the enterprise zone. That is, despite the best efforts of scholars to find a positive link between empowerment zone designation and improved outcomes, most studies find little effect. For example, a 2006 study by the GAO measured the effect of empowerment zone designation on rates of poverty, unemployment, and economic growth by comparing the zones with comparison census tracts with comparative characteristics.[129] In respect of poverty, the GAO found that while some decreases in poverty had occurred, "these changes could not be tied definitively to the EZ/EC program."[130] The same applied to unemployment rates. The picture in terms of economic growth was even less encouraging: "Urban EZs saw a decrease in the number of businesses, while the number in comparison areas remained about the same. But urban EZs saw an increase in the number of jobs, while their comparison areas saw a decrease [sic]" (while the report says "decrease," its graphs show an increase of roughly the same levels for both comparison and EZ tracts, so the wording appears to be incorrect).[131]

As a whole, therefore, the effect of the empowerment zone designation cannot be attributed to significant improvements on these measures. Oakley and Tsao used a different "fixed-effects" model that assessed the impact of the EZ in Baltimore, Chicago, Detroit, and New York. Their analysis shows that "across the four zones, zone designation made no difference at all" to levels of poverty, unemployment, or aggregate household income. Moreover, they find that "even where there were positive outcomes, they were modest."[132] In contrast to GAO and Oakley and Tsao's unimpressive results, Rich and Stoker find that "several cities did produce improvements that likely can be attributed to the EZ initiative."[133] However, they note that the results "are not consistent across outcomes or cities." In a recent elaboration of their work, Rich and Stoker identify significant variation in outcomes among cities' empowerment zone programs, which they attribute to disparities in the quality of local governance that was high in places such as Philadelphia and Baltimore, low in New York and Chicago, and lamentable in Atlanta.[134] Yet, despite their efforts to highlight areas of program success, they evenhandedly conclude that "the gains were modest. None of the local EZ programs fundamentally transformed distressed urban neighborhoods."[135] At best, therefore, the evidence is suggestive of a small positive effect of the program. However, considering that the proportion of urban areas covered by the zones was tiny in comparison to the extent of poverty, unemployment, and dereliction in America's cities, such shifts represent slight improvements at the margins.

Thus, Clinton's key urban policy initiative had its roots in the unabashedly neoliberal enterprise zone program, as reflected in the tax incentives and deregulatory elements at the heart of the program. However, as John Mollenkopf notes, the commitment of social service spending and the role of the Community Empowerment Board reflect the policy's liberal roots, not least in the model cities program.[136] Moreover, the program's commitment to direct civic participation in the drafting of strategic plans and in the creation of local community trust boards to afford residents a say in how funds were used is a significant departure from the enterprise zone and urban development corporation model examined in Chapters 1 and 2. However, even enterprise zone pioneers, such as Stuart Butler—who attacked the empowerment zones—recognize that Clinton's urban policy was a far cry from the Democratic programs of the past.

> *Timothy Weaver:* So would it be fair to say that they've [Democrats] come somewhat down the spectrum in your direction, away from the Great Society?
>
> *Stuart Butler:* Oh yes. I think when you look at Clinton . . . the empowerment vision is very strong with Clinton and welfare reform was a perfect example of that: change the incentives,

change the dynamics; encourage people to become independent. That was exactly what people on the right were saying. But he also has this third way, smart government at the detailed level vision, which is what drew him to the detailed planning. He wanted the planning to come up as opposed to top down, which is a big difference. But he still wanted to use all elements of government in a "smart," creative way and to hold town hall meetings to talk about it. I mean, this is so Clinton!

TW: So that was too much?

SB: It was certainly a hell of a lot better than in the past. But it still contained a vision of activist, detailed government which I am skeptical, and I remain skeptical, of as a long run strategy for dealing with the inner cities. *But I must say it's more a question of degree and argument at the margin, than a fundamental disagreement.*[137]

Thus, while differences are clear, Clinton's urban policy was imprisoned by neoliberal thinking, which prevented a clean break with the past, made tax incentives central, and limited the overall amount of the spending he was prepared to commit to urban areas. Moreover, the elimination of general revenue sharing, UDAG, local public works programs, and antirecession fiscal assistance during Clinton's period in office undercut cities' ability to recover from the 1980s.[138] But most important, the overall economic and labor market framework of the Clinton administration, which was more fundamentally aligned with neoliberalism—deficit reduction, welfare reform, free trade—meant that the urban poor and working classes, most of whom were not touched by the empowerment zone spending, were worse off at the end of the 1990s than at the beginning. Moreover, not only was it Clinton's failure to articulate and forge an alternative political economy in the 1990s, but in addition, some of his reforms accelerated the financialization of the American political economy that inflated the bubble that burst in 2000–2001 and the rise in inequality that has only now become the subject of sustained criticism.

Remarkably similar tendencies can be identified with respect to the Labour Party's urban policy under Tony Blair. For the location of his first major speech outside of the House of Commons as prime minister, Blair selected the Aylesbury Estate, a public housing development in the borough of Southwark in southeast London, not far from Docklands. Many on the estate were unemployed, lived in poverty, and were perpetrators or victims of crime. As such, for Blair, Aylesbury was the ultimate symbol of the failures of Tory Britain: "For eighteen years the poorest people in our country have been forgotten by government. There will be no forgotten people in the Britain I want to build."[139] In the speech, Blair suggested that "the decline of old industries and the shift to an economy based on knowledge and skills has [sic] given rise to a new class: a workless class. In many countries—not just Britain—a large minority is playing no role in the formal economy, dependent on benefits and the black economy. . . . Today the greatest challenge for any democratic government is to refashion our institutions to bring this new workless class back into society and into useful work, and to bring back the will to win." Blair's Alyesbury speech reveals a concern for the plight of the poor and unemployed that suggests a bridge to his social democratic predecessors. However, his emphasis on the "workless class . . . playing no role in the formal economy [and] dependent on benefits" places Blair rhetorically in line with the neoconservative and neoliberal thinking of his Conservative predecessors. Looking back at the speech, Blair draws the link with his erstwhile American third-way collaborator: "It echoed many of the sentiments of Bill Clinton."[140]

Blair's urban policies interwove two strands of concern central to New Labour's worldview: application of neoliberal techniques and ideology, on one hand, and efforts to address the plight of the "deserving" poor on the other. As with the Clinton administration, clear continuities between Blair's government and the policies associated with the previous government can be identified. For example, Labour retained the Single Regeneration Budget (SRB), a program introduced in 1994 by the Conservatives that awarded funds to urban areas on a competitive basis, rather than automatically based on need. It used the public-private partnership mode of governance to tackle holistically problems of health, education, crime, housing, and economic distress. Shortly after Labour came to power, the government announced the creation of regional development agencies (RDAs) that would determine how the SRB funds were spent. Like urban development corporations, RDAs were statutory bodies, governed by appointed boards that would use billions of pounds-worth of public funds to promote economic development but would not be subject to mechanisms of local democratic accountability. Thus, the blurring of public and private continued unabated.[141] However, one important innovation that Labour did introduce was to direct 80 percent of the SRB to Britain's fifty most deprived areas.[142]

In addition to Labour's continued commitment to interurban competitive bidding in the form of the SRB, which was retained until 2004, was Labour's more controversial acceleration of the Large Scale Voluntary Transfer Program, "the logical extension of the right-to-buy legislation, which had reduced the overall size of council housing stock by encouraging sitting tenants to purchase their homes at a significant discount."[143] This program therefore extended the privatization of British public housing by encouraging local authorities to transfer ownership and management of their remaining housing to "housing associations," which are private non-profit entities eligible for public-sector grants and private-sector financing.

But in addition to retaining some elements of Conservative urban policy, Labour developed a plethora of schemes of their own. I will focus here on the "urban renaissance," the 1999 Urban White Paper, and Labour's approach to neighborhood "renewal." In 1998, Deputy Prime Minister John Prescott appointed the highly acclaimed architect Richard Rogers as chairman of the Urban Task Force (UTF). Its mission, articulated in a report entitled "Towards an Urban Renaissance," was to "identify causes of urban decline in England and recommend practical solutions to bring people back into our cities, towns and urban neighbourhoods. It will establish a new vision for urban regeneration founded on the principles of design excellence, social well-being, and environmental responsibility within a viable economic and legislative framework."[144] Thus, from the outset, Britain's urban problems were seen as rooted in the loss of the middle classes to the suburbs, a pattern that had occurred in the United Kingdom to a measurable but far smaller extent than in the United States. Even more important than the lure of the leafy suburb, however, was the new challenge of globalization: "In the 21st century, it is the skilled worker, as well as the global company, who will be footloose. Cities must work hard to attract both."[145] Thus, the globalization thesis, so influential in shaping economic policy, was also central to urban policy.

Despite the rhetoric of "holistic solutions," plans for an "urban renaissance" were largely property led. This flows from Rogers's view that "if you live in well-designed public spaces and buildings you have a much better chance of having a better quality of life."[146] In addition to improving the urban fabric, the report also called for a "change in urban attitudes so that towns and cities again become attractive places to live, work and socialize."[147] While the task force report finds fault in urban attitudes and culture, in poor design, and even in high levels of unemployment, it does not see these tendencies as inherently linked to fundamental deficiencies in the British political economy. Therefore, the solutions are found in the recycling of land and buildings to bring derelict and underutilized brownfield sites back into use, improving the urban environment by better design and attractive public spaces, and "effective management" of development.

While the report claims that "local authorities will lead the urban renaissance," it recommends the introduction of "Urban Priority Areas where regeneration can be undertaken by dedicated companies, assisted by streamlined planning decision-making, easier land acquisition, tax incentives and additional resources."[148] But while the middle classes and business investors would be lured into the cities by attractive architecture and tax incentives, those whose behavior is not consistent with the renaissance would be subject to strengthened sanctions. Moreover, the aim "to create neighborhoods with a mix of tenures and incomes" explicitly involves bringing wealthier people into poorer parts of the city but makes no parallel suggestion for bringing poorer people into wealthier parts of town through, for example, new public housing provision.

The funding for significant investment in Britain's towns and cities was envisaged to come from a mix of private and public sources: "One of the most efficient uses for public money in urban regeneration is to pave the way for investment of much larger sums by the private sector."[149] Here the public-private model, which had been adopted by the Conservatives in the United Kingdom and embraced by the Clinton administration in the United States, was now to be central to British urban policy.

As a whole, therefore, the report suggests a series of win-win policy initiatives whereby the public good is served by the attraction of private investment. However, as urbanist Neil Smith points out, it is difficult to see how the vision of the urban renaissance does not involve an updated version of gentrification, with the agents of change now being the corporations, the state, or a combination of the two.[150] As Smith notes, "Urban policy no longer aspires to guide or regulate the direction of economic growth so much as to fit itself to the grooves already established by the market in search of the highest returns, either directly or in terms of tax receipts."[151]

The central recommendations of the Urban Task Force were adopted by the government in its Urban White Paper (UWP), entitled *Our Towns and Cities—The Future: Delivering an Urban Renaissance*.[152] Of particular importance is the creation of the urban regeneration companies (URCs), which have a number of key parallels with the Conservatives' urban development corporations. The URCs were created as the primary vehicles to deliver the goals established in the UWP. Their purpose was to "work with a range of private and public sector partners . . . to develop and bring investment back to the worst areas of cities and towns."[153] URCs were established with the permission of the Department of the Environment, Transport and the Regions (DETR) and operate as private, nonprofit companies governed by shareholders that include representatives from local authorities, regional development agencies, and the private sector. The URCs are funded by a combination of public funds that are used to leverage private capital. Three pilot areas were established in 1999—named Liverpool Vision, New East Manchester, and Sheffield One—with nineteen more being created in the following decade. Unlike the development corporations, the URCs are nonstatutory and do not have planning powers; their role is to mobilize public and private resources to promote physical urban development.

Like the urban development corporations of the 1980s and 1990s, URCs have no clear mechanism for democratic control. Indeed, the Office of the Deputy Prime Minister (ODPM), the department that assumed responsibility for urban policy once the DETR was reconfigured in 2001, would only support URCs whose board was chaired by a "representative of the private sector." Moreover, the ODPM explicitly limited the role of local elected officials: URC boards must have "no public sector majority and no local authority influence or control."[154]

But while the Labour government was determined, like its Conservative predecessor, to limit local governmental control over urban policy, it also emulated the Clinton administration's efforts to enhance the involvement of local communities. In particular, the creation of local strategic partnerships (LSPs) was intended, at least in part, to enhance local participation,[155] as were the New Deal for Communities boards, which have clear parallels with the community trust boards that ran elements of the Clinton administration's empowerment zone (see Chapter 5). However, while community *involvement* is encouraged, this does not necessarily result in enhanced *power* to determine the basis of urban policy. Indeed, as urban scholar

Annette Hastings points out, the guidance regarding LSPs suggests that local people are encouraged to share their experiences but "contrary to expectations about an empowerment model of community engagement, it seems rather that their role has been conceived of as influential, well-resourced 'expert advisers.' "[156] Moreover, the impact of "local people" on the LSPs was likely in any case to be limited by the presence of representatives from business and the voluntary sector.

Given that the involvement of the private sector in urban redevelopment planning has in various ways been enhanced *by design* through institutions such as the urban regeneration companies, it is clear that the demands of capital are now thoroughly intertwined with the needs of citizens. Indeed, in light of the requirements that the URC boards must be chaired by a member of the private sector and that at least half the seats be held by business representatives, it is clear that local citizen control is severely limited. While the creation of the LSPs does serve to rein in this tendency somewhat, their public-private character means that urban policy development and delivery occur in the absence of any formal democratic mechanism by which those driving local economic development can be held to account. Governing arrangements such as these both signify the neoliberalization of urban policy and guarantee that strategies inimical to the neoliberal project will be subject to private-sector veto.

What is perhaps most striking is that the move toward institutions such as UCDs under the Conservatives, which was in large part a political project aimed at neutering the power of Labour-run local authorities, was extended under New Labour with the intention of doing the same thing. In reflecting on this tendency, Hazel Blears MP, secretary of state for communities and local government (2007–2009), provides an insight into early New Labour thinking:

> It's very difficult to get a handle on what an LSP is. . . . at least your local councilors are visible . . . some of them. I think there was a real feeling in the early days of our government that parts of local government just didn't work and were pretty dysfunctional. And we spent a lot of time creating almost parallel organizations to circumvent and bypass local government . . . because we were desperate to push on, to create other structures. And I think as local government improved over the years, which I think it did, we should have been faster to give them more autonomy and more power over the things

that really mattered. I think some people, and I'd like to think I wasn't one of them, they'd got into a kind of mindset, that if it was local government it was automatically bad and I think that was quite damaging.[157]

Two final continuities with Conservative urban policy are worth noting. First, in 2002, Gordon Brown's Pre-Budget Report announced the designation of "enterprise areas" located in the 1,997 most deprived wards in the United Kingdom. Within each of these areas, private-sector activity is encouraged through exemptions on stamp duty (a property transaction tax), tax relief for "community investments," access to a private-public venture capital fund, and support for local minority-run businesses.[158] In describing the thinking behind this creation, Brown suggested, "Inner cities and established industrial areas should be seen as new markets with competitive advantages—their strategic locations, their often untapped retail markets, and the potential of their workforce. And right now we want to put in place the right incentive structure to stimulate business-led growth in our inner cities and estates and encourage much bigger flows of private investment."[159] Second, despite having wound them down shortly after taking office, the Labour government decided in 2003 to reintroduce UDCs in the form of the Thames Gateway Urban Development Corporation.[160] Labour's embrace of the ideas, policy tools, and institutional designs, promoted by the previous government, prompted Michael Heseltine, who originally created UDCs in the 1980s, to suggest that the Conservatives had "won the argument" over urban policy:

> *Timothy Weaver:* Since the Labour Party came in in 1997, do you
>   feel that some of your ideas have been picked up by it?
> *Michael Heseltine:* Well, I think they've all been; I can't think of
>   anything they've done that's new . . . oh, they've changed the
>   names.[161]

But despite the conspicuous continuities, it would be wrong to suggest that Labour's urban policy is indistinguishable from the Conservatives' approach.[162] As Stuart Wilks-Heeg puts it, after Labour came to power in 1997, "the ideological assumptions underpinning urban policy [were] more eclectic than under the Conservative Party."[163] One crucial distinction is evident with respect to the concern for the "socially excluded." Unlike the

Conservatives, Labour expressed a serious desire to tackle poverty and social injustice, which combined to leave some urban areas "largely by-passed by national economic success."[164] This led to the creation of the Social Exclusion Unit (SEU), which aimed to identify, measure, and tackle social deprivation. In contrast to the view of the urban task force that "successful urban regeneration is design-led,"[165] the SEU contended that "there has been too much emphasis on physical renewal" and therefore calls for "investing in people, not just buildings."[166] This in turn gave rise to the Neighborhood Renewal Unit and the New Deal for Communities that committed approximately £11 billion over eleven years to improve services and to support "regeneration" in Britain's most deprived areas. At their core, these initiatives view "communities" of about 4,000 or 5,000 as the key units of society whose members are excluded due to deficiencies on a number of dimensions. Most important are deficits in the skills required to compete in the global economy, but levels of crime, quality of housing, and health are also considered problems to be addressed as part of this "joined-up process." This focus on the poorest people and places in British society represents an unambiguous shift in emphasis from the previous government and from traditional neoliberal priorities.

However, New Labour's communitarian impulse is in some important respects a departure from its own social democratic tradition and may have far more in common with neoconservatism and neoliberalism than is obvious at first glance. First, its approach discreetly brushes aside structural explanations of poverty, unemployment, and deprivation in favor of the notion that community "breakdown" resulting in low levels of social capital is the key problem to be solved.[167] Second, this "devolves" responsibility for these problems to the local level. This in turn implies that individuals ought to bear responsibility for the well-being of their communities. Third, despite talk of the community being free to make its own decisions, in some cases, significant amounts of NDC funds went unspent because community plans were rejected by the government, sometimes because they included plans for democratically elected local authorities to play a role.[168] Hence, the dispersal of funds was contingent on proposals that corresponded to the government's priorities. As East London Labour MP Jon Cruddas explained, New Labour's urban policy did "attempt to correct the worst excesses" of the "neoclassical economic model," but the money was usually linked to whether you would embrace privatization, academies, and planning: "It was a very centralized form of discretionary funding usually tied into a neoliberal approach to the role of the state."[169]

As a whole, therefore, New Labour's emphasis on social exclusion does represent a clear break from the past, but its method for addressing these problems in many respects advances the neoliberal project by providing a "flanking, compensatory mechanism for the inadequacies of the market mechanism," on one hand, while actively advancing neoliberal modes of governance on the other.[170]

Conclusion: Neoliberalism 2.0?

Did the arrival of the third-way governments of Clinton and Blair represent a significant shift away from neoliberalism? Unsurprisingly, Anthony Giddens, the sociologist who most famously advanced the third-way concept in a book by that title in 1998, argues that "third way politics is not a continuation of neoliberalism, but an alternative philosophy to it."[171] Yet even in theory, the third way rests upon an unapologetic embrace of markets that "allow free choices to be made by consumers" and "generates far greater prosperity than any rival system."[172] As such, it labels as "archaic" the view that market "excesses need constantly to be reined back by the state." Therefore, the "left has to get comfortable with markets, with the role of business in the creation of wealth, and the fact that private capital is essential for social investment."[173] Beyond this recognition of the importance and centrality of markets, the third way, for Giddens, offers the promise of a bolstered civil society, a more efficient state, investment in human capital, and a new social contract "based on the theorem 'no rights without responsibilities.' "[174] He also asserts a concern for inequality but sees the "5 percent or so at the bottom of society as being detached from the wider society" as "casualties of the welfare state" rather than of the failures of market economies.[175]

As to the question of how to tackle inequality, Giddens is supportive of progressive taxation but is content with the reductions in progressivity brought about by neoliberal reforms in the 1980s. Indeed, he suggests that "social democrats should continue to move away from heavy reliance on taxes that might inhibit effort or enterprise, including income and corporate taxes. Seeking to build up the tax base through policies designed to maximize employment possibilities is a sensible approach."[176] Finally, with respect to urban policy, Giddens follows Michael Porter's[177] recommendation that cities become more competitive by looking to "new forms of collaboration between business, government and the non-profit sector." While government does have a role to play, Giddens warns that it "should recognize that its own initiatives can inhibit changes." This description seems very similar to the approach launched by the Conservative Michael Heseltine in Docklands and elsewhere (see Chapters 2 and 6), and as such, the distinctiveness of the third way, even theoretically, is unclear.

While Giddens's rendering of the third way does indeed depart from the most extreme versions of neoliberalism, with its explicit emphasis on civil society and egalitarianism, it does not propose to alter the overall political economy. Rather than suggest ways for transforming neoliberal globalization in a different image, it seeks instead to help people better contend with it, and often its remedies (e.g., welfare reform) are fundamentally consistent with neoliberal goals while others (e.g., investment in human capital) are not as easily reconciled with neoliberalism, although are not inimical to it either. As such, it is less a third way than neoliberalism 2.0 or "left neoliberalism"—an updated version that maintains and extends many of the neoliberal institutional innovations of the 1980s but sees a greater role for the state in supply-side investments and in offering help for those willing to "take responsibility for themselves" while the "undeserving" are left to fend for themselves.

If one has to strain to identify theoretical distinctions between neoliberalism and the third way, in practice, the differences are marginal. Some scholarly accounts of the Clinton administration see the president as firmly committed in his first two years to a genuinely third-way agenda and argue that Clinton was forced in a rightward direction only after the 1994 Republican takeover of Congress.[178] However, it is clear from the platform construction process and from his preelection policy positions on deficit reduction, welfare reform, and urban policy that any clean break from the neoliberal Carter-Reagan-Bush years was circumvented by Clinton's own ideological preferences and electoral calculations and by Democrats in Congress as much as it was the result of being forced to compromise with right-wing Republicans after 1994. Thus, as Stephen Skowronek writes, "Whatever Clinton's true leanings, the overriding feature of his first term is that its major policy accomplishments—the deficit-cutting budget of 1993, GATT, NAFTA, the crime bill, and the welfare overhaul—all 'played against type,' that is, contrary to the positions presumed to be held by liberalism's traditional constituents."[179] Moreover, the two significant areas of Clinton's agenda that clearly distinguished it from the Reagan-Bush years were the commitment to major investment spending and health care. However, the investment spending was shelved, along with a "middle-class" tax cut, as deficit reduction crowded out other priorities in 1993 (i.e., *before* the GOP takeover of Congress),[180] and health care reform proved an abject failure. As his urban policy illustrated, Clinton failed to articulate a substantially different approach from neoliberal priorities.

The contribution of Tony Blair's three terms as prime minister highlights a very similar pattern. In many respects, although New Labour did more to address the social injustices associated with neoliberalism than did the Clinton administration, it often did so through mechanisms that reinforced and institutionalized neoliberal modes of governance, as Labour's urban policy illustrates. As such, the Clinton and Blair governments have in many ways advanced the neoliberal project by ruling out fundamental alternatives in favor of ameliorative tinkering at the margins, on one hand, while institutionalizing key neoliberal reforms, on the other.[181] In this sense, they have made what might have been a fleeting blip a historical development from which we are yet to emerge. The expansion of the public-private partnership at the urban level is a classic example and key institutional tool of this development. That it takes Warren Buffett to point out that the "rich won" the class war speaks volumes about the failure of the New Democrats and New Labour to articulate and effect an alternative political-economic framework. As such, Peck and Tickell are right in their assessment that the hard-nosed edge of neoliberalism advanced by Thatcher and Reagan has "gradually metamorphosed into more socially interventionist and ameliorative forms, epitomized by the Third-Way contortions of the Clinton and Blair administrations."[182]

The final question to consider is why such a shift occurred. Scholars of American politics have mostly explained this phenomenon through reference to Clinton's weak position vis-à-vis Congress, which forced a reluctant Clinton to the right.[183] Skowronek's explanation sees Clinton's placement in political time as being a primary constraint on his options, since he has "as a practical matter, been located on a field largely defined by his opponents."[184] Marxist scholars, on the other hand, see actors such as Clinton and Blair as engaging in a political project "to reestablish the conditions for capital accumulation and to restore the power of economic elites."[185]

With respect to the Blair government, Mark Wickham-Jones argues that the neoliberal embrace was needed to signal to the electorate that the

Labour Party *really had* changed.[186] Others, such as Colin Hay and Richard Heffernan, maintain that the party had adopted a strategy of "preference accommodation" as part of a pragmatic bid to "catch up" with the median voter who had moved to the right.[187] Still others, such as Bob Jessop, maintain that the shift resulted from a pragmatic view about the rise of "globalization" which meant a structural dependence on capitalism.[188]

While each of these accounts is attractive in a number of respects, they tend to overdetermine the constraints—emerging from the nature of political institutions or from the neoliberal mode of capitalist reproduction—under which Clinton and Blair operated. It is undoubtedly the case that they were both hemmed in to such a degree that their freedom to depart from a politics of *neoliberalism by default* was limited, but this was due in part to their acceptance of the neoliberal *belief* that there was no alternative, either because the economic structure or electoral "reality" demanded the adoption of neoliberal policies.[189] Indeed, there are cases in urban policy (the urban renaissance, urban regeneration companies, the new markets initiative), economic policy (independence to the Bank of England, Labour's sticking to Conservative spending plans for the first two years of Blair's first term, reductions in business taxes in both countries), and social policy (with welfare reform as the most conspicuous example), which suggest that ideology played a necessary if not sufficient role. Urban policy is especially revealing in this regard, since it did not have salience with the electorate and so cannot be said to have been driven by efforts to "signal credibility."

As Mark Blyth notes, "While the Democrats defeated the ideas of business in order to build embedded liberalism, business was able to dismantle embedded liberalism only once the Democrats had lost sight of what they were defending. Disembedding liberalism was above all else, then, a struggle over ideas, a struggle that the Democrats lost."[190] The same could equally be said of New Labour. Ultimately, Blair and Clinton were limited as much by their own acceptance of neoliberal ideas as by the crowded political field with which they had to contend. At times, it appeared that they were articulating more forcefully the necessity of the continuation of neoliberalism than Reagan and Thatcher, while at other times, they attempted to remedy the failings of this approach. The contradictions in this stance arose from conflicted ideological commitments as much as anything else. Blair's description of himself provides the perfect summary of his predicament. In his words, "I remain on the progressive side of politics, but I am fiscally more conservative and, on markets, liberal."[191] Their contribution to political development was to embed the fundamentals of neoliberalism while providing selective compensation to the "deserving" middle and working classes but that ultimately sowed the seeds for the record inequality, stagnating median wages, and the Great Recession that have only recently come into full view.

PART II

Neoliberalism in the Trenches:
Urban Politics in Philadelphia and London

Chapter 4

Neoliberalism in the Trenches: Philadelphia 1951–1991

> My mail ran 1,000 to 1 against my decision, [but Liberty Place is] a
> symbol of the future of this city.
> —Mayor Wilson Goode, 1986

Looking out over the Philadelphia skyline, bejeweled with glittering sky-scrapers, one might be tempted to conclude that three decades of corporate embrace by the city's ruling elites had paid off. A stroll around Center City on a Saturday night reveals a vitality uncommon to many American downtowns, which have become hollowed out and soulless after 6 P.M. Moreover, in 2009, the city's population grew for the first time since the 1950s.

Yet these signs of revitalization obscure the grim reality of life for many in the neoliberal trenches. In 2000, after seven years of uninterrupted growth, Philadelphia's median household income of $30,055 had fallen by 7 percent over the decade since 1990.[1] Meanwhile, the poverty rate stood at 22.9 percent, nearly 3 percentage points higher than in 1990. That the 6 percent unemployment rate was relatively low illustrates the degree to which work, for many Philadelphians, failed to offer a route out of poverty. Moreover, racial disparities abound: on each of these measures, African Americans and Hispanics fare far worse than their white counterparts. In the decade since 2000, poverty and unemployment are the highest they have been in the past thirty years, while median wages have fallen still further. Unsurprisingly, the income distribution of Philadelphia households has grown more imbalanced as the number of the city's residents in the bottom two quintiles of the income distribution increased, while the middle-and the upper-middle households declined.[2] Notably, the number of households in the top quintile registered a slight increase. Thus, racial and class polarization characterized Philadelphia at the dawn of the twenty-first century. While significant segments within Philadelphia, in particular the wealthy and corporations, have benefited from the neoliberal turn at the federal, state, and city levels, the poor, the working class, and even the middle class have not. Since the 1980s, their standards of living have dropped compared to the very wealthy whose incomes rocketed.

While these changes are undoubtedly products of national, even international, political-economic shifts, they also have distinctly local political roots. The pro-corporate governing regimes of three successive mayors between 1980 and 2000 sowed the seeds for the developments that are now bearing fruit. This chapter provides an account of the political-economic basis of these trends. In the United States, this neoliberal transformation did not assume the top-down pattern of *neoliberalism by design* (see Chapter 6), not least because the institutions of federalism hampered the ability of neoliberal elites at the national level to impose a blueprint. In contrast, the Philadelphia case highlights the ways in which neoliberalism has been driven by local responses to economic and political shifts of international, national, *and* local origin. As with many other American cities, neoliberal policies and institutions emerged gradually and in patchwork fashion and were often promoted by liberals pushed in a pro-market, business-friendly direction by their assessment of the viable alternatives rather than because of ideological zeal. Hence, Philadelphia's political-economic development is best characterized as *neoliberalization by default*. I focus here on the key developments in Philadelphia between 1951 and 1991; Chapter 5 examines Philadelphia under Mayor Rendell (1992–2000) and considers the parallels between his governing philosophy and that of President Clinton.

As Paul Kantor notes, many approaches to the study of urban politics and history either focus on the internal city-level dynamics of coalition building or tend to see urban policy as a function of market imperatives.[3] This chapter takes a different view. It argues that in order to understand the pro-business bias in Philadelphia's local policy, which emerged in the 1980s, we must place the city's development in political, economic, and ideological context and chart the interplay between national urban policies and local urban politics over time while acknowledging the independent and interactive elements of both. Furthermore, this chapter shows that the full significance of the Anglo-American neoliberal turn can only be fully understood through a detailed account of how national political processes and economic trends shape political, social, and economic change in cities. For it is especially in these urban trenches that the battle of ideas waged at the elite national and international levels, detailed in Chapters 1 and 2, becomes concrete. The benefits from the bursts of economic growth in the 1980s and the long, although ill-fated, expansion of the 1990s did not simply trickle down but were filtered through a series of political institutions at the federal, state, and local scales in ways that exacerbated existing inequalities between the city and the suburbs, as well as created new inequalities within urban places. In short, neoliberal policies have distinct urban characteristics that need to be studied in order to understand the full significance of the neoliberal turn.

While my primary interest here lies in the last two decades of the twentieth century, it is crucial to recognize that neoliberal policy entrepreneurs did not encounter a smooth surface on which to etch their designs. Rather, they confronted a blemished landscape pockmarked with historically patterned institutional, racial, ideological, and political contours. Therefore, an understanding of the 1980s and 1990s requires casting the analysis back to the emergence of a cadre of Democratic political reformers who captured the city's institutions in 1951 and brought a century of Republican machine politics to an end. In what follows, I show how the political development of Philadelphia during the 1980s is rooted in the slow-moving processes of deindustrialization, economic restructuring, and demographic change (mainly involving the shift of whites to the suburbs and of blacks into the city), which were coupled with the sharp retrenchment of urban federal aid, all of which began in the preceding decades.[4] These transformations combined to push the city from a New Deal/Great Society liberal trajectory to a neoliberal one.

The primary transformation was political economic. A series of federal policies on trade, the macroeconomy, and toward cities had accelerated deindustrialization, particularly in cities such as Philadelphia.[5] The second shift was demographic. An influx of African Americans looking for work and politically structured "white flight" for those who could afford to leave the city fostered a racialized politics that came to a head under Frank Rizzo's mayoralty in the 1970s. Third, the city's fiscal situation, for a time buttressed by federal spending, deteriorated as aid was cut and poverty and labor costs rose. Finally, the ideological critique of postwar liberalism gathered pace toward the end of this period as political, business, and media elites increasingly championed neoliberal ideas in response to the "urban crisis."[6]

These structural and ideological shifts interacted with racially charged local political coalition building that promoted economic strategies that emphasized pro-business developmental policies at the expense of allocational and redistributive policies. Moreover, these tendencies, themselves partly fostered by political acts, were exacerbated by federally inspired but state-administered enterprise zones in the 1980s and, as shown in Chapter 3, by Bill Clinton's national empowerment zone program in the 1990s.

Precisely at the time Philadelphia politicians battled desperately—even myopically—to prevent businesses from abandoning the urban core, the economic and social costs of unemployment, poverty, and stagnating wages rose while the federal government withdrew its financial support. Moreover, in a classic illustration of how policy creates politics, programs such as enterprise zones served to encourage precisely the kinds of concessions to business that undermined the ability of the city to address persistent shortfalls in its social service spending.

It would be mistaken, however, to overemphasize the role of supra-urban forces as public choice and neo-Marxist accounts sometimes do.[7] In seeking to account for the political-economic development of cities such as Philadelphia, attention should be given to the interaction of these external forces with the internal dynamics and institutions at the urban scale. In Philadelphia, the biracial, pro-development governing coalitions constructed by mayors William Green (1980–1984), Wilson Goode (1984–1992), and Ed Rendell (1992–2000) consisted of an alliance between white liberals, blacks, and business interests. The glue that held these groups together was racial and ideological hostility toward former police commissioner Frank Rizzo, mayor from 1972 to 1980 who ran for the role in each election until he died during the 1991 mayoral campaign.[8] Rizzo's coalition rested largely on a white ethnic vote and various factions who benefited from his patronage politics. He was largely responsible for the growth in authoritarian policy practices by which blacks were routinely terrorized, and a startling number of civilians were shot by on-duty police officers.[9] Moreover, corporate interests were only selectively and temporarily brought into the governing regime. Thus, Rizzo earned the hostility of blacks, liberal whites, and business executives, who united to defeat him on a number of occasions throughout the 1980s.

Most striking was the formation of the electoral and governing coalition under Mayor Wilson Goode, Philadelphia's first black mayor. While Goode was from the reformist wing of the black political spectrum and had strong ties to business, he was no diehard neoliberal. Yet, as has often been the case as black regimes take power,[10] the political-economic environment, conditioned by these transformations, afforded few progressive opportunities to Goode. As such, Philadelphia's political development during the 1990s illustrates a pattern of *neoliberalism by default*, that is, a process by which pro-market policies are adopted because political, economic, and/or ideological forces constrict the range of plausible alternatives on offer. This stands in contrast to the pattern of *neoliberalism by design* that characterizes the transformation of London Docklands (see Chapter 6). This is not to say that alternative coalitions could not have been built around social democratic or progressive policies—as the cases of Santa Cruz, Burlington, Chicago, and Boston illustrate—but instead to suggest that Goode took the path of least resistance.[11]

As such, it is important to emphasize that these pro-growth developmental forces did not come to rule automatically. Rather, each member of the coalition had something to gain from cooperation, although, as will be shown, some gained more than others. Moreover, business in particular took steps in the early 1980s to ensure that it would not again find itself on the fringes of power. Thus, it is the interaction of these local political concerns, long-term demographic and economic shifts, and the changing shape of federal policy that explain the particular political development of Philadelphia. Undergirding each of these factors, however, is the role of ideology, which is key to understanding why neoliberal policies are routinely followed at national and local levels despite their inability to generate increased revenues or improve working and living conditions for the majority of the population.

Urban scholars have offered a range of theoretical frameworks that may be invoked to make sense of how cities such as Philadelphia would be expected to behave under these circumstances. I will briefly review some of the most influential theories in order to clarify the key theoretical issues at stake when dealing with the Philadelphia case. Urban theorists working in the public choice vein, such as Paul Peterson, suggest that a city's economic policies are conditioned by its position in an inherently competitive system where the city, without the sovereignty that states enjoy, is forced to pursue a business-friendly strategy in a bid to generate a competitive advantage with its rivals and bolster its tax revenues.[12] Under this account, attempts to develop redistributional policies would be suicidal. Thus, such scholars would predict that Philadelphia, faced with such constraints, would pursue the kinds of pro-market neoliberal policies that were being pushed at the time by the Republicans.

A rather less apolitical account is provided by Logan and Molotch, who maintain that city policy is shaped by urban elites who benefit from the transformation of the city into a growth machine, which is achieved through the manipulation of place to enhance the "exchange value" (i.e., price) of land. This is often done through the creation of a "good business climate," undergirded politically through the ideological claim that growth is universally beneficial and hence normatively desirable.[13] In contrast to Peterson, Logan and Molotch claim that "cities pursued growth not because they had to, but because those who controlled their policies used them for this purpose—that is, used them as growth machines to benefit their own fortune building."[14] Thus, in the Philadelphia case, one would expect pro-growth policies to result from the capture of the political process by a coalition of elites who stood to gain from the enhanced exchange value of land.[15]

Still others, such as Clarence Stone, place the politics of coalition building in a central role.[16] Like Logan and Molotch, Stone recognizes the degree to which, in a capitalist society, business elites tend to enjoy a privileged position in the relationship between the local state and society.[17] However, Stone's concept of the urban regime places politics at the heart of the process of building of coalitions necessary for governance. While business is likely to be a key player in any constellation of governing forces, business interests alone cannot succeed without the political support of City Hall, which in turn will depend on a mayor's support among various constituencies within the city. Hence, the policy agenda of urban regimes is not simply *determined* by capital but rather is contingent upon the degree to which constituent elements of a governing coalition are able to cooperate around a shared agenda. Outcomes vary depending on the relative strength of business and nonbusiness interests. Therefore, one cannot assume that pro-growth politics will always emerge or that cities will deterministically embrace pro-business strategies.[18] But while urban scholars have recognized the role of ideology, it rarely takes center stage. As noted in the Introduction, students of neoliberalism such as David Harvey and Jason Hackworth—while grappling with ideational phenomena—render ideas as "epiphenomenal," that is, as simply reflecting material interests.[19] As Hackworth argues, neoliberalism " 'won' because its powerful institutions and individual pro-ponents organized enough people and interests to believe that there is no alternative."[20] As such, this analysis improves on the extant urban politics literature by illustrating how actors' ideas about the realm of the possible, developed independently of business interests, are central to explaining the emergence of neoliberalism.

Moreover, while Peterson underestimates the role of local deci-sion making, Stone arguably underestimates the effect of national and international-level forces. Thus, this book argues that we must view urban politics and policy as both local and national in origin. Hence, we need to place the economic, political, and ideological processes—operating at the local, national, and international levels—in their proper historical context in order to chart urban political development in the United States and the United Kingdom.

As such, this chapter and the next use Philadelphia's political develop-ment to illustrate the ways in which the penetration of business influence varies significantly over time. Indeed, there will be a brief examination of the degree to which business was frozen out during the Tate and Rizzo years from 1962 to 1980. Moreover, it examines the apparent conundrum of pro-business positions being adopted by City Hall in the absence of business lobbying. Enterprise zones are a case in point. This investigation will proceed first with a brief overview of Philadelphia's demographic and economic transformation over the twentieth century, followed by a detailed discussion of the impact of federal urban policy since the end of the Second World War. This will give way to an in-depth examination of coalition building and political development, which pays particular attention to the emergence of Philadelphia's black urban regime in the 1980s.

Philadelphia in Transition

By the late nineteenth century, Philadelphia had become one of America's leading industrial cities. It had been the largest city in the British colonies until the opening of the Erie Canal in 1825, which ensured New York would become the largest port in the Americas. Philadelphia's population exploded from around 120,000 in 1850, to 1.3 million in 1900, and to 1.9 million by 1930.[21] Since then, the city's population hovered around the 2 million mark before declining from 1.95 million in 1970 to 1.52 million in

Table 4. Population in Philadelphia by Race

Year	Total Population	White Total	White Percentage	Black Total	Black Percentage
1940	1,931,334	1,677,957	86.9	250,907	13.0
1950	2,071,605	1,692,637	81.7	376,041	18.2
1960	2,002,512	1,467,479	73.3	529,240	26.4
1970	1,948,609	1,278,717	65.6	653,791	33.6
1980	1,688,210	983,084	58.2	638,878	37.8
1990	1,585,577	848,586	53.5	631,936	40.0
2000	1,517,550	683,267	45.0	655,824	43.2
2010	1,526,006	626,221	41.0	661,839	43.4

Source: U.S. Census Bureau.
Note: Data regarding Philadelphia's Hispanic population is not included in this table. Between 2000 and 2010, the Hispanic population grew from 128,928 to 187,611 (i.e., from 8.8 percent to 12.3 percent of the population). By comparison, in 1980, just 64,323 (3.8 percent) Hispanics lived in Philadelphia. This shift is likely to have a profound effect on ethnic and class politics in Philadelphia.

2000. Since 2000, the city's population grew slightly to 1.53 million (see Table 4). Meanwhile, the Philadelphia region as a whole grew steadily from around 2 million in 1900 to reach around 6 million by 2010. Yet, as Jerome Hodos points out, Philadelphia's development diverged from New York's, which was to become a global city, and occurred instead through a "paradoxical combination of simultaneous growth and decline," which resulted in Philadelphia's becoming a "second city."[22] However, merely looking at the population trends that detail the growth and decline of Philadelphia during the postwar period obscures the issue of who was arriving and who was leaving. Here, the crucial issue is race.

As Table 4 shows, the absolute number of Philadelphia's African Americans rose dramatically in the three decades after 1940. Most of these migrants came from the South to find work. However, this was precisely the time when manufacturing and other low- to mid-skilled occupations were declining. From 1970 onward, Philadelphia's black population remained fairly stable. In contrast, the white population plummeted by approximately 200,000 during the 1950s and again in the 1960s. That decline accelerated until the late 2000s, when the white population began to increase. However, by the end of the decade, that increase had reversed, so by 2010, Philadelphia had become a "majority-minority" city for the first time in its history.

Many of the newly arriving masses came to work in Philadelphia's diverse manufacturing sector, but like most "frostbelt" cities, Philadelphia's manufacturing days were numbered. While industrial production would fall precipitously from the 1960s, the roots of the decline can be traced to the Great Depression, although wartime production requirements postponed the reckoning that was to come.[23] The proportion of Philadelphia's private labor force working in manufacturing declined from 48 percent in 1947 to 24 percent in 1980;[24] by 2000, that proportion shrank to just 10 percent.[25] That which remained increasingly specialized in chemicals and pharmaceuticals. But as Philadelphia's manufacturing sectors lost ground, employment in other sectors expanded significantly, particularly in the service sector.[26] The share of the working population engaged in this diffuse category economy grew dramatically from around 22 percent in 1970 to 49 percent in 2000.[27]

The shifting patterns of capital and labor in and out of Philadelphia did not, of course, occur in a political vacuum. While apolitical shifts in technology, for example, undoubtedly accelerated the most recent wave of globalization, federal, state, and local policies, which reflected the political and ideological strategies of elites at each level of government, were just as influential. Before dealing with Philadelphia's internal politics, it is therefore necessary to set the context of postwar federal urban policy.

The Impact of Federal Urban Policy

As Chapter 1 notes, a number of federal and state policies played a central role in promoting the shift of industry out of central cities and to the suburbs and to the South and West of the United States. This came in the form of both "fiscal welfare,"[28] by which tax subsidies are channeled to business at the expense of other groups, and a host of fiscal policies that encourage investment outside of "frostbelt" cities. As Michael Peter Smith points out, these twin processes "have directly contributed to urban fiscal crises in declining central cities by subsidizing capital flight to new points of production."[29] Indeed, accelerated depreciation allowances in particular accentuated capital flight from older cities: between 1962 and 1981, "this subsidy was worth $90 billion. In 1982 alone it was worth $20 billion."[30] This suggests that economistic explanations for the particular patterns of investment and disinvestment that focus on "capital logic" must be treated with a degree of skepticism since they fail to account for the role of government in promoting these patterns *before the fact*. But while government policies had encouraged people and businesses to leave the city for the suburbs and beyond, they also facilitated the transformation of central Philadelphia.

The story of federal funding to Philadelphia is also one of long-term unintended consequences. Urban renewal is a prime example. While the initial hope was that urban renewal would be the savior of cities, enabling the transformation of an outmoded and dying industrial core into a forward-looking, dynamic postindustrial engine, the reality proved less felicitous. One example is the destruction of Philadelphia's "Skid Row" to make way for the creation of the federally funded Independence Mall and the Vine Street Expressway.[31] Skid Row was a "blighted neighborhood," comprising twenty-five square blocks situated on the northeastern edge of Center City, which attracted groups of itinerant unskilled, homeless laborers during the industrial period, in search of work and inexpensive housing. As such, it represented an important source of cheap labor. For the first two decades of the twentieth century, the city took a largely ambivalent approach to the area since "the work already done by this group was necessary to the needs of the political economy of the time."[32] However, during the 1920s and 1930s, demand for casual, migratory labor diminished. Moreover, after the Second World War, the expansion of employment opportunities and the emergence of the New Deal welfare state reduced the number of younger people who would have become itinerant laborers. Thus, as a group, those who remained were "older, more disabled, and less attached to the labor force than their predecessors."[33]

In the 1950s, Philadelphia's elites decided that Skid Row was antithetical to the aims of urban renewal. The Greater Philadelphia Movement (GPM), an influential pro-growth business association, organized a Skid Row Study Committee in 1956, which proposed that much of Skid Row should be cleared and replaced with the expressway and the "stately" Independence Mall. Concerned that "blighted" people would remain even after the obliteration of the blighted area, the GPM secured the destruction of Skid Row's flophouses, cheap hotels, Christian missions, bars, liquor stores, and theaters, which were replaced by the Metropolitan Hospital, the administrative offices of the Philadelphia Police Department, the Vine Street Expressway, and Independence Mall.

The destruction of Skid Row illustrates some of the unintended ramifications of urban renewal. In Philadelphia, as in many other places, federal money was used by local development agencies and pro-growth coalitions to clear the way for urban redevelopment. But while boosters hoped that the expressway would attract people to the city, it also enabled them to make a fast getaway to their often federally subsidized suburban homes. Moreover, it reduced provision of affordable accommodation for a fragile population. Heralded as one of the most successful applications of urban renewal, Philadelphia's urban core was transformed. Acts such as these "stimulated a downtown boom that replaced the old center with new office buildings, restaurants, tourist parks, hotels, specialty shops, university campus facilities, and thousands of luxury housing units."[34] But they also displaced the poor and working class in order that housing could be built for the higher earners associated with the postindustrial mode of production.

With a declining population, deindustrialization, and competition from the suburbs, Philadelphia entered the 1970s in a fragile state. Not only were revenues in decline, but the demands for city services were increasing, not least because many of those who left the city were hitherto employed and paying city taxes. Had the economic composition of the city remained the same, only smaller, the balance between revenues and necessary expenditures would not have been so askew. Fortunately for the city, however, direct federal aid helped to make up for the mismatch between revenues and expenditures. Throughout the early to mid-1970s, despite Republican presidents in the White House, federal funding to Philadelphia rose steadily and peaked in 1977 (see Table 5). As with the austerity measures normally associated with the Reagan administration, however, the shift initially occurred under President Carter, a Democrat.

Elsewhere, the cuts came sooner. Although Philadelphia initially escaped the executioner's blade, the neoliberal assault on cities was heralded by President Ford's refusal to bail New York out of its fiscal crisis in 1975.[35] The president's move yielded one of the most memorable newspaper headlines of the 1970s: "Ford to City: Drop Dead," screamed the *New York Post*. While Ford's prescription was not quite fatal, the patient had to swallow medicine of the likes of which the Chicago Boys would have been proud.[36] In the face of Ford's refusal to help out, the city was forced to go to the financial markets to secure emergency loans. These were granted on condition of major restructuring, which resulted in the ceding of budgetary authority to an unelected Financial Control Board, cuts to city services, and mass layoffs of city workers. Philadelphia's reckoning would not be far behind. President Carter's embrace of pro-market neophyte neoliberalism was reflected in his choice of Paul Volker as chairman of the Federal Reserve. The resultant "Volker Shock," whereby interest

Table 5. State and Federal Aid to Philadelphia, 1970–1991

Year	State and Federal Revenues in Original Figures (in Millions of Dollars)	State and Federal Revenues Adjusted to 2000 Dollars (in Millions)	Year-on-Year Percentage Change in 2000 Dollars
1970	67.6	300	
1971	77.7	330	10.0
1972	149.7	613.8	86.0
1973	261.8	1015.3	65.4
1974	261.8	914.4	−9.9
1975	300	960.2	5.0
1976	344.5	1042.6	8.6
1977	396.2	1125.8	8.0
1978	419.4	1107.6	−1.6
1979	410.6	973.9	−12.1
1980	436.6	912.4	−6.3
1981	440.7	834.9	−8.5
1982	457.4	816.2	−2.2
1983	463.8	801.9	−1.8
1984	437.9	725.8	−9.5
1985	439.8	703.8	−3.0
1986	464.8	730.3	3.8
1987	421.4	638.8	−12.5
1988	435.4	633.8	−0.8
1989	506.5	703.4	11.0
1990	518.4	683	−2.9
1991	573.4	755.5	10.6

Source: City of Philadelphia Budget.

rates rose dramatically in a bid to tame inflation, induced a massive contraction in the American economy. As such, Carter's reframing of urban policy further reflected his role as a bridging figure between New Deal liberalism and neoliberalism.

As we have seen, a matrix of political-economic and demographic and social conditions left Philadelphia especially exposed. For a while, federal and state aid stemmed the tide. Carter's first year in office, however, marked the zenith of federal funding to cities. As direct urban federal funding under Reagan declined dramatically and was routed through the states, Philadelphia's ability to cover its costs became virtually impossible. The city had to try to find a way to cope without sufficient support from Harrisburg or Washington.

It is important to note, however, that while direct state and federal grants to the city were cut severely, federal spending on individuals did increase somewhat by the early 1990s. Some of this rise came in the form of grants to cover Medicaid and Aid to Families with Dependent Children and through direct payments to individuals such as Social Security, housing assistance, and Medicare.[37] Therefore, while the Reagan and Bush administrations succeeded in cutting grants to *places* such as Philadelphia, payments to *people* in cities continued to rise. The next section considers the interaction between these structural changes and local efforts to build stable coalitions, to explain the policies and politics that emerged.

Coalition Building and Political Development in Philadelphia

Philadelphia emerged from the 1970s in the midst of highly unfavorable structural forces: rising unemployment, disinvestment, loss of population, and cuts in federal funding. As with the United States as a whole and indeed in the United Kingdom, the 1970s represented the hinge period during which time, in the face of economic lethargy and rising inflation, the contradictions and limits of liberalism would reach a breaking point.[38] Political and economic elites responded with the embrace of a series of neoliberal policies. However, these policies ran up against institutions and politics still very much embedded in postwar liberalism. In some respects, these changes reflected the attempt to reconcile the legacy of the reforming elites of the 1950s and 1960s with the consequences of economic restructuring and federal retrenchment.

While business mobilized in the 1950s and early 1960s, its influence faded somewhat in the 1970s, at times frozen out of the political process by mayors Tate and Rizzo. However, business influence returned forcefully in the 1980s. The interaction between national-level political and economic forces—such as federal urban funding and economic restructuring and national-regional population shifts—and local-level factors—such as the role of race in coalition building—shaped the degree of business penetration into Philadelphia politics. Crucially, the alliance between middle-class African Americans and business, which began in the 1960s and intensified in the late 1970s, set in motion a series of positive feedback effects that culminated in the election of Wilson Goode, Philadelphia's first black mayor, who won office in 1983 with the substantial backing of business. Moreover, the turn to neoliberal policy prescriptions reflected and in turn propelled an ideological shift based upon the claim that market forces would lead to more efficient and equitable outcomes than had been produced through Keynesian-style government intervention.

To fully understand political developments since the 1980s, one must understand the historical dynamics that shaped the coalitional and institutional terrain in which the pivotal alliance between blacks and business elites was formed. Following a century of almost uninterrupted Republican rule, in 1951, Philadelphia elected Democratic reformer Joseph Clark. Since then, the city's political-economic trajectory has traversed three distinct periods. The first "reform" period was presided over by Clark (1952–1956) and Richardson Dilworth (1956–1964).[39] The political alliances formed during this time led to the creation of key pro-business institutions and the transformation of the city government, which would have significant ramifications for Philadelphia in the 1980s and the 1990s. The second "machine" period witnessed a return of machine politics under Mayors James Tate (1962–1972) and Frank Rizzo (1972–1980). As Philadelphia languished economically and became polarized along racial lines, Rizzo's attempt to change the city charter to enable him to run for a third term as mayor provided an opportunity for the emergence of a third "liberal/neoliberal" period governed by William Green, Wilson Goode, and Edward Rendell.

Joseph Clark's coalition came into office to replace a regime characterized by patronage-based machine politics. Both Clark and Dilworth were committed to dismantling the institutions and politics associated with Philadelphia's infamous reputation as a "corrupt and contented" city.[40] They realized that key business groups would have to be at the heart of any governing coalition. At the time, Philadelphia's economic elites consisted of two key groups. The first consisted of the established business leaders of the industrial era, represented by the Chamber of Commerce. In contrast, the second group comprised a new generation of leaders who were associated with service sector industries such as banking, legal services, and insurance. In 1948, these "Young Turks" formed the pro-growth GPM "to get the city moving again" via the redevelopment of Center City.[41]

The GPM did not simply seek investments in infrastructure and a more coordinated economic policy, however; it also sought to remake the institutions of city government. In 1951, as a result of a series of revelations of corruption and the subsequent suicides of several Republican officeholders, the city's economic and legal elites bolted from the GOP, fearing that Philadelphia's notoriety for political scandal and physical deterioration would be inimical to their interests.[42] They joined with the Democrats to support a new city charter that strengthened the mayor, established a civil service, enhanced the role of the City Planning Commission, and limited the power of the City Council.

The Democrats under Dilworth also aimed to bring African Americans into their electoral coalition through supporting the Fair Employment Practices Commission that the Republicans opposed.[43] As such, business groups joined Democratic Party ward leaders, union members, African Americans, and liberal activists and intellectuals to elect Clark mayor and elevate Dilworth to the district attorney's office. As Guian McKee points out, this alliance "neatly mirrored the New Deal coalition that had defined Democratic politics since the 1930s."[44] It also highlighted the racial tensions that existed within the city: while almost two-thirds of blacks voted for Clark in 1951, Italian and Irish Philadelphians gave the Democrats just half of their vote.[45]

As with New Deal liberalism, the influence of business in Philadelphia under Clark and Dilworth resulted in government activism and investment in Philadelphia's industrial base, in infrastructure such as the public transportation system, and in public housing. Moreover, there was an explicit role for labor. This is perhaps best reflected in the creation of the Philadelphia Industrial Development Corporation (PIDC), a quasi-autonomous institution sponsored jointly by the Chamber of Commerce and the city of Philadelphia. The PIDC's board was composed of representatives from city government, labor unions, and the Chamber of Commerce, although neighborhood organizations and groups that represented African Americans were not included due to their relatively tangential position in Philadelphia's governing coalition of the time.[46] This corporatist approach highlights a key distinction between liberalism and neoliberalism. While business has a central role in both, in the former, business was more rooted by place and advocated for investments in public as well as private goods. Moreover, the demands of business were balanced somewhat by those of labor, whose influence on Philadelphia's governing regime was far more significant in the 1950s and 1960s than during the 1980s and 1990s.

The reform era came to an end, however, as fissures within the fledgling Democratic coalition were exposed in the early 1960s. Philadelphia's fragmented Democratic Party increasingly struggled to reconcile the reform agenda of liberal whites and business with the interests of labor and blacks who were losing ground as deindustrialization accelerated. Moreover, both Democratic and Republican politicians cynically exploited divisions between whites and blacks on the issues of housing and workplace integration. This, along with the growing disillusionment with the civil rights movement, led to splits between black moderates, like Charles Bowser and Leon Sullivan, and radicals such as local NAACP President Cecil Moore, who sought to build a black political base independent from the Democrats, who he considered insufficiently committed to ending racial discrimination.[47]

When Dilworth resigned in 1962 in order to make an abortive run for governor, he was replaced by City Council President James Tate, a politician out of the traditional pro-union Philadelphia mold with strong ties to Philadelphia's white working class.[48] Local Democratic elites, with the support of business, opposed Tate in his run for the nomination for the 1963 mayoral election. Unable to rely on the support of Democratic elites, liberals, or business, Tate built a biracial working-class coalition to carry him to victory in the 1964 mayoral election. While Tate knew he could rely on the support of unionized working-class whites, he labored to attract the votes of African Americans, who by 1960 composed 26.4 percent of Philadelphia's population. Given the class-based and ideological divisions within the black community, African American votes were by no means guaranteed, as Moore's unsuccessful attempt to establish himself as a spokesman for the black community demonstrates. He wrote both to Tate and to Republican candidate Jim McDermott to offer a substantial bloc of black votes in exchange for a commitment to increase the number of black appointees. As Countryman notes, however, this "scandalized" most black leaders in the city, who were loyal Democrats. Ultimately, black voters overwhelmingly backed Tate with an estimated 73.5 percent of the black vote. In contrast, Tate only received 45.3 percent of the white vote. However, with the support of labor and the lion's share of black voters, Tate won the election with 54.5 percent of the vote. Thus, while "black Philadelphians had clearly become the most loyal Democratic voters in the city," white voters had begun to desert both the city and the Democratic Party.[49]

Given their growing electoral clout, blacks were increasingly able to benefit from political incorporation into the electoral coalition. Throughout Tate's first term, he delivered approximately 39 percent of the city's jobs to African Americans[50] and steered federal Great Society funds to black neighborhoods. While poorer blacks benefited from Tate's largesse, those from the middle class resented their systematic exclusion from political office. Meanwhile, he rewarded the support of the municipal unions with generous contracts.[51] These policies, along with a series of tax increases, alienated the business community. As a result, the GPM threw its support behind Democrat-turned-Republican district attorney Arlen Spector in the 1967 race for mayor. Nevertheless, with the support of middle- and working-class African Americans and the white working classes, Tate narrowly won reelection.

These voting patterns illustrate the fact that the black electorate of the 1960s was heterogeneous. As such, the notion of a monolithic "black vote" is inapposite in those elections where race was not a primary dividing line. Keiser notes that, during the 1960s, African American support was divided along class and ideological lines into three camps: a working-class group linked to Tate and the Democratic Party through patronage politics, a radical group that rejected liberalism and biracial alliances, and a liberal group led by the clergy that sought alliances with liberal reformers and business.[52] This political heterogeneity was masked, however, as these groups united as race came to define the 1971 election. Having served out his maximum two terms, Mayor Tate was not in a position to run again. As such, the Democratic primary of that year was crucial.[53] The contest exposed the deep cleavages within Philadelphia's Democratic coalition that had been on display nationally in the 1968 presidential election. This time, Frank Rizzo's approach had echoes of George Wallace's candidacy. He confined his appearances to white neighborhoods and promised them that they would not have to put up with "unwanted" public housing developments. Rizzo also expressed his opposition to busing and trumpeted his "tough-on-crime" credentials. He infamously remarked that his approach "would make Attila the Hun look like a faggot."[54] The three-way race splintered the anti-Rizzo forces, which handed victory to Rizzo, who won with a plurality on 48 percent of the vote. In the general election, Rizzo faced Republican Thatcher Longstreth, one of the few in his party to back the Fair Employment Practices Commission. Liberal whites and African Americans defected from the Democratic Party and joined with business interests to back the Republican. On a record turnout of 77 percent, Rizzo won by just under 50,000 of approximately 750,000 votes cast.[55]

As mayor, Rizzo was fortunate to govern during a period of relative largesse from the federal government. While the Nixon administration's distribution of federal funding tended to disadvantage cities in the Northeast, Philadelphia was an exception to this rule.[56] Indeed, Nixon continued to funnel federal funds to Philadelphia as a result of Rizzo's endorsement of Nixon for president in 1972. Moreover, Nixon considered Rizzo's influence on the conservative realignment to be considerable: "Frank Rizzo was a leading member of what I called The Silent Majority. He played an indispensable role in helping me build support among ethnic voters who had for years been part of the coalition that Franklin Roosevelt had brought to the Democratic Party. These voters were among those who made it possible for President Reagan to win landslides in 1980 and 1984."[57] In the lead-up to the 1972 presidential election, Nixon saw Rizzo as a key ally in building support for his campaign among white ethnic voters in Philadelphia in order to deliver Pennsylvania for the GOP. Nixon ordered his campaign manager to "work out a system so that Mayor Rizzo receives a call from us each week." The only other people who enjoyed such an arrangement were Nelson Rockefeller and Ronald Reagan.[58] As part of Nixon's courtship of Rizzo, the president caught his aides off-guard when he promised in a meeting with Rizzo that he would announce his flagship General Revenue Sharing program in front of Independence Hall with Frank Rizzo by his side, which Nixon duly did.[59] But Rizzo did not merely receive symbolic gestures from Nixon; Philadelphia also received a disproportionate share of General Revenue Sharing funding. The city enjoyed twice the per capita funding than Chicago, and in the first eighteen months of the program, Philadelphia received $65 million, equivalent to 10 percent of the city's budget.[60]

Three major political developments during the Tate-Rizzo "machine" period were highly significant for Philadelphia's later neoliberalization. The first was the alienation of economic elites from City Hall. While business wielded influence at the heart of government in the reform period from 1952 to 1962, during the Tate and Rizzo years (1962–1980), its effect on city policy was highly variable. Tate's contact with business reached its nadir after he broke off relations with the GPM after it backed his Republican opponent in the 1967 election. During Rizzo's first term, relations between City Hall and business improved somewhat as he "held the line on taxes."[61] Shortly after he was reelected, however, business leaders were appalled when Rizzo disclosed a deficit of $86 million and asked for a 30 percent increase in the real estate and property taxes. Moreover, Rizzo further infuriated the corporate sector when he blamed the city's fiscal woes on the "ineffectuality" of the city's business executives.[62] Finally, business leaders were hostile to Rizzo's patronage politics through which he solidified trade union support through generous pension plans and favorable city contracts.

The second major development was the emergence of a unified black electorate of sufficient size to have electoral clout. Although significant variation existed ideologically and programmatically among black Philadelphians during the 1960s and 1970s, these differences were cast aside when faced with the common enemy of Frank Rizzo. Not only did blacks mobilize in an effort to prevent him from winning the Democratic nomination, but they were also prepared to cross party lines and vote Republican, despite the party's association with racial violence and the Ku Klux Klan.[63]

The third significant shift involved the solidification of the coalition between business elites and blacks. Notably, Countryman's otherwise excellent account of racial politics in Philadelphia pays scant attention to this alliance.[64] While the links between African Americans and business were evident from the 1960s onward, as reflected in Leon Sullivan's Opportunities Industrialization Centers,[65] this connection was given an electorally consequential boost in the final anti-Rizzo campaign of the 1970s.

In 1978, when Rizzo sought to change the charter to enable him to run for a third term, he appealed to voters in straightforwardly racial terms. He implored his supporters to "vote white" on the charter question. This horrified both business leaders and black voters. With cities such as Charlotte and Atlanta attracting corporate investment through a message of racial accommodation,[66] Philadelphia could not be allowed to go down the opposite path. Therefore, the Greater Philadelphia Partnership (GPP; a reincarnation of the GPM) joined with prominent members of the black community to form the "Charter Defense Committee." Crucially, it provided funds for "highly successful voter registration drives in the city's black neighborhoods and for radio advertisements opposing the charter change."[67] The success of the registration drive was dramatic: it added over 100,000 black voters to Philadelphia's rolls, which raised the African American proportion of city voters by 6 percentage points to 38 percent. The GPP's investment paid off. Two-thirds of voters rejected the proposed change. In predominantly black wards, the turnout was 63 percent. "Displaying unprecedented unanimity, voters in predominantly black wards cast 96 percent of their ballots against Rizzo's proposal to change the charter."[68]

It was in the white heat of Philadelphia's racial cauldron that the dominant biracial coalition of the next forty years was forged. These three key developments—the alienation of business elites from the Tate-Rizzo mayoralties, the emergence of a unified and growing black electorate, and the alliance between corporate-sector business elites (represented by the GPP) and African Americans—would form the coalitional basis for the election of the city's first black mayor, Wilson Goode, in 1983. Thus, as we have seen, Philadelphia did not simply follow a Petersonian logic whereby pro-developmental policies were adopted wholesale. Indeed, at times, Philadelphia pursued policies that were often at odds with such assumptions. Ultimately, the foundations for neoliberalism were laid by a combination of racial politics, ideology, and material constraints. All three were crucial.

The Neoliberal Turn: 1979–2000

Bill Green's Mayoralty

With Rizzo defeated, the 1979 Democratic primary race enabled other political figures to emerge from his shadow and mount a serious challenge for the nomination. Given the growth in the African American proportion of the electorate to 38 percent, black leaders convinced Charles Bowser to run as their candidate against Bill Green. Bowser had run as an independent moderate in 1975, but his 1979 campaign took on a more radical complexion as he attempted to connect Green to Rizzo's racist organization. However, Green refused to be drawn and stuck to a message of racial tolerance. Although Bowser was able to win all the predominantly black wards and two white majority wards, he did not stimulate as high a turnout among blacks as was achieved to defeat Rizzo's charter change.[69] Thus, Green defeated Bowser with 53 percent of the vote.

With the Democratic nomination secured, Green then courted the black vote in preparation for the general election against Republican David Marston. Green's efforts were complicated by the decision of prominent black leader Lucien Blackwell to run as an independent and Marston's pledge to guarantee the role of managing director to an African American. Both Marston and Blackwell assiduously courted Bowser's endorsement. In the face of this competition for black votes, Green matched Marston's commitment in exchange for the endorsements of Bowser and Samuel Evans, another senior figure in Philadelphia black politics. This would be enough to win the election. Not only did he garner 53 percent of the vote in a three-way race, but Green also won approximately 50 percent of the vote in the thirteen wards in which at least 90 percent of registered voters were black.[70] True to his word, Green appointed Wilson Goode, an African

American from the moderate reformist wing of the black political spectrum, to be Philadelphia's first black managing director.

As Green entered office, Philadelphia was bleeding jobs and population. During the 1970s, Philadelphia's population had fallen by over 260,000 from 1.95 million to 1.69 million. Moreover, life for those within the city limits was tough. In 1980, unemployment stood at 12.4 percent of the labor force, and poverty rates had risen from 15 percent in 1969 to 22 percent in 1979. For African Americans, the picture was especially bleak. While the black unemployment rate in 1973 stood at 7.2 percent (just 0.4 percentage points higher than for the population as a whole), by 1980, 20.4 percent of black Philadelphians were unemployed. This would peak at 23.7 percent in 1983.[71] For those in work, median household income was $13,169 in 1979 ($39,599 in 2010 dollars), 73 percent of the regional median.[72]

Mayor Green immediately took steps to confront the racial and economic legacies bequeathed by Rizzo. As Keiser notes, beyond the symbolically important appointment of Goode, Green also tackled the key issue of concern for black Philadelphians: police harassment and brutality.[73] His administration instituted a new set of directives intended to curb the use of deadly force. These reduced the number of civilians shot by the police by 53 percent in the first two years.[74] Moreover, Green's police commissioner, Morton Solomon, ordered the destruction of thousands of files gathered by Rizzo's "spy squad," a unit established to collect intelligence on the mayor's enemies, real and imagined.[75] Green's approach to the city police was not wholly driven by the need to solidify his biracial coalition, however. The new mayor also had to tackle the deficit, which had swollen to $167 million during the Rizzo years, and a sinking municipal bond rating. In a bid to balance the budget, Green laid off 1,200 city workers, 700 of whom were police officers.

However, Green was willing to go only so far in alienating the police force. He refused to support Lucien Blackwell's proposals to create an affirmative action program for police hiring, intended to address the fact that in 1980, just 17.5 percent of the police force was African American while 37.8 percent of the city's population was black. Green also disappointed his coalition partners by vetoing legislation that required the city to set aside 15 percent of all contracts for minority-owned firms. Nevertheless, the City Council overrode Green's veto. Thus, in some respects, African American support for Green had paid off. Many of the worst excesses of the Rizzo administration with regard to police harassment and brutality had been addressed. However, long-held racially biased employment practices had not been tackled. Moreover, Green did little to take on social and economic inequalities associated with racial discrimination and deindustrialization.

Federal Policy: Cuts and Enterprise Zones

Philadelphia had been a beneficiary of the urban components of both the New Deal and the Great Society. Moreover, the city even benefited from the federal government's largesse during the Nixon administration, not least due to the Nixon-Rizzo connection. Nixon's revenue sharing policy was initially popular with fiscally strained cities such as Philadelphia, in part because they would be used for ordinary city services, thereby limiting the extent to which cities had to rely upon tax increases to cover the growing costs.[76] As with the trajectory of neoliberalism more broadly, however, the Carter presidency proved to be pivotal for urban policy. While Carter increased Community Development Block Grant (CDBG) funding to cities in his first year as president, instituted the Comprehensive Employment Training Act (CETA), and initiated the Urban Development Action Grant (UDAG), his administration's stance toward postindustrial cities was characterized by a pro-market bias. As Barnekov and Hart note, "There was a growing belief that despite the impressive number of jobs and amount of private investment that UDAG had apparently generated in distressed urban areas, the benefits of the program were not reaching the most deprived groups in America's cities. The program had become, some believed, 'a lush picnic basket for private developers.' "[77] By the end of his term, Carter's Presidential Commission on the National Agenda for the 1980s considered the decline of older rustbelt cities to be "inevitable" and argued that a policy of revitalization for such cities was "ill-advised." Rather, federal policy should focus on people rather than places.[78] Hence, just as planners on the British left, such as Peter Hall, were looking for market-led solutions to urban problems, so too were Democrats in the United States turning to neoliberal remedies.

The effect of this shift in federal urban policy for Philadelphia would be severe. This was felt most directly through the reductions in direct federal aid. As with all large cities, especially those dealing with the wrenching upheavals wrought by deindustrialization, federal grants-in-aid were highly important sources of revenue. As Table 5 shows, aid to Philadelphia reached its zenith in 1977 before falling steadily throughout the 1980s.[79] Cuts to programs such as CETA resulted in Philadelphia laying off employees in the midst of the 1981 recession. Altogether, Adams estimates that federal aid to Philadelphia declined from more than $250 million in 1981 to $54 million in 1990.[80] Unsurprisingly, the proportion of the city's tax base accounted for by federal aid fell from 25.8 percent in 1979 to just 7.5 percent in 1988.[81] Crucially, and in contradistinction to the claims made by proponents of delivering federal funding via the states, Pennsylvania failed to make up for the difference.[82] Any city facing the loss of a taxpaying population in combination with higher unemployment, rising numbers of people in poverty, and a significant payroll of public employees, would find itself facing deficits. For Philadelphia, the additional burden of the cuts in aid from the federal and state government would place the city under severe fiscal strain. These factors worked to constrict the range of policy options open to a series of mayors, which fostered a politics of *neoliberalism by default.*

The influence of federal and state policy was not exclusively confined to cuts, however. As noted in Chapter 1, the key urban policy innovation of the 1980s was the enterprise zone, a concrete application of neoliberal ideas. While President Reagan failed in numerous attempts to pass substantive enterprise zone legislation in Congress, enterprise zones were taken up with remarkable speed by the states. Indeed, by the mid-1990s, forty states had developed their own enterprise zone programs.[83] Pennsylvania was no exception.

In February 1982, Republican Governor Richard Thornburgh announced the creation of "Enterprise Development Areas" by administrative order. These areas would compete to win enterprise zone designation, which would provide benefits for business, including state corporate tax credits and low interest loans. Moreover, the program was designed to bring private interests into the heart of economic development policy. According to program guidelines, applicants would "be asked to furnish, from the private sector, commitments by business and industry to locate, expand, or start up in the proposed areas . . . and commitments by financial institutions to invest in those businesses and industries."[84] Furthermore, the guidelines also suggested that local governments would improve their chances of winning designation if they offered their own business incentives: "Help from local government can include property tax relief; regulatory relief, including changes in zoning and building codes; streamlined permit procedures; and enhanced police and fire protection."[85] However, to characterize the Pennsylvania program as unequivocally neoliberal would be misleading. After all, it aimed to funnel resources from programs associated with liberal policies, such as existing state-administered block grants and training programs, into the zones.

Pennsylvania's enterprise program also illustrates the ways in which states take preemptive action in response to the federal government's proposed plans. In October 1983, Thornburgh indicated that Pennsylvania's decision to create its own program "will put certain Pennsylvania communities in a better position to compete for, and participate in, proposed federal enterprise zone programs, which would offer a range of federal tax incentives to boost the economy."[86] Hence, in part prompted by Reagan's signaling, the state created a new institution, largely in the neoliberal image, in anticipation of a federal program that never emerged from Congress.

Moreover, this strategy cascaded down the levels of government. In response to the enterprise zone proposals at the state and federal levels, Philadelphia developed its own enterprise zone plans in 1982. In an illustration of the interest of major corporations in enterprise zones, Smithkline Beckman co-hosted a conference on enterprise zones with the city of Philadelphia in March 1982 with Mayor Bill Green in attendance. The mayor's address to the conference implied that while he did not oppose the plan per se, he was clearly concerned about the potential pitfalls associated with the concept: "A real enterprise zone will be an area where the core business is not at war with the core community, but one in which both cooperate for their mutual advantage."[87] The implication was that existing businesses on the "wrong side" of the enterprise zone boundary may be harmed by businesses moving into the zones and having a competitive advantage from the zone benefits.

A policy paper developed on behalf of Green by the City Planning Commission (CPC) also struck a cautious note: "Philadelphia believes that by itself the EZ program will fall short of its goals for job creation and neighborhood revitalization. . . . Only used in conjunction with other targeted incentives will Enterprise Zones help to revitalize the nation's distressed communities."[88] The CPC was clear that "tax cuts and regulatory relief measures are not sufficient, by themselves, to overcome the problems that lead to economic distress."[89] Indeed, voicing the concerns of many enterprise zone skeptics (see Chapters 1 and 2), the report suggested that the proposed enterprise zone tax incentives "may simply produce windfalls for large corporate entities or minor relocations in existing business activity."[90]

Despite the desperate decline of Philadelphia's industrial base, as described above, the CPC argued that the city had taken significant steps toward retaining businesses in the city that were yielding "significant results." Programs such as the American Street Corridor Plan had harnessed local and federal dollars through the alphabet soup of federal initiatives: EDA Title IX, CBDG, CETA, and the City Capital Program. Therefore, it feared that the elimination of "EDA and cuts to UDAG . . . would dramatically curtail Philadelphia's ability to continue to expand its present revitalization initiatives."[91]

The overall tenor of the report is caution laced with skepticism. Its major message was that investment in infrastructure, increasing the availability of capital to business, and workforce development are the key requirements for an economic recovery. If these elements could be integrated into enterprise zone plans, then the city would support them with gusto. The report's author, R. Duane Perry, thought this unlikely, however, given the ideological opposition to such plans in both the White House and in Harrisburg.[92] But despite his skepticism, Green did not wish to miss out on the opportunity of winning either state or federal enterprise zone designation. Thus, he wrote to Governor Thornburgh to propose that Philadelphia and Pennsylvania "combine the strength of our resources and initiate a coordinated approach to developing an Urban Enterprise Zone program which will complement the proposed federal program."[93]

Given the scale of Philadelphia's difficulties, it is easy to understand the city's reservations about enterprise zones. Yet as Perry explains, enterprise zones seemed to be the best the Reagan administration had to offer. And in light of the city's economic woes, the mayor had to be seen to be doing something rather than nothing.[94] The city's commerce director, Richard A. Doran, expressed a similar view: "It's unrealistic to believe that you can take a vacant piece of land and that a major American business with thousands of jobs will make a decision to locate a plant there just because it's going to get a tax credit."[95] He argued that major investment would be the key but recognized that Reagan was not likely to provide the money. Therefore, Doran concluded that it was worth supporting the scheme.

Beyond City Hall, enthusiasm for enterprise zones was muted at best. Many within Philadelphia's African American community opposed the plans outright. John Bowser, executive director of the Urban Coalition, suggested that far from encouraging new business activity, enterprise zones might do the opposite: "If I had a business in [a new] enterprise zone, I'd put a garage on it and call it an 'expansion,' and in six months I'd sell it and move to the Sun Belt and set up another operation. That's maximizing my profits; that's the theory of the free enterprise zone."[96] Moreover, the *Philadelphia Tribune*, a leading black newspaper, feared the zones would put downward pressure on wages and effectively "bring the Third World home."[97] Yet other black politicians were more circumspect. For example, Philadelphia U.S. Representative William Gray (D-PA), a leading African American politician, expressed serious doubt about the efficacy of enterprise zones at a breakfast meeting sponsored by the Greater Philadelphia Chamber of Commerce: "The enterprise zone is not a cure-all, or panacea, for urban problems and cannot make up for the tremendous cuts in funds for human service programs." Nevertheless, he ultimately supported the idea: "It is a concept worth pursuing and should be viewed not as a substitute for other federal programs, but a complement."[98] He co-sponsored an enterprise zone bill in Congress. Sensing a degree of support for the zones among some black Philadelphians, Peter Liacouras, the new Temple University president, pledged to work with African American community groups and clergy to win enterprise zone designation in North Philadelphia.[99]

As with business groups at the national levels in the United Kingdom and the United States, Philadelphia business groups did not initially push for enterprise zones. A comprehensive account of local business sentiment conducted by First Pennsylvania Bank suggested little appetite for the scheme among the several hundred businesses surveyed. As Kenneth T. Mayland, the bank's vice president and corporate economist, stated, "The bottom line of our report is that, in this area at least, urban enterprise zones would be substantially less successful than their proponents tout."[100] The survey revealed that the key factors that shape location decisions were the availability and skills of the labor force, access to public transportation, and the levels of crime. All these factors ranked far higher than tax incentives and financial aid. These views dovetailed with those of Gerald Carlino, senior economist of the urban regional section at the Federal Reserve Bank of Philadelphia. Carlino's view was that place-based programs had not succeeded in the 1960s and 1970s: "We have been preoccupied for so long with 'place prosperity,' and it hasn't worked. That's what urban enterprise zones do, try to revive a place. I'm more interested in people prosperity. If a firm moves into a poor section of the city, do you think the local people would be hired? Probably not."[101] Despite the reservations of community leaders, politicians, and some in the business community, three enterprise zones were established in Philadelphia in 1983, located in the American Street Corridor, Hunting Park West, and West Parkside. Each of these areas was home to different social groups within Philadelphia. American Street was home to white ethnic and Hispanic residents and had been the site of numerous public investments, including through the Model Cities program. The Hunting Park West zone, the largest and most industrialized of the zones, included white ethnics and African Americans. In contrast, the West Parkside zone was almost exclusively African American and home to the largest concentration of black-owned businesses and residents in the program.[102] In addition to the incentives provided by the state, the city also provided its own real estate tax abatement, at first for domestic properties but later applied to businesses as well, and a security rebate program, jointly funded with the state, through which applications were eligible for up to $5,000 in security improvements.[103] Thus, the enterprise zone, a program with little local political or business support, was created in Philadelphia *by default* in anticipation of a federal program that never emerged. Knowing that little federal money was likely to emerge out of Washington, D.C., people like Bill Green felt the need to do something rather than nothing, so proceeded with the policy. Having been created, the zone grew with the aid of institutions such as the Enterprise Center, a nonprofit founded by the Wharton Small Business Development Center, which helped to run the West Parkside zone.[104]

From Green to Goode: The Election of Philadelphia's First Black Mayor

During Bill Green's tenure as mayor, his tough stance on the deficit, illustrated by his unwillingness to cave in to union demands, did little to halt the exodus of labor and capital out of Philadelphia. After all, Green had the misfortune of governing in the aftermath of the 1980 recession and during the even deeper recession in 1981–1982, as Federal Reserve Chair Paul Volker sought to tackle spiraling inflation through a sharp contraction in the money supply, resulting in soaring interest rates. This neoliberal formula did succeed in bringing inflation down, as it had in Britain. However, the collateral damage of these decisions was recession and mass unemployment, which stood nationally at 11.4 percent as Green entered office and rose thereafter. In Philadelphia, unemployment was 8.3 percent in 1981 and remained above that level for two years, rising above 10 percent in 1983 before falling to 7 percent in 1985. Given that the costs of such action fell disproportionately on cities such as Philadelphia, it is hardly surprising that Green was "largely unable to stem the tide of decline."[105]

At the same time, Philadelphia's business interests were becoming increasingly concerned about their inability to shape the city's social and political life. Having become fragmented and marginal to government during the Tate and Rizzo administrations and buffeted by recession under Green, the Chamber of Commerce sought ways to strengthen its influence. In 1982, the Chamber of Commerce commissioned a "Long Range Planning Committee," which concluded that greater coordination and penetration into City Hall was required.[106] As described above, business had been divided into a number of organizations with different interests. While the Chamber of Commerce represented traditional manufacturers, the Greater Philadelphia Movement spoke for emergent corporate interests. The Long Range Planning Committee aimed to weave together these strands into a new group: Greater Philadelphia First Corporation (GPFC), which was founded in 1983. The GPFC consisted of a committee of twenty-seven local CEOs whose role was "to coordinate local corporate initiatives in donations, economic development activities, regional cooperation, and political reform."[107] Each member of the committee agreed to pay $50,000 in annual dues "to create a pool of funds that the new coalition could use to promote various economic development projects in the region."[108] Thus, as Green's term came to an end, business, which had already forged strong links with segments of the black community, was rolling out a coordinated, well-funded, and widespread political operation. One of their first acts was to back Wilson Goode.

As with many prominent black politicians of the 1980s, Goode earned his credentials through involvement with the institutions that emerged from Lyndon Johnson's Great Society.[109] Goode was a founding member of the Black Political Forum and further developed his links with the local community as executive director of the Philadelphia Council for Community Advancement (PCCA) from 1967 to 1978. The PCCA was created by the business community during Dilworth's administration to distribute funds from the Ford Foundation and the federal and city governments. Through its provision of technical support for nonprofit low-income housing schemes, the PCCA "strengthened the political ties between the reform-business alliance and blacks."[110] A highly religious man, Goode's role as deacon of his church also enabled him to build relationships with Philadelphia's politically influential black clergymen. Goode's work with the PCCA also "enabled him to meet many of the young banking, business, and elite executives who were in line to assume leadership positions in the city over the next 10 years."[111] Indeed, as early as 1967, Goode was selected by the Greater Philadelphia Movement to participate in its Community Leadership Seminar Program (CLSP). Moreover, the Chamber of Commerce bestowed its Outstanding Young Leaders Award on Goode, and two years later, he served as chairman of the CLSP's Program Committee.

In 1977, Goode gained statewide prominence when he was appointed by Governor Milton Shapp to the Public Utility Commission (PUC), and soon after, Shapp made him chairman. Countryman argues that during his time on the PUC (1977–1980) and as the city's managing director (1980–1983), Wilson Goode "transformed himself from community activist and political insurgent into a respected technocrat."[112] When Green unexpectedly announced that he was not going to seek reelection, Goode decided to run. In order to secure the all-important Democratic nomination, however, Goode would have to overcome Frank Rizzo, who was able to run again for a third term since it would be nonconsecutive to his previous two-term mayoralty.

As had occurred with Rizzo's race against Green, a coalition of blacks and business groups coalesced to deny Rizzo the nomination. The difference this time, however, was that African Americans now stood to move from the politics of protest to the politics of incorporation, from being a key element of the electoral coalition, to occupying a central place in the governing regime. As such, Goode received enthusiastic support from most segments of black Philadelphia. More important, however, was the overwhelming support of the CEOs from Philadelphia's major corporations, including Smith & Kline, Provident Bank, the Philadelphia Saving Fund Society, Rohm & Hass, and ARCO Chemical Company, which formed a coalition to support Goode's campaign.[113] These groups were both repelled by Rizzo's patronage politics and racialized rhetoric and attracted to Goode's pro-business ideology. They believed that a Goode administration would promote their interests, thus enabling Philadelphia's transformation into a postindustrial, corporate city.[114] In contrast, a Rizzo mayoralty would be inimical to the goals of the city's business elites. As a board member of the GPM put it, a "Frank Rizzo victory would have given the city such a bad black-eye that it would be impossible to attract new industry."[115]

With the support of the city's blacks, white liberals, and business groups, Goode won comfortably. He captured 98 percent of the black vote but received the support of just 22 percent of whites. Rizzo, in a desperate bid to revive his image, toned down his racist rhetoric and magnanimously endorsed Goode in the general election. This set up a three-way race including Republican businessman John Egan—former chairman of the Philadelphia Stock Exchange—and independent Thomas Leonard. While one might have expected business to support the Republican candidate, just one GPFC board member made a personal contribution to Egan. In contrast, eleven GPFC executives personally contributed to Goode's campaign.[116] With such strong backing, Goode won handily with a 123,000 vote margin and 55 percent of the vote, compared to Egan's 27 percent and Leonard's 8 percent.[117] Thus, having been central to the expansion of black voter registration in the 1978 charter campaign, business then played a key role in supporting their candidate for mayor.

Goode soon repaid the favor. Shortly after his election, he established an "Economic Roundtable," which provided a venue for business leaders to lobby to city officials directly.[118] Thus, just two years after business took concerted steps to address concerns about its own divisions and political access, the mayor himself created an institution that solved the problems both of coordination and of political penetration. Moreover, Goode solicited the advice of the Chamber of Commerce on ways to streamline government and on senior-level administration appointees.[119] Within two weeks of his election victory, Goode appointed David W. Brenner as director of the Commerce Department. As the former chairman of the Greater Philadelphia Chamber of Commerce and a senior partner at the accounting firm Arthur Young & Co., Brenner was the consummate business executive.[120] Furthermore, Goode's other cabinet appointees all had close ties to the business community. Leo Brooks, the city's managing director, was a board member of the Chamber of Commerce; Dianne L. Semingson, director of the Office of City Representative, was an executive of the Arco Chemical Co.; Richard G. Gilmore, the city's new finance director, was an executive of Girard Bank; and city solicitor, Barbara W. Mather, was recruited from the Center City law firm Pepper, Hamilton, & Scheetz. As such, Goode's team reflected his business-friendly stance.

After Goode entered City Hall, Philadelphia's Center City transformation proceeded apace. A number of high-profile projects reflected the pro-business orientation of the administration. For example, the new mayor gave considerable support to the proposals of Willard G. Rouse III, a major private developer and member of Goode's economic roundtable, "who played a central role in reshaping Center City."[121] Philadelphia's emergence from the recessions of the early 1980s sparked the rapid growth downtown of finance, insurance, and business services, which in turn fueled a property boom. Rouse was at the center of these developments. In 1984, he proposed the construction of Liberty One, an office building that, at 945 feet, would tower over the William Penn statue atop City Hall, which had enjoyed an unimpeded view as a result of a gentleman's agreement and pressure from the CPC to not build higher than the statue.[122] Rouse's proposals stimulated a high-profile debate about the kind of city Philadelphia ought to be. Planner Edmund Bacon led the charge against the plans, asserting that "the center of the city belonged to all the people not to any individual or corporation."[123] Nevertheless, Goode, a proponent of commercial development, backed Rouse's proposals, despite acknowledging that "my mail ran 1000 to 1 against this decision."[124] William Penn lost his view.

In the case of the convention center and downtown development, Goode deployed the standard argument of pro-growth mayors that the only way to tackle problems of poverty and inequality in the neighborhoods would be through downtown growth. The assumption was that the benefits of growth would eventually trickle down to the middle and working classes. Bartlet argues that these developments indicate the "extent to which the city's role [in city planning] has changed from active partner to cheerleader and legitimator of Center City development."[125] This shift signified the accommodation of key urban Democratic elites to the neoliberal interpretations that had been germinating since the 1950s and that sprouted up during the tumultuous years of the 1970s. By the mid-1980s, these ideas and policy prescriptions that were the preserve of Republicans in the United States and Conservatives in the United Kingdom had begun to form the consensus among local Democratic and Labour Party leaders.[126] Wilson Goode's mayoralty acted as a staging post along this transformational path.

The city's African Americans, whose unemployment rate of 17.1 percent in 1980 stood 9 percentage points above that of whites, hoped that they could immediately benefit from the construction boom. As such, their allies in City Council introduced a hiring preference ordinance (Bill 649) to counter discrimination against minorities and women in the building trades. Bill 649 would have required contractors on projects of over $1 million to make a good-faith effort to draw 45 percent of their workforce from the city, 25 percent from minority groups, and 5 percent from women. Despite the strong support for the measure among black community groups, Goode sided with the Chamber of Commerce and the construction unions, which argued that such an ordinance would prompt retaliation in the suburbs, which, in the long run, would harm the interests of Philadelphia-based construction workers.[127] The unemployed, the poor, and the excluded would have to wait. Any harm done to business interests, they were told, would ultimately harm their prospects for a brighter future.

But as Keiser argues, the Goode administration was not simply "a corporate centered regime."[128] During his tenure as mayor, Goode brought African Americans into government, used set-asides for black contractors who worked on city jobs, and channeled a $60 million block grant for low-income housing in North Philadelphia. Moreover, although business strongly supported the administration's efforts to build a trash-to-steam plant in South Philadelphia, Goode's plans were thwarted by the City Council.[129] However, these progressive currents did not alter the drift in a neoliberal direction. Although no ardent Hayekian, Goode, like all city mayors, had to take business interests into account, as Clarence Stone's work illustrates.[130] Yet, this did not necessitate a straightforward capitulation to corporate demands.[131] The case of Goode's administration reveals that the policy direction depended additionally on the mayor's ideological acceptance of the "pro-growth" logic. In this regard, Goode's example follows that of Maynard Jackson in Atlanta and Coleman Young of Detroit.[132] As Adolph Reed points out, "Black regimes adhere to the pro-growth framework for the same reasons that other regimes do: It seems reasonable and proper ideologically; it conforms to a familiar sense of rationality; and it promises to deliver practical, empirical benefits."[133] Hence, the degree of corporate penetration into Goode's administration should not be taken as confirmation of Paul Peterson's "city limits" argument that suggests that cities must follow pro-business policies at the expense of redistributionist ones.[134] Indeed, Rizzo's mayoralty showed that neoliberalism was not inevitable. Instead, it was the coincidence of severe cuts in federal aid, Goode's own class position that nurtured a pro-business ideology, and limits to biracial progressive alliances that advanced the neoliberal agenda *by default*.

However, Goode's reputation for competence among ordinary citizens and business elites came under severe strain with the MOVE incident. Since the MOVE incident is not central to this account, I will not dwell on the details here. Suffice it to say that in May 1985, a dispute between the city and a radical back-to-nature group reached a grizzly conclusion in which the police dropped a bomb on the house in which the group was staked out. Shamefully, the police commissioner and the fire commissioner made the tactical decision to let the fire burn rather than to extinguish it immediately. Eleven people, including five children, died as a result, and sixty-one houses were destroyed.[135] In the aftermath of MOVE, it seemed almost inconceivable that Goode would be reelected given his failure to prevent the crisis escalating so dangerously. However, his resistance in the face of industrial action by the city's public employees union won him plaudits among corporate elites who then backed his campaign.[136] In July 1986, 15,000 uniformed and 13,200 nonuniformed officers went on strike for a pay raise and to resist attempts by the city to audit union health and welfare accounts. Goode refused to buckle in the face of rotting trash, closed libraries, and shuttered city pools. Cheered on by the *Inquirer* and the business community, Goode secured union acquiescence on the audit and managed to limit the rise in wages to a modest increase.[137]

In the primary election, Goode faced District Attorney Ed Rendell. Although black support for Goode had waned somewhat as his first term drew to a close, African Americans turned out faithfully to enable the mayor to win the primary with 57 percent of the vote. Seeking to benefit from the drift of whites to the GOP, Frank Rizzo switched parties to run as a Republican in the general election. Once again, this galvanized the African American vote in support of Goode. On election day, Goode benefited from a 70 percent turnout among blacks, 97 percent of whom voted for him. However, Goode secured only 18 percent of the white vote. Combined, however, the alliance between business, Democratic whites, and African Americans was enough for Goode to beat Rizzo by 18,000 votes.[138]

Although the high turnout among African Americans was vital to Goode's victory, as Keiser points out, he could not have won "without the support of Democratic party ward leaders who persuaded their friends, families, and city jobholders to vote for him."[139] Thus, although Goode had originally been elected as a "reform" mayor in 1983, his 1987 victory was partly based on his strategic use of patronage politics. In particular, Goode appointed former union leader Robert Brady to be deputy mayor of labor and backed Brady's successful bid to become chairman of the Democratic City Committee. Goode subsequently handed Brady control of patronage positions in the court system and the Parking Authority. This strategy successfully drew "white ethnic" Democratic ward leaders: "Only one member of the city's 29-member Democratic delegation to the state house and senate defected to the Rizzo team."[140]

Goode's second term was largely dominated by a spiraling budget deficit, which led the city close to default by the end of his term, juxtaposed with the continued rise of gleaming skyscrapers. Cuts in federal aid combined with the rising costs associated with high unemployment and poverty left Philadelphia unable to raise money on the municipal bond market. City costs were further strained due to the legacy of Rizzo's patronage politics. While the Nixon administration's largesse helped Rizzo to cover the costs of his deals with the unions, when the federal government withdrew its support, Philadelphia faced a fiscal crisis common to so many American cities. Goode's response was to initiate a typically neoliberal tactic: to raise taxes on people and decrease them on business. With respect to the latter, he attempted with some success to reduce the General Business Tax. His attempts to balance the budget through an increase in personal taxes, however, were resisted by the City Council. Keiser argues that this was because his rivals in City Hall hoped to be in a position to gain credit for solving the crisis themselves.[141] Thus, Goode's primary strategy was to do what he could to make Philadelphia more attractive to business, as his continued support for the enterprise zone program illustrates.

Enterprise Zones Under Goode

During Goode's period in office, support for the city's enterprise zone program gained momentum. In July 1984, the city received $250,000 in state funds for the three enterprise zones. The program would be overseen by the Commerce Department, an institution of city government with strong business connections run by Goode appointee Joseph R. James, a former executive director of the Philadelphia Citywide Development Corporation.[142] A year later, progress began on one of the first enterprise zone sites. The city of Philadelphia reached an agreement to buy the 74-acre Midvale-Heppenstall Steel Co. plant in Hunting Park for $5 million for conversion into an industrial park. In a plan supported by the PIDC, the city would buy the land from the Hunting Park Corporation, which would demolish the site as part of the deal. The aim was to use enterprise zone tax abatements, low-interest financing, inexpensive rents, and industrial zoning to lure investors.[143] Despite the enterprise zone incentives, however, the deal fell through in April 1986.

Nevertheless, progress was evident on a number of fronts. The *Philadelphia Inquirer* and the *Daily News* published a number of stories reporting positive developments within the zones. In June 1986, the *Inquirer* reported on City Commerce Director David W. Brenner's sanguine view of the zones: "We have finally found something that can make a difference in turning around deteriorated neighborhoods."[144] Moreover, Joseph James claimed that between June 1983 and January 1986, 1,881 jobs were created in the three enterprise zones, and 2,933 jobs were retained. He said that forty-four businesses started up, forty-eight firms expanded, and sixty were retained.[145] However, newspaper reports suggested that these numbers included businesses *outside* the zones. In light of this, some community groups and business leaders began to suspect that the enterprise zones were having less impact than was being touted.

William Harrington, the head of West Parkside's Philadelphia Business Cooperation Office, reported that "basically, nothing much is happening" in the enterprise zone, which he considered to be a case of "the emperor having no clothes." Moreover, Ralph R. Widner, executive director of the Greater Philadelphia First Corporation, noted that there had been "sporadic activity but not a broad, overwhelming pattern." Furthermore, John Claypool, executive director of the Greater Philadelphia Economic Development Coalition, noted that despite some gains in American Street, "it hasn't turned the corner."[146] In retrospect, Claypool argues that the enterprise zone incentives had "virtually no effect" on business creation or development in American Street that occurred over the longer term.[147] Despite these reservations, however, the perceived benefits among Philadelphia's pro-growth coalition of political elites, the local media, and (some) business groups that stood to benefit from the zones' financial incentives led to lobbying in favor of the zones. This resulted in the expansion of the existing enterprise zones and to the application by the Goode administration to the state to create a new zone, the Port of Philadelphia Enterprise Zone, which eventually won official designation in 1989.

In a series of editorials, the *Philadelphia Inquirer* implored the city, the commonwealth of Pennsylvania, and the federal government to press ahead with enterprise zones despite mounting evidence of their limited impact on rates of employment and business development. Indeed, in October 1989, an *Inquirer* editorial waxed lyrical about the policy's promise. Conceding that the enterprise zone is "perhaps an imperfect concept," the paper declared that "it is the only route by which cities like Philadelphia are likely to get help in creating the kinds of opportunities that its jobless can qualify for."[148] The newspaper's stance reveals the degree to which neoliberal shibboleths came to dominate elite opinion and constricted the range of imaginable policy prescriptions available to tackle unemployment and promote growth.

Almost a year later, the *Philadelphia Daily News* dug deeper into the claims of job creation made by enterprise zone promoters to reveal their shaky foundations. While the city claimed that 1,878 jobs had been retained or created in the American Street enterprise zone, the *Daily News*'s researchers could only identify a total of 1,213 jobs retained or created. What city officials had failed to acknowledge in their tally were the jobs lost when employers "like the National Drying Machinery, with 85 jobs, moved elsewhere."[149] As Sherri Wallace has argued, the absence of rigorous record-keeping or analysis undermined the credibility of the city's claims about the net effect of enterprise zone incentives.[150] Nevertheless, the *Inquirer* continued to publish editorials favorable to enterprise zones. Just two days after the *Daily News*'s story, the *Inquirer* argued that enterprise zones bridged the partisan divide: "Liberals like them because they recognize the need to provide special help to inner-city neighborhoods, and conservatives like them because they look to the free-enterprise system, rather than social programs, to uplift the downtrodden." It also quotes Michael Gallagher, one of the city's enterprise zone administrators, as saying that "everyone should get on the phone to Washington because this is, in effect, the city's only real hope of getting help out of the federal government."[151]

The apparent consensus in favor of enterprise zones, which emerged despite the absence of decisive evidence that they "worked," was illustrated by the positions of the two leading mayoral candidates in Philadelphia's 1991 election. Both Ed Rendell and Frank Rizzo—who this time ran on the Republican ticket—supported them. In this respect, the ideas and political calculations behind Rendell's candidacy foreshadow Bill Clinton's. That is, Rendell's position was emblematic of the New Democratic ideology that explicitly rejected key elements of New Deal and Great Society liberalism and largely accepted the key tenets of neoliberal economic policy, although it lamented some of its social effects. As a mayoral candidate in July 1991, Rendell testified before a subcommittee of the House of Representatives Ways and Means Committee in favor of a federal enterprise zone bill. He argued that federal enterprise zones would be "a lifeline for what has become an almost permanent underclass in Philadelphia and other urban cities."[152] Rendell claimed that Philadelphia's "three state-designated enterprise zones have been able to stimulate investment and create or retain jobs in these areas." On the basis of this apparent success, he argued that "the program would be infinitely more effective if federal tax incentives were available." Notably, in respect of his support for capital gains tax reductions, Rendell's position was closer to preferences of Republicans rather than to Democratic versions of the bill. In a typically Clintonesque move, Rendell asserted that "Philadelphia, and all older American cities, are not looking for a handout or a bailout, but we do need federal help to serve as a catalyst for the economic recovery that is so desperately needed in our depressed areas."[153] But this was not mere rhetoric. As we shall see in Chapter 5, Rendell repeatedly pursued policies that fell squarely outside the tradition of liberal city mayors and far closer to the neoliberal visions of Republicans and Conservatives.

Conclusion

The transformation of Philadelphia from a thriving industrial city to a bifurcated corporate metropolitan region during the 1970s and 1980s is not simply an economic story. Rather, it is a historically contingent political-economic tale in which race, class, and ideology interact in unexpected and consequential ways. Most crucial were the links forged between "good government" African Americans and the business community. In part, this was a marriage of convenience rooted in animosity toward Frank Rizzo. While blacks feared his racialized politics, business groups considered Rizzo a danger to their profitability. But Wilson Goode and his supporters were not simply corporate stooges. Rather, his coalitional calculus provided a privileged role for business. Moreover, his administration—now replete with recruits from the corporate world—largely accepted the view that since the federal government had withdrawn its support from a decaying city, there was simply no choice but to embrace Philadelphia's pro-business corporate future. Goode's ideology was, therefore, compatible with neoliberal prescriptions, as his support for downtown development and enterprise zones illustrates. In this sense, electoral politics, economic change, and ideology combined to push Philadelphia down a path of *neoliberalism by default.*

In Goode's somewhat reluctant turn toward neoliberal prescriptions are faint echoes of the "there is no alternative" view deployed by both Thatcher and Reagan to mask the ideological nature of their ambitions (see Chapters 1 and 2). During the late 1980s and the 1990s, however, those echoes grew louder as this presentational sleight of hand was gradually taken to be good policy by those on the "left" in the British Labour Party and in the "New Democrats" (see Chapter 3). They too would argue that their respective parties would have to abandon their ideological and programmatic positions in light of emergent globalization and its attendant demands for "flexible labor markets" and tax and regulatory regimes that foster "business friendly climates." For the cities, this would mean the adoption of the Paul Peterson *City Limits* view.[154] Wilson Goode's mayoralty resulted in a key step in that direction. Yet, as has been shown above, Goode's break with New Deal/Great Society liberalism was partial and incomplete—he continued to support investment in the neighborhoods and was blocked by the City Council in his attempts to balance the budget.

Philadelphia's transition to a postindustrial political economy delivered few economic benefits for the city's working and middle classes. Between 1979 and 1989, median wages (in 2010 dollars) rose only modestly from $39,599 to $43,264. Moreover, the poverty rate, which had been approximately 15.5 percent in 1969, rose to 20.6 percent in 1979 and fell only slightly to 20.3 percent by 1989. Clearly, this period had been kind to the wealthy and corporate elites, but many were doing worse in real terms and relative to others. But while Philadelphia's path toward neoliberalism during the 1980s took a serpentine form, Ed Rendell's rise to office signaled an ideological and strategic posture that made for a more direct route. As the next chapter elaborates, Philadelphia's development during the 1990s reveals the sharp bifurcation of urban America by which vast poverty and plenty characterize the neoliberal city.

Chapter 5

"America's Mayor" Comes to Power in Philadelphia: The Consolidation of the Corporate City Under Ed Rendell

> I do not believe that, even if it could, the federal government should reinstate massive and unrestricted revenue-sharing for cities. That would only provide a short-term crutch, not a long-term cure, for the deep structural problems that confront us.
> —Mayor Edward Rendell, testimony before Congress, April 24, 1992

At the turn of the 1990s, Philadelphia stood at the crossroads with one foot planted in its industrial past, while another stood in an uncertain corporate future. The primary and general elections of 1991 were the pivots upon which the city's transformation turned, with incoming mayor, Ed Rendell, the pivotal figure. As Wilson Goode's second mayoral term came to a close, the city faced a financial crisis that he was neither willing nor able to resolve. This task was left to Rendell, a politician more of the neoliberal persuasion than his predecessor, his commitment to state-led investment in infrastructure, education, and housing notwithstanding. Still, under his leadership, many of the ideas and institutions of the liberal past were eschewed in favor of a political agenda hitherto associated primarily with the right.

This chapter will examine the key conflicts that drove Philadelphia's political development during the 1990s and consider the politics surrounding, as well as the local effect of, President Clinton's signature national urban initiative: the empowerment zones. I argue that the creation of the Philadelphia Intergovernmental Cooperation Authority (PICA, Pennsylvania's financial watchdog), the defeat of the unions, privatization, and city-promoted gentrification constitute significant milestones along the path of Philadelphia's neoliberalization. The creation of PICA and privatization were two institutional developments that aimed to insulate political-economic decisions from Philadelphia's citizens, especially those in labor unions. These acts were not merely born out of economic necessity but reflect contingent choices, some ideological, others strategic. Yet, Philadelphia faced major financial pressures that limited the range of policy options open, even to those politicians who might have favored a progressive approach. As such, this period is replete with examples of the politics of neoliberalism *by design* and *by default* that are grounded not simply in material imperatives but, crucially, in ideological assessments about what the material realities that the city faced implied about which policies ought to be adopted.

Some theoretical approaches to urban politics seek to explain Rendell's neoliberal tendencies primarily on materialist grounds. For example, scholars such as Paul Peterson, who work in the public choice vein, might explain support for these policies as a function of the city's efforts to enhance its competitive advantage. Peterson does not expect ideology or other "political variables" to be "relevant to the analysis, because the internal political arrangements of the city are not treated as decisive factors affecting local policy."[1] He finds "the primary interest of cities to be the maintenance and enhancement of their economic productivity. To their land area, cities must attract productive labor and capital."[2] In order to attract capital, Peterson notes, cities "can minimize their tax on capital and on profits from capital investments" (essentially, the enterprise zone strategy) and "discourage labor from organizing so as to keep industrial labor costs competitive" (the privatization strategy).[3] As numerous scholars point out, Peterson's account rests on a remarkably thin view of urban politics in which decisions appear to be induced by market imperatives.[4]

As an empirical matter, there are examples of variation with respect to policy choice, as reflected in the differing urban regimes present in the United States (and elsewhere), even if the spectrum of viable policy options is bounded due to the inherent nature of American capitalism.[5] This would suggest that more room for maneuver on urban policy exists than Peterson's analysis allows. Furthermore, Logan and Molotch's work has shown that neoliberal urban policy prescriptions may result, not from politicians' rational calculations but rather from the capture of "mobilized interests" who wish to use the city as a growth machine to promote their interest in enhancing the profitability of land through growth. In contrast to Peterson's vision, growth machines are contingent entities that are sustained only through constant political mobilization and struggle. In Logan and Moloch's view, ideological reproduction is central to the ongoing maintenance of regimes: "Perhaps most important of all, local publics should favor growth and support the ideology of value free development."[6] For Logan and Molotch, "The overall ideological thrust is to deemphasize the connection between growth and exchange values and to reinforce the link between growth goals and better lives for the majority."[7] Yet, in this account, ideology is deployed cynically and expediently by local growth machines. While they persuasively expose the canard that growth in all its forms stands to benefit all of the city's residents, Logan and Molotch's view of ideology is overly sparse: "For many places and times, growth is at best a mixed blessing *and the growth machine's claims are merely legitimating ideology, not accurate descriptions of reality.*"[8]

As noted above, this understanding unnecessarily reduces ideology simply to a tool to be deployed to promote certain actors' materially derived ends. Moreover, it seems to limit the role of politicians to being ciphers for business interests. Thus, the politicians who stand to make electoral (or modest financial) gains are operating in bad faith, are suffering from false consciousness, or are part of a vast conspiracy. This chapter argues that politicians such as Rendell do not simply deploy ideology strategically in order to manipulate their opponents—although he undoubtedly does so at times. While it is undoubtedly the case that ideas are used strategically by politicians as rhetoric, reducing them to *mere* rhetoric excludes the possibility that certain ideas have motive force as they work to build coalitions between those who stand to gain materially from a given set of governmental arrangements and those who do not.

As will be illustrated below, the effect of the city's transformation—rooted in the 1980s restructuring and propelled by Rendell's agenda—has not been to enhance the well-being of the majority of Philadelphians; quite the contrary. While the wealthy top 20 percent of the income distribution saw their incomes rise during the 1990s, virtually every other segment of society saw their incomes fall. Median household income fell by 9 percent between 1990 and 2000, from $43,264 to $39,325 (in 2010 dollars) even as it grew by 4 percent for the nation as a whole.[9] This is particularly striking given the extremely positive perception of Philadelphia's progress under Rendell. Moreover, in the first decade of the twentieth century, these trends accelerated. In 2010, Philadelphia's median household income was just $34,400. However, the proportion of households that earned over $100,000 increased from 6.3 percent in 2000 to 11.3 percent in 2010. This occurred alongside a rise in the family poverty rate from 18.4 to 20.0 percent over the same period.[10] This bifurcation not only is reflective of trends throughout American society but also chimes with the pattern of change in London Docklands, as shown in Chapter 6.

In Chapter 1, enterprise zones were used to chart the ideological shift of congressional Democrats during the 1980s and early 1990s. Gradually, the Democratic Party's position shifted from one of ambivalence to outright support of the policy. By 1992, Democrats began actively sponsoring enterprise zone legislation in Congress. As with their positions on welfare, deficit reduction, and trade, Democrats' preferences regarding urban policy reflected their partial embrace of neoliberal ideas. With New Deal/Great Society liberalism abandoned, a new neoliberal consensus had been born. To be sure, both periods of "consensus" should not be overstated: Democrats and Republicans had substantial differences then as now. As Chapter 3 shows, the emergence of a neoliberal order was not simply an American phenomenon. In the British context, the programmatic and rhetorical commitments of the Labour Party were similarly transformed along neoliberal lines as Tony Blair's New Labour sought to emulate Bill Clinton's formula for success.

As Chapter 4 illustrated, city elites in Philadelphia responded to the neoliberal turn in national policy through a partial embrace of pro-market policies. As we saw, in the face of population losses, high unemployment, and significant cuts in federal funding, the Goode administration adopted a combination of neoliberal pro-growth strategies (enterprise zones, tax abatements, and Center City corporate development) and limited race-conscious liberalism (public housing investment, set-asides for black contractors, and appointments of blacks to city government posts). As such, Philadelphia drifted down the path of *neoliberalism by default*, although the scattered remnants of the liberal past slowed its journey. Despite Goode's pro-business approach, Philadelphia's economic growth was insufficient to compensate for rising costs and declining federal and state revenues. To make matters worse, internal political conflict undermined Goode's proposals to balance the budget. Thus, by the end of his term, the city faced a fiscal crisis. This chapter describes how Mayor Ed Rendell accelerated Philadelphia's economic transition to a corporate-based economy through the implementation of a program that more consciously eschewed the liberal policy tradition in favor of neoliberalism.

In the wake of the 1992 Los Angeles riots, there was a glimmer of hope that a more generous set of urban policies would emerge in Washington. However, Bill Clinton's aim to "reinvent government," "end welfare as we know it," and eliminate the deficit snuffed it out: the best he could offer was the empowerment zone, a plan that combined the classic neoliberal aim of reducing business taxes with an ostensible concern with local empowerment. Although the empowerment zone did bring $79 million to Philadelphia, this was a drop in the ocean compared with the employment, infrastructural, and social service needs of the city and in comparison with what the city received under revenue sharing during the Rizzo years.

Philadelphia's Fiscal Crisis

The mayoral election of 1991 took place in the context of Philadelphia's "fiscal crisis," defined by economist Robert Inman as occurring when "a city's potential to raise revenues is insufficient to cover the city's legally required expenditures."[11] As Chapter 4 indicated, the roots of Philadelphia's fiscal maladies were intertwined with a series of long-term political and economic developments that date back to the 1960s and 1970s and that resulted in increased demands vis-à-vis expenditures and decreased revenues. Yet political, business, and media elites framed the crisis as created by the unreasonable demands of greedy municipal unions, ignoring the effect of declining revenues.

The gravity of the city's financial difficulties became apparent in September 1990 when the city sought to borrow $375 million through the municipal bond market to cover its short-term obligations. The scale of the proposed borrowing—$188 million more than the previous year—prompted a closer examination of the city's finances, which revealed that the additional $187 million was required to cover $73.3 million in accumulated debt from six years of budget deficits and an anticipated debt of $132.6 million.[12] In light of Philadelphia's financial fragility, Standard and Poor's downgraded the city's bond rating two steps from BBB+ to BBB−, the lowest "investment-grade" bond in their rating system and lower than any other American city's rating at the time.[13] Worse still, Moody's downgraded Philadelphia's bond rating from an investment grade of Baa to speculative grade ("junk bond") status of Ba in June 1990 and then to the even lower grade of B in September 1990.[14] Hence, when Philadelphia went to the bond market to raise the necessary funds, investors balked.

In respect of expenditures, three in particular stand out: spending on poverty, wage payments, and employee benefits. As noted above, the coalition-building measures undertaken by Mayors Tate and Rizzo during the late 1960s and 1970s, for whom union support was key, resulted in generous pay and pension awards to public employees. This increased real labor costs, between 1967 and 1985, an average annual rate of 3.3 percent.[15] For some time, economic growth, high levels of federal grants-in-aid, and tax increases kept the city's finances in balance despite these commitments. However, they also generated long-term obligations that could not be matched in the face of declining revenues.

Much of the commentary on Philadelphia's fiscal crisis, particularly in the press and by politicians, focused almost exclusively on the rising costs of labor. Initially, this was part of a concerted effort on the part of business groups, politicians, and right-wing think tanks to create the perception that American institutions had become beholden to labor power and narrow interest groups, which had caused the fiscal crisis. The institutions of the welfare state were signifiers of the dominance of "big-government liberals." According to this view, stagflation could only be lanced if unions could be brought to heel, the welfare state dismantled, and the privilege of capital vis-à-vis labor restored. Thus, unemployment was the fault of the unemployed, poverty the result of the deficiencies of the poor, and cities the authors of their own demise. While Republicans were the preeminent standard bearers of this narrative, over time, an expanding group of Democrats increasingly subscribed not only to this rhetorical posture but to its policy implications as well, rejecting alternatives offered by fellow politicians, the U.S. Conference of Mayors, and the labor movement.

Indeed, as Inman points out, the increase in non-labor spending under Mayor Goode "went largely for increases in the city's poverty budget."[16] Over the 1970s and 1980s, poverty rates in Philadelphia had mushroomed from approximately 15.5 percent in 1969 to 20.5 percent by 1979 and did not fall during the 1980s despite strong national economic growth. In 1989, the poverty rate stood at 20.3 percent. Furthermore, this increase was not merely the result of wealthier people leaving the city; in fact, by 1989, there were 47,000 more people in poverty than there had been in 1969: Philadelphians were getting poorer.[17] As such, the city's expenditures on poverty had to rise in absolute and relative terms because of declining federal and state assistance.

Analysis completed by the Pennsylvania Economy League showed that Philadelphia's spending was not unusually profligate. Compared to other large cities, such as Atlanta, Chicago, Houston, and Pittsburgh, Philadelphia's spending in fiscal year (FY) 1987 on sewerage, parks and recreation, police and fire, and highways and administration was below average.[18] The key difference was that the city spent far more on state mandates, such as on courts and health and welfare services, than similarly situated cities in other states. While these cities' mandated costs were covered through increased state financial support, the commonwealth of Pennsylvania failed to do the same for Philadelphia. This left the city in the position of making up the difference through a combination of increased borrowing and higher taxes levied on a shrinking tax base.[19]

In terms of revenues, Philadelphia's financial position was eased during the 1970s through increasing federal grants-in-aid, which peaked in 1977.[20] However, during the 1980s, the city's coffers were emptied by cuts in state and federal grants-in-aid and a declining tax base as a result of deindustrialization, as Chapter 4 has shown. In real terms, between 1979 and 1989, the revenue Philadelphia received from the state and federal governments was cut by 27.1 percent. That is, in 1979, the city was granted $410.6 million. Adjusted for inflation, this was equivalent to $694.5 million in 1989 dollars. However, on average, state and federal revenues appropriated to Philadelphia decreased in real terms each year, except for a small increase in 1986 and a large one in 1989 (see Chapter 4). Still, by 1989, the amount the city received was just $506.5 million, $188 million less than the value of what the city garnered in 1979. If state and federal revenue had kept pace with inflation, Philadelphia's financial imbalance of $375 million would have been reduced by half. That is, Philadelphia would have been $187 million wealthier per year. One could quite reasonably argue that cities such as Philadelphia should have enjoyed a real-terms *increase* in state and federal aid commensurate to the rising costs associated with higher poverty rates. That funding was *cut* in real terms while Philadelphia endured two of its most wrenching decades aggravated the city's already difficult fiscal situation and illustrates the far-reaching influence of ideologically motivated neoliberal reforms.

Despite the magnitude of the cuts in federal aid, scholars and commentators have tended to define the "crisis" as a function of the growth in spending on public-sector workers. For example, while Inman notes that "the decline in federal and state aid has been significant," he argues that "two factors seemed decisive: poverty and rising public employee compensation. The fiscal future of Philadelphia turns on managing these two budget items. Additional aid for city poverty and more realistic labor contracts are the answer. The resulting saving would be well spent on cutting taxes."[21] In a similar vein, while Rendell recognized that the Reagan-Bush years had hurt the city, he insisted that "our problems come from a quarter century of mismanagement."[22] But in light of the significant real terms cuts in federal and state aid during the 1980s, it is clear that rising expenditure on the public sector was but one of a series of contributing factors, albeit a major one. That it gained primacy reflects increasing dominance of neoliberal discourse, which sought reflexively to hold labor, the poor, and "big government" responsible for all urban ills. This tendency represents a key ideological victory for neoliberals and the culmination of a decades-long project.

Finally, while Inman was certainly right to call for additional aid for city poverty, he did not address the issue of why Philadelphia experienced such high levels of poverty in 1990 despite significant national economic growth. While it is true that Philadelphia's finances would have been improved through higher poverty funding, lower rates of poverty would have at least the same budgetary effect and improved people's lives. And this does not even take into account the plethora of costly social ills that are highly associated with, if not directly caused by, poverty. The failure to place these trends in their historical context, which pays attention to the neoliberalization of the American political economy, is especially unfortunate since it created a vacuum into which neoliberal bromides rushed.

In response to decreasing intergovernmental revenues and increasing expenditures on wages and poverty, the Green and Goode administrations increased borrowing and local taxes. The overall tax burden rose, although local property taxes fell slightly, during the 1970s and 1980s.[23] However, Goode's attempts to raise $165 million through a 10.5 percent increase in the resident wage tax in his FY 1989 budget were effectively vetoed by prominent African American councilperson John Street, who had his own plans for tackling the deficit for which he hoped to accrue the credit. [24] Ultimately, the City Council approved an increase of just $52 million, which undermined Goode's attempts to improve Philadelphia's fiscal situation.[25] The responsibility for resolving the problem would have to wait for his successor, Ed Rendell.

The above discussion has shown how, during this period, Philadelphia found itself in an especially unfavorable environment. Not only was urban and economic policy at the national level inimical to the city's interests, but the city was also embedded in an institutional matrix that undermined its ability to deal with the social and economic consequences of the neoliberal turn. National policies on enterprise zones, law and order, welfare, and the failure to address unemployment interacted negatively with the consequences of the "new federalism," which was especially harmful to cities like Philadelphia that are embedded in states hostile to urban interests. As Gyourko and Summers maintain, with inadequate national and state assistance, Philadelphia committed a disproportionate amount of its resources to provide services to the poor: "an activity that belongs at higher levels of government."[26] Therefore, the argument that labor costs were the chief factor that undermined the city's fiscal stability is unpersuasive; stubbornly high poverty rates and cuts in federal and state assistance were at least as important.

The Creation of PICA

The impact of the battle over the definition and interpretation of the fiscal crisis resulted in two especially consequential outcomes that highlight the neoliberalization of Philadelphia during the 1990s, which fell on either side of Rendell's election victory: the creation of PICA and the defeat of the municipal unions. I shall take each in turn.

As discussed above, the failure to sell the necessary bonds to balance the budget opened the door to the creation of PICA, an institution not unlike the Financial Control Board that was created to oversee New York City's finances in the wake of the 1975 fiscal crisis. Investors had made clear that the city would only be lent money either at exorbitant rates of interest (one suggested 29 percent) or if the city agreed to financial oversight. PICA was largely the brainchild of Councilperson John Street, who formed a committee to investigate state cooperation, which issued a report calling for the creation of the PICA, largely along the lines proposed by Street. The city also asked Pennsylvania to allow the city to impose a 1 percent sales tax to pay for the secured bonds. With little fanfare, on April 23, 1991, the Pennsylvania House of Representatives passed Bill 209 to create PICA. It was signed on June 5 by Democrat Governor Robert Casey.

PICA's role was to secure the sale of $350 million or more in bonds on behalf of the city, the proceeds of which would be distributed if the city demonstrated its financial rectitude in a Five-Year Plan. PICA's board consisted of five members appointed respectively by the governor, the president pro tempore of the Senate, the minority leader of the Senate, the Speaker of the House of Representatives, and by the minority leader of the House of Representatives. Given the political composition of Pennsylvania's offices of state, the expectation was that there would be three Democrats and two Republicans.[27] However, key decisions on loans, hiring, and the beneficiaries of bond work required the consent of four-fifths, which handed effective veto power to one of the two Republicans. Thus, an unelected board—rather than a democratically accountable body—would supervise Philadelphia's financial decisions. Hence, PICA gained de facto veto power over the city's budget. As such, it is a neoliberal institution par excellence.[28]

PICA's ability to reject city budgets was the mechanism by which the local welfare state was partially eroded. Its creation also marked a major shift in governing authority, by which Philadelphia's city government ceded power to Pennsylvania. This institutional reconfiguration, itself far from inevitable, would influence political decision making in Philadelphia for decades to come. Throughout the fall of 1991, Wilson Goode's attempts to develop a workable plan were repeatedly rejected by PICA. In September, his administration submitted a draft plan that called for a two-year wage freeze for city employees, a reduction in benefits to 1990 levels, and a series of tax increases. However, the board rejected the proposals as inadequate while Rendell dismissed the proposals as "purely speculative."[29] Later that month, Republican board member John Egan insisted any bond offering would only occur on condition that City Hall inform PICA about any labor contracts or expenditures worth over $1 million. Egan made this gambit despite the absence of any such provision in the legislation that brought PICA into being. This led to a period of brinkmanship between members of City Council, who sympathized with unions' concerns, and PICA, cheered on by the *Philadelphia Inquirer*, which steadfastly insisted on oversight of labor negotiations. Ultimately, the city agreed to Egan's proposals.[30]

Goode subsequently attempted to assuage PICA's concerns through a plan that would reduce the city's workforce by up to 1,400 (6 percent of the total) and cut spending on homelessness, the Community College of Philadelphia, and the subsidy to local museums.[31] During the fall of 1991, the city sidestepped PICA and secured a number of short-term loans (at double-digit rates of interest) that enabled it to meet its obligations. It also borrowed money from its own pension fund in order to cover its expenses. With Goode unable to provide a permanent solution, it became clear that the task of restoring the city's finances would have to be met by incoming Mayor Ed Rendell, a task he accepted with relish.

Before examining Rendell's Five-Year Plan, it is worth noting that the creation of PICA altered the institutional terrain on which conflict over deficit reduction was resolved. Now the elected members of City Council and union leaders would have to bargain not only with the mayor but with an institution designed to exact concessions from pro-labor forces. In this sense, those with a neoliberal agenda were given the upper hand, not least because those with veto power on the Five-Year Plan were insulated from political accountability. Thus, PICA served to provide political cover for those seeking to take unpopular decisions—hence Rendell's characterization of PICA as "a tremendous aid and benefit to the citizens."[32] Furthermore, once created, the institution sought to expand its power, and those within Philadelphia who stood to benefit from such changes used PICA to their advantage in negotiations. Hence, PICA's creation, a case of *neoliberalization by design* from above, resulted in *neoliberalism by default* from below.

"America's Mayor" Comes to Power

Edward G. Rendell had been district attorney during Wilson Goode's first term in office. He left the position to make an abortive run to challenge Goode for the Democratic mayoral nomination in 1987. Rendell had another opportunity to win the nomination four years later when Philadelphia's mayoral two-term limit ensured that Goode could not run again. Goode's improbable reelection after the MOVE fiasco demonstrated not only that black candidates were viable but that black voters were likely to be pivotal to any election outcome and would likely play a key role in any governing coalition. However, as Chapter 4 illustrated, Philadelphia's African Americans were no monolithic bloc. Rather, like their white counterparts, they divided along class and ideological lines, contradicting those who assume that black political preferences are homogeneous.[33]

In Philadelphia, the fissures within black politics were obscured somewhat by the presence not simply of Goode but also because of the electoral
choices on offer—that is, between Goode, a black candidate who appealed
primarily to middle-class blacks, and Rizzo, a white candidate whose politics were seen as inimical to black interests. Therefore, to view overwhelming support of Goode as simply a reflection of racial solidarity or as
confirmation of homogeneous political preferences is misleading. After all,
some African Americans had voted against black candidates in Democratic
primaries (for example, against Charles Bowser in 1983) in the past and
had splintered along class lines (for example, around Tate's candidacy). As
such, there was no reason for Rendell to believe that he could not attract
the support of African American voters.

As Richard Keiser maintains, by the end of Goode's term, two biracial
coalitions existed within the city. The first was based on the patronage-
style spoils system under which labor leaders united with prominent black
politicians who were influential in the local Democratic organization, such
as Lucien Blackwell, John Street, and Dwight Evans. This group tended
to appeal to working-class blacks. The second biracial coalition comprised
primarily middle-class African Americans who coalesced with business
leaders and liberal whites. Although Keiser argues that "Goode walked the
line between both, and depending on the issue," the evidence presented
above suggests that Goode tended far more toward the latter "good government'" group than the former.[34]

In the Democratic primary, Rendell faced challenges from both strands
of Philadelphia black politics. From the patronage-oriented, working-class
faction came Lucien Blackwell, a prominent member of City Council. Fear-
ful that a Blackwell victory would result in a return of old-style machine
politics and racial polarization, middle-class reformers searched for an
alternative candidate. Congressman William Gray III, the third-ranking
Democrat in the U.S. House of Representatives, an influential player in
Philadelphia's black political establishment, and a long-term rival of Blackwell, persuaded his protégé George Burrell to enter the race. As part of a
strategy to increase Burrell's credibility, Gray implored him to commit to
remaining in the race for the duration.[35] Against the two black candidates
were local lawyer Peter Hearn—who was considered to be an unlikely
winner—and Ed Rendell.

During the 1991 campaign, Rendell staked out a series of positions with
respect to economic policy that fell squarely within the neoliberal framework, which formed the backbone of the New Democrat strategy and the

new direction taken by some—but by no means all—Republicans. Rendell's neoliberal ideological commitments were made especially clear on three fronts: his enthusiasm for enterprise zones, his opposition to increased federal funding for Philadelphia, and his support for privatization.

As noted in Chapter 4, Rendell's positions on federal funding and enterprise zones were illustrated in congressional testimony. Not only did he use this venue to lobby for enterprise zones, which he described as a "lifeline for what has become an almost permanent underclass in Philadelphia," he also argued in favor of measures—such as on capital gains tax relief—that were closer to Jack Kemp's policy preferences than to Representative Charles Rangel's (D-NY) proposals.[36] Rendell insisted that Philadelphia was "not looking for a handout or a bailout" but rather federal funds that "serve as a catalyst for the economic recovery."[37] This, of course, chimed with Bill Clinton's rationale for enterprise zones, which was framed in terms of enabling "poor people [to] participate in the free enterprise system," who, after all, "want a hand up not a handout. They want empowerment, not entitlement."[38]

In his first official trip after taking office, Rendell attended a meeting of the U.S. Conference of Mayors in which he abstained on a resolution for $15 billion in spending targeted toward urban areas with acute unemployment, which put Rendell at odds with Boston Mayor Raymond L. Flynn, president of the conference. The plan, backed by Rep. John Conyers Jr. (D-MI) and by Senator Tom Harkin (D-IA), would have granted $291 million to Philadelphia had it become law. While Rendell's position was presented as straightforward pragmatism, he also implied that it was part of a strategy to undermine the city's unions. On the prospect of the city receiving such a level of financial aid, Rendell remarked, "Obviously, it would be a godsend . . . But if we got $291 million, what would the unions say?"[39] Rendell's "tough" stance was lauded by the *Philadelphia Inquirer*, which ran an editorial suggesting that his refusal to call for increased federal aid "shows integrity."[40]

Soon after, Rendell was more explicit: "I do not believe that, even if it could, the federal government should reinstate massive and unrestricted revenue-sharing for cities. That would only provide a short-term crutch, not a long-term cure, for the deep structural problems that confront us."[41] Rendell's position in respect of the future of federal funding represented the rhetorical coup de grâce to urban liberalism. According to Donna Cooper, Ed Rendell's deputy mayor for policy and planning and political adviser, Rendell's position was more grounded in principle than in strategic positioning: "He just thought that cities should be self-sufficient and independent, and thrive on their own; and that the federal government's role should be to intermittently help cities overcome challenges."[42]

In January 1993, with a Democrat now in the White House, Rendell rejected a more modest proposal from the U.S. Conference of Mayors for an increase of $3 billion for general revenue sharing. Rendell called for a pragmatic approach: "With a promise to reduce the deficit, there's just no way that they can do that. So you don't ask them to do something that's politically impossible to do."[43] But was it? As the passage of urban aid bills in the Senate before Clinton's election revealed, there was a bipartisan coalition in Congress that could have supported a substantial urban aid bill. Moreover, it is by no means clear that it was politically necessary for the Democrats to insist on eliminating the deficit. So it is unclear that the path Clinton took, backed by Rendell, was the only plausible course of action available. Yet, having made the decision to focus on the deficit, the Clinton administration constricted the range of urban policy options on offer.

Moreover, in Rendell's (and Clinton's) reckoning, the only way that a robust Democratic coalition could be built and sustained would be to reject the notion of "entitlement" as it referred to individuals and cities. As Donna Cooper explained, "They [Rendell and Clinton] were similar guys in that there were problems with, in their minds, entitlement. Whether it's city entitlement or poor people entitlement, that it really undermines the coalition of Democrats because [it includes] a set of white people who don't get access to entitlements, and therefore they don't like them, like welfare; or there's a set of suburban Democrats who don't like cities being entitled. . . . They [Rendell and Clinton thought] there should be a level playing field."[44] The effect of the decision—rooted in interpretations of the economic and political "realities"—to limit urban investment and financial support meant that neoliberal approaches, such as privatization, were adopted *by default* in some cases and strengthened those who wanted to transform Philadelphia *by design*.

Notably, even before Clinton had taken the oath of office, urban politicians such as Rendell were calibrating their policy demands in reaction to Clinton's deficit-reduction agenda. As shown in Chapter 3, senior officials in the Clinton administration, such as Robert Reich, Clinton's secretary of labor, and Joseph Stiglitz, chairman of the Council of Economic Advisors, argued that this commitment was a fetter on the administration's ability to fashion progressive policies.[45] Part political strategy, part ideological attachment to what Stiglitz terms "market fundamentalism," Clinton's position on the deficit would have profound effects for cities. Just as with Reagan, city politicians were told that policies that would restore the levels of federal aid commensurate with the needs of their populations were politically unacceptable. Therefore, as with welfare, macroeconomic policy, and education, there was little to distinguish between the urban policies of the Republicans and the Democrats. Neoliberal ideas had determined the realm of the possible and, in Rendell's eyes, the desirable.

In this guise, Rendell appeared to have adopted the neoliberal critique that cities do not deserve support from higher levels of government and that such support ultimately makes matters worse. In the aftermath of the Los Angeles riots in spring 1992, a coalition in favor of increased urban aid was built, which included the National League of Cities, the U.S. Conference of Mayors, the NAACP, the National Organization for Women, and numerous members of Congress, including Republicans such as Senator Christopher Shays (R-CT) and Arlen Specter (R-PA). This burgeoning coalition included tens of thousands of protesters who marched on Washington in May 1992 under the banner "Save Our Cities: Save Our Children." However, like Clinton, rather than try to build a coalition around an alternative, Rendell's response eschewed attempts to shift the political debate and refused even to join the coalition, on seemingly ideological, as well as pragmatic, grounds.

Ultimately, the Senate passed a $2 billion bill that would have increased funding to Head Start, summer jobs and training programs, a summer school program for disadvantaged youngsters, and "weed and seed" law enforcement initiatives. This got pared down to $1 billion as President Bush threatened a veto. This vote, however, suggests that the one barrier to major increases to urban aid was the presence of a Republican in the White House. Yet, as Chapter 3 shows, ideological hostility from a Democratic president would undermine attempts to restore aid to the cities. Congress was ready to act, but the president was not.

Despite Rendell's antigovernment rhetoric, he lobbied hard for federal programs that he felt both could contribute to Philadelphia's economic development but would also be consistent with Clinton's ideology. As Rendell put it in 1993, "Clinton did campaign as a new type of Democrat, and I think he believes he's a new type of Democrat. That's why these old proposals like revenue sharing and CETA and things like that are inconsistent with what he says."[46]

In addition to his support for enterprise zones and his opposition to the restoration of federal grants-in-aid, Rendell also used the 1991 campaign to set out his proposals for privatization, a paradigmatic ideological project of neoliberal thinkers generally. Within a year of taking office, he had privatized thirteen city services, including maintenance of City Hall, security in city museums, city warehouse operations, and some street maintenance.[47] In addition to the alleged savings to the city budget that privatization offered, Rendell also viewed it as a means by which to discipline the public sector: "The knowledge that your department can be bid out is an enormous motivating factor.. . . Ironically, privatization is the most effective way we know to restore both productivity and the taxpayers' faith in government."[48]

Rendell's support of privatization was part of a far broader strategy intended to reduce the power of the city's unions. In debates and speeches, Rendell proposed that the city could reduce its deficit by privatizing its trash collection services. Echoing Osborne and Gaebler's influential *Reinventing Government*,[49] Rendell argued that "we must change the way we do business and run the city as it should be run. If we do that, we can cut back our spending and still improve city services." His view was that trash collection should be put out for competitive tendering and that the union that hitherto ran the services—District 33 of the American Federation of State, County, and Municipal Employees (AFSCME)—should bid alongside private companies. Rendell noted that "if the union wanted to do that and they were even close to the cost savings of the private sector, I would keep the union. If they couldn't and wouldn't, then I would privatize."[50]

Rendell's promotion of privatization signaled the bipartisan ideological realignment of American politics that is a central feature of this book. For, as in the case of enterprise zones, welfare, carceral policy, and fiscal policy, the new coalition in favor of privatization included Democrats and Republicans (as it included Labour and Conservative MPs in the United Kingdom). But the consensus was not all consuming. That is, in Philadelphia, party identification was no guide as to who supported privatization, a policy that just a few years earlier was considered outside of the mainstream. Ironically, privatization was *opposed* by Republicans Frank Rizzo, Ron Castille, and John Egan. Upon entering the race as Rizzo's replacement as the Republican mayoral nominee, Egan argued that privatization was just "a big lie for covering up 25 years of mismanagement," declaring "I'm not against it. I'm absolutely against it."[51] He also described plans for privatization as a "political gimmick

. . . that blames workers for years of mismanagement and political chica-
nery."[52] Moreover, Democrats such as Lucien Blackwell staunchly opposed
the scheme. Yet other Democrats, such as Peter Hearn, and Republican Sam
Katz joined Rendell in lining up behind privatization.

In the primary election, the city's African American voters divided along
ideological and class lines. Some have argued that the split black vote
handed victory to Rendell. For example, Keiser argues that given Blackwell's
standing in the "Black community," "he would have won the Democratic
Party primary, in which blacks were the majority of registered voters, *if he
had been the only Black candidate.*"[53] However, in the election itself, Rendell
emerged victorious with 46 percent of the vote, 6 percentage points more
than the share of the vote secured by both African American candidates.[54]
Keiser's assumption that all black Philadelphians would have rallied around
the sole black candidate seems odd in light of his careful attention to the
ideological and class-based cleavages within the black politics in Philadelphia. Moreover, his claim is especially doubtful in light of the fact that one-
fifth of the black electorate voted for Rendell, a further indication of political heterogeneity among Philadelphia's African American voters.[55] These
patterns reflect the splintering within black politics, often along class lines,
by which consensus along programmatic lines is gradually eroded.

In the Republican primary, voters were also presented with a crowded
field. As Chapter 4 illustrated, Frank Rizzo was a permanent feature of
Philadelphia politics during the 1970s and 1980s. The same was true in the
following decade. In February 1990, Rizzo announced that he would run
for the Republican nomination, setting up a race between him, financial
consultant Sam Katz, and district attorney and Vietnam veteran Ron Castille. In a closely fought election, Rizzo narrowly beat Castille by 1,500 votes
with 35.5 percent to Castille's 34.4 percent. With 36,764 votes, Katz came
in third place with 27.4 percent. This set up a tough fight between Rizzo
and Rendell.

Rendell could safely assume that Rizzo's candidacy would appeal to pro-
union "ethnic" white voters in South Philadelphia and the Northeast. With
his defection to the Republican Party, Rizzo was responsible for the shift of
an estimated 40,000 to 50,000 voters who switched their registration to the
GOP in order to vote for him.[56] Rendell, therefore, had to stitch together a
coalition similar to that which twice delivered Goode to City Hall. However, Rendell's ability to build a biracial coalition was hampered by the
hostility of black ministers who had been alienated by Rendell's decision to

run against Goode for the Democratic nomination in 1987, despite having made an apparent commitment not to run.[57] Moreover, leading African Americans were wary of Rendell's plans for the privatization of city services, which Rizzo opposed.

Rizzo also directly courted the black community, through a tough stance on drug dealing in predominantly African American neighborhoods. Given Rizzo's racist image and the history of almost unanimous black opposition, it seems implausible that Rizzo could have realistically hoped to secure the support of a significant number of black voters. However, Paolantonio suggests that, as a result of Rendell's pro-privatization position, many black voters considered throwing their weight behind Rizzo.[58] Ultimately, however, Rendell's alienation of the black ministers was balanced out by the political capital he accrued through his prosecution of police brutality cases as district attorney.[59] Thus, Rendell's hopes of attracting substantial support among working- and middle-class blacks were realistic. This was reflected in a June 1991 poll that found that 73 percent of black voters backed Rendell compared with 13 percent supporting Rizzo. Overall, Rendell enjoyed a commanding lead, with 67 percent to Rizzo's 25 percent with 8 percent undecided.[60]

As indicated above, Rendell's support for privatization was illustrative of a far broader antipathy toward municipal unions and his belief that Philadelphia's future lay firmly in the service and corporate sector. These positions, of course, were two sides of the same coin. In order to enhance the city's competitive advantage, it had to introduce a series of neoliberal reforms. It is not therefore surprising that Rendell was the beneficiary of considerable financial support from the business community, which he courted assiduously. While Rendell received the majority of his campaign contributions in the form of small donations from individuals, he also received substantial financial support from local law firms, developers, and New York investment houses. For example, the Rubin Group, formed by Center City developer Ronald Rubin and which included leading businesspeople from the region, gave $35,000 to both Rendell and Burrell in March 1990.[61] Ultimately, the group backed Castille in the Republican primary. However, the donations to Rendell and Burrell suggest that ideology rather than party was the Rubin Group's overarching concern. This is also evident from Rendell's strong business backing when it came to the general election.

In addition to funding from the Rubin Group, Rendell received considerable donations from Philadelphia law firms. For example, Ballard, Spahr,

Andrews & Ingersoll, the former law firm of both Rendell and his chief of staff, David Cohen, donated $50,000 to the campaign. Meanwhile, Dilworth, Paxson, Kalish & Kauffman contributed $25,000, and Pepper, Hamilton & Scheetz gave $20,000. Additionally, Rendell was also the beneficiary of significant contributions from New York City investment houses. Bear Sterns & Co. donated $25,000 through its political action committee while Goldman Sachs & Co. gave $5,000. Moreover, Goldman's executives contributed an additional $16,000 to the Rendell campaign. None of these firms made contributions to Rizzo's campaign.[62] Local business interests also gave financial assistance to Rendell through loans. By the end of the campaign, Rendell had some $237,521 in unpaid debts. The *Philadelphia Inquirer* reported that Thomas J. Knox, a multimillionaire businessman, lent Rendell $35,000, while Rendell owed $20,000 to local developer Michael Karp. Another $50,000 was lent by the city law firm of Brobyn & Forceno.[63]

With a significant war chest and a large lead in the polls, Rendell entered the summer of 1991 in a commanding position. His chances of victory were sealed, however, when on July 16, 1991, Rizzo died of a heart attack. After almost three weeks of deliberation and just three months before the general election, Philadelphia's Republican elite backed Joseph E. Egan to be their candidate against Rendell. A former president of the Philadelphia Industrial Development Corporation, Egan had strong business and union ties. Despite his party identification as a Republican, Egan found himself to the left of Rendell. While Egan had one foot moored in the compromise between labor and business, symbolized by the New Deal, Rendell sought to sail in the opposite direction into unambiguously neoliberal waters.

Ultimately, Rendell won by a landslide, with 59.5 percent of the votes to Egan's 27.4 percent.[64] However, his winning margin obscured two significant qualifiers. First, despite his impressive victory, Rendell garnered almost 40,000 fewer votes than Rizzo received as the losing candidate in 1987 and over 50,000 fewer than Goode secured. Second, turnout in black wards lagged behind that in predominantly white wards by between 6 and 22 percent. Nevertheless, Rendell's victory still rested on the reconstitution of the biracial regime nurtured by Goode. While the lower turnout no doubt reflects the almost foregone conclusion of the election in the wake of Rizzo's death, the fact that every winning mayoral candidate since Rendell has received well under Rendell's 1991 election total indicates a fundamental weakening of Democratic Party support in the city, which was triggered by Rizzo's supporters' defection to the GOP in the 1980s.

During the campaign, Rendell used his tough stance on the deficit and the unions, as well as his promotion of privatization, to establish his neoliberal *bona fides*. Clearly, candidates' respective positions on these issues cannot be assumed to stem purely from their ideological preferences. After all, there are structural and electoral reasons that might explain the range of policy preferences illustrated above. For instance, Rizzo's key electoral strategy was to appeal to the city's white working-class voters. As such, a pro-union stance would be expected. Similarly, Rendell's neoliberal policy prescriptions might be explained as a straightforward gambit to win business support. Yet, this does not necessarily rule out ideological explanations per se. I argue that Rendell's proposals were part of an overall strategy to build an ideological basis of support for a set of policies that he believed would take the city in the right direction. His refusal to join other city mayors, such as David Dinkins of New York or Boston's Raymond Flynn, in their bid for increased federal urban spending, is a case in point. Indeed, the electoral logic could just as easily suggest that he not take on entrenched interests such as the unions and assume a more conciliatory posture. In this way, electoral coalitions can be built upon ideological foundations just as they might be established through direct appeals to voters' material interests.

Indeed, Donna Cooper, Rendell's ally in government, suggested it was his policy priorities that attracted business support, not the other way around. Hence, there was no need for him to respond to the pressure of capital; Rendell was their kind of Democrat to begin with: "A lot of people gave money to Ed Rendell because they liked what he had to say; that it was fresh, that it was new. A lot of these guys were Democrats, but they are sick of 'the Democrats.' . . . I was with a former CEO of Exxon Mobil, a Republican; he goes: 'I love Ed Rendell because he's one of the few pragmatic Democrats in America.' . . . Nobody's getting anything from giving him money."[65] Thus, as Ed Rendell entered office in January 1992, the further neoliberalization of city policy, embraced somewhat reluctantly under Wilson Goode, looked set to continue. Yet given his position on enterprise zones, urban aid, and privatization, it seemed that Rendell's economic policy posture was not simply adopted out of perceived necessity but out of a preference for a leaner, more efficient City Hall propelled by market mechanisms and weakened unions. Alternatives presented by other mayoral candidates and by national institutions such as the U.S. Conference of Mayors were rejected on grounds not only of political expediency but also on principle.

Rendell's arguments against federal "handouts" and in favor of public-sector "reform" helped to naturalize neoliberal critiques and policy solutions in ways that made particular choices seem like the only alternative that common sense would dictate. This view came to animate the administration's approach to labor and its Five-Year Plan to reduce the city's deficit.

Rendell's Defeat of the Unions and the Five-Year Plan

When Rendell came into office on January 6, 1992, he turned the parlous state of the economy to his advantage in his battle with the municipal unions, which were increasingly portrayed as having been the main contributors to the "crisis." Just days before Rendell took office, John Street brokered an agreement within City Council around an ordinance that required the city to "consider any authority [i.e., PICA] views concerning financial impact on the city" in labor contract negotiations and gave PICA access to detailed information regarding contract negotiations.[66] Thus, PICA's influence ultimately extended beyond the powers granted to it in the enabling legislation.

Rendell's most immediate task was to produce a Five-Year Plan to reduce the deficit that would be acceptable to PICA. Others have provided detailed analysis of the negotiations that preceded the plan; therefore, an extensive discussion need not detain us here.[67] It is worth noting, however, that during the negotiations, Philadelphia's revenue streams were further undermined when Pennsylvania Governor Robert Casey presented his own austerity budget that cut state funding to the city by $74 million.[68] The major elements of the plan were cuts to city services and reductions in pay and benefits to city workers.

In a live televised address, Rendell treated the citizens of Philadelphia to the tried and tested "there is no alternative" bromide: "Our Five Year Plan makes the only choice there is—to cut the cost of city government." Unions were held responsible for the city's financial situation and were told they would need to make substantial concessions as a result. As Rendell's chief of staff put it, "Without sacrifices by labor and reform of the government structure, I don't know of anyone who can design a way to resolve the city's financial crisis."[69] To support his position, Rendell pointed out that the unions had made substantial gains during the 1990s. He noted, for instance, that union contracts accounted for 65 percent of the city's operating budget and that workers received a pay increase of 8 percent in early 1992.[70] Moreover, the Five-Year Plan proposed a reduction in what Rendell claimed were overly generous holidays and sick days. Rendell failed to acknowledge, however, that the unions had, in fact, made a series of concessions in preceding years on each of these fronts. For instance, in the early 1980s, previous austerity measures resulted in mass layoffs. Furthermore, in 1988, the union contract began with a first-year bonus in lieu of a wage increase, with smaller raises given in each of the following years. Finally, despite the cries of political corruption, union pay awards after 1972 were settled by outside arbitration.

In contrast to the claims that union workers were overpaid, two detailed studies published in spring 1992 suggested that Philadelphia public employees were not paid significantly more than their counterparts in other major cities. In fact, they tended to be paid below the mean salary of most other comparable cities. For example, a police officer paid at the top of the pay scale made $32,221 in 1991, roughly $4,400 a year less than the $36,673 average for officers in the other nineteen of the nation's twenty largest metropolitan areas.[71] To provide some perspective, median wages in Philadelphia in 1989 were $24,603. These figures fail to take into account longevity pay—the money an officer gets in addition to base pay, depending on the number of years served—as the Rendell administration keenly pointed out. However, the maximum longevity pay was $2,300 a year, after thirty years of service. Therefore, even with longevity pay factored in, the total salary at maximum base pay and longevity wages would still fall below the average wage in the nation's largest cities. A similar picture holds true for firefighters, who enjoyed a starting salary of $28,333 (slightly above average); sanitation workers (slightly below average); custodians (slightly above average); and social workers (below average).

These stubborn facts forced Cohen to resort to the standard critique that *all* public-sector workers were overpaid. Dismissing these figures as "irrelevant," he argued that "I think the critical factor is what you have to pay a custodial worker in the private sector."[72] This is undoubtedly so, but mainly because the private-sector custodial worker would have lower wages and fewer benefits. Therefore, the overall effect on the city's finances and local economy of replacing public employees with private ones may not be as favorable as they seem at first glance. Indeed, were one to follow scholars such as David Imbroscio and view the issue of public-sector wages and privatization through a "Public Balance Sheet" lens, which takes a far broader view of the social costs involved, one might arrive at a different conclusion.[73]

It is also worth noting that these figures appear to contradict the claim made by Buzz Bissinger in his popular account of Philadelphia during Ed Rendell's first term, *A Prayer for the City*. He claims that "the taxpayer cost of employee compensation had more than doubled in the last ten years, from roughly $25,000 a year per employee to more than $50,000 a year."[74] Bissinger provides no citation or further evidence in support of his figures. When considered against the data cited in the report, his claim seems doubtful. This is especially consequential since Bissinger's account of the crisis now constitutes the commonsense exegesis of Philadelphia's financial woes among Philadelphia's cognoscenti. This is not to say, however, that there were not examples of waste, fraud, and abuse within elements of the union movement that exacerbated Philadelphia's fiscal difficulties. There were, as Bissinger readily points out. Rather, the point is that rising union wages and benefits were neither extraordinary nor the sole cause of the city's accumulated fiscal debt. Yet, in the absence of increases in federal or state support, cutting labor costs was one of the few things the administration could immediately do to address the deficit. In this sense, the city's hand was forced to some degree. However, the extractions that Rendell drew from the unions were far greater than were necessary, and the relish with which they were imposed suggests that the battle with the unions was about power and ideology as much as it was about fiscal discipline.

In sum, Rendell's plan called for a five-year wage freeze, a reduction in the workforce by 300, and city takeover of union-run health care plans. Thus, the city's workforce of 24,000 would have their wages frozen until 1996, and starting salaries for firefighters and police officers would be reduced. Moreover, Rendell proposed that the number of vacation days would be cut from fourteen to nine and the number of paid sick days halved, thus undoing gains made by labor in previous negotiations. The mayor further suggested that additional savings would accrue from a city takeover of the union medical plans. Rendell's goal was not only to reduce labor costs but also to restructure the institutional relationship between City Hall and the city's four municipal labor unions. He also called for efficiency savings, the closing of fire houses, and the introduction of charges for services citizens hitherto received for free. However, no tax increases were proposed; the deficit would be eliminated through cuts alone.

The total savings that would result from the plan would be $1.1 billion over five years. According to city officials, reductions in labor costs—$509 million—would account for just under half of the savings, although union leaders contested this, arguing that in fact, city workers would shoulder $940 million of the burden.[75] Moreover, to assume this would only have a positive effect on city finances fails to take into account the effect on spending on those unemployed, on lower wages, or with effectively lower salaries due to rising health care costs.

Unsurprisingly, the PICA board members, Wall Street traders, and the Philadelphia Chamber of Commerce received the plan enthusiastically. Michael Johnston, an assistant vice president of Moody's Investors Service, saw Rendell's proposals as offering a "different kind of plan that "seem[ed] to be an effort to do something serious."[76] Perhaps more unexpectedly, the plan was quickly approved in City Council under the stewardship of John Street, who pushed the proposals through with relatively little debate. Having made passage through City Council, Rendell was further encouraged by positive noises from the PICA officials. However, he would have to face down the unions before his plan could go ahead.

Given potential losses to wages, benefits, and control of health care, union leaders stridently opposed the plan. Their initial line of attack was to challenge the legality of PICA itself, claiming it was inconsistent with Philadelphia's Home Rule Charter. This legal challenge was unsuccessful, however, because John Street had considered this potential objection and crafted the PICA legislation carefully enough to ensure that there would be no valid legal challenge to the institution.

Their next step was to try to extract concessions from the Rendell administration in negotiations during the spring of 1992. However, Rendell quickly gained the upper hand in the media war. As Jenkins points out, his strategy was to undermine the unions' case through appeals to the public, both directly through speeches and announcements, and via the press, to "manipulate the conflict between the city and its unions . . . replacing it with a conflict between the greedy, inefficient unions and a city that was fighting for survival."[77] Concerned about the potential of union spin in the media, Alan Davis, the city's chief negotiator, suggested that the administration should wage a ruthless propaganda battle: "We will be prepared with whatever propaganda machines we have going—editorial boards—so that we win this thing publicly. . . . We'll have to engage in media education here."[78] Part of this "education" was to leak a letter—labeled "confidential" to gain reporters' attention—that detailed the unions' apparently outrageous work rules to sympathetic members of the media on the day on which the labor contracts were due to expire. The desired effect was achieved: the story was picked up in the *Philadelphia Daily News*, the *Philadelphia Inquirer*, and the *Wall Street Journal*, which ran a story entitled "Philadelphia (Horror) Story" that detailed the most egregious examples from the letter.[79] This was accompanied by an editorial that illustrates the success of Rendell's efforts to blame the city's struggles on the alleged rising power and influence of municipal service unions: "The memo . . . provides an eye-opening example of what's wrong with the management of many major cities. City governments have become increasingly dominated by powerful labor unions, which exist to maximize the benefits and salaries of their members. The taxpaying residents are largely forgotten, except when they're asked to pay more to support the city's growing bureaucracy. It is little wonder that so many people and businesses are throwing up their hands and fleeing our great urban centers."[80] The third prong of the administration's attack was the strategic use of layoff and privatization threats. Bissinger describes the process: "There was universal agreement that the machinery of layoff notices should start in earnest on all fronts, with all the notices leaked in various stages through the media to whip up as much hysteria as possible. The strategy called for not just one layoff bomb, but a series of smaller ones, with different numbers of workers laid off each time, leaving virtually every worker in the city in dread and fear as to whether his name or her name would be included in the next round."[81] As Bissinger notes, the administration's manipulation stretched to threatening the privatization of garbage collection as a ploy to try to divide the union despite the fact that, in Rendell's words, "There's no way we're going to do it."[82]

On the basis of the Five-Year Plan, PICA approved the sale of $475 million in bonds for the city, thus resolving Philadelphia's fiscal crisis in one stroke. After a brief interregnum, during which a Pennsylvania Labor Relations Board–mandated "fact finding" was conducted (and suspended on order of the State Supreme Court), negotiations collapsed and Rendell offered the unions his "last, best offer." Although a strike was called, it lasted for a mere sixteen hours.[83] Fearful of the threat of privatization, the unions—despite their reputation for intransigence—largely accepted the city's proposed changes. Wages were frozen for two years and increased by 2 percent in the third year and 3 percent in the fourth, the number of paid holidays was reduced from fourteen to ten, health benefits to employees were reduced to $360 per month, the city gained access for the first time to union books for their health and welfare programs, and the city enhanced its ability to contract out work and lay off workers.[84] As such, the city stood to save $374 million over the course of the four-year contract. The scale of the union capitulation, as well as the manipulative means by which it was achieved, is summarized by Bissinger, who had unparalleled access to the discussions: "It was solely on the basis of a bluff that the city had taken the initial steps to contract out certain portions of the sanitation work performed by Sutton's union [District Council 33]. . . . When someone later asked Cohen what the city got from the unions in return for the sanitation provision, his answer was both brief and blunt: 'Everything.'"[85] Rendell emerged from the conflict a strengthened figure. He earned plaudits in the national press, including in a front-page article in the *Wall Street Journal*, which waxed lyrical about how the "bootstrap mayor" had "used fiscal toughness and good-natured boosterism to pull this city from the brink of financial and spiritual ruin."[86] Moreover, Rendell's policy positions and ideological posture did not go unnoticed in Washington, D.C. Shortly after his defeat of the unions, Vice President Al Gore dubbed Rendell "America's Mayor."[87] In November 1996, *American City and Country* named him "Municipal Leader of the Year" because "his 'tough love' policies have helped turn the city around."[88] In many respects, this high praise was richly deserved. After all, Philadelphia's position had materially improved: within eighteen months of securing his deal with the unions, Philadelphia had a balanced budget, and by FY 1996, the city enjoyed a $118 million surplus. Furthermore, the city's bond rating rose back to investment-grade status in 1992 by Fitch and in 1995 by Moody's.[89] However, many of Philadelphia's citizens clearly suffered through lost jobs, curtailed benefits, and lower wages. Moreover, antipathy toward labor and to the institutions of the welfare state had been stimulated and then exploited by the Rendell administration. Finally, Rendell, the media, and business had successfully persuaded the public and key elites that the fiscal crisis was the fault of inefficient government and the excesses of labor, thus achieving a historic goal of right-wing neoliberals. However, as has been shown above, this account is a partial one.

Yet for Rendell's critics, a nagging question remains. Did he have any real alternatives to the course he took? After all, the city was in financial dire straits, and some steps had to be taken to ameliorate the deficit. While deindustrialization, endemic unemployment, and persistent poverty had undermined the city's finances, it was not apparent what short-term steps the city could have taken to reverse or reduce these factors. So what might Rendell have done differently? First, he might have thrown his political heft behind the coalition calling for increased federal aid, rather than undermining it—to be sure, this would not have solved all the city's problems, but it could have protected services from cuts. Second, he could have sought fewer concessions from the unions. Third, rather than cutting the business privilege tax on gross receipts and introducing the ten-year property tax abatement on new construction, the administration could have maintained Philadelphia's tax regime at its existing level. Moreover, the city might have enacted "linkage" policies like those deployed in Boston whereby a per foot fee was assessed on office development, the proceeds of which were put into a fund for affordable housing.[90] Fourth, Rendell could have pursued more proactive local alternative economic development policies[91]—for example working more closely with the Philadelphia Industrial Development Corporation to promote hi-tech manufacturing, as had been tried in Chicago. However, none of these alternatives were even attempted.

The political response to Philadelphia's fiscal difficulties—the creation of PICA, privatization (albeit limited), and the defeat of the municipal unions—institutionalized key neoliberal goals. Indeed, those on the right had considered the devolution of power to the states as a method for undermining the institutions of the New Deal and the Great Society. Moreover, these shifts were not forced onto unwilling city officials. To the contrary, while John Street was instrumental in the creation of PICA, Rendell relished the fight with the unions and was an enthusiastic advocate for privatization. Thus, while supra-local structural forces—such as deindustrialization, declining federal funding, and demographic change—were crucial, the neoliberalization of the inner city came as much from below as from higher levels of government. Yet, as earlier chapters have indicated, there are clear instances of federally driven neoliberal innovations: enterprise zones and empowerment zones. Here, too, Rendell was an enthusiastic promoter.

From Enterprise Zones to Empowerment Zones

As Chapter 4 noted, Rendell testified before Congress in favor of enterprise zones as a mayoral candidate in 1991. His testimony was consistent with his "new economic agenda," which as historian Michael Katz points out, "reflected faith in the discipline of the market."[92] In contrast to the equivocal tone struck by mayors Green and Goode, Rendell tenaciously promoted the zones. Indeed, he expressed a specific preference for reductions in capital gains tax in addition to cuts in federal business taxes, a position that chimed with the original neoliberal vision for enterprise zones, as reflected in the proposals promoted by Jack Kemp in the United States and Geoffrey Howe in Britain. At the time, Democrats in Congress were resisting Republican efforts to include cuts to capital gains tax in federal enterprise zone legislation.

Three months after Rendell took office as mayor of Philadelphia in 1992, he returned to Washington to once again testify in favor of enterprise zones. He reported that Philadelphia's four zones had "stimulated investment and created jobs."[93] Indeed, despite ample evidence to the contrary, Rendell heralded enterprise zones as "the most successful and comprehensive example of how the federal government can help the cities help themselves."[94] His account of Philadelphia's fiscal crisis corresponded rhetorically and analytically with the neoliberal position stretching back to the approaches to New York City and Chile in the mid-1970s. Rendell stated, "We can't borrow our way out of our crisis; we can't tax our way out of our crisis. We have to grow our way out of our crisis." The method for doing so was through the use of supply-side market mechanisms, such as enterprise zones.

In the aftermath of the Los Angeles riots in spring 1992, initial calls for major federal urban investment ultimately gave way to a rearticulation of neoliberal and conservative diagnoses and remedies. In Philadelphia, local political elites echoed Rendell's view that any response to urban difficulties should not come in the form of major federal legislation. The *Philadelphia Inquirer*'s "urban manifesto" claimed, "There is simply no support out there for policies that further increase dependency and discourage work." As a result, there "should not be a whole raft of new federal programs or any kind of Washington-based assault on the problem." Moreover, it went on to suggest that urban distress and unrest was rooted in "the loss of family values and accountability." As such, it declared that "the chief aim of government should be to help restore those lost values and to increase accountability."[95]

The key recommendations of the manifesto were welfare reform, independent schools, a "reform" of public housing, and enterprise zones. Given the nature of these policy prescriptions, the newspaper noted that "much of what we have written above is consistent with the ideas being articulated by Bill Clinton, the prospective Democratic presidential nominee. But it also borrowed ideas that Jack Kemp, President Bush's Secretary of Housing and Urban Development, has been articulating."[96] In short, it reflected the accommodation to neoliberal ideas that just over a decade before were regarded as extreme to moderate Republicans and Democrats.

During Rendell's first year in office, a lacuna emerged between the claims of enterprise zone enthusiasts, such as Ed Rendell and the *Philadelphia Inquirer*'s editorial board, and the empirical evidence regarding their success. Ironically, it was the *Inquirer*'s own staff who raised doubts about the efficacy of the enterprise zone. Just days after the publication of the "urban manifesto," the paper reported that enterprise zones "may help, but few think it would transform city neighborhoods by themselves." The story went on to report that "a 1989 Urban Institute study concluded that even if the 50 proposed enterprise zones were a complete success, they would help only 1.5 percent of the poor."[97]

Of greater significance, the *Inquirer* published a major story in 1992 on enterprise zones reviewing empirical evidence and the views of businesspeople and economists. It noted that over time, "many Democrats had reluctantly come aboard" to support the policy. In respect of the Philadelphia zones, the article reported that "the city's Department of Commerce says that 128 companies have started or expanded operations in Philadelphia's four enterprise zones—Hunting Park West, American Street, West Parkside and Ports of Philadelphia—since 1983."[98] Moreover, "about $40.6 million in public monies has been invested in those companies, along with $147.7 million in private money." Furthermore, "the city says, 3,130 jobs have been created and 11,820 jobs retained." However, the story pointed out that these numbers are suspect: "No rigorous system exists for determining how many jobs actually were created, and, two years ago, city officials acknowledged that figures for one enterprise zone, the American Street corridor, had been overstated by about a third because they included companies that had gone out of business, moved, or never hired all the people they had expected to."[99] The *Inquirer*'s report reflected the more general tendency of enterprise zone advocates to overstate the likely impact of the program. As Chapter 1 showed, a typical move was to only count "jobs created" while ignoring the number of jobs that had left, thus leaving the casual observer with a false sense of the effect of the policy on *net* job creation.

In another article, the *Inquirer* noted the "modest" impact of enterprise zones, pointing out that the number of jobs retained and created was "too small to have much effect on neighborhoods where more than 60 percent of the residents live below the poverty line." Even these statistics, however, are insufficiently detailed to estimate the value-added effect of the enterprise zones, since they do not deal with the issue of how many of these jobs would have been created or retained had the enterprise zone incentives not existed. Further, without additional analysis, it is not known whether the jobs created were those associated with city firms that had moved into the zones to receive the benefits of the incentives. In this case, they would not contribute to the overall number of jobs in Philadelphia but merely represent a shuffling of the deck. However, it may be that these jobs either came from outside Philadelphia or are genuinely new jobs (i.e., not transplanted from somewhere else)—unfortunately, the data do not exist to make an accurate assessment. Indeed, Wallace suggests that the figures are not available because the administration placed a moratorium on enterprise zone data, since they had proved less successful than had been anticipated.[100] Finally, even if one assumes all these jobs were net gains, as the *Inquirer* pointed out, they pale in comparison to the 53,000 manufacturing jobs that the city lost in the 1980s.

Despite the obvious limits to the enterprise zone approach, the Clinton administration and mayors such as Ed Rendell continued to press for federal enterprise zone legislation. As was detailed in Chapter 3, Clinton supported enterprise zones as governor of Arkansas and as a candidate for president. Shortly after the 1992 presidential election, Clinton and Al Gore began to develop the modified "empowerment zone" idea. As detailed in Chapter 3, empowerment zones were established under the Omnibus Budget Reconciliation Act of 1993. Each city that won empowerment zone status would be awarded $100 million of Title XX Social Services Block Grant funding for community programs, and businesses in the designated areas would receive a wide range of tax incentives.

As noted above, Rendell was fiercely committed to winning empowerment zone designation for Philadelphia. This was for a series of political, financial, and ideological reasons. During his first term in office, Rendell became increasingly concerned about the charge that, as Bissinger puts it, "he was a downtown mayor driven by the edifice complex."[101] The perception was that Rendell was neglecting the "neighborhoods," often a code word for the city's black residents. Yet, his reelection hopes rested on nurturing this biracial coalition. Thus, a high-profile program such as the empowerment zone—targeted on the poorer sections of the city—would serve this purpose. Second, given the tenuous state of the city's finances, the mayor naturally wanted to ensure that Philadelphia was the beneficiary of the only major urban policy initiative on offer from the Clinton administration. This issue was especially acute given the Department of Housing and Urban Development's (HUD's) cuts to housing programs and the commitment to welfare reform. Finally, the empowerment zone policy chimed with Rendell's ideological preference against top-down, "big-government" spending programs and in favor of policies that used public money to foster private investment. Rendell felt that any additional spending from the federal government would have to be combined with pro-market measures. Thus, in all these regards, empowerment zones were ideal.

Such was Rendell's commitment to Philadelphia's winning empowerment zone designation, he was prepared to forfeit some of the $100 million through submitting a bistate bid with Camden, New Jersey.[102] This virtually guaranteed Philadelphia and Camden's winning EZ status; its primary competition came from Kansas City, which straddles Kansas and Missouri. The political logic suggested Clinton's preference for Philadelphia. The Democrats could not hope for any Electoral College votes from Kansas, thus leaving them with no more than Missouri's eleven to gain. Indeed, Robert Nelson, chair of the North Central Community Trust Board, reports that the Clinton administration actively encouraged Rendell to improve Philadelphia's bid when the original draft of the application failed to live up to expectations: "As we understand it, the proposal that first went in did not meet the standards . . . and Bob Dole's district in Kansas was really the top bi-state application . . . and I remember being in this building at three o'clock in the morning having to amend the proposal. We know what happened, somebody from the President's office said, 'look, Ed, your proposal did not pass muster. . . . I want to give it to you, but Bob Dole's Kansas application was better and you have to find a way to substantiate why we can choose you.'"[103]As such, with the political die already cast, Philadelphia's empowerment zone status was "ours to lose," as described by Jeremy Nowak, a member of the committee that drafted the proposal.[104] Thus, from the outset, national political consideration played a key role in Philadelphia's empowerment zone.

To Rendell's delight, the Philadelphia-Camden bid was successful, making it one of ten urban areas to be granted empowerment zone status in the first round.[105] However, the city only secured $79 million of the $100 million available to each area as $21 million went to Camden. Although $79 million was no mean amount for a cash-strapped city, it paled in comparison to the resources required to tackle the scale of Philadelphia's poverty, unemployment, and myriad social problems. Moreover, as a result of cuts to the federal HUD budget, the total amount the city received from the federal government was due to be reduced in 1994. As David Cohen, Rendell's chief of staff, put it, Clinton's budget was "a mixed bag for Philadelphia—more good than bad, but definitely a mixed bag."[106] Cuts came in the form of a reduced Community Development Block Grant, operating grants, and modernization programs for public housing. Thus, the extra $79 million would have to help make up for cuts elsewhere.

The empowerment zone legislation stipulated that poverty levels should be 20 percent or above in each census tract, 25 percent in at least 90 percent of census tracts, or 35 percent in at least 50 percent of census tracts. Given the story of systematic neglect outlined above, a wide range of Philadelphia's census tracts were of eligible status. The 1990 census shows that Philadelphia contained eighty-four census tracts with poverty rates of 30 percent or higher. Yet, only twelve were granted EZ status. Thus, out of a total of over 300,000 people living in poverty in 1990, only the areas occupied by 20,154 would directly benefit from empowerment zone designation.[107] Put another way, the program targeted areas in which just 6.7 percent of the city's poor lived.

This raises the important political question of why city officials chose some tracts over others. In the original plan, two areas were slated for zone status: an area in West Philadelphia and the American Street area of North Philadelphia.[108] However, in the final draft of the application, an additional zone was included: North-Central Philadelphia, which included Councilman John Street's district. Why? One account, provided by Nemon, stresses the role of community power combined with well-placed political support: "Vocal residents in North Central Philadelphia, using their political backing on the City Council, were able to sway city officials to include census tracts in their area."[109] However, the evidence suggests this has far more to do with Rendell's politically astute coalition-building efforts.

In his position as president of the City Council, Street held great sway over what could (and what could not) be achieved politically in the city. As such, Rendell had a keen political interest in maintaining the support of his colleague from North Philadelphia. Nowak describes the relationship thus:

"Ed's job was to make John feel good, and John Street would deliver."[110] Thus, in order to overcome the potential for stasis that is encouraged by Philadelphia's fragmented institutional structure, decisions made by the mayor's office had to be tailored so as to garner Street's support or at least to avoid his opposition. When it came to the empowerment zone, Rendell initially was "reluctant to include a census tract that Street wanted. However, Rendell became almost terrified that the omission would offend the City Council President."[111] Thus, in the final application, not two but three areas were included: West Philadelphia, American Street, and North-Central Philadelphia (Street's district).[112] Nowak argues that the process of selection as a whole was driven by political calculation. He reports that all the areas proposed for inclusion were chosen to build and reinforce political coalitions, as opposed to any objective criteria: "Options were never driven by data."[113]

Unlike with enterprise zones, there have been numerous systematic attempts to evaluate the successes and failures of the Philadelphia empowerment zone (PEZ). Before reviewing these studies, it is worth considering the ways in which funds were distributed. According to the PEZ's publication, *Momentum*, the largest segment of the $79 million (44 percent) had been spent on "economic development";[114] $11.7 million (15 percent) had been spent on "safety and quality of life" projects, such as investment in a police mini-station and childcare; $5.6 million (7 percent) had been used to finance the rehabilitation of 304 housing units; and $6.4 million (8 percent) went to "program administration." The remaining $20.1 million was invested in perhaps the most successful and enduring of all the PEZ initiatives: a neighborhood funding stream that uses its interest to fund small-scale, community projects. This has included funding the creation of the community lending institutions that have made 223 loans to 139 businesses and nonprofits, as well as job training of 108 residents.

Momentum claims "460 + businesses moved into the EZ" between 1995 and 2005 and that the PEZ has created "2,112 jobs for EZ residents" in the same period, although it gives no account as to whether this is a net growth of jobs.[115] This implies that businesses were attracted and jobs created *as a result* of the program. More systematic studies, however, have recognized any worthwhile evaluation of the PEZ would need to separate out the effects of the empowerment zone *in particular* from the effects of economic trends in general. A number of attempts to identify the independent effects of the empowerment zone have been made by comparing trends within the PEZ census tracts with trends within "comparison" census tracts with similar demographic characteristics.[116]

For example, the General Accounting Office (GAO) found that while the Philadelphia EZs experienced a decrease in the level of unemployment between 1990 and 2000 (from 23.6 percent to 19.4 percent), the comparison area also experienced a decrease, although not a statistically significant one.[117] A similar result was found with respect to poverty. Between 1990 and 2000, poverty in the PEZ areas fell by 8.4 percentage points from 52.1 percent to 43.7 percent. However, this apparently impressive change pales somewhat when one considers the fact that the poverty rate of the comparison area also fell, although by 5.1 percentage points (from 43.07 to 37.97). Even this attempt to hold all things constant in order to observe the effects of the empowerment zone may be flawed, since the comparison areas selected in the 1990 sample appear to be significantly dissimilar to the PEZ tracts. For example, the initial poverty rate in EZ tracts was 8.5 percent *higher* than in the comparison tracts. This may help to account for the fact that by 2000, poverty fell by less in the comparison tracts than in the Philadelphia EZ tracts, since it is likely that levels of poverty are more difficult to reduce the closer one gets to zero. Nevertheless, this evidence is at least suggestive that the empowerment zone may have had an independent, although modest, effect on poverty and unemployment. Yet, even after these efforts, poverty in 2000 was still at 43.7 percent with unemployment at 19.4 percent.

This improvement is in marked contrast to a rather bleaker picture of economic growth: "The Philadelphia portion of the EZ experienced little change in the number of businesses between 1995 and 2004 [an increase of 0.75 percent], while its comparison area experienced a large increase [of 7.2 percent]. Both the Philadelphia portion of the EZ and the EZ comparison area saw a similar decline in the number of jobs available."[118] As shown above, this is markedly different from the business growth noted by the Philadelphia empowerment zone publications. Perhaps this may be because they failed to cite the number of businesses that left or folded during that period, choosing only to highlight business growth rather than the net effect of gains and losses.

The numbers on jobs are perhaps the most surprising of all: Philadelphia's EZ areas experienced a decline in the number of jobs of 26.5 percent while the comparison area witnessed a 27.9 percent decline.[119] Thus, it appears likely that the EZ had little or no effect on increasing the net numbers of jobs. From conversations with PEZ staff, it is apparent that the difficulties of establishing the direct effect of the PEZ on changes in the numbers of jobs or businesses are well known. As the PEZ Commercial Corridors Business Organizer Rojer Kern stated,

> It has been very difficult to try to keep track of, say, actual job creation. . . . All things being equal, development was happening on Girard Avenue. So the work of the Girard Coalition to improve the streetscape and to improve the perception of safety on the corridor and all of that I think has been important, but then how can you really say how important it has been? Just because you say you're putting in cameras and cleaning the streets and doing sidewalk renovation, does that really mean that a business will come to an area? Well, yes it does, but . . . how can you prove that you actually did that?[120]

The consensus among PEZ officials was that the best examples of business development in the empowerment zone could be found in the American Street area. However, could the arrival of these businesses be tied directly to the benefits offered by the empowerment zone itself? "That, you really can't say," Kern reported.[121] These kinds of results are typical across the EZ cities.[122]

In the most recent attempt to measure the effect of the program on PEZ tracts and measure it against comparison tracts, Rich and Stoker deploy a range of innovative measures that the GAO did not employ. Their overall conclusion was that Philadelphia's zones fared better than those in most other cities. However, despite their best efforts, Rich and Stoker's findings "directly align with the GAO study all but for the unemployment indicator (we found that the EZ tracts and the control tracts fared about the same), though the GAO found statistically significant effects for all three indicators in Philadelphia and none of ours were statistically significant."[123]

On the whole, therefore, these studies suggest that, at best, the EZ designation had a modest positive effect but, at worst, had no effect whatsoever. Perhaps more troublingly from a policy perspective is the fact that it is extraordinarily difficult to establish the "pure" effects of the EZ itself. As such, one would be hard-pressed to make a convincing case that, according to these objective criteria, the empowerment zones made a significant difference for the people living within them. As has been shown above—and in previous chapters—the muted effects of the empowerment zone are strikingly consistent with the underwhelming effects of enterprise zones. Yet, political support for the approach was sustained throughout the 1990s.

In reflecting on the empowerment zone's impact, Donna Cooper, Rendell's deputy mayor for policy and planning, who oversaw the empowerment zone, suggested that these figures were unlikely to have picked up the full effect of the empowerment zone measures since they only go up until 2000 (or up to 2004 for data on business development).[124] Therefore, I examined the data in the PEZ and comparison census tracts to see what changes had occurred to unemployment, poverty, and median incomes between 2000 and 2007. In respect of unemployment, both the PEZ tracts and the comparison enjoyed a decline. However, the drop in unemployment in the comparison tracts of 2.2 percentage points—from 16.1 percent to 13.9 percent—was greater than in the PEZ tracts, where unemployment fell by 1.6 percentage points from 19.3 percent to 17.7 percent.[125] In Philadelphia as a whole, unemployment fell very slightly from 10.9 percent to 10.7 percent. Therefore, the PEZ appears to have had little or no effect on reducing unemployment over the period not captured by the GAO study; in fact, the comparison area did slightly better. This suggests that the apparent gains made in PEZ tracts between 1990 and 2000 were not sustained and may have been driven by changes before the PEZ was established in 1995.

In terms of poverty, the PEZ tracts do slightly better than the comparison tracts, although poverty rose in both and overall poverty rates were far higher in PEZ tracts. Levels of family poverty in the comparison tracts rose by 4.8 percentage points (from 31.7 percent to 36.5 percent) while poverty increased in the PEZ tracts by 2.9 percentage points, from 39.4 percent to 42.3 percent by 2007. Thus, in respect of poverty rates, zone designation does not appear to have made a major impact. At best, they may have played some role in reducing the rise in poverty that had occurred.

Differences with respect to income are more striking, with empowerment zone tracts faring markedly worse than the comparison areas. In the comparison tracts, median incomes fell by 7.0 percent from $21,617 in 2000 to $20,098 in 2007 (in 2007 constant dollars). However, median incomes in the EZ census tracts declined by 11.6 percent from $20,928 to $18,497. Overall, therefore, these data show that the assumption that a longer time horizon would reveal an improved picture than the one painted by the GAO study is not borne out. These data are summarized

Table 6. Summary of Changes in Unemployment, Poverty, and Median Income in Empowerment Zone and Comparison Census Tracts, 2000–2007

	Unemployment	Poverty	Median Income
Change in EZ census tracts (2000–2007)	Decrease of 1.6 percentage points (19.3 to 17.7 percent)	Increase of 2.9 percentage points (39.4 to 42.3 percent)	Decrease of 11.6 percent ($20,928 to $18,497)
Change in comparison tracts (2000–2007)	Decrease of 2.2 percentage points (16.1 to 13.9 percent)	Increase of 4.8 percentage points (31.7 to 36.5 percent)	Decrease of 7.0 percent ($21,617 to $20,098)
Difference in EZ census tracts	Worse by 0.6 percentage points and higher levels overall	Better by 1.9 percentage points and higher levels overall	Worse by 4.6 percentage points and lower levels overall

in Table 6. This would therefore suggest that as a policy to reduce unemployment and poverty and to raise median incomes, the empowerment zone has not succeeded. It also draws attention to the fact that recent declines in median wages were also associated with lower unemployment, suggesting that, even before the Great Recession, work increasingly did not pay. These figures further imply that any urban policy that can credibly claim to offer transformation of poor urban areas must be bound together with a diagnosis and strategy that places cities in the broader political-economic framework.

This is not to say, however, that the Philadelphia empowerment zone did no good. It did. After all, the city had an interest in satisfying certain constituencies, which at times meant the provision of public goods from which all potentially benefited. Its notable achievements include the inclusive approach during the drafting period of the Strategic Plan, the development of community lending institutions that provide capital to those previously excluded by discriminatory practices, job training programs, the upscaling of previously dilapidated buildings, and the rehabilitation of housing units. All these measures are likely to make certain poor areas more attractive to businesses and more pleasant for residents. Moreover, it is generally agreed that under the direction of Eva Gladstein in 1999, the PEZ operated far more effectively than in its first five years.

Three further elements of the PEZ are noteworthy. The first is that the level of community involvement in the empowerment zone, which was initially impressively high, waned over time. Initially, the community trust boards (CTBs) had been elected. However, by 1999, the CTBs introduced new governance rules that eliminated elections and limited boards to fifteen members in each, five of whom would be directly appointed by the mayor.[126] The limits to genuine participation were unsurprising given that the areas in which the PEZ would operate would contain many people who were poor and, as a result, worked multiple jobs, not to mention fulfilling family commitments. As such, these citizens were not in a position to participate in the planning and implementation given the time required to attend the often long and arduous meetings. Thus, "the poorer residents, faced with their daily obstacles to survival, essentially did not participate in the decision-making bodies of the PEZ."[127]

The second notable feature of the Philadelphia empowerment zone was the infamous misuse of public funds, first revealed by a 1998 HUD audit, which raised questions about the use of 30 percent of the spending it reviewed—about $150,000. The audit reported that the city "did not provide HUD with a realistic picture of actual progress, and the impression exists that the benefits . . . were greater than actually achieved."[128] A more blatant case of wrongdoing triggered a Federal Bureau of Investigation (FBI) probe into the use of federal empowerment zone funds surrounding one of the largest developments in the zone, an entertainment center that was to be built on Cecil B. Moore Avenue in the North-Central Philadelphia empowerment zone (in John Street's district). In short, the FBI investigation led to a nine-month prison sentence for Jamel Cato, executive director of the North Philadelphia Financial Partnership, who pled guilty to the charge of embezzling almost $350,000 of empowerment zone funds in July 1999.[129]

Finally, there is the case of Paula Taylor Peebles, a political ally of John Street, who ran organizations that were granted projects worth $2.6 million of empowerment zone money. Peebles's organizations received these funds despite the city's being aware that one of her organizations owed the city $625,686 in real estate taxes and water, sewer, and gas bills.[130] As a result, the city solicitor filed a lawsuit seeking return of the money. Why did she receive the money? For Robert Nelson, chair of the CTB in the PEZ in which these projects were awarded, politics played a central role. She was, he maintains, "the squeaky wheel that got the oil."[131] The issue led City

Controller Jonathan Saidel to state, "I am very concerned that the oversight from the city, as well as the Mayor's office, is not what it should be."[132] Both the widespread misuse of funds and the stunted degree of community involvement illustrate the limits to the "empowerment" approach. Putting decision-making authority into the hands of people at ever lower levels of government does not equal empowering the poor or the needy. Indeed, it can just as easily result in empowering local power brokers who no more have the interests of local residents at heart than those at higher levels of government. As such, these examples cast doubt on Rich and Stoker's conclusion that the PEZ was an exemplar of "good governance."[133]

Despite the limited impact of empowerment zone designation on the key measures on jobs, unemployment, and poverty, Rendell remained a staunch supporter. When it emerged in 2001 that the population in the zones had dropped during the 1990s by 17 percent, Rendell was bullish. He suggested that the loss of population was "irrelevant" as an indicator of success and argued that "our zone held its own compared with other zones."[134] Moreover, nationally, a bipartisan consensus in favor of the empowerment zone approach remained, and the program was expanded under George W. Bush.

Philadelphia's Political-Economic Development Under Rendell

In this final section, we will zoom back out from the small tracts of land covered by the empowerment zone to consider briefly the major changes in Philadelphia's political-economic development that occurred under Rendell's tenure as mayor.

As Stephen McGovern notes, after his victory over the unions and the reduction in the deficit, Rendell focused on tourism as a dynamo of Center City economic development.[135] While Mayor Goode focused on downtown office development, Rendell's innovation was to "shift the target of government assistance . . . to what he anticipated would be the next growth areas—arts, culture, entertainment and tourism."[136] Concrete expressions of this conviction arose in the form of a hotel-building boom, a new convention center (which had been initiated prior to Rendell's election but was completed under his leadership), the renovation of Independence Mall, and a revitalized Broad Street, dubbed the Avenue of the Arts. Rendell described the latter project as "one of the most, if not the most, important things we're doing now in Philadelphia."[137] McGovern estimates that the total price tag for developments that included a world-class orchestra hall, a theater, and the renovation of the Academy of the Arts would be $318 million. As McGovern argues, Rendell's "substantial record of achievement" illustrates his "considerable skill in molding the necessary political alliances and accumulating essential resources to move large." The result was to bolster Rendell's public standing since "Philadelphia seemed to be on the move again."[138]

Jerome Hodos points to a further consequential transformation that occurred in Philadelphia during the 1990s: the globalization of Philadelphia that "is both *happening to* the city and, increasingly, being *actively pursued* by regional elites" who want to promote foreign direct investment.[139] The effect of this shift has been to increase the commitment to the idea of regionalism, which undergirded Rendell's strategy of making the city appeal via tourism and marketing to economic elites who live beyond the city limits. In this way, there is a premium placed on the city's image as a cultural hub.

Finally, by the end of the 1990s, state and federal support began to increase markedly. Some of the rise in state support reflects the distribution of proceeds from bond sales overseen by PICA, so these trends include rises in debt as well as grants. Moreover, along with the federal funding came increased federal mandates. The data are summarized in Figure 1.

As Wolman et al. note, Philadelphia's standing in the public mind was enhanced greatly during the Rendell years. They developed a composite index of the level of municipal distress for the 145 largest cities in the United States as of 1990. The forty-eight cities in the bottom third of the distribution were defined as "distressed central cities."[140] They sent this list to "urban experts," asking them to identify those cities perceived "to have experienced the greatest economic 'turnaround' or revitalization over the course of the past decade."[141] According to the experts, out of the forty-eight, Philadelphia was ranked the eleventh most successful city of the decade. Yet, the empirical evidence suggests that, on a range of metrics, Philadelphia fared far *worse* than the performance of the mean city among the forty-eight identified. These metrics included changes in per capita income, median household income, poverty rates, unemployment rates, and participation in the labor force. In contrast to the experts' assessments, Philadelphia ranked thirty-ninth. Wolman et al. also developed an index that used

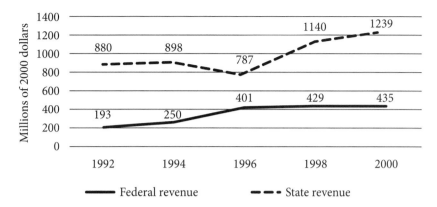

Figure 1. State and federal revenues in the city of Philadelphia. Sources: U.S. Department of Commerce, *Statistical Abstract of the United States* (Washington, D.C.: U.S. Census Bureau, 1995, 1997, 1999, 2001, 2003).

a far wider range of factors to capture economic, social, and demographic well-being. On this measure, Philadelphia ranked thirty-seventh overall.[142] Moreover, on both measures, not only did Philadelphia compare unfavorably with other cities, but its position had worsened since 1990.[143] Thus, the mismatch between perception and reality is significant.

Quite obviously, Center City Philadelphia underwent a dramatic change, as the skyline, the proliferation of restaurants, and the revived "Avenue of the Arts" reflect. Yet, as Wolman et al.'s findings show, these signs of growth can be deceptive. The mismatch that they identify stems in part from the exceptionally good press that Rendell received. It also reflects the ways in which neoliberal political-economic development produces enormous benefits to the wealthy but has served the middle and bottom ends of the income distribution poorly. This is due to the twin features of the neoliberal political economy that, on one hand, have failed to move the city toward full employment, even during the years of regional and national economic expansion. On the other hand, as Adams et al. show, the growth of the tourism and hospitality industries, a corollary to downtown development, has produced jobs that tend to be low paid.[144] One other development that offers a brighter ray of hope is the role of medical and education institutions that provide employment in cities such as Philadelphia. As Adams notes, "meds and eds" account for 26 percent of all jobs and 23 percent of all wages in Philadelphia.[145] Within these institutions, there exist

Table 7. Key Demographic and Economic Data for Philadelphia in 1990, 2000, and 2010

	1990	2000	2010[a]
Total population	1,585,577	1,517,550	1,526,006
Per capita income[b]	20,172 (12,091)	20,905 (16,509)	20,170
Median household income[b]	43,264 (24,603)	39,325 (30,746)	34,400
Unemployment rate (percentage)	9.7	10.9	15.8
Labor force participation rate (percentage)	58.4	55.9	55.1
Poverty rate for individuals (percentage)	20.3	22.9	26.7

Source: U.S. Census Bureau.
[a] American Community Survey, one-year estimates, 2010.
[b] In 2010 dollars; numbers in parentheses are originals.

a variety of jobs at a number of pay scales that undoubtedly have helped prevent median wages slip further than they already have. However, these institutions also enjoy tax-exempt status, and so their contribution to the city's economy has to be weighed against the potential loss of revenues. Moreover, "meds and eds" have not provided the kinds of jobs in sufficient numbers to alter the trajectory of political-economic change in Philadelphia. Overall, during the past three decades, manufacturing jobs have been replaced by lower numbers of more poorly paid jobs in the service sector alongside a thin sliver of extremely highly paid jobs that have gone to the lucky few who are fortunate enough to enjoy the fruits of downtown development, so skillfully delivered by Mayor Rendell and his predecessors.

As Table 7 indicates, Philadelphia's transition into a postindustrial economy has resulted in stagnating (or declining) incomes, high rates of unemployment, and rising levels of poverty. These trends were not reversed during the years of growth that preceded the Great Recession. The erosion of the national and local welfare state, an abandoned commitment to full employment, and a hollow national urban policy have failed so many within American cities such as Philadelphia. Yet, Center City, a playground for the wealthy, boomed. One illustration of this is the American Community Survey data that show that as median wages fell and poverty rose during the 2000s, the proportion of Philadelphia's families that earned over $150,000 grew from 2.4 percent in 2000 to 3.0 percent in 2005 and, despite the recession, reached 4.9 percent in 2010. To be clear, these trends are not the result of enterprise or empowerment zones. Rather, the key point is that the neoliberal policy prescriptions—including but not limited to such policies—have failed to arrest these problems and almost certainly have exacerbated them.

Conclusion

Philadelphia entered the 1990s in a precarious state. While Mayor Goode had shepherded Philadelphia into a new corporate era, as the transforming skyline attested, his second term came to an end with the city finances in disarray and his governing capacity undermined. In the fiscal crisis that ensued, the city's governing authority was eroded by the creation of PICA. Moreover, the ideological interpretation of the causes of the crisis laid most of the blame at the municipal unions' door. In this account, their defeat would be a necessary condition for Philadelphia's prospects of recovery. The man elected to apply the medicine would be the affable Rendell, who defeated the unions with aplomb. Having done so, Rendell used his governing coalition to complete Philadelphia's transformation into the neoliberal city that began in the 1980s. This included the embrace of locally derived initiatives, such as privatization as well as state or federal programs such as empowerment zones and enterprise zones. While the political-economic transformation of Philadelphia was not a purely contingent "choice" made by individuals but rather intimately connected to the national and global economic trends, these forces were refracted through the city's governing institutions, which were subject to political control.

Although Rendell took significant steps to promote the neoliberalization of Philadelphia, Hackworth's claim that "Rendell successfully dismantled the local welfare state" is perhaps exaggerated.[146] The local welfare state, although wounded and disheveled, limps on and provides crucial services to hundreds of thousands of residents. Hackworth is correct, however, to emphasize the ideological function of the Rendell mayoralty. Rendell largely won the argument that intransigent unions and a bloated City Hall were responsible for Philadelphia's financial misfortunes. In this sense, Rendell, the bond markets, and the local media went some way in dismantling the "ideological infrastructure" that buttressed the welfare state.[147]

The effect of this transformation has been to produce a more sharply bifurcated city, in which two worlds exist alongside one another. In one world, the restaurant boom, the new hotels and shiny apartment buildings, and acres of office space represent unequivocal gains. Philadelphia, in this world, is a city reborn. In the alternative world, however, the poor (often working) struggle as the middle class sees its standard of living slip. The people who inhabit this world benefited little from the "roaring nineties" and the massive expansion that preceded the Great Recession of 2008–2009. As such, Philadelphia serves as a case study that reveals the full extent of neoliberal political-economic development in ways that analysis at the national level may miss. Meanwhile, as federal and state governments become ever meaner, the city's governing capacity is eroded. As such, its ability to address the acute and growing poverty, endemic joblessness, and rising inequality is curtailed. The traditional functions of government have been outsourced to "third-sector" organizations that have neither the means to address the extent of these problems nor the democratic authority to act.[148] Looking forward, there are few bright spots on the horizon. The latest census figures reveal more of the same while the ideological climate appears to be more hostile than ever to alternatives that stand outside the neoliberal frame. The challenge, therefore, must be to construct an alternative ideological infrastructure for progress in the twenty-first century alongside a series of credible alternative policy ideas. This cannot be done, however, until we have a full understanding of the inadequacies and injustices of the present.

Chapter 6

Neoliberalism by Design: Poverty and Plenty in London's Docklands

> Ten years ago today we set out together a future vision of economic revival which accepted as its first base the beneficence of the capitalist system. Ten years later the sight we survey exceeds our wildest dreams. The future we saw then is successfully at work today.
> —Geoffrey Howe, London Docklands, June 26, 1988[1]

> It comes home to you that this is no longer a democratic idea, you've got no democratic rights at all . . . I can't vote them out if I don't like it. . . . They're an autonomous authority.
> —Local Docklands resident reflecting on the London Docklands Development Corporation[2]

Over the course of the 1980s and 1990s, London's docklands was radically remade in the neoliberal image. Once the site of the British Empire's principal port, "docklands" was central to global trade in the eighteenth and nineteenth centuries. Indeed, the very names East India Dock and Canary Wharf signal Britain's imperial past. Although London is no longer the capital of an empire powered by global trade, the area known today as "Docklands" now serves as a crucial node in the global network of financial capital. Canary Wharf, now the pulsing heart of Docklands, is home to the global headquarters of HSBC and Barclays and the European headquarters of Citigroup. Their neon logos emblazon the skyscrapers that rose up over the past three decades, monuments to the power of global capital and the triumph of neoliberal ideas. Yet, despite the wealth that is generated on the banks of the river Thames, this area of East London is pockmarked with some of the most deprived wards in Britain.[3] As such, echoes of the Dickensian past, wherein the poor and rich lived cheek by jowl, reverberate along the streets. In Docklands, a tale of two cities applies in the same place.

While the soaring inequalities wrought by state-led gentrification in Docklands, undergirded by neoliberal ideas, echo patterns of change in Philadelphia, the parallels end there. For in marked contrast to Philadelphia's tentative, gradual, and, at times, reluctant turn to neoliberalism—more often than not occurring *by default*—the neoliberalization of London Docklands was faster, less compromised, and more radical. This was largely due to the willingness and ability of Conservative government ministers to harness the power of central state institutions to impose their neoliberal blueprint. While the vast majority of local people and political institutions wanted to resist such changes, their capacity to do so was curtailed by the weakness of local authorities in Britain's intergovernmental system. As such, the radical remaking of Docklands is a paradigmatic example of the politics of *neoliberalism by design*. This chapter uses Docklands to provide a grounded illustration of this concept by examining the ways in which state power was deployed to make Docklands the jewel in Margaret Thatcher's crown.

"Docklands" refers to the area of East London that abuts the Thames. For generations, Docklands was home to a thriving port. Although it provided jobs for many of its inhabitants, many were poor and remained so well into the twentieth century. At its heart lies the Isle of Dogs, the iconic peninsular formed by a meander in the river Thames. It is the site of Canary Wharf and West India Dock, which in 1802 was the first to open; 180 years later, it became home to the world's first enterprise zone.

The transformation from global port to financial hub did not occur seamlessly. Indeed, after the bombing of the docks during the Second World War, the decline of the British Empire, and the rise of containerization, the area experienced massive unemployment and dereliction. During this interregnum, debate raged about what ought to be done with the docks. During the 1970s, numerous plans were developed and initiatives launched as the national government and the Greater London Council alternated between Conservative and Labour rule. The deadlock was broken decisively, however, when Margaret Thatcher's Conservative Party was swept to power in 1979.

As noted in Chapter 2, Thatcher's government contained two influential cabinet members who were personally committed to the economic, political, and institutional transformation of urban areas in general and of Docklands in particular: Chancellor of the Exchequer Sir Geoffrey Howe and Secretary of State for the Environment Michael Heseltine. Their respective visions reflected the twin features of neoliberalism that are emphasized in this book. While Howe's Hayekian prescription of tax cuts and deregulation led him to the enterprise zone program, which consciously sought to reduce the role of the state, Heseltine's urban development corporations (UDCs) saw a role for state intervention but with a neoliberal twist.

While Keynesian interventionism envisaged the national or local state taking managerial steps to raise aggregate demand as a means to securing full employment, Heseltine's interventionism involved the deployment of central state authority to remove local control over a particular area and place power instead in the hands of a quasi-public body that would act with a "single-minded determination" to actively promote private-sector growth within the area. Howe's and Heseltine's approaches, therefore, disagreed on the means (that is, the degree of state intervention) but agreed on the ends: the privatization of public space and the state-assisted growth of private enterprise. It should be added that both policies sprang from the normative belief that the local area and the nation as a whole would be vastly improved by removing the shackles of the local state that, in their view, hampered entrepreneurial initiative. Moreover, both prescriptions resulted in the strengthening of private capital through upward transfer of resources and power.

Thus, neoliberal ideology informed policy prescriptions regarding London Docklands just as they did with respect to national urban policy and likewise with economic, social, and industrial policy more generally. However, while neoliberal ideas played a central role in policy development, such ideas did not in and of themselves determine a given political-economic outcome. As we saw in Chapters 1 and 2, the national institutional constellations through which political entrepreneurs navigated had a profound effect on policy outcomes at the national level in both the United States and the United Kingdom. Moreover, as the Philadelphia case demonstrates, national urban policy ideas had to further permeate through local institutions and interact with urban political coalitions. These divergent institutional structures help to explain the "variegated" character of neoliberalization.[4]

In the United States, the institutional structures that confronted the neoliberals afforded their opponents the opportunity to thwart enterprise zone proposals at the national level. The sheer number of veto points arrayed by the separation of powers and divided government, which was further aggravated by Democratic control of the House of Representatives, meant that President Reagan could not get his enterprise zone program through despite his personal commitment to the idea. But while American political institutions at the national level proved insurmountable, federalism provided an alternative route. As Chapters 4 and 5 illustrate, Pennsylvania was spurred into action in anticipation of a national enterprise zone program and instituted its own. Further down the ladder of government, Philadelphia's enterprise zone emerged as officials responded to signals from the state and the White House that a national initiative was in the offing.

In stark contrast, centralized national political institutions in the United Kingdom enabled neoliberals to go further and faster than their American counterparts. Although scholars have noted that, despite the strength of the British executive, major political change has nevertheless proved elusive in certain policy domains,[5] this is not so with respect to urban policy or with regard to cities' institutions of government. As Chapter 2 noted, this is for two reasons. First, cities in the United Kingdom have no independent constitutional standing, and traditions of city government are not well established. Most important, British cities are subject to the doctrine of *ultra vires*, which prohibits local authorities from engaging in activities that are not explicitly approved by Parliament.[6] While powers periodically have trickled down to the local level, British cities have rarely enjoyed the relative autonomy of American cities. Remarkably, this even applies to London. The Greater London Council's (GLC's) very existence was contingent on the acquiescence of the central government, which created it in 1964 and abolished it in 1986. Furthermore, during these years, the GLC had fewer powers than most American and continental European cities. Thus, the government in Westminster has the authority and capacity to mandate institutional or policy change in particular places to a far greater degree than can an American administration in Washington, D.C. Moreover, when the target of change is a particular *place*, rather than particular societal groups (for example, victims of crime, old-age pensioners, and users of the National Health Service), opponents to change are hampered in the degree to which they can construct coalitions to resist change. As this chapter will show, this lack of local capacity and authority had major implications for the political development of Docklands.

The second reason why radical change of a neoliberal kind was possible in urban policy during the 1980s was due to the advantageous institutional locus of the key urban policy entrepreneurs. That the primary proponent of enterprise zones was the chancellor of the Exchequer was highly significant. After the prime minister, the chancellor is arguably the most influential member of the government and the Treasury the most powerful department of state. Had the enterprise zone proposal come from another government department or from local government, the Treasury would have been in an extremely strong position to veto it. However, Geoffrey Howe's personal interest in both enterprise zones and the future of London Docklands proved crucial. Moreover, Howe also supported the establishment of the UDCs, proposed by Michael Heseltine. As one of the government's "big beasts," a particular favorite of Margaret Thatcher in the early 1980s, and well regarded by his officials at the Department of the Environment (DOE), Heseltine was able to overcome significant local opposition to his plan, which included a petition to the House of Lords from Docklands' community organization and local authorities, to introduce the London Docklands Development Corporation.

These two factors—weak cities and powerful central government backing—meant that resistance from within national institutions of government and from local institutions from below was more easily circumvented in Britain than in the United States. As such, Docklands was reinvented in the neoliberal image. It became the quintessential geographical referent of neoliberal ideas—the urban corollary of supply-side economics. As will be shown below, this was precisely how the proponents of enterprise zones and UDCs saw them. They hoped that the Docklands example would illustrate the wisdom of their ideas and attract more recruits to the cause.

Over time, the strident tone and content of the government's urban policy softened. The need for community consultation, if not local control, was acknowledged. Economic development in Docklands would now proceed through the auspices of "public-private partnerships," whereby once-ignored local residents became ostensibly important "stakeholders." Although this shift was effected under Margaret Thatcher's successor, John Major, it was pursued with added vigor by the "New" Labour Party that was swept into office in the 1997 landslide election.

The re-creation of London Docklands provides a test case for the competing theoretical accounts of political development. At first glance, it appears to be prima facie evidence in support of scholars, such as Susan Faintstein, who emphasize the role of interests rather than ideas or institutions.[7] After all, it is plain that private interests would become the primary beneficiaries of the privatization of public land, tax incentives, and deregulation. Furthermore, it is certainly true, as Doreen Massey points out, that the interests of financial capital have been furthered significantly by the transformation of London Docklands both in absolute terms and relative to labor.[8] However, the sequencing of events matters greatly. As this chapter shows, there is little evidence that either the enterprise zone or the creation of the London Docklands Development Corporation arose as the result of business lobbying or pressure. Indeed, politicians and officials had to go to great lengths to encourage businesses to locate in Docklands. Rather, the transformation of Docklands is a clear case of how ideas, when carried by politicians with sufficient institutional clout and personal skill, can effect consequential and enduring institutional change at a specific scale.[9]

The political development of London Docklands further illustrates a far broader point about the need for social scientists to look beyond national institutions and particular policy domains in evaluating the extent of political change. The creation of the London Docklands Development Corporation (LDDC), a nondemocratic institution that assumed the lands and planning powers of elected and accountable local authorities, shows how "durable shifts in governing authority" can occur at lower levels of government with consequential effects.[10] Furthermore, the abolition of the Greater London Council in 1986 signaled the degree to which the mechanisms of local popular control in London Docklands were doubly undermined by the Conservatives' ideological onslaught. These consequential shifts occurred despite local resistance. The ideological commitment and coherence of the Conservative government meant that it was willing and able to deploy the institutions of the state to achieve ideological ends. As such, this is a clear case of *neoliberalization by design*.

This chapter will place the radical reinvention of London Docklands by the Conservatives in historical context through a brief discussion of the wrangling over the future of the docks that occurred in the 1970s. It will then detail the introduction of the enterprise zone and the LDDC, the two major institutional signifiers of the area's neoliberalization, and focus on the key venture of the time: Canary Wharf. Following this will be an examination of the abortive attempts by local actors to establish alternatives to the neoliberalization of Docklands and of the gradual softening of the LDDC's stance. The discussion then shifts to an investigation of the changes brought about by the election of a Labour government in 1997. Finally, the transformation of social and economic conditions in Docklands will be considered to provide a basis for an evaluation of the winners and losers of the experiment.

Declining London, Deteriorating Docklands

Although contemporary London's status as a "global city" has now been cemented,[11] in the 1970s the city was in a precarious state. Indeed, this was something London held in common with Philadelphia. Although the two cities occupy different places in their respective national markets and in the global economy, illuminating parallels can be drawn in respect of their economic and demographic trajectories. Between the 1850s and the advent of the Second World War, both cities experienced rapid population growth. While Inner London grew from around 2 million to around 5 million in 1939 (Greater London's population rose to a peak of 8.6 million in that year), Philadelphia grew from 565,000 in 1860 to around 2 million by 1940. Although Philadelphia's population stabilized during the 1950s and 1960s, it would witness a massive decline from the 1970s onward. In London, however, the major shift of jobs and population to the suburbs that came to characterize American urban change began in earnest from the 1940s and continued until the late 1980s: between 1931 and 1981, Inner London's population fell from 4.9 million to 2.4 million (51 percent). During the 1940s and 1950s, Inner London's loss was Outer London's gain. However, from the 1960s until 1986, London's total population declined to a low of 6.8 million.[12] In the 1970s alone, London's population declined by 841,000 or 11 percent. Thus, as the engine of postwar growth ground to a halt, London's future global city status was by no means ensured.

No doubt part of Inner London's population decline was due to "the Blitz," the sustained Nazi bombing campaign that terrorized the capital and numerous other British industrial centers between September 1940 and May 1941. Docklands was particularly hard hit. Its port infrastructure was pummeled and its population plummeted. In the Isle of Dogs alone, the prewar population of 21,000 was reduced to just 9,000 by 1945.[13] Neverthe-less, as London recovered, so did Docklands. By 1951, the Isle of Dogs population had grown to 10,000, and work was so abundant that during the 1950s and 1960s, there was a shortage of skilled labor. Moreover, by 1950, labor reforms had reduced the exploitation of workers as the casuali-zation of work was abolished.[14] Thus, as Hobbs notes, "For a brief period . . . the docker enjoyed a measure of autonomy rare in industrial society."[15] But a period of near-full employment, rising wages, and falling poverty began to fracture at the turn of the 1960s. In response to the rise of contain-erization, the Port of London Authority made the strategic decision to invest in the expansion of the Tilbury Port further down the Thames in Essex. In 1969, St. Katherine's Dock was the first to close. In a sign of future trends, it was sold to developer Taylor Woodrow, which used the site for office development and the construction of a hotel. Throughout the 1970s, the remaining docks closed gradually until the Royal Docks, the last to go, were sold off in 1981. These changes, regional, national, and international in scope, placed enormous pressure on Docklands. Between 1955 and 1981, employment in Docklands fell from 31,000 to just 4,100, and barge traffic declined from 13 million tons a year in 1963 to only 3 million in 1978.[16]

What to Do with Docklands?

During the 1970s, a number of abortive efforts to revive or "regenerate" the docks were proposed. The first of these was undertaken by Peter Walker, the Conservative secretary of state for the environment, who appointed consulting firm Travers Morgan to conduct a comprehensive study of London Docklands. As Walker acknowledged, the aim of the study was to consider how local industries could be replaced in order to reshape the area to "bring the West End into the East End."[17] However, Walker did not require that Travers Morgan simply deliver a blueprint. Instead, he asked for a series of options that ranged from the creation of a water park with large open spaces for recreation, an office development with a mix of affordable and luxury housing, a plan that focused on shopping and entertainment complexes, and a vision based upon a significant investment in private housing.[18] But while these competing visions were explored, the report ultimately favored what it called the "City New Town" version. This envisaged the creation of 60,000 new service and office jobs, 1,000 industrial jobs, and a population increase of 100,000 who would live in housing that would be equally divided between public and private.[19] Notably, the study team that Travers Morgan assembled included high-ranking officials from the central government and the GLC. However, as Brownill notes, "Neither local politicians nor the public were included."[20]

In response to the docks' decline and the consultation process that was launched after the publication of the Travers Morgan report, a number of community groups sprang up to channel local opinion to government.[21] One such group was the Joint Docklands Action Group (JDAG), an umbrella organization for a series of highly localized planning-oriented groups. JDAG, allied with elements of the local trade union movement and the Labour Party, sought to fashion alternative visions to those that sought to promote property-led redevelopment of the area.

Given the exclusion of the public from the planning process until after the publication of the report in early 1973, it is understandable that it was met with derision by local groups that saw each of the options as irrelevant to their needs and largely based on a program of gentrification. That the Tower Hotel opened on the now-defunct St. Katherine's Dock in the same year as the report's publication only contributed to calls for "Homes before Hotels" and "People before Profits," as the protesters' slogans read.[22] Indeed, as Hebbert argues, the alienation of the local population, which was exacerbated by this process, promoted the rise of "grassroots radicalism" that would later be a thorn in the side of the London Docklands Development Corporation in the 1980s.[23]

The degree of local hostility to the plans forced the government to think again. The Labour Party's taking control of the GLC in April 1973 was the final straw. Soon afterward, the Conservative government in Westminster abandoned the Travers Morgan proposals. As with economic policy, Ted Heath's government was willing to change course in the face of opposition.[24] In this case, Heath's government was not prepared to impose a vision for Docklands over the opposition of the local councils.[25] This would be in stark contrast to the Thatcher government that famously was "not for turning." Thus, in 1974, the government accepted the recommendations of the Labour-led GLC and local councils to establish a new planning body, the Docklands Joint Committee (DJC), which would coordinate the activities of the Docklands' councils and provide a place at the table for the Port of London Authority and the local Trades Union Congress representatives. Explicit in the DJC's mandate was public consultation. This would be achieved by the creation of the "Docklands Forum," a body designed to gather, articulate, and convey the views of community members, which it did through its elected members that sat on the on the Docklands Joint Committee.[26]

In 1976, the DJC produced the London Docklands Strategic Plan (LDSP). The plan's key goals were to provide employment, a mix of housing intended to create a "social balance," and improved transport infrastructure. Whereas the Travers Morgan report focused almost solely on office and service sector development, the LDSP saw a continued role for industry. As such, it was viewed by the GLC as "a compromise between the interests of the private developers and the local workforce and community in Docklands."[27] Although some progress did occur, most notably in the building of hundreds of mixed-income housing units, the DJC had difficulty in both acquiring land that existing public utilities were reluctant to relinquish and securing the necessary financing.[28] The latter problem was aggravated by the stringent limits placed on central government spending by the International Monetary Fund (IMF) as part of the conditions on the loans it granted to the United Kingdom in 1976 (see Chapter 2 for details). While some notable changes had been introduced in the three years after the plan's publication, it was clear in light of massive increases in unemployment that a more radical approach would be required. While different visions were aired, the election of Margaret Thatcher's Conservative Party in 1979 ensured that a neoliberal design rather than a socialist one would win out.

The Enterprise Zones, Canary Wharf, and the LDDC

More than anywhere else in Britain, London Docklands was the place where neoliberal ideas were rendered concrete. The site for the two major urban policy innovations of the 1980s—the enterprise zone and the UDC—London's docks were the launching pad for the Thatcher government's ideological flagship. Standing in the heart of the enterprise zone and the LDDC is Canary Wharf, a development that today signifies the dominance of finance in the British political economy.

The Isle of Dogs Enterprise Zone

Enterprise zones were Chancellor of the Exchequer Geoffrey Howe's self-proclaimed "hobby-horse."[29] In his autobiography, Howe notes that Margaret Thatcher was reluctant to include his enterprise zone idea in the

Conservative Party election manifesto because "for her it smacked too much of 'regional policy,'" that is, the kind of approach that she associated with the managerialism of previous Labour and Conservative governments.[30] But Howe was "determined that the idea should survive, so [he] transformed it into a major speech," which he gave to the Bow Group in June 1978.[31] His choice of location for the speech—the famous Waterman's Arms pub on the Isle of Dogs—was no coincidence. As he describes it, "There, in the midst of dockland dereliction at its most depressing, I launched the idea of Enterprise Zones."[32] In his speech, Howe argued that the Docklands' "urban wilderness" was indicative of the "developing sickness of our society" in which "the burgeoning of State activity now positively frustrates healthy, private initiative, widely dispersed and properly rewarded."[33] In terms reminiscent of neoliberals in the United States, Howe argued that the "frustrating domination of widespread public land ownership and public intervention into virtually all private activities, has produced a form of municipal mortmain which will not be shifted without a huge effort of will."[34]

For Howe, the "British disease" of overregulation and economic decay could be overcome by the "fundamental reform of our tax system" and "the sensible deregulation of our economy."[35] As Chapter 2 noted, the Thatcher government recognized that it would take time to accumulate the necessary political capital to transform the entire British economy along these lines. But in Docklands, as in other urban areas, Howe saw an opportunity "to set up test market areas . . . to prime the pump of prosperity, and to establish their potential for doing so elsewhere."[36]

Thus, in Howe's view, the introduction of enterprise zones was not only a way of "trying out our ideas" but also a "kind of trial run intended to foster support for the other possible changes, which we sought to introduce more broadly in the British economy."[37] In retrospect, Howe considered his enterprise zone idea as "the trail-blazer for several other policies of the 1980s."[38] But the government's ambitions for the enterprise zones went still further. As Howe explained when he returned to Docklands to deliver a speech to the Bow Group in 1988, which commemorated his first public promotion of enterprise zones, his aim was to use the concept to help win the ideological battle over the future organization of the British economy:

> Equally the enterprise-zone concept was about fostering and encouraging a general change in attitudes towards economic freedom in this country. We knew that if radical solutions were going

to be popular, we had to make them attractive to the ordinary citizen. That would enable us to launch initiatives whose subsequent success would confirm those initial reactions. The zone concept was easily comprehensible, and would, we hoped, help win the political argument about the market at the same time as it cured the real problems of some inner-city sites.

As the years since 1979 have rolled on, so the enterprise culture we wanted has come into being. Now it is the established political wisdom of our time.[39]

Once he became chancellor upon the Conservative Party's election victory in 1979, Howe put his plans into action. In his 1980 budget, he announced that the government would establish "about half a dozen enterprise zones, with the intention that each of them should be developed with as much freedom as possible for those who work there to make profits and to create jobs."[40] Ultimately, the Conservatives enacted eleven enterprise zones with the most prominent of all located in the Isle of Dogs, in the heart of Docklands. Thus, once the place where the idea was born, Docklands now became the vehicle to showcase the ideas that underpinned the Thatcher government's neoliberal ideology.

The principal benefits available to businesses that located inside enterprise zones were two sacred cows for neoliberals both in America and Britain: relief from local and national taxes and reduced regulation. In particular, the enterprise zones offered the following benefits: exemptions from local authority rates (local taxes); 100 percent income tax or corporation tax allowances on construction and investment in all industrial and commercial buildings, which allowed developers to offset building costs against taxes owed; abolition of planning controls; exemption for firms from compulsory government statistical requirements; and "inward-processing relief" (i.e., duty-free import and reexport of unfinished goods originating outside what was then the European Community).[41] These benefits lasted for ten years.

A key difference between the American enterprise zones and those in Britain was the extent of the benefits offered to business. As Chapter 1 notes, there is a high degree of variation among the state enterprise zone programs in the United States. The most generous of the state initiatives, such as Indiana, Michigan, and Virginia, offer either total or substantial relief from state taxes. But none of these, since they are creatures of the states, can offer reductions or exemptions from federal taxes.[42] Moreover, federal regulations were still in effect in the zones. By contrast, the British zones, although not as radical as some of their most ardent supporters had hoped,[43] offered not only national *and* local tax exemptions but also a far more laissez-faire regulatory regime. When combined with the significant public investment delivered by the LDDC and with nationwide reductions in business taxes and regulation, these measures provided prospective investors with potent incentives to develop the land.

Some initial enterprise zone enthusiasts hoped that the tax and regulatory incentives would spark a revival in light industry in the Isle of Dogs that would provide jobs for local people.[44] However, the primary form of new activity that emerged was commercial and residential property development. Reg Ward, the first chief executive of the LDDC, was remarkably open about his disagreement with those who envisaged the enterprise zone as reviving or retaining industrial activity: "Philosophically one was actually against simply using the Enterprise Zone to re-establish the past. . . . So against the . . . intentions of government and civil servants I directed the Enterprise Zone really at [the] commercial sector and we were very fortunate in pulling that off."[45] Indeed, by way of example, Coupland points out that while Advanced Textile Products "had an impressively designed modern warehouse . . . it was fully computerized, employing only one person."[46] Since then, the building converted into office space. Moreover, one of only two other notable industrial development sites in the area—Cannon Workshops—was partially demolished to make way for Canary Wharf, the signature commercial development of the Thatcher era.

The Docklands enterprise zone is located almost exclusively on the northern half of the Isle of Dogs in the London boroughs of Tower Hamlets and Newham. It occupied 425 acres of land, that is, just under 10 percent of the entire Docklands area. The most comprehensive evaluation of the Isle of Dogs enterprise zone was conducted by the Department of the Environment in 1995.[47] It revealed that employment within the zone had grown from 641 in 1981 to a total of 10,300 by the end of 1991.[48] Two-thirds of these jobs were in the services sector, while the other third was in manufacturing. Moreover, the number of "establishments" within the zone had increased over the period from 90 to 433.[49] In respect of costs to the Exchequer, the report only disaggregated some by zone. For example, the estimated net cost of the capital allowances for the first round of enterprise zones from 1981 to 1993 was £489 million; unfortunately, the report does not provide the figures for the Isle of Dogs enterprise zone. There are, however, data on the cost of foregone rates (taxes). As one might expect, the Isle of Dogs zone is by far the most costly in this regard. The total was £92.89 million, 26.4 percent of the total amount forgone for all ten of the enterprise zones created in the first round.[50] In addition to the forgone revenues was approximately £850 million of public investment as of 1994. A 1998 report estimated that the total amount of public expenditure within the zone would be still higher.[51] Value-for-money estimates for London Docklands as a whole will be given below since the 1998 report does not disaggregate the enterprise zone figures from the total figures. Suffice it to say that, even when one considers the substantial leveraging that occurred, the cost to the public was extraordinary.

Canary Wharf

A vast office development in the heart of the Isle of Dogs enterprise zone, Canary Wharf's name dates back to the nineteenth century when goods arriving at West India Dock from the Canary Islands were stored there.[52] At the time of its 1980s reinvention, the Canary Wharf development was the largest completed by a single developer anywhere in Europe. But while its central structure—One Canada Square—would eventually become an icon of Tory Britain, the scheme's progress was plunged into uncertainty as international property markets deteriorated. Nevertheless, the Conservatives' financial reforms, in addition to specific steps the government took to ensure the viability of the scheme, resulted in Canary Wharf's remarkable success. Ultimately, it became central to London's rise as one of the world's most important financial centers, one of the world's few "global cities."

The original Canary Wharf project was conceived during the property boom of the mid-1980s. In 1985, G. Ware Travelstead, an American developer who headed First Boston Real Estate, compiled a consortium of U.S. banks to make an audacious proposal to build an 8.8 million square foot office development for financial and advanced services at a cost of £1.5 billion.[53] But as Fainstein reports, while the enterprise zone's tax and regulatory incentives might have piqued the interest of Travelstead and his backers, they were not sufficient. Rather, Travelstead made his proposals contingent upon the LDDC's commitment to extend the Docklands Light

Railway to Bank Station in the heart of the city of London and to undertake extensive road improvements at an estimated cost of £250 million.[54] However, despite the LDDC's agreement to both of these proposals, the consortium withdrew from negotiations in the summer of 1987. Although considerable design work and land acquisition had been completed, Travelstead was unable to secure the necessary financing as the estimated costs continued to spiral and withdrew its bid.

However, the project was not doomed. To the relief of government officials, the deal was salvaged almost immediately, as Toronto-based Olympia & York (O&Y) stepped in to assume control of the project. O&Y was founded by Paul Reichmann, who was impressed by the Thatcher government's economic reforms and who eventually became personal friends with the prime minister, who reportedly encouraged Reichmann to invest in Docklands. Indeed, Eric Sorensen, chief executive of the LDDC from 1991 to 1998, confirmed that Thatcher "had a particularly good relationship with Paul Reichmann . . . and I think the quality of that relationship was a very important part of the process of getting Canary Wharf going."[55]

O&Y's entrance into the London property market came on the back of its considerable success in developing the impressive World Financial Center in lower Manhattan's Battery Park City. In Docklands, the company committed to develop 4.6 million square feet by 1992 and 7 million afterward, proposed to pay £8.2 million to the LDDC for the land and to contribute £150 million to the upgrading of the Docklands Light Railway. Later, O&Y further pledged to contribute £400 million to the extension of the Jubilee Line, provided that it was routed through Canary Wharf. The LDDC agreed and the development proceeded. Thus, in May 1988, construction on One Canada Square began; by November 1990, the tallest building in Britain was complete.

It is worth noting, given the bargain price it sold the land for, that the LDDC potentially missed a historic opportunity to recoup funds from the development. Fainstein points out that the DOE, which was involved in the negotiations, raised the question of receiving a share in the profits from the development but decided against it on the grounds that the department and the LDDC "considered that to do so might jeopardize the whole development."[56]

Shortly after One Canada Square was completed, however, O&Y ran into major financial difficulties. The company faced a liquidity crisis as the transatlantic property market deteriorated in 1990. Despite the apparent oversupply of office space in Canary Wharf, O&Y continued to commit billions of dollars' worth of investment to the site. The Reichmann family attempted to liquidate some of its holdings but could not sell any of its real estate for a price greater than the debt owed on the property. Although Reichmann's financial difficulties in Battery Park City were obvious, he decided to take out an advert in the *Sunday Times* in a bid to reassure investors of Canary Wharf's ongoing credibility. In it, Reichmann argued that "on a scale of one to 10, if you say the risk with Battery Park was nine, here it would be one." Despite these entreaties, Reichmann failed to persuade prestigious financial firms in the city of London to move east to Canary Wharf. Although large American firms—Morgan Stanley, Bear Stearns, and Texaco—had been attracted successfully to the new site, British firms had been unimpressed.

At the time, some suggested that Reichmann failed to appreciate "the mystique of the City of London." One developer suggested that he went wrong because, like other North Americans, Reichmann had "no sense of place, or of history. He didn't realize that British people and businesses are tied by invisible threads to places: to the Bank of England or just to a set of streets, some shops, a restaurant."[57] This quaintly romantic vision would, of course, be exploded by subsequent events and almost certainly failed to articulate the role played by snobbery,[58] but by mid-1992, it appeared to explain the damning facts on the ground: 53 percent of Canary Wharf's office space was unlet. Furthermore, the lower than anticipated number of office workers also depressed retail vacancy rates.

In light of O&Y's ongoing difficulties on both sides of the Atlantic, the company's commercial paper (promissory note) was downgraded by a Canadian bond-rating agency that estimated that the value of O&Y's listed investments had fallen by 40 percent between 1990 and 1992. Following the downgrade, the company failed to make bond and mortgage payments on its holdings in New York and Canada. In a bid to avoid bankruptcy, O&Y took out loans worth $58 million to ensure that Canary Wharf would be equipped for the arrival of new tenants in mid-1992. However, by this time, O&Y had filed for bankruptcy protection in Canada, and its lenders had begun to assume possession of the company's Canadian holdings. In Britain, the government took a direct interest in trying to shore up O&Y's Canary Wharf venture. Not only had vast amounts of public money been spent on making Docklands viable, Thatcher was also adamant that her government's flagship urban innovation should not fail. She asserted that the government had a "moral obligation" to continue its support.[59] The government even considered moving the DOE to the site and eventually did move the headquarters of London Underground to Canary Wharf. But this desperate action was taken too late to salvage O&Y. The array of British banks that had invested approximately £550 million in the project refused to issue any more of the funds that were required to continue progress on the Jubilee Line. The creditors' patience had run out. Canary Wharf was therefore taken into administration and placed into the hands of accounting firm Ernst & Young by a British bankruptcy court.

For a brief period, therefore, Canary Wharf appeared to be a monumental failure. It has been suggested that some officials in Whitehall began referring to One Canada Square as the "Margaret Thatcher Memorial Tower." Others crowed that O&Y had "paid the price for Thatcherism." For the government's detractors, O&Y's collapse—which threatened to make a white elephant out of Canary Wharf—seemed for a moment to be an indictment of the avarice, hubris, and callousness that characterized Thatcherism. But what at first appeared to be Docklands' terminal decline proved to be but a brief interregnum.

What the critics neglected to take into account were the longer-term implications of the structural reorganization of the financial services industry that occurred during the 1980s. These began with the abolition of exchange controls in 1979, one of Geoffrey Howe's first acts as chancellor. Of even greater consequence were the reforms ushered in by Nigel Lawson, Margaret Thatcher's second Chancellor of the Exchequer, in 1986. Known as "the Big Bang," Lawson's deregulatory reforms weakened the city of London's grip on finance by allowing international ownership of British firms. It also abolished "fixed commissions" at the London Stock Exchange. This removed the separation between brokerage firms and securities firms. Not only did these changes inject vitality into the conservative world of finance, dominated by "old-boy networks," but they also attracted inward investment of capital from major foreign banks, which over the medium term would increase demand for modernized buildings with large electronic trading floors. This produced a wave of what journalist Anna Minton calls "'Big Bang' architecture" in the city and, most extensively, in Docklands. These reforms set the stage for London's emergence as a major hub in the network of global finance with Docklands at its heart.[60]

Thus, while the particular fluctuations of the global economy had undermined O&Y, deeper changes to the structure of Britain's financial services industry, over time, created demand for new office complexes with sophisticated technological capabilities. The government's intervention encouraged the supply to be located in Docklands. In a remarkable comeback, it was Paul Reichmann who played a central role in Canary Wharf's recovery. Having reportedly lost $10 billion, Reichmann leveraged his remaining $100 million to lead a group of investors to obtain a 10 percent share in the newly formed Canary Wharf Group (CWG). As the British economy recovered in the mid-1990s, CWG was able to attract new financial firms to Docklands through lower rental rates than the City of London and with the promise of lax planning regulations that enabled the rapid construction of purpose-built skyscrapers with the advanced fiber-optic connections that met the high-technology requirements of financial services organizations.

Perhaps the most symbolically important signal of Canary Wharf's rebirth was the arrival of the investment arm of Barclays Bank to the complex. In Fainstein's estimation, "this move marked the acceptability of the address to British firms."[61] Others would soon follow. In 1996 and 1998, respectively, deals were struck to build two forty-four-floor towers to house Citibank's European headquarters and HSBC's global headquarters, which would add an additional 3.5 million square feet. In the meantime, the Canary Wharf Group boasted that its existing 4.5 million square feet of office space was 98 percent occupied. By 1997, Canary Wharf's working population reached 19,000. In the same year, newly elected Labour Prime Minister Tony Blair chose Canary Wharf as the location for his first Anglo-French summit. Thus, as Docklands' economic status was secured, so too was its political importance. Blair could do no better in illustrating New Labour's settlement with financial capital than to host the summit in the very place that symbolized the rebirth of British finance.

In a sign of New Labour's embrace of finance, Canary Wharf went from strength to strength. By October 2000, Canary Wharf Group entered into the Financial Times Stock Exchange (FTSE)100 as the largest property company in Britain. Since then, development on and around Canary Wharf has continued apace. City Airport—much resisted by local residents—was completed in 1987 and expanded during the 1990s. The One Canada Square shopping mall has expanded significantly, attracting luxury retailers such as Tiffany & Co. and Jaeger. Moreover, once a minnow competing with the city of London, the Canary Wharf Group expanded its operations to the Square Mile with the construction of Drapers Gardens, which in 2010 was successfully let to BlackRock, the world's largest asset management firm. In the same year, 97.1 percent of CWG's property space was fully let, and the market value of its properties was an estimated £411.5 million. In its annual report, the company anticipated, despite the subdued British economy, that "rental rates levels at Canary Wharf will increase in 2011."[62] Thus, with the central forty-eight-story skyscraper, One Canada Square, now joined by several other towers, which host the most prominent financial, legal, and energy companies of our time, Canary Wharf today stands as a tribute to neoliberalism—the physical manifestation of an ideological and class triumph.[63]

The London Docklands Development Corporation

The creation of the UDCs, the other major urban policy development of the 1980s, also had major implications for Docklands. The LDDC was one of the first two UDCs to be created by the Conservative government under the Local Government Planning and Land Act (LGPLA) of 1980. Its creator was Michael Heseltine, secretary of state for the environment. Compared to enterprise zones, UDCs reflected a more ambitious view about the role government should play in promoting neoliberalization. While enterprise zone promoters aimed to sever the "dead hand" of the state that was responsible for Docklands' moribund condition, UDC enthusiasts considered that, with insulation from local democratic pressures, the state could be the midwife of capitalist revival.

Having concluded that the existing Docklands' bodies—the local authorities and the DJC—were incapable of tackling the scale of the problem at hand, Heseltine's UDCs were quasi-autonomous nongovernmental organizations (QUANGOs), run by unelected boards, and answerable to the secretary of state. The LDDC, in Heseltine's view, would be free from ideologically motivated opposition and would have the freedom to focus on the economic transformation of the area. Heseltine justified usurping local authorities' power on the basis that "there is a need for a single-minded determinism not possible for the local authorities concerned with their much broader responsibilities."[64]

As the Local Government Planning and Land Act stated, "The object of an urban development corporation shall be to secure the regeneration of its area," by "bringing land and buildings into effective use, encouraging the development of existing and new industry and commerce, creating an attractive environment and ensuring that housing and social facilities are available to encourage people to live and work in the area."[65] The act empowered the secretary of state to vest land in the UDCs and provided them with development control, which in practice meant that the corporations could grant themselves planning permission by resolution.[66] Put simply, the act enabled the central government in Westminster to transfer local public ownership of the land into the hands of the UDC, which in turn would sell it to private corporations. The Docklands case illustrates how this was done. In Heseltine's view, it was through institutions such as the LDDC that the "culture of the enterprise system" was "forcibly injected" into local actors' attitudes.[67]

Far larger than the enterprise zone, the LDDC covered 5,500 acres of land located in the boroughs of Tower Hamlets, Newham, and Southwark. The ability of these local, democratically accountable political institutions to shape this development was curtailed by Heseltine's decision to place the local authorities' land and planning powers into the hands of the LDDC. In 1981, Heseltine named Nigel Broackes as the first chairman of the LDDC. Described by the *Times* newspaper as "Britain's most elegant tycoon," Broackes was the chairman of Trafalgar House, a property, shipping, and engineering conglomerate.[68] Given that Broackes was "well known within the City and market institutions," it followed that "under this kind of control the UDCs have tended to pursue market-oriented strategies within their designated areas."[69] Early on, Broackes pithily summed up his approach with a rhetorical question he put to the *Guardian* newspaper in 1981: "Why face aggravation from Councils opposed to the profit motive and home ownership?"[70] Broackes earned the scorn of local residents, whom he described as "surplus population."[71]

Broackes was joined by Chief Executive Reg Ward, a quixotic maverick who described himself as a "dreamer with both feet planted firmly in the air."[72] Ward's antipathy to planning and his insistence on nothing less than a clean break from Docklands' industrial past made him an ideal, if heterodox, partner for Heseltine. Ward's unequivocal rejection of urban planning echoes the neoliberal critique of regulation more broadly: "I believe our planning system inhibits thinking, inhibits opportunities, doesn't create them. It is also detached from the realities of the marketplace . . . at the LDDC we have gone for an organic approach, rather than a traditional masterplan, and if you don't react to it conceptually then you are really not for us."[73] As local efforts were afoot to try to salvage what was left of industry on the Isle of Dogs, Ward remained trenchant in his opposition to plans that envisaged a future for dock work or manufacturing more generally: "Whilst it was socio-economically attractive to espouse bringing back the docks [and] manufacturing industry, the reality was that they had both gone and there was no reason why [they] should ever conceive of returning."[74] With respect to the local population, Ward averred that "their future didn't lie in the past but lay in an entirely new range of activities."[75] This position was not simply based on a sober empirical evaluation of the range of possibilities but rather on an ideologically informed view that presented assertions about the inevitable decline of industry as facts. Ward and the LDDC were also opposed to the construction of more public housing in favor of selling public land to private interests for the development of high-end commercial and residential property. These choices were presented as the only available alternative for Docklands. In this way, the central planks of the ideological infrastructure that buttressed neoliberalization were laid.

As a result, the vast majority of development in Docklands involved office construction and luxury housing. But in contrast to what would be expected from a "growth coalition" perspective, key real estate developers were initially resistant. It would take time and persuasion by ideologically motivated political actors to attract private-sector investment. In the words of Broackes: "To start with, the house builders were not interested, but we managed to persuade people like Wimpey and Barratts and Comben (major house builders) to try a pilot scheme."[76] This is corroborated by a director of a leading house-building firm who explained that the industry did not consider that Docklands had potential: "I think we were just frightened to death by the scale of it to be frank with you."[77] As such, "the LDDC barely broke even on its land sales; on the Isle of Dogs its initial offerings sold for about £80,000 per acre."[78]

But by the mid-1980s, Docklands was hot. A speculative boom trebled land values, with some parcels sold at £3 million per acre. As a result, the vast majority of the 24,000 housing units completed in Docklands was intended for owner occupation and sold at prices well beyond the reach of the local population. In the feverish atmosphere in post–Big Bang Britain, house prices shot up overnight. The example of the price of two-bedroom flats in the Clipper's Quay development is illustrative. In June 1985, the flats were priced at £47,500. By January 1986, the price had risen to £74,500. Thirteen months later, in March 1987, the cost of the same flats stood at £199,950, an increase of over 300 percent in just twenty-one months. These kinds of price explosions even drew the criticism of house builders and developers who in one case suggested that the LDDC should have prevented "the dramatic increase in land values" driven by the "greed of housing developers and speculators."[79] It would seem that the inflation in the overall economy had not been slayed after all but rather transferred into property prices. But boom inevitably turned to bust on Black Monday in October 1987, when stock prices plummeted and residential and commercial land prices collapsed. However, over the 1990s and 2000s, the economy recovered, and successive governments allowed property prices to spiral once more.

In 1998, the newly constituted Department of the Environment, Transport and the Regions (DETR) conducted a study of Docklands that enables an evaluation of the overall effects of the government's intervention via the enterprise zone and the LDDC. The total estimated public-sector costs associated with the project were £3.9 billion.[80] Approximately £1.81 billion of this amount was associated with transportation and infrastructural spending, and £1.06 billion of this cost arose from foregone tax receipts. Just £243 million (6 percent) was dedicated to social housing and community facilities. Total private-sector investment was estimated at £8.7 billion. DETR estimated that, although 84,000 jobs had been created within the LDDC's boundaries, only 23,000 could be attributed to the enterprise zone and the LDDC's activities. As a result, the cost per net additional job for the local economy of the boroughs of Tower Hamlets, Southwark and Newham, was estimated at £56,000 at 1998 prices, although the report claims that this cost may fall "to perhaps £36,000 at end state," that is, by 2010 or 2015.[81] In light of these extraordinary costs, it is highly doubtful that they equate to good value for money. Moreover, given that the vast majority of beneficiaries were the wealthy, this seems to be a case of upward transfer of resources, a hallmark of the neoliberal turn.

And yet, neoliberals see Docklands as a testament to the righteousness of their ideas. Clearly, the area has been radically transformed and is now the site of tremendous innovation and economic activity. Indeed, in some regards, local Docklanders undoubtedly benefited from improved transportation infrastructure and a modest increase in affordable housing, what might be called positive externalities. Thus, as Fainstein points out, "Within the terms of the LDDC's mandate, Canary Wharf can now be seen as a total success in relation to the goal of reviving the economy of the Isle of Dogs."[82] However, the overwhelming beneficiaries were those who came from outside the area to live and work. For those whose jobs had disappeared with the docks, the new gleaming towers of finance and retail offered few opportunities.

Was There an Alternative?

Mrs. Thatcher was (in)famous for her claim that "there is no alternative" (TINA) to her wrenching economic reforms. This formulation has been used countless times to frame opponents to change as intransigent fantasists. This rhetorical move was also favored by architects of New Labour as they sought to brand opponents as simply unrealistic.[83] As Imbroscio notes, this ostensible realism has also been deployed by American liberals (and neoliberals) who have argued over the years that cities have no choice but to abandon progressive policies in favor of ones that march to the tune of capital.[84] So, too, for London Docklands. Proponents of change argued that the past was dead and that nothing other than a radical shift would do. But despite these attempts to manipulate the terms of the public debate, local residents and political groups attempted not only to register their disapproval but also to forge an alternative vision for Docklands.

The institutional design and the operational style of the LDDC systematically excluded local people and their representatives from the process. Having insulated itself from local popular control, the LDDC failed to provide the formal opportunity for public participation. The LDDC board was accountable only to Parliament, met in secret until 1986, and was not required to publish minutes or agendas.[85] As a result, especially in the early years, local people were barely consulted about major redevelopments on their doorsteps. Of course, this was the point. Local democratic control was seen as inimical to the area's success. Reg Ward—always plainspoken—provides an insight into the LDDC's attitude: "Local people then were an obstacle best avoided and little was done to assist or include them."[86] As one LDDC executive explained, "We didn't have time to be nice to people, to consult with people, because we actually had to demonstrate that this experiment set up by Michael Heseltine was the way forward."[87] As a board member acknowledged, "For part of one whole generation . . . there was nothing we could do to alter their future . . . there would be a significant sector of people who would gain nothing."[88] Thus, from the outset, the aim was not to use public investment and intervention to help those communities ravaged by deindustrialization.

In his seminal 1978 enterprise zones speech, Howe described Docklands as an "urban wilderness." But this stands in contrast to the reality on the ground. While it is clear that the closing of the docks (not complete until after the speech) and the decline in concomitant dock-related industries had decimated the local economy, thousands still lived in the area, many of whom had work and were actively engaged in trying to forge a future for themselves and their families. Indeed, leafing through the archival documents, one finds a plethora of civic organizations engaged in serious, long-term activism *and* planning.[89]

As early as 1979, archival evidence reveals that those who opposed the creation of the LDDC were actively engaged in making their views known and proposing alternatives, such as the implementation of the 1976 Strategic Plan for London Docklands. Submissions to the government were made from an array of groups, including the Surrey Docks Society, the Newham Community Renewal Programme, the Lambeth Inner City Consultative Group, and the Docklands Forum.[90] The replies from the DOE illustrate its keenness to sugarcoat the proposals and send a clear signal that no alternatives would be considered. In a response to Reverend Paul Regan of the Newham Churches Renewal Programme, a DOE official assures him that "none of this [the creation of UDCs] means disenfranchising the local population."[91] Yet, as early as 1980, it was becoming obvious that the government intended to move forward with the creation of the LDDC irrespective of intense local opposition. In a letter from Michael Heseltine to Kevin Halpin, chairman of the Docklands Forum, the secretary of state turned down the invitation to discuss the plans: "I have to say, however, that a meeting would not change my views and I hope very much for the greater good of Docklands as a whole, we can work together to ensure that the UDC, when set up, can get ahead with all speed."[92] In a final example, the DOE received an eighteen-page petition organized by the East End Docklands Action Group signed by 162 local residents. It stated, "There is no need for a UDC as the plans already exist to develop adequate housing, industry, leisure, and health facilities and public transport in Docklands.

All that is needed for the implementation of these plans is the finance that has been promised."[93] But this fell on deaf ears.

Still, opponents did take full advantage of one parliamentary avenue open to them: the House of Lords. In a concession to get the Local Government Planning and Land Bill through Parliament without the need for a public inquiry to set up UDCs, the government allowed the bill to include provisions for petitions to the House of Lords. The bitter irony—that the only refuge for those seeking to exercise their democratic right to object to decisions taken by public officials was the unelected and unaccountable Upper Chamber—was surely not lost on the LDDC's detractors. Petitions were filed by numerous local business organizations, trade union councils, local authorities, and individuals. They included but were not limited to the Newham Chamber of Commerce; the GLC; the councils of Newham, Southwark, and Tower Hamlets; the Surrey Docks Child Care Project; the Tower Hamlets Trade Council; and the Association of Island Communities. This list both signals the breadth of opposition to the creation of the LDDC and highlights the depth of civic life in Docklands.

Their lordships devoted considerable time—forty-six days of hearings —to the petition, which delayed the official establishment of the LDDC by more than a year.[94] The Select Committee Report confirmed that the Docklands Joint Committee's progress on implementing the LDSP had been rather limited, especially in respect of housing and employment.[95] But contrary to claims that before the enterprise zone and the LDDC, the Docklands was in terminal decline, the report noted that a "substantial amount of progress has been made since 1976 in areas other than industry and housing."[96] Examples included major infrastructure development, the creation of the London Industrial Park, the creation of the new Billingsgate Fish Market, and the new printing works for News International. However, the lords ultimately concluded that, these welcome developments notwithstanding, "the area is very badly in need of regeneration."[97] Thus, the authors essentially accepted the TINA view: "The boroughs tend to look too much to the past and too exclusively to the aspirations of the local population and too little to the possibility of regenerating Docklands by the introduction of new types of industry and new types of housing." Although the report did require proper consultation, it provided no mechanism by which it would be guaranteed or consequential: it stated that the local population should "know what the Corporation is thinking, so they can express their views on any proposal and it must make it clear that such views, even if not accepted, are always seriously considered."

As to the central question of what body should promote regeneration, the committee was clear: "A UDC is more likely to attract private investment into the area than the boroughs and the DJC."[98] While the committee sympathized with locals' concerns, it ultimately backed the government's position: "The Committee [is] conscious that to transfer development control over so wide an area from democratically elected councils to a body appointed by the Secretary of State is a step which is not easily justified, especially in an area such as Docklands where the attachment to local democracy was shown to be so strong; but . . . the Committee think[s] that the Government [has] made out their case. Accordingly, the Committee recommends that the principle of a UDA and a UDC for the London docklands should be accepted."[99]

The House of Lords' decision was in part based on the sanguine view that opposition to the LDDC "will gradually die away" since the "Chairman designate [Nigel Broackes] of the UDC has made it clear that he is well aware that if a UDC is to be a success, it must work in harmony with the boroughs and give due consideration to the views of the local population."[100] In light of the difference between Broackes's contrition before the committee and his subsequent views about the local community illustrated above, it was evident the waning of the local community's opposition would not be so gradual. However, the residents did more than simply oppose. Most notably, they attempted to forge an alternative vision through the "People's Plan."[101]

A plethora of well-organized and committed local groups devoted considerable time and resources into organizing around the key challenges presented by the LDDC. The most notable of these were the Association of Island Communities (AIC) and the Docklands Forum. They were supported financially by local councils and had good links with the local Labour Party and the GLC, which by the early eighties was led by then-socialist and provocateur Ken Livingstone. A constant thorn in Margaret Thatcher's side until she abolished it, the GLC, in partnership with the Newham Docklands Forum, developed the "People's Plan for the Royal Docks." The plan presented an alternative strategy for housing and economic development in Docklands based on the principle of "popular planning," which opened the process to local residents, employers, and community groups. In respect of employment, the plan proposed to reuse part of the docks for cargo handling.[102] This suggestion was based upon the findings of a report by Roger Tym that the docks could be viable if they focused on servicing short sea routes within Europe.[103] The plan also called for new public housing and a childcare scheme that would both create jobs and support local working families. Not surprisingly, the plan was rejected out-of-hand by the LDDC. So, too, were other proposals that sought to find compromise between the "needs-based" People's Plan and the market-oriented LDDC vision. For example, the London Borough of Newham accepted the LDDC's proposals for City Airport, unlike the People's Plan, but pressed for more action on affordable housing and employment. However, the LDDC's willingness for land to be used for luxury flats and commercial real estate won out.

During the latter half of its time, however, the LDDC did make more sincere efforts to engage the local community, although this was always discretionary.[104] This reflected a rhetorical shift in government policy toward "social regeneration," which occurred in the aftermath of a third successive Conservative Party general election victory in 1987. There were also substantive changes in the LDDC's approach, the most notable of which was the new Community Services Division, which was set up with an initial budget of £60 million.

But the most important reason for the LDDC's more cooperative stance was the changing local political climate that emerged in the mid-1980s. The first significant shift came about when the Liberal Party gained control of the Tower Hamlets council in 1986. Far more consensual than their radical Labour predecessors, the Liberals were prepared to work with the LDDC. Even more significant was the effect of the Conservative victory in the 1987 general election. Stephen Timms, then chair of planning in the London borough of Newham and later a member of Tony Blair's cabinet, explained the strategic shift that occurred:

> There had been a bit of a hope that we would get the Tories out [in 1987] and that all these horrible things that we had to deal with would be abolished and that we could go back to how things were. It didn't turn out like that of course, not by a mile, and so we then had to think: well, what was our response? The response that I took forward as chair of planning, and then later leader [of Newham Council], was that we needed to negotiate on behalf of our community to get the best out of what was being proposed. The very

pragmatic, not particularly ideological approach. We had lost and
we needed to make the best of it.[105]

Thus, without the institutional avenues traditionally open in well-
functioning democratic systems, the LDDC's detractors gradually gave up,
were co-opted, or splintered into warring factions increasingly suspicious
not only of the LDDC but also of each other. One local resident summed
up the disempowering effect of institutions such as the LDDC: "It comes
home to you that this is no longer a democratic idea, you've got no democratic rights at all . . . I can't vote them out if I don't like it. . . . They're an
autonomous authority."[106] But perhaps most crucially, the most powerful
political force locally and nationally—the Labour Party—not only began to
accept the new political reality of dealing with the Conservatives but also
came to accept key tenets of the neoliberal worldview.

New Labour, New Docklands?

The LDDC was wound up in 1998, a year after Labour came back into
power under Tony Blair's leadership. Responsibility for Docklands was
placed in the hands of English Partnerships, another nondepartmental public body, and the London borough of Newham, to which the LDDC's planning powers were restored. As noted in Chapter 3, New Labour's urban
policy revolved around two key planks: a design-oriented approach that
sought to bring about an "urban renaissance" primarily aimed at making
the inner cities attractive to the middle classes[107] and a "social exclusion"
approach intended to tackle deprivation.[108] While the latter was not exclusively an urban policy per se, since so many deprived wards are located
within urban areas, it was a de facto urban policy. As such, the Labour
government was less concerned with grand place-based initiatives in its
early years but rather focused on developing "strategic partnerships"
intended to bring various government resources to bear. This approach
envisaged a role for local authorities not dissimilar from the one envisaged
by their Conservative predecessors.

As Johnstone and Whitehead maintain, Labour embraced the Tories'
commitment to competitive bidding for urban spending but tried to direct
it toward deprived areas. Under the inherited Single Regeneration Budget,
80 percent of the resources were sent to the fifty most deprived wards in

the United Kingdom.[109] These included wards in Docklands. But while Johnstone and Whitehead see both "an acceptance and rejection of Thatcherism" in Labour's urban policy,[110] Ward and Jones maintain that "New Labour's approach to British cities has distinct neo-liberal undertones, albeit couched in 'new language'. Heavy state intervention is justified in terms of 'freeing' markets."[111] And as the case of the LDDC illustrates, this approach is entirely consistent with the Conservative past.

But Johnstone and Whitehead's characterization should not be summarily dismissed as false. Clearly, the "third way" involves significant departures from Thatcherism. In the British context, the introduction of the minimum wage by Labour and record investment in the National Health Service would be cases in point. However, the key issue that concerns us here is the degree to which Labour's urban policies reflect neoliberal approaches more generally than in their Thatcherite mode. In this context, the answer is clear. While Labour's concerns were *in part* directed toward the poor and working class, the party was also committed to promoting the role of finance, assuming that the two were unrelated or could even be reinforcing. Its refusal until 2008 to increase the top rate of tax on individuals and its tax cuts for corporations reflect this. Former Labour cabinet minister, John Denham, highlights the obvious tension within this approach: "Rather than attempt to extend elements of social justice into the private sector economy we have preferred to run social justice and the market as parallel activities, relying on the free-market economy to provide the wealth from which the social justice can be created."[112] Moreover, Labour's understanding of inner-city poverty and unemployment reflects the neoliberal view that such phenomena arise out of individual deficiency rather than as a result of structural failures entrenched in the political economy.[113] The answer, therefore, is to address those deficiencies at a micro level rather than consider a macroeconomic reorientation. Hence the creation of the Social Exclusion Unit, the Neighborhood Renewal Unit, the introduction of "welfare to work,"[114] and the urban regeneration companies. All these institutions were designed, in Tony Blair's words, "to give people a hand up, not a hand-out."[115]

With respect to governance, Labour once again emulated its neoliberal predecessors. Largely, responsibility has not returned to the local authorities but instead to supra-local quangos such as neighborhood renewal teams, local strategic partnerships, and regional development agencies.[116] Each of these institutions is insulated from local popular control and involves *by design* a built-in role for business. Moreover, that the transformation of the Labour Party nationally was mirrored at the local level in Docklands reflects the accommodations that New Labour made with ideas once associated only with the right. For instance, as Buck et al. point out, the Labour council in Southwark "now accepts the revolution the LDDC wrought, and is pushing towards its logical conclusion through the pursuit of private investment and a more affluent population."[117] Moreover, in Newham, the Labour leader (and later mayor) Sir Robin Wales and Chief Executive Wendy Thompson both promoted the government's "modernization" agenda, which built directly on the LDDC's work during Labour's first term (1997–2001). At its heart, this understanding of modernization is rooted in the classically neoliberal belief that interurban competition and partnership with the private sector, rather than local democratic institutions, are required to deliver the kind of change "consumers" desire. As Hoskins and Tallon note, this involves the unremitting gentrification—sold as "urban renaissance"—of the Docklands boroughs, as reflected in the skyrocketing rise of house prices in the borough of Tower Hamlets, home to Canary Wharf.[118]

As Hamnett observes, even the 2000 election of Ken Livingstone as mayor of London (2000–2008) did not alter the government's approach to Docklands and to finance more broadly: "Livingstone has committed himself to strengthening London's role as a major international financial center rather than trying to resist it."[119] As a result, the poor are either being squeezed out of the East End or are "slowly being encircled with luxury riverside developments and conversions which are increasing the divisions between rich and poor in the new London."[120] Indeed, Tower Hamlets Labour MP Jim Fitzpatrick is a great supporter of the LDDC, Canary Wharf, and the role of finance, despite the hostility of many constituents:

> I got into a lot of bother with my local party because I commended
> Lord Heseltine and his vision for . . . the LDDC initiative . . .
> because the LDDC was much hated. The freedom of planning con-
> trols that they had unfettered the right to be able to build what
> they wanted, where they wanted without having to formally con-
> sult with local communities meant that they were almost at war
> with many on the Isle of Dogs, around the Canary Wharf ferry
> area and Tower Hamlets. . . . But in reality, without the LDDC,
> Canary Wharf would have taken 20–25 years instead of the 10

years it took to construct and I don't think one can undervalue the significance and the importance not just to Docklands and East London but to London both as our nation's capital and [as] one of the world's major financial centers.[121]

Despite the plethora of initiatives that Labour launched to address problems of deprivation, conditions in the Docklands local authorities remained extremely alarming. The British government produces an "Index of Multiple Deprivation" for every local authority in England, which is a composite measure of deprivation that includes income and employment; health and disability; education, skills, and training deprivation; barriers to housing and services; living environment; and crime. In 2010, Tower Hamlets ranked as the third most deprived local authority in London (out of 33) and the seventh most deprived in England as a whole (out of 326). Furthermore, the percentage of children living in "income-deprived households" in Tower Hamlets was 59.1 percent, the highest rate in England, and unemployment stood at 15 percent.[122] Meanwhile, between 1995 and 2000, house prices in the borough rose by 161 percent, the highest rise of any local authority in the country.[123] Moreover, the average wage of those who worked (but did not necessarily live) in the area in 2009 was £64,000.[124] As with Philadelphia, the neoliberal turn has delivered wealth to the lucky few but failed to help the middle and has failed to arrest, or perhaps even contributed to, grinding poverty.

Conclusion: Interpreting the Transformation of Docklands

How should one interpret the reinvention of Docklands in the neoliberal era? Answers to this question are a source of controversy among urban scholars. While most agree that the enterprise zone and the LDDC reflected the Tories' pro-market ideological convictions, a number of academics have suggested that these policies reflect a jumble of contradictory positions, rather than a coherent neoliberal program. For example, Sue Brownill's most recent work softens the more strident tone she struck in her original findings on Docklands, produced in the mid-1990s, when the future of the development was in doubt.[125] Brownill argues that to describe even the "early years" of the LDDC (1980–1987) as a period of neoliberalization "would be an oversimplification."[126] Looking at Docklands over the past four decades as a whole, Brownill sees not simply an ideological assault but rather a "place where different discourses, different governance arrangements, and different practices of planning co-existed and interacted."[127] Thus, Docklands is less a neoliberal animal than a hybrid creature reflected in the different ideological and political compromises layered over time.

Brownill is certainly not alone in this view. For example, her work draws on Mike Raco's finding that such developments "contain within them competing and conflicting agendas" that produce a "hybridity of development discourses."[128] Furthermore, in respect of Docklands specifically, Cochrane maintains that UDCs "were not pure children of Thatcher because they drew on a clear cut interventionist agenda."[129] Along similar lines, Barnes et al. detect what they see as a contradiction between the principles of Thatcherism and the development of Docklands: "The Conservatives' strategy was not wholly the market-orientated exercise in free enterprise and 'non-planning' it purported to be. It required, and later demanded, state intervention on an unprecedented scale."[130]

What these authors have in common is a fundamental misunderstanding of neoliberal political development that not only risks reducing ideology to mere rhetoric but also underestimates the indispensable role of the state in furthering the neoliberal project. On the first point, it should come as no surprise that there is often a significant gap between rhetoric and reality and between theory and practice. Politicians are perennially concerned about the effect of their decisions on their own or their party's electoral prospects. This may mean, therefore, that when circumstances demand, they take positions that appear to be in conflict with their previously stated goals. But this does not necessarily mean that ideological concerns are either irrelevant or always trumped by short-term political gain. The more fundamental objection to Brownill's, Raco's, and Barnes et al.'s position—that the myriad examples of state intervention suggest hybridity rather than neoliberalism—is that it rests on the notion that the state, for neoliberals, is always something to be curtailed. One can point to numerous statements by Thatcher and Reagan to the effect that each action the state takes is inimical to the freedom of its citizens. But this *is* pure rhetoric and should be taken as such.

Neoliberals' objection is not to the state per se but rather to the behavior of the state. Thus, the goal is not the destruction of the state but rather its *reorientation*. To the extent that the state intervenes to promote markets, privilege capital, and resist claims on private property, it is a most welcome weapon in the neoliberal armory—recall Hayek's notion of "planning for competition."[131] Moreover, the case of Docklands underscores Peck and Tickell's understanding of "roll-back" and "roll-out" neoliberalism, wherein the state is on one hand stripped away only to be replaced by new state institutions that function according to alternative politically and ideologically motivated criteria.[132] However, the key difference illuminated by the Docklands case is that these two functions occur *simultaneously* in time and space. The enterprise zones "rolled back" the state while the LDDC "rolled out" new state institutions whose goal was to promote the transfer of public land into private hands.

Finally, the political-economic development of Docklands illustrates the decisive role of ideas carried by politicians who drove the project forward. What initially appears as a straightforward case of what Fainstein calls "property-led development" undertaken by the kind of pro-growth coalition envisaged by Logan and Molotch turns out to be more complex.[133] Although capital interests were the undisputed victors of Docklands' redevelopment, it was not they who pressed for it. As was the case for U.S. federal urban policy, capital triumphed but did not lead the charge. Rather, this was a *political-ideological* effort, which had durable institutional effects. This is why it is imperative to pay close attention to the *sequencing* of political development, not simply to the outcomes and the key beneficiaries. The objective of neoliberals in the British context was to enhance the central state's power *for the purpose* of achieving ideologically determined goals— that is, the preference for an increased role for business, private property, and markets in urban areas. As such, the LDDC represents an interesting manifestation of neoliberal urban policy, which points to what at first glance appears to be a contradiction between neoliberalism in theory and practice but instead is simply what David Harvey and Brenner and Theodore call "actually existing neoliberalism."[134]

But if ideas provided the motive, institutions presented the opportunity.[135] Unlike the American case—where federalism, separation of powers, and divided government stymied the efforts of neoliberals at the national level to radically transform places like Philadelphia from the White House—Conservative politicians in Britain were able to exploit the capacity of centralized state institutions to remake Docklands anew. But the significance of the deployment of political institutions that the Docklands case highlights is not limited to their role in smoothing the path for change; they also become the tools to advance the neoliberal agenda, as the LDDC illustrates. Not only was the purpose of the LDDC to turn over public land into private hands, but its role as a quasi-nongovernmental organization enabled these fundamentally political decisions to be taken without any formal mechanism for popular democratic control. Hence, ideas and institutions interacted to produce *neoliberalism by design*. In Philadelphia, by contrast, politicians cast in a non-neoliberal mold *reacted* to changing economic and ideological dynamics and opted for *neoliberalism by default*.

One might be tempted to conclude that Canary Wharf, lying at the heart of the enterprise zone and the Docklands Development Corporation, is a tribute to Thatcherism or a relic of a bygone era. However, to associate the triumph of financial capital exclusively with the Thatcher government would be blinkered. For as shown in Chapter 3, the shift from a Keynesian to a neoliberal political economy is not simply the work of those in Conservative (or Republican) circles but rather one ushered in and consolidated by politicians, media, and businesspeople themselves, from across the party political divide. Once the province of the right wing of the Conservative Party, over time, the benefits of ever greater tax relief and deregulation, including the penchant for "flexible" labor markets, became common sense among elites in the Labour Party and the Democrats. The results, as we have seen, for people in London Docklands and in Philadelphia have diverged along class and racial lines. For those in the sky rises, the neoliberal era has been an unqualified boon. But little has trickled down into the neoliberal trenches. For these urban outcasts, the neoliberal political economy offers little.

Conclusion. The Neoliberal Persuasion

> In one sense we dismantled parts of the state that the right wouldn't touch . . . the way we locked ourselves into a model of indentured consumption through the housing market . . . Brown, Blair they bought into the whole Greenspan model of self-correcting laws of economics in terms of perfecting the neo-classical frameworks, which meant that there was no reason to assume that this wouldn't go on. So it was rational to keep on borrowing, because growth was locked in. Now if the music stops, and you hit the buffers, who will pick up the cheque?[1]
>
> —Jon Cruddas, Labour MP for East Ham

> You're basically improving the quality of life for people who are getting poorer. That's the situation of America.[2]
>
> —Donna Cooper, deputy mayor of Philadelphia for policy and planning under Ed Rendell

Out of the tumult of the 1970s, the ideas and programmatic commitments that had held sway since the 1930s and 1940s were abandoned. In the decades that followed, the institutions associated with New Deal and Great Society liberalism in the United States and those that emerged from the postwar settlement in the United Kingdom were recast in a neoliberal mold. If these institutions and commitments have not been dismantled in their entirety since then, they have been radically reconfigured.

This book has argued that the neoliberal political-economic order that was forged in the 1970s and 1980s by radicals in the Conservative Party in Britain and by Republicans in America set into motion a new trajectory of political-economic development. That the opposition Labour and Demo-cratic Parties in their respective countries became persuaded by and ulti-mately adopted many of the key ideas, policy instruments, and institutional forms bequeathed by their predecessors confirms that this change consti-tutes a "durable shift" not only in governing authority and capacity[3] but also in the relationship between the state, market, and citizen. While this claim finds support among British academics[4]—although certainly not unanimity—scholars of American political development have tended to view the New Deal/Great Society order as more or less intact, if buffeted by waves of conservative attack.[5] While Jacob S. Hacker and Paul Pierson have adopted a political-economic approach to chart the emergence of the "winner-take-all" politics that has resulted in spiraling inequity, they pay scant attention to the role of ideas and do not connect this development with neoliberalism.[6] As Jamie Peck points out, it is ironic that the United States is one of the few places in which "mainstream" scholarly analysis tends not to engage neoliberalism as a conceptual tool.[7] Perhaps it is impos-sible to see the elephant in the room because it is so close up.

As has been demonstrated, a focus on national urban policy and local urban politics clarifies the degree to which the ideas propagated primarily by right-wing politicians of the 1970s and 1980s played a key role in shaping national policy and transforming urban political institutions and in deter-mining local political-economic outcomes. Part I illustrated how urban pol-icies reflect and in some cases advance the economic and social goals of national governments. In particular, the enterprise zone and the urban development corporation served to distill neoliberal ideas into concrete institutional designs. Part II provided a grounded account of how the battle to neoliberalize the British and American political economies was waged in the urban trenches. The case of London Docklands illustrated the unambig-uous, top-down pattern of *neoliberalism by design* through which local democracy was hollowed out as power was wrested from local authorities and placed in the hands of unaccountable political appointees at the Lon-don Docklands Development Corporation (LDDC) by the British state. Moreover, it was the location of the flagship enterprise zone, the ultimate place-based articulation of neoliberalism. These early innovations were cru-cial for the subsequent emergence of Canary Wharf, in the heart of Dock-lands, as a key node in the international network of global financial capital, which in turn promoted the financialization of the British political economy.

The effect of these activities has been to concentrate power in the hands of the financial class. One is tempted to suggest that the Docklands example underscores Marx's claim that the "executive of the modern state is but a committee for managing the common affairs of the whole bourgeoisie."[8] However, as my analysis shows, the bourgeoisie was not knocking on doors in Washington, D.C. or Westminster to demand enterprise zones or urban development corporations. Instead, these innovations were part of political-ideological projects that did not emerge from, although no doubt resulted in, the restoration of class power in the hands of the "1 percent." This underscores the argument made throughout that the relative influence of ideas, interests, and institutions—almost always operating simultaneously—varies according to the particular point on the trajectory of change.

In Philadelphia, meanwhile, the road to neoliberalism was more serpentine, characterized by a pattern of *neoliberalism by default*. There, almost identical ideas interacted with the slow-moving processes of deindustrialization, racial change, and the logic of coalition building. The overall result is urban political development along distinctly neoliberal lines, reflected in the institutional innovations of the enterprise and empowerment zones, privatization, Philadelphia Intergovernmental Cooperation Authority (PICA), and the socioeconomic patterns outlined above.

Seen together, Docklands and Philadelphia showcase the argument that political development occurs at different spatial levels and to different extents. Moreover, the case of national urban policy shows that the overall size of the state does not necessarily tell us a great deal about the character of the state. That is, national urban spending directed to Philadelphia declined massively but was increased markedly for Docklands. However, the extent of neoliberalization was greater in Docklands than it was in Philadelphia. Hence, one must attend to the *purposes* to which the powers of state institutions are deployed. The study of cities provides an ideal vantage point from which to view the reorientation of state purposes that occurred under neoliberalism.

Moreover, although urban policy was the central mechanism by which Docklands' neoliberal trajectory was launched, the impact of national urban policy in Philadelphia was primarily felt in the form of cuts. While this constrained political elites and made entrepreneurial government more likely, it was the specifics of coalition building in Philadelphia that determined the particular form of political development that emerged.

The result of these processes, whether by design or default, has been the increasing urban bifurcation along class and racial lines, which has reversed some of the gains made by minorities and the working class in the 1960s and 1970s. The benefits from the bursts of economic growth in the 1980s and 1990s did not simply trickle down but were filtered through a matrix of political institutions at the federal, state, and local scales that exacerbated existing inequalities between the city and the suburbs and created new urban inequalities. In short, neoliberal policies have distinct urban characteristics, which must be studied in order to understand the full significance of the neoliberal turn.

The Great Recession of 2008 raises the question of whether the end of neoliberalism is in sight. After all, it laid bare the full contradictions, inequities, and destructive tendencies of neoliberal capitalism. Yet, the primary political beneficiary of this development appeared to be the right, in the form of David Cameron's Conservative-led government in the United Kingdom and the Republican takeover of the House of Representatives in the United States in 2010 and the Senate in 2014. Both are committed to a radical program of austerity that would make Reagan and Thatcher blush. Although President Obama launched a half-hearted stimulus package that prevented total collapse, the American political class appears to have accepted high unemployment for years to come on the basis that "there is no alternative" that is either possible or desirable.[9] That the Democrats and the Labour Party had so little to offer in terms of an alternative to neoliberalism reflects the degree to which they contributed to its construction, especially with respect to the unleashing of finance. As Labour MP Jon Cruddas puts it, "Brown, Blair they bought into the whole Greenspan model of self-correcting laws of economics in terms of perfecting the neo-classical frameworks, which meant that there was no reason to assume that this wouldn't go on. So it was rational to keep on borrowing, because growth was locked in. Now if the music stops, and you hit the buffers, who will pick up the cheque?"[10] Both the New Democrats and New Labour were happy to go along for the ride and had little to say when the car hurtled into the ditch.

The full effect of the financial crisis on American cities remains to be seen. However, it is already clear that the neoliberals throughout the land are using it to reorient the local state to meet their objectives, as recent experience in Detroit attests.[11] Moreover, even during a period of economic growth, the best that could be done was to improve "the quality of life for people who are getting poorer."[12] In a time of austerity, the chances of even meeting this grim standard are reduced.

Still, with the election of Barack Obama in 2008, there were hopes that the Chicagoan might reorient urban policy in a progressive direction. Yet, despite creating the White House Office of Urban Affairs, no major new initiatives were launched until 2013, when President Obama announced the creation of "promise zones." Nine of the first thirteen would be focused on high-poverty urban areas in San Antonio, Philadelphia, Los Angeles, Camden, Hartford, Indianapolis, Minneapolis, Sacramento, and St. Louis (the others being three rural and one tribal community), with seven more in the offing. Much like enterprise zones and empowerment zones, the promise zone idea seeks to address the problems of poverty and unemployment through a combination of tax incentives for business and the prioritization of needy areas for the targeting of existing federal resources. A key difference is found in its ambitious "wrap-around" approach that seeks to capitalize on the lessons of the Harlem Children's Zone. However, the program does not involve additional federal spending. Illustrating his programmatic and ideological connection to Reagan and Clinton, Obama suggested that those in the federal government will help poor areas, "not with a handout, but as partners with them, every step of the way."[13]

In two key respects, the promise zones reflect the dominance of neoliberal thinking regarding urban policy that continues through the Obama administration. First and most obviously, they involve tax incentives and "cutting red tape," two themes central to the enterprise zone idea. Second, framing the role of the federal government in terms of "partnership" highlights the distance traveled since the New Deal. The government's role— once heralded as the guarantor of "freedom from want"—has been diluted to one of "partner." In this rendering, the government's responsibility for taking serious steps to address the needs of the 45.3 million people who lived in poverty in 2013 is evaded. With the government's role so diminished, the president's new initiative seems to hold little more than the promise of irrelevance. It is also worth noting that the adoption of promise zones reflects the remarkable endurance of a policy regime that has consistently failed to produce positive results.

Meanwhile, in Britain, Chancellor George Osborne has emulated his predecessor, Geoffrey Howe, almost identically, by introducing twenty-five new enterprise zones to stimulate urban prosperity.[14] Much like Howe's original vision, businesses in Osborne's zones enjoy a 100 percent business rate (tax) discount for up to five years, "enhanced capital allowances," "radically simplified planning approaches," and assistance in the availability of "superfast broadband."[15] Thus, tax cuts and deregulation as a means to stimulate the economy are back in vogue. As was widely reiterated at the time of the announcement, the experience of the 1980s enterprise zones suggested that they would "likely . . . be ineffective at stimulating sustainable economic growth in depressed areas."[16]

The chancellor ploughed on, nevertheless. The British government predicted that enterprise zones would create 54,000 additional jobs by 2015, an annual rate of 18,000. However, consistent with the enterprise zone experience in the United Kingdom and beyond, the number of jobs created was set to fall well below expectations—by December 2013 (twenty months into the program), just 4,649 jobs had been created. This forced the Department for Communities and Local Government to admit that just 6,000 to 18,000 jobs in total will be created by 2015. As the House of Commons Public Accounts Committee noted, such results were "particularly underwhelming."[17] Moreover, due to lack of business interest in the scheme, the Office for Budget Responsibility, a statutory body that monitors government spending, reduced its forecast for the costs of tax relief in enterprise zones by 80 percent, from £30 million in 2015–2016 to just £6 million.[18] The lack of business take-up of tax incentives reinforces a key theme developed throughout this book: policies that on first sight appear to be driven by the interests of capital are often instead rooted in the ideological preferences of officeholders. The same could as easily be said about George Osborne's self-defeating program of austerity that cut spending but failed to shrink the nation's debt.[19]

The absence of any sophisticated critique of the neoliberal variety of capitalism suggests that widening inequalities, high levels of unemployment, and grinding poverty are set to continue. While the recent Occupy movement has brought issues of political economy and inequality into focus, it is unclear so far how its critique of capitalism can be fashioned into a credible, politically feasible program of political transformation. Moreover, the privatization of public space, itself a neoliberal innovation, has been used as a weapon of capital to secure a legal injunction preventing any protest from occurring at Canary Wharf.[20] As such, along with the ideological barriers that have been erected by neoliberals over the past forty years, the very heart of financial capital is physically protected by judicial and political power.

What is crystal clear, however, is that any credible articulation of an alternative will not occur overnight but will be a decades-long process. The task, therefore, before those who regret these processes of division is to follow the lead of the early neoliberals and construct, as they did, an alternative ideological infrastructure with a matching set of policies that present realistic alternatives to the widening income disparities, chronic unemployment, and stagnating median wages that have resulted from the faithful adherence to trickle-down economics. "Improving the quality of life for people who are getting poorer" surely cannot be enough.

A p p e n d i x

Archival Sources

Bill Clinton Presidential Library, Little Rock, Arkansas
Conservative Party Archives, Oxford
Docklands Forum Archives, Docklands, London
Jack Kemp Archives, Pepperdine University, Malibu, California
  (since moved)
Margaret Thatcher Archives, Cambridge
Neil Kinnock Archives, Cambridge
Peter Shore Archives, LSE
Port Authority of London Archives, Docklands, London
Ronald Reagan Presidential Library, Simi Valley, California
U.K. National Archives, Kew, London

Interviews Conducted

United Kingdom

Hazel Blears MP	Secretary of state for communities and local government (2007–2009)
Sue Brownill	Urban scholar and Docklands activist in the 1980s
Bob Colenutt	Docklands activist in the 1980s

John Cruddas MP	MP for Dagenham and Rainham in Docklands since 2001
Jim Fitzpatrick MP	MP for Poplar and Limehouse (Canary Wharf) since 1997, minister for London (2005–2007)
Mike Gapes MP	MP for Ilford South (near Docklands) since 1992
Sir Peter Hall	Prominent planner and brainchild of enterprise zones
Lord (Michael) Heseltine	Secretary of state for the environment (1979–1993 and 1990–1992) who introduced urban development corporations
Lord (Geoffrey) Howe	Chancellor of the Exchequer (1979–1983) who introduced enterprise zones
Lord (Richard) Rogers	Chair of Tony Blair's Urban Taskforce and proponent of the "urban renaissance"
Lord (Clive) Soley	Opposition spokesman on housing and local government in the 1980s
Eric Sorensen	Chief executive of the London Docklands Development Corporation (1991–1998)
Stephen Timms MP	Chief secretary to the Treasury (2006–2008) and MP for East Ham in Docklands since 1997

United States

William Barnes	National League of Cities
Marc Bendick	Urban expert, testified before Congress on enterprise zones
Santiago Burgos	Director of program operations and planning, Philadelphia empowerment zone
Stuart Butler	Heritage Foundation, brought enterprise zone idea to the United States
Mary Cannon	Policy adviser to Jack Kemp
John Claypool	Former director of the American Street Corridor Project in Philadelphia's enterprise zone and empowerment zone
Donna Cooper	Chief policy adviser to Mayor Ed Rendell, oversaw the Philadelphia empowerment zone

Eva Gladstein	Executive director of the Philadelphia empowerment zone (1998–2005)
Joe Houldin	Philadelphia Industrial Development Corporation
Steve Horton	Ran Philadelphia's Enterprise Zone Program
Robert Inman	Wharton professor and expert on Philadelphia's finances
Rojer Kern	Commercial corridors business organizer, Philadelphia empowerment zone
Jeremy Nowak	Coauthor of Philadelphia's empowerment zone bid and urban expert
Duane Perry	Author of report to Mayor Bill Green on the Philadelphia enterprise zone (1981) and policy analyst in the Philadelphia Commerce Department in the mid-1980s
James Pinkerton	Policy adviser to Ronald Reagan and George H. W. Bush
Susan Wachter	Undersecretary of housing and urban development under Bill Clinton
Sherri Wallace	Urban scholar who conducted research on Philadelphia's enterprise zone in the 1990s

Notes

Introduction

1. Demetrios Caraley, "Washington Abandons the Cities," *Political Science Quarterly* 107.1 (April 1, 1992): 1–30.

2. For seminal works on the third way, see David Osborne and Ted Gaebler, *Reinventing Government: How the Entrepreneurial Spirit Is Transforming the Public Sector* (New York: Addison-Wesley, 1992); Anthony Giddens, *The Third Way: The Renewal of Social Democracy* (Cambridge: Polity Press, 1998).

3. John H. Mollenkopf, "Urban Policy at the Crossroads," in *The Social Divide: Political Parties and the Future of Activist Government*, ed. Margaret Weir (Washington, D.C.: Brookings Institution Press, 1998), 473.

4. Margaret Weir, "Political Parties and Social Policy Making," in *The Social Divide: Political Parties and the Future of Activist Government*, ed. Margaret Weir (Washington, D.C.: Brookings Institution Press, 1998), 1–45.

5. For an articulation of alternatives open to cities, see David L. Imbroscio, *Urban America Reconsidered: Alternatives for Governance and Policy* (Ithaca, N.Y.: Cornell University Press, 2010).

6. For an account of the Clinton administration's "market fundamentalism," see Joseph E. Stiglitz, *The Roaring Nineties: A New History of the World's Most Prosperous Decade* (New York: Norton, 2003).

7. This point is especially well made in Karen Orren and Stephen Skowronek, *The Search for American Political Development* (Cambridge: Cambridge University Press, 2004).

8. Rogers M. Smith, "Which Comes First, the Ideas or the Institutions?" in *Rethinking Political Institutions: The Art of the State* (New York: New York University Press, 2006), 91–113; Robert C. Lieberman, "Ideas, Institutions, and Political Order: Explaining Political Change," *American Political Science Review* 96.4 (2002): 697–712; Robert C. Lieberman, "Ideas and Institutions in Race Politics," in *Ideas and Politics in Social Science Research*, ed. Daniel Béland and Robert Henry Cox (Oxford: Oxford University Press, 2011), 209–227.

9. Scholars working in the historical institutionalist vein have paid close attention to this challenge. See, for example, Paul Pierson and Theda Skocpol, "Historical Institutionalism in Contemporary Political Science," in *Political Science: The State of the Discipline* (New York: Norton, 2002), 639–721; Margaret Weir, "Ideas and Politics: The Acceptance of Keynesianism in Britain and the United States," in *The Political Power of Economic Ideas: Keynesianism Across Nations*, ed. Peter A. Hall (Princeton, N.J.: Princeton University Press, 1989), 53–86;

Peter A. Hall, ed., *The Political Power of Economic Ideas: Keynesianism Across Nations* (Princeton, N.J.: Princeton University Press, 1989); Marie Gottschalk, *The Prison and the Gallows: The Politics of Mass Incarceration in America* (Cambridge: Cambridge University Press, 2006); Paul Pierson, *Dismantling the Welfare State? Reagan, Thatcher, and the Politics of Retrenchment* (Cambridge: Cambridge University Press, 1994).

10. Political time and secular time were out of sync, thus preventing significant urban policy innovation at the national level. See Stephen Skowronek, *The Politics Presidents Make: Leadership from John Adams to Bill Clinton* (Cambridge, Mass.: Belknap Press of Harvard University Press, 1997).

11. Daniel Stedman Jones, *Masters of the Universe: Hayek, Friedman, and the Birth of Neoliberal Politics* (Princeton, N.J.: Princeton University Press, 2012); Monica Prasad, *The Politics of Free Markets: The Rise of Neoliberal Economic Policies in Britain, France, Germany, and the United States* (Chicago: University of Chicago Press, 2006); David Harvey, *A Brief History of Neoliberalism* (New York: Oxford University Press, 2005); Gérard Duménil and Dominique Lévy, *Capital Resurgent: Roots of the Neoliberal Revolution* (Cambridge, Mass.: Harvard University Press, 2004); Kees van der Pijl, *The Making of an Atlantic Ruling Class* (London: Verso, 1984).

12. Richardson Dilworth, ed., *The City in American Political Development* (New York: Routledge, 2009).

13. Paul Kantor, *The Dependent City Revisited: The Political Economy of Urban Development and Social Policy* (Boulder, Colo.: Westview Press, 1995); Robert O. Self, *American Babylon: Race and the Struggle for Postwar Oakland* (Princeton, N.J.: Princeton University Press, 2003); Thomas J. Sugrue, *The Origins of the Urban Crisis: Race and Inequality in Postwar Detroit* (Princeton, N.J.: Princeton University Press, 2005); Doreen Massey, *World City* (Cambridge: Polity Press, 2007).

14. For example, Pierson, *Dismantling the Welfare State?*

15. Orren and Skowronek, *The Search for American Political Development.*

16. Daniel Béland and Robert Henry Cox, "Introduction: Ideas and Politics," in *Ideas and Politics in Social Science Research*, ed. Daniel Béland and Robert Henry Cox (Oxford: Oxford University Press, 2011), 3.

17. Ibid., 3–4.

18. For an example of this approach, see Christopher Hood, *Explaining Economic Policy Reversals* (Buckingham, U.K.: Open University Press, 1994).

19. R. C. R. Taylor and P. A. Hall, "Political Science and the Three New Institutionalisms," *Political Studies* 44.5 (1996): 936–957. At least three kinds of institutional approaches exist: rational choice, historical institutionalist, and sociological. I focus here on historical institutionalism since it is most relevant to the methodological approach I employ below.

20. Smith, "Which Comes First, the Ideas or the Institutions?"

21. William W. Goldsmith, "Enterprise Zones: If They Work, We're in Trouble," *International Journal of Urban and Regional Research* 6.3 (1982): 441.

22. Susan S. Fainstein, *The City Builders: Property Development in New York and London, 1980–2000*, 2nd ed., rev. (Lawrence: University Press of Kansas, 2001).

23. Gérard Duménil and Dominique Lévy, "Neoliberal Income Trends," *New Left Review* 30 (December 2004): 105–133; Duménil and Lévy, *Capital Resurgent*; Harvey, *A Brief History of Neoliberalism*; Mike Geddes, "Marxism and Urban Politics," in *Theories of Urban Politics*, ed. Jonathan S. Davies and David L. Imbroscio, 2nd ed. (Los Angeles: Sage, 2009), 55–72.

24. E. E. Schattschneider, *Politics, Pressures, and the Tariff* (Hamden, Conn.: Archon Books, 1963); Pierson, *Dismantling the Welfare State?*; Theda Skocpol, *Protecting Soldiers and Mothers: The Political Origins of Social Policy in the United States* (Cambridge, Mass.: Belknap Press of Harvard University Press, 1992); Marie Gottschalk, *The Shadow Welfare State: Labor, Business, and the Politics of Health Care in the United States* (Ithaca, N.Y.: ILR Press, 2000).

25. See Pierson and Skocpol, "Historical Institutionalism in Contemporary Political Science." For an examination of institutional accounts of urban politics, see Vivien Lowndes, "New Institutionalism and Urban Politics," in *Theories of Urban Politics*, ed. Jonathan S. Davies and David L. Imbroscio, 2nd ed. (Los Angeles: Sage, 2009), 91–105.

26. Weir, "Ideas and Politics: The Acceptance of Keynesianism in Britain and the United States."

27. Stephen Skowronek, *Building a New American State: The Expansion of National Administrative Capacities, 1877–1920* (Cambridge: Cambridge University Press, 1982).

28. Skocpol, *Protecting Soldiers and Mothers*; Gottschalk, *The Shadow Welfare State*.

29. Daniel P. Carpenter, *The Forging of Bureaucratic Autonomy: Reputations, Networks, and Policy Innovation in Executive Agencies, 1862–1928* (Princeton, N.J.: Princeton University Press, 2001).

30. Eric Schickler, *Disjointed Pluralism: Institutional Innovation and the Development of the U.S. Congress* (Princeton, N.J.: Princeton University Press, 2001).

31. Howe was concerned that "the grey men whose job it is to consider the 'administrative difficulties' of any new idea would be ready enough to start manufacturing the small print that could stop the initiative in its tracks." Geoffrey Howe, *Enterprise Zones and the Enterprise Culture* (London: Bow Publications, 1988), 12.

32. Grant Jordan, "Enterprise Zones in the UK and the US: Ideologically Acceptable Job Creation?" in *Unemployment: Policy Responses of Western Democracies* (London: Sage, 1984), 125–147.

33. Lieberman, "Ideas, Institutions, and Political Order."

34. Hall, *The Political Power of Economic Ideas*; Colin Hay, *The Political Economy of New Labour: Labouring Under False Pretences?* (Manchester, U.K.: Manchester University Press, 1999); Colin Hay, "Ideas, Interests and Institutions in the Comparative Political Economy of Great Transformations," *Review of International Political Economy* 11.1 (2004): 204–226; Sheri Berman, *The Social Democratic Moment: Ideas and Politics in the Making of Interwar Europe* (Cambridge, Mass.: Harvard University Press, 1998); Weir, "Ideas and Politics: The Acceptance of Keynesianism in Britain and the United States"; Peter A. Hall, "The Role of Interests, Institutions, and Ideas in the Comparative Political Economy of the Industrialized Nations," in *Comparative Politics: Rationality, Culture, and Structure* (Cambridge: Cambridge University Press, 1997), 174–207; Smith, "Which Comes First, the Ideas or the Institutions?"; Béland and Cox, *Ideas and Politics in Social Science Research*; Lieberman, "Ideas and Institutions in Race Politics."

35. Pierson, *Dismantling the Welfare State?* 178.

36. Ibid.

37. Desmond S. King and Stuart M. Wood, in *Continuity and Change in Contemporary Capitalism* (Cambridge: Cambridge University Press, 1999), 372.

38. Mark Blyth, *Great Transformations: Economic Ideas and Institutional Change in the Twentieth Century* (Cambridge: Cambridge University Press, 2002). Also see Lieberman, "Ideas, Institutions, and Political Order."

39. Smith, "Which Comes First, the Ideas or the Institutions?" 111.

40. Ibid., 109.

41. Ibid.

42. Peter A. Hall, "Policy Paradigms, Social Learning, and the State: The Case of Economic Policymaking in Britain," *Comparative Politics* 25.3 (1993): 281, 284.

43. Ibid., 283–284.

44. Ibid., 284.

45. Ibid., 289.

46. In doing so, I follow Hay, *The Political Economy of New Labour*; Richard Heffernan, *New Labour and Thatcherism: Political Change in Britain* (New York: St. Martin's Press, 2000); Andrew Gamble, *The Free Economy and the Strong State: The Politics of Thatcherism*, 2nd ed. (London: Macmillan, 1994).

47. Lieberman, "Ideas and Institutions in Race Politics," 217.

48. Neil Brenner, Jamie Peck, and Nik Theodore, "Variegated Neoliberalization: Geographies, Modalities, Pathways," *Global Networks* 10.2 (2010): 184.

49. This definition is influenced strongly by David Harvey's: "Neoliberalism is in the first instance a theory of political-economic practices that proposes that human well-being can best be advanced by liberating individual entrepreneurial freedoms and skills within an institutional framework characterized by strong private property rights, free markets, and free trade. The role of the state is to create and preserve an institutional framework appropriate to such practices." See Harvey, *A Brief History of Neoliberalism*, 7.

50. Neoliberalism also diverges from conservatism since it does not share the same reverence for traditional institutions and rejects gradualism in favor of radical change often through "shock therapy."

51. Pierson, *Dismantling the Welfare State?*; Skowronek, *The Politics Presidents Make*.

52. Judith Stein, *Pivotal Decade: How the United States Traded Factories for Finance in the Seventies* (New Haven, Conn.: Yale University Press, 2010).

53. Margaret Weir, *Politics and Jobs: The Boundaries of Employment Policy in the United States* (Princeton, N.J.: Princeton University Press, 1992).

54. Ibid., 161.

55. Daniel T. Rodgers, *Age of Fracture* (Cambridge, Mass.: Belknap Press of Harvard University Press, 2011).

56. Jamie Peck and Adam Tickell, "Neoliberalizing Space," in *Spaces of Neoliberalism: Urban Restructuring in North America and Western Europe*, ed. Neil Brenner and Nikolas Theodore (Malden, Mass.: Blackwell, 2002), 33–57.

57. See, for example, Jones, *Masters of the Universe*.

58. Paul Pierson and Theda Skocpol, eds., *The Transformation of American Politics: Activist Government and the Rise of Conservatism* (Princeton, N.J.: Princeton University Press, 2007). Hacker and Pierson label many of the changes I attribute to neoliberalism as part of the "winner-take-all-economy." See Jacob S. Hacker and Paul Pierson, *Winner-Take-All Politics: How Washington Made the Rich Richer—and Turned Its Back on the Middle Class* (New York: Simon & Schuster, 2010).

59. See, for example, Sue Brownill, "London Docklands Revisited: The Dynamics of Waterfront Development," in *Transforming Urban Waterfronts: Fixity and Flow* (New York: Taylor & Francis, 2011), 121–142.

60. Harvey, *A Brief History of Neoliberalism*.

61. Jamie Peck, *Constructions of Neoliberal Reason* (Oxford: Oxford University Press, 2010).

62. Quoted in ibid., 3–4.

63. Friedrich A. von Hayek, *The Road to Serfdom* (Chicago: University of Chicago Press, 1944), quoted in Peck, *Constructions of Neoliberal Reason*, 48.

64. Franklin D. Roosevelt, "State of the Union Message to Congress," January 11, 1944.

65. Sean Wilentz, *The Age of Reagan: A History, 1974–2008* (New York: Harper, 2008).

66. See, for example, Susan S. Fainstein, Norman I. Fainstein, Richard C. Hill, Dennis Judd, and Michael Peter Smith, *Restructuring the City: The Political Economy of Urban Redevelopment*, rev. ed. (New York: Longman, 1986); David Harvey, "From Managerialism to Entrepreneurialism: The Transformation in Urban Governance in Late Capitalism," *Geografiska Annaler. Series B, Human Geography* 71.1 (1989): 3–17; Neil Smith, "New Globalism, New Urbanism: Gentrification as a Global Urban Strategy," in *Spaces of Neoliberalism: Urban Restructuring in North America and Western Europe*, ed. Neil Brenner and Nikolas Theodore (Malden, Mass.: Blackwell, 2002), 80–103; Neil Brenner and Nikolas Theodore, eds., *Spaces of Neoliberalism: Urban Restructuring in North America and Western Europe* (Malden, Mass.: Blackwell, 2002); Geddes, "Marxism and Urban Politics"; Jonathan S. Davies, "Back to the Future: Marxism and Urban Politics," in *Critical Urban Studies: New Directions* (Albany: State University of New York Press, 2010), 73–88.

67. Davies, "Back to the Future: Marxism and Urban Politics," 76.

68. Notably, Davies's sophisticated Marxist account "demands no conspiracy" between the capitalist class and city officials. Instead, officials "respond to territorial imperatives, as they perceive them, rather than to orders from a self-conscious elite." This view does seem to leave room for the role of ideas in that perceptions of territorial imperatives presumably could vary and therefore may be contingent rather than materially given. However, Davies does not delve into this issue. Ibid., 77.

69. John R. Logan and Harvey Luskin Molotch, *Urban Fortunes: The Political Economy of Place* (Berkeley: University of California Press, 1987).

70. Ibid., 60.

71. Ibid., 85. Emphasis added.

72. See Clarence N. Stone, "Systemic Power in Community Decision Making: A Restatement of Stratification Theory," *The American Political Science Review* 74.4 (December 1, 1980): 978–990; Clarence N. Stone, *Regime Politics: Governing Atlanta, 1946–1988* (Lawrence: University Press of Kansas, 1989).

73. Hackworth, *The Neoliberal City: Governance, Ideology, and Development in American Urbanism* (Ithaca, N.Y.: Cornell University Press, 2007), 10.

74. Ibid., 11.

75. Ibid., 17–18. Emphasis added. It seems that Hackworth does think ideas matter in a greater sense than this but does not demonstrate how.

76. Peck, *Constructions of Neoliberal Reason*, 7.

77. Ibid., 16.

78. H. V. Savitch and Paul Kantor, *Cities in the International Marketplace: The Political Economy of Urban Development in North America and Western Europe* (Princeton, N.J.: Princeton University Press, 2002).

79. Caraley, "Washington Abandons the Cities."

80. Margaret Weir, Harold Wolman, and Todd Swanstrom, "The Calculus of Coalitions: Cities, Suburbs, and the Metropolitan Agenda," *Urban Affairs Review* 40.6 (2005): 730–760.

81. Paul Kantor and H. V. Savitch, "Can Politicians Bargain with Business?" *Urban Affairs Review* 29.2 (1993): 230–255.

82. Both Paul Kantor and William Sites emphasize the role of national responses to international dynamics. See Kantor, *The Dependent City Revisited*; William Sites, *Remaking New York: Primitive Globalization and the Politics of Urban Community* (Minneapolis: University of Minnesota Press, 2003).

83. Richardson Dilworth, ed., *The City in American Political Development* (New York: Routledge, 2009); Joel Rast, "Why History (Still) Matters Time and Temporality in Urban Political Analysis," *Urban Affairs Review* 48.1 (2012): 3–36; Clarence N. Stone and Robert Whelan, "When the Twain Meet: Urban Politics and APD," *Clio: Newsletter of Politics and History* 22.2 (Fall/Winter 2011–2012): 3.

84. Harvey, *A Brief History of Neoliberalism*.

85. Fainstein, *The City Builders*.

86. Smith, "New Globalism, New Urbanism: Gentrification as a Global Urban Strategy."

87. Jamie Peck and Adam Tickell, "Neoliberalizing Space."

88. Brownill, "London Docklands Revisited: The Dynamics of Waterfront Development"; Mike Raco, "Sustainable Development, Rolled-out Neoliberalism and Sustainable Communities," *Antipode* 37.2 (March, 2005): 324–347.

89. Bob Jessop, "Liberalism, Neoliberalism, and Urban Governance," in *Spaces of Neoliberalism: Urban Restructuring in North America and Western Europe*, ed. Neil Brenner and Nikolas Theodore (Malden, Mass.: Blackwell, 2002), 105–125; Smith, "New Globalism, New Urbanism: Gentrification as a Global Urban Strategy"; Martin Jones and Kevin Ward, "Excavating the Logic of British Urban Policy: Neoliberalism as the 'Crisis of Crisis Management'," in *Spaces of Neoliberalism: Urban Restructuring in North America and Western Europe*, ed. Neil Brenner and Nikolas Theodore (Malden, Mass.: Blackwell, 2002), 126–147.

90. Brenner, Peck, and Theodore, "Variegated Neoliberalization."

91. Adolph L. Reed, *Stirrings in the Jug: Black Politics in the Post-Segregation Era* (Minneapolis: University of Minnesota Press, 1999), 99.

92. Harold Wolman, Edward W. Hill, and Kimberly Furdell, "Evaluating the Success of Urban Success Stories: Is Reputation a Guide to Best Practice?" *Housing Policy Debate* 15 (January 2004): 965–997.

93. Hacker and Pierson, *Winner-Take-All Politics*.

Chapter 1

1. See, for example, Paul Pierson, *Dismantling the Welfare State: Reagan Thatcher and the Politics of Retrenchment* (Cambridge: Cambridge University Press, 1994).

2. As I will explain in detail below, the bill was pocket-vetoed by President H. W. Bush because it contained tax increases.

3. I borrow this term from Mark Blyth, *Great Transformations: Economic Ideas and Institutional Change in the Twentieth Century* (Cambridge: Cambridge University Press, 2002).

4. Stein, *Pivotal Decade*.

5. Rodgers, *Age of Fracture*; also see Tony Judt, *Ill Fares the Land* (New York: Penguin Press, 2010).

6. David Vogel, *Kindred Strangers: The Uneasy Relationship Between Politics and Business in America* (Princeton, N.J.: Princeton University Press, 1996); Blyth, *Great Transformations*; Peck, *Constructions of Neoliberal Reason.*

7. Although as Weir points out, the American version of Keynesianism was compromised from the outset with the failure of the 1946 employment act. See Weir, *Politics and Jobs.*

8. Leonard S. Silk, "Nixon's Program—'I Am Now a Keynesian,'" *New York Times,* January 10, 1971, E1.

9. Gerald Ford, Speech to Congress, October 8, 1974.

10. Ibid.

11. See John H. Mollenkopf, *The Contested City* (Princeton, N.J.: Princeton University Press, 1983).

12. Skowronek, *The Politics Presidents Make.*

13. Dennis R. Judd and Todd Swanstrom, *City Politics: Private Power and Public Policy,* 4th ed. (New York: Longman, 2004), 179. For more on Carter's urban policy, see Chapter 3.

14. Mollenkopf, *The Contested City,* 275.

15. Judd and Swanstrom, *City Politics,* 183.

16. Ronald Reagan, Remarks at the Conservative Political Action Conference Dinner, March 20, 1981, http://www.reagan.utexas.edu/search/speeches/speech_srch.html.

17. Ronald Reagan to Milton Friedman, March 13, 1981, Ronald Reagan Presidential Papers, Ronald Reagan Library, Simi Valley, California.

18. Quoted in Judd and Swanstrom, *City Politics,* 182.

19. U.S. Department of Housing and Urban Development, *The President's National Urban Policy Report* (Washington, D.C.: Government Printing Office, 1982), 14.

20. Caraley, "Washington Abandons the Cities."

21. Ibid., 11.

22. Robert W. Poole, *Cutting Back City Hall* (New York: Universe Books, 1980), 10.

23. Ibid. Italics in original.

24. Peter Geoffrey Hall, "Green Field and Grey Areas" (presented at the Royal Town Institute Annual Conference, Chester, U.K., June 15, 1997).

25. Peter Geoffrey Hall, "Enterprise Zones: British Origins, American Adaptations," *Built Environment* 7.1 (1981): 6.

26. Ibid., 5.

27. Ibid., 6.

28. Sir Peter Hall, interview by author, London, July 21, 2009.

29. Ibid.

30. Ibid.

31. Geoffrey Howe to Margaret Thatcher, June 27, 1977, Margaret Thatcher Archives, at http://www.margaretthatcher.org/archive/browse.asp?t = 3.

32. Geoffrey Howe to Margaret Thatcher, July 20, 1978, Margaret Thatcher Archives, at http://www.margaretthatcher.org/archive/browse.asp?t = 3.

33. Margaret Thatcher to Geoffrey Howe, August 2, 1978, Margaret Thatcher Archives at http://www.margaretthatcher.org/archive/browse.asp?t = 3.

34. Geoffrey Howe to Margaret Thatcher, March 12, 1979, Margaret Thatcher Archives, at http://www.margaretthatcher.org/archive/browse.asp?t = 3.

35. Stuart M. Butler, *Enterprise Zone: A Solution to the Urban Crisis?* (Washington, D.C.: Heritage Foundation, 1979).

36. Ibid.

37. John Chamberlain, "New 'Zones' Could Save Our Cities," syndicated nationally by King Features in *The Detroit News, New Haven Register,* and *Baton Rouge State Times,* March 23, 1979, published in "Heritage in the News: Special Enterprise Zones Issue," *Heritage Foundation* (September 1980).

38. Ibid., 2.

39. Stuart Butler, interview by author, Heritage Foundation, Washington, D.C., February 3, 2009. Butler is British, so he is referring here to being a student of American history.

40. Butler, *Enterprise Zone: A Solution to the Urban Crisis?* 12.

41. Ibid., 2.

42. See, for example, Jane Jacobs, *The Death and Life of Great American Cities* (New York: Modern Library, 2011); Jane Jacobs, *The Economy of Cities* (New York: Random House, 1969).

43. Martin Anderson, *The Federal Bulldozer: A Critical Analysis of Urban Renewal, 1942–1962* (Cambridge, Mass.: MIT Press, 1964).

44. Stuart M. Butler, *Enterprise Zones: Greenlining the Inner Cities* (New York: Universe Books, 1981), 86.

45. Stuart M. Butler, "The Conceptual Evolution of Enterprise Zones," in *Enterprise Zones: New Directions in Economic Development,* ed. Roy Green (Newbury Park, Calif.: Sage, 1991), 35.

46. Stuart Butler, interview by author, Heritage Foundation, Washington, D.C., February 3, 2009.

47. Quoted in Jones, *Masters of the Universe,* 320.

48. David L. Birch, *The Job Generation Process* (Cambridge, Mass.: M.I.T. Program on Neighborhood and Regional Change, 1979); David L. Birch, *Job Creation in America: How Our Smallest Companies Put the Most People to Work* (New York: Free Press, 1987).

49. Butler, "The Conceptual Evolution of Enterprise Zones," 36.

50. Michael Allan Wolf, "Through the Legal Looking-Glass," in *Enterprise Zones: New Directions in Economic Development,* ed. Roy Green (Newbury Park, Calif.: Sage, 1991), 61–62.

51. "Heritage in the News: Special Enterprise Zones Issue," *Heritage Foundation* (September 1980).

52. A search of newspaper articles from 1979 to 1980 but not included in the newsletter also reveals that most stories on enterprise zones mention the Heritage Foundation, Butler, and/or the United Kingdom.

53. Sir Peter Hall, interview by author, London, July 21, 2009.

54. Butler, "The Conceptual Evolution of Enterprise Zones," 30–31.

55. Karen Mossberger, *The Politics of Ideas and the Spread of Enterprise Zones* (Washington, D.C.: Georgetown University Press, 2000), 60–61.

56. Butler, *Enterprise Zones,* 10–11.

57. See, for example, Kenneth T. Jackson, *Crabgrass Frontier: The Suburbanization of the United States* (Oxford: Oxford University Press, 1985); Dolores Hayden, *Building Suburbia: Green Fields and Urban Growth, 1820–2000* (New York: Pantheon Books, 2003); Self, *American Babylon*; Peter Dreier, John H. Mollenkopf, and Todd Swanstrom, *Place Matters: Metropolitics for the Twenty-First Century,* 2nd ed., rev. (Lawrence: University Press of Kansas, 2004).

58. Butler, *Enterprise Zones*, 11.

59. Kantor, *The Dependent City Revisited*, 162.

60. Judd and Swanstrom, *City Politics*, 224.

61. Butler, *Enterprise Zones*, 14.

62. Ibid., 22.

63. Butler, *Enterprise Zone: A Solution to the Urban Crisis?* 1–2.

64. For an excellent account of the role of think tanks in framing the "urban crisis" and in advancing a critique of liberal governance, see Alice O'Connor, "The Privatized City: The Manhattan Institute, the Urban Crisis, and the Conservative Counterrevolution in New York," *Journal of Urban History* 34.2 (2008): 333–353.

65. William E. Simon, *A Time for Truth* (New York: Reader's Digest Press, 1978), 12.

66. Butler, *Enterprise Zone: A Solution to the Urban Crisis?* 2.

67. Butler, *Enterprise Zones*, 139.

68. Ibid., 140. Emphasis his.

69. Stuart Butler, interview by author, Heritage Foundation, Washington, D.C., February 3, 2009.

70. For excellent analysis of these debates, see Michael B. Katz, *The Undeserving Poor: America's Enduring Confrontation with Poverty*, 2nd ed., rev. (New York: Oxford University Press, 2013).

71. Stuart M. Butler, "For 'Enterprise Zones,'" *New York Times*, June 13, 1980, A29.

72. Butler noted the "danger of discretion at the federal level" but concluded that government involvement in designation was the "only workable approach." See Butler, *Enterprise Zones*, 146.

73. Ibid., 132.

74. Ibid., 146.

75. For a good explanation, see Butler, *Enterprise Zone: A Solution to the Urban Crisis?*

76. In order to secure congressional support for enterprise zones, particularly in the Senate, proponents added measures to include rural enterprise zones, which also have poverty and unemployment criteria. Since my focus here is on urban policy and politics, I focus on the criteria for the urban zones.

77. Hall, "Enterprise Zones: British Origins, American Adaptations," 6.

78. Butler, *Enterprise Zones*, 152, 153.

79. Ibid., 136.

80. Marc Bendick, Congressional Testimony, House Ways and Means Committee, *Tax Incentives Targeted to Distressed Areas Hearing* on HR 1955, 98th Cong., 1st Sess., November 17, 1983.

81. Hall, "Enterprise Zones: British Origins, American Adaptations," 6.

82. Quoted in James Traub, "Jack Kemp Faces Reality," *New York Times Magazine*, May 7, 1989.

83. Butler, *Enterprise Zones*, 129, 143.

84. Luix Overbea, "Enterprise Zones: Coming Urban-Aid Experiment," *Christian Science Monitor*, June 1, 1981, 12. Pryde was an influential enterprise zone proponent who frequently testified on behalf of them before Congress.

85. Ronald Reagan, Reagan-Anderson Presidential Debate, Baltimore, September 21, 1980, American Presidency Project, http://www.presidency.ucsb.edu/ws/index.php?pid= 29407#axzz1Xw JpGOPx.

86. Stuart Butler, interview by author, Heritage Foundation, Washington, D.C., February 3, 2009.

87. In the House, Representatives Robert Garcia (D-NY) and, eventually, Charles Rangel (D-NY) were also important, as were Rudolph Boschwitz (R-MN) and John Chafee (R-RI) in the Senate.

88. Stuart Butler, interview by author, Heritage Foundation, Washington, D.C., February 3, 2009.

89. See Hacker and Pierson, *Winner-Take-All Politics*, and Peck, *Constructions of Neoliberal Reason.*

90. Interestingly, Kemp was an advocate of supply-side economics whose own tax-cutting agenda became Reagan's as part of a deal by which Kemp agreed to drop out of the 1980 Republican primary to make way for Reagan. According to Anderson, "Reagan endorsed Kemp's tax proposal as part of a political deal and got Kemp's support. And Kemp gained tremendous public exposure that put him on the shortlist of the Republican presidential hopefuls for 1988." See Martin Anderson, *Revolution: The Reagan Legacy* (Stanford, Calif.: Hoover Institution Press, 1990), 163.

91. Developed by Arthur Laffer and which supposedly shows the relationship between tax levels and revenues and which claimed that the United States could cut taxes and raise revenues, since it was beyond the peak of the curve at which the optimal rate of taxation leads to the highest possible tax revenues.

92. David E. Rosenbaum, "Reagan Calls His Version 'Urban Enterprise Zones,'" *New York Times*, November 23, 1980, 42.

93. Anderson, *Revolution.*

94. David Broder and Kathy Sawyer, "Jack Kemp: Galileo of GOP Economics; Reagan Backer Promotes Tax Cut—and His Own Political Future," *New York Times*, May 20, 1980, sec. 1.

95. Jack Kemp, memo to the White House, May 1984, Jack Kemp Archives, Pepperdine University, California.

96. It required that potential zones had at least 4,000 residents, with a certain percentage unemployed and/or in poverty, and made the following tax provisions: local governments in whose jurisdiction the zones were located were to reduce property taxes by 20 percent, exclusion from Social Security taxes for zone employees, capital gains tax relief for individuals and corporations, cuts in income tax for qualified businesses, accelerated depreciation, and a ten-year carryover on losses for qualifying businesses.

97. Quoted in Nadine Cohodas, "Urban Enterprise Zone Plan Stresses Business Tax Breaks," *CQ Weekly* 38 (May 9, 1981): 806.

98. Butler, *Enterprise Zones*, 131.

99. Ibid.

100. A companion bill in the Senate (S. 2823), sponsored by Rudolph Boschwitz (R-MN), drew the support of 16 sixteen Republican co-sponsors but no Democrats.

101. Lou Cannon, "Reagan Makes Appeal to Blacks; Don't Pigeonhole Me Reagan Asks Blacks," *Washington Post*, August 6, 1980, A1.

102. Douglas Neeland, "Reagan Urges Blacks to Look Past Labels and Vote for Him," *New York Times*, August 6, 1980, A1.

103. "Text of Presidential Debate Between Anderson and Reagan," *CQRW* 38 (27 September, 1980): 2864.

104. Mossberger, *The Politics of Ideas and the Spread of Enterprise Zones*, 60–61.

105. Cohodas, "Urban Enterprise Zone Plan Stresses Business Tax Breaks," 806.

106. "Public Sector Jobs; Holes in Cities," *The Economist*, August 15, 1981, 22.

107. Ibid.

108. William Barnes, *Some Thoughts on the Enterprise Zones*, Discussion Paper (Washington, D.C.: National League of Cities, August 1981), 10.

109. Ibid.

110. William Barnes, interview by author, National League of Cities, Washington, D.C., April 14, 2009. Bendick supports this assessment. Marc Bendick, interview by author, Washington, D.C., April 13, 2009.

111. AFL-CIO Executive Council Statement on Enterprise Zones, issued February 16, 1981, quoted in U.S. House Hearings by the Subcommittee on Economic Stabilization of the House Committee on Banking, Finance and Urban Affairs, *Urban Jobs and Enterprise Zone Act of 1981*, 97th Cong., 1st Sess., July 8, 1981, 99.

112. Editorial, "Help the Urban Poor Escape," *New York Times*, December 8, 1980, A26.

113. U.S. Senate Hearings by the Subcommittee on Savings, Pensions, and Investment Policy of the Senate Finance Committee, *Urban Enterprise Zones*, 97th Cong., 1st Sess., July 13, 1981, 56.

114. Ibid., 148.

115. U.S. House Hearings by the Subcommittee on Economic Stabilization of the House Committee on Banking, Finance and Urban Affairs, *Urban Jobs and Enterprise Zone Act of 1981*, 97th Cong., 1st Sess., July 8, 1981, 5–6.

116. It is worth noting that there were some proto-neoliberal tendencies in the way the War on Poverty played out locally. For instance, federal funds were often used to support community groups that promoted "black capitalism" undergirded by "bootstrap" rhetoric. See, for example, Kent B. Germany, *New Orleans After the Promises: Poverty, Citizenship, and the Search for the Great Society* (Athens: University of Georgia Press, 2007).

117. Ibid., 80.

118. Ibid., 81, 84.

119. Ibid.

120. U.S. Senate Hearings by the Subcommittee on Savings, Pensions, and Investment Policy of the Senate Finance Committee, *Urban Enterprise Zones*, 97th Cong., 1st Sess., July 13, 1981, 56.

121. Ibid., 244–245.

122. Ronald Reagan, State of the Union Address to Congress, Washington, D.C., January 26, 1982.

123. "Text of Reagan Message on Enterprise Zones," *CQWR* (March 27, 1982): 705.

124. In terms of co-sponsorships, both bills show increased support on both sides of the aisle, albeit tilted in a Republican direction. While Chaffee's bill attracted the support of 24 Republicans and 4 Democrats, Conable's bill had no fewer than 104 Republicans and 28 Democrats.

125. Herbert H. Denton, "Top Business Officials Voice Doubts on Reagan Urban Enterprise Zone," *Washington Post*, February 11, 1982, A5.

126. Bob Dole to James Baker, January 8, 1982, Enterprise Zones (2), Box 8, Ronald Reagan Presidential Papers, Ronald Reagan Presidential Library, Simi Valley, California,

127. U.S. Senate Hearings by Committee on Finance, *Enterprise Zones: 1982*, 97th Cong., 2nd Sess., April 21, 1982, 152.

128. Ibid., 151. Emphasis added.

129. U.S. Senate Hearings by Committee on Finance, *Enterprise Zones: 1982*, 97th Cong., 2nd Sess., April 21, 1982, 479.

130. Marc Bendick, interview by author, Washington, D.C., April 13, 2009.

131. Marc Bendick, "Employment, Training, and Economic Development," in *The Reagan Experiment: An Examination of Economic and Social Policies Under the Reagan Administration*, ed. John L. Palmer and Isabel V. Sawhill (Washington, D.C.: Urban Institute Press, 1982), 247–269.

132. The conflict over his testimony precipitated his leaving the Urban Institute in 1984, although not on bad terms. Marc Bendick, interview by author, Washington, D.C., April 13, 2009.

133. U.S. Senate Hearings by Committee on Finance, *Enterprise Zones: 1982*, 97th Cong., 2nd Sess., April 21, 1982, 131. In 1968, Chisholm was the first African American woman to become a member of Congress.

134. Ibid., 131–134.

135. Ibid., 130–131.

136. Its spokesperson, Ruth Messenger, reported that the organization "strongly supports the concept of the EZ legislation." Ibid., 244.

137. Editorial, "Give Enterprise Zones a Chance," *New York Times*, March 26, 1982, A26.

138. U.S. House Hearings by the Subcommittee on Economic Stabilization of the House Committee on Banking, Finance and Urban Affairs, *Enterprise Zones*, 97th Cong., 2nd Sess., July 13, 1982, 489.

139. Ibid., 491.

140. U.S. House Hearings by the Subcommittee on Economic Stabilization of the House Committee on Banking, Finance and Urban Affairs, *Enterprise Zones*, 97th Cong., 2nd Sess., July 13, 1982, 18.

141. "Urban Enterprise Zones," *Congressional Quarterly Almanac* (1982): 68.

142. Although many urbanists took this as a rank insult, some wore the moniker as a badge of honor. William Barnes of the NLC helped to found "the Wily Stalkers Marching and Eating Society." William Barnes, interview by author, National League of Cities, Washington, D.C., April 14, 2009.

143. John Herbers, "The Administration Seeks to Cut Aid to Cities, Charging It Is Harmful," *New York Times*, June 20, 1982, A1.

144. U.S. General Accounting Office, *Revitalizing Distressed Areas Through Enterprise Zones: Many Uncertainties Exist* (Washington, D.C.: U.S. General Accounting Office, July 15, 1982), ii.

145. Ibid., iii.

146. Ronald Reagan, State of the Union Address to Congress, Washington, D.C., January 25, 1983.

147. The bill drew the co-sponsorship of 154 Republicans and 105 Democrats.

148. U.S. House Hearing by House Ways and Means Committee, *Tax Incentives Targeted to Distressed Areas*, 97th Cong., 2nd Sess., November 17, 1983.

149. Ibid., 149.

150. Ibid., 109.

151. Peterson, *City Limits*.

152. U.S. House Hearing by House Ways and Means Committee, *Tax Incentives Targeted to Distressed Areas*, 97th Cong., 2nd Sess., November 17, 1983, 109.

153. Ibid., 116.

154. "'Enterprise Zone' Program a Sound Approach to the Nation's Urban Problems?" *Congressional Digest* 64 (May 1985): 147.

155. Ibid., 221.

156. Howard Kurtz, "Targeting Federal Aid Raises the Question, Who's in the Bull's Eye?" *Washington Post*, December 6, 1983, A15.

157. Ronald Reagan, State of the Union Address to Congress, Washington, D.C., January 25, 1984.

158. Howard Kurtz, "Zone Opposition Hit at Mayors' Meeting," *Washington Post*, June 18, 1984, A3.

159. Steven R. Weisman, "The White House; the Night Ducks, All in a Neat Row, Died," *New York Times*, June 27, 1984, A16.

160. Robert Rothman, "House Democrats Still Stymie Reagan Enterprise Zone Plan," *CQ Weekly*, September 29, 1984, 2369–2371.

161. Ronald Reagan, "Remarks Accepting the Presidential Nomination at the Republican National Convention in Dallas, Texas," August 23, 1984.

162. The First Reagan-Mondale Debate, October 7, 1984, found at Commission on Presidential Debates, http://www.debates.org/pages/trans84a.html.

163. Ronald Reagan, State of the Union Address to Congress, Washington, D.C., February 6, 1985.

164. Simply analyzing roll call votes for the bill as a whole reveals relatively little about preferences about enterprise zones specifically. Fortunately, there was an enterprise zone amendment sponsored by Rep. Garcia that shows significant support for the measures on both sides of the aisle: the amendment was adopted 366–32, with the breakdown of Republicans being 169–0 and Democrats 197–32. See Steve Blakely, "House Democrats Still Stymie Reagan Enterprise Zone Plan," *CQ Weekly*, June 14, 1986, 1360.

165. Ronald Elving, "Major Provisions of Housing Authorization Bill," *CQ Weekly*, January 2, 1988, 19–20.

166. Barry Rubin and Margaret Wilder, "Urban Enterprise Zones: Employment Impacts and Fiscal Incentives," *Journal of the American Planning Association* 55 (December 1989): 418–431.

167. Karen Mossberger, "State-Federal Diffusion and Policy Learning: From Enterprise Zones to Empowerment Zones," *Publius: The Journal of Federalism* 29.3 (1999): 31–50.

168. Text of the Republican Platform in "Republican Party Issues Detailed, Long Platform," *CQWR* 46 (August 20, 1988): 2383.

169. Ibid.

170. Barbara Vobejda and Ann Devroy, "Rep. Kemp Is Considered to Lead HUD," *Washington Post*, December 6, 1988, A1.

171. U.S. General Accounting Office, *Enterprise Zones: Lessons from the Maryland Experience* (Washington, D.C.: U.S. General Accounting Office, 1983), 3.

172. Ibid., 3.

173. Ibid. The other factors ranked above the enterprise zone incentives were market access, community characteristics, site characteristics, receptiveness to business in general, governmental cooperation, and the condition of local infrastructure.

174. Ibid., 41.

175. Ibid., 58.

176. Editorial, "Gently into the Enterprise Zone," *New York Times*, March 13, 1989, A18. It is important to note, as legislators did in 1989 hearings, that prior and subsequent enterprise zone proposals did include tax incentives that were more substantial than those offered in the Maryland zone. However, empirical analysis on a range of state zones largely reflects these conclusions.

177. Ibid.

178. "Not so EZ," *The Economist*, January 23, 1989, 16.

179. George H. W. Bush, State of the Union Address to Congress, Washington, D.C., February 1989.

180. David E. Rosenbaum, "Darman Balances Hard Decisions and Hard Numbers," *New York Times*, February 12, 1989, A30.

181. Ibid.

182. Jack Kemp, "Lighting Candles from Harlem to Watts," *Washington Post*, September 17, 1989, C7.

183. Gwen Ifill, "Enterprise Zone Tax Break Urged; Seeking Teeth in Plan Kemp Delays Picking Sites for Revitalization," *Washington Post*, March 23, 1989, A16.

184. U.S. House Hearing by House Ways and Means Committee, *The EZ Improvements Act of 1989*, 100th Congress, 2nd Sess., October 17, 1989, 62–63.

185. Ibid., 63.

186. They included $500 tax credit for each new worker who was neither disadvantaged nor rehired, tax credit for each new disadvantaged worker of up to $3,000, property tax credit of 80 percent of the increase in value from improvements for five years, and 100 percent guaranteed loans.

187. Eleanor Chelimsky, the GAO's assistant comptroller general, was routinely attacked on these grounds. With ersatz disbelief, Rangel noted, "A lot of us wonder why you went to Maryland." U.S. House Hearing by House Ways and Means Committee, *The EZ Improvements Act of 1989*, 100th Congress, 2nd Sess., October 17, 1989, 129.

188. See Chelimsky's written testimony in ibid., 2.

189. Ibid., 3.

190. Ibid., 5.

191. Ibid., 282–294.

192. Ibid., 181.

193. Ibid., 87.

194. Ibid., 273.

195. Ibid., 212–213.

196. Ibid., 87.

197. Gwen Ifill, "Enterprise Zones Get Surprise Backer; Rostenkowski's Change of Heart Bodes Well for a Kemp Measure," *Washington Post*, July 9, 1990, A9.

198. James Pinkerton, interview by author, Washington, D.C., April 13, 2009. Others involved in the "new paradigm" included David Osborne, senior PPI fellow and author of

Reinventing Government, and Elaine Kamarck, future White House aide during the Clinton administration. Interestingly, PPI and the Heritage Foundation held a joint conference on the "new paradigm" in 1990. See Kenneth S. Baer, *Reinventing Government: The Politics of Liberalism from Reagan to Clinton* (Lawrence: University of Kansas Press, 2000), 167.

199. Peter Applebombe and Jason DeParle, "Ideas to Help Poor Abound, but a Consensus Is Wanting," *New York Times*, January 29, 1991, A1.

200. "Lexington," "A Sword Called Empowerment," *The Economist*, June 2, 1990, 28.

201. George H. W. Bush, State of the Union Address to Congress, Washington, D.C., January 29, 1991.

202. Jack Kemp, "How We Trap America's Poor Iin the 'Other Economy,'" *Washington Post*, May 6, 1991, D1.

203. Kemp, "How We Trap America's Poor in the 'Other Economy.'" The Steiger Amendment reduced the capital gains tax from 49 percent to 28 percent.

204. Peck and Tickell, "Neoliberalizing Space"; Raco, "Sustainable Development, Rolled-Out Neoliberalism and Sustainable Communities."

205. Ibid.

206. Jill Zuckman, "Riots Resurrect Enterprise Zones," *CQ Weekly* 50 (May 9, 1992): 1593.

207. Jack Kemp, "A New Agenda for Ending Poverty; Give People a Stake in Their Own Communities," *Washington Post*, May 3, 1992.

208. Samuel Brunelli, "Enterprise Zones Work," *Washington Post*, May 15, 1992.

209. David S. Cloud, "House Passes Urban Aid Bill with Deal on Capital Gains," *CQ Weekly* 50 (July 4, 1992): 1927.

210. Barbara Vobejda, "Leader of Mayors' Conference Calls Aid Plan 'Not Worthy of the Name'; Hill Supporters Defend $ 5 Billion Plan for 50 Enterprise Zones," *Washington Post*, January 3, 1992, A4.

211. Ibid.

212. It included an expansion of individual retirement accounts, a phase-out of the personal exemption for higher earners, a series of real estate tax breaks, a repeal of a luxury tax, and tax-free savings bonds.

213. David S. Cloud, "Tax Bill Gets Bipartisan Nod from Senate Finance Panel," *CQ Weekly* 50 (August 1, 1992): 2251–2254.

214. Ann Devroy, "Kemp Urges Veto of Senate Tax Proposal; HUD Secretary, Bush Differ on Urban Zones," *Washington Post*, July 31, 1992, A4.

215. Jill Zuckman, "Enterprise Zone Alchemy: 90s Style Urban Renewal," *CQ Weekly* 50 (August 8, 1992): 2354.

216. Devroy, "Kemp Urges Veto of Senate Tax Proposal," 4.

217. Editorial, "Worst Bill of the Year," *Washington Post*, July 31, 1992, sec. A.

218. The proposals were also supported by a few Democrats, including Joseph Lieberman (D-CT).

219. John R. Cranford, "Bentsen Forestalls Efforts to Derail Urban Aid Bill," *CQ Weekly* 50 (August 15, 1992): 2435–2436.

220. Of those voting in favor, forty-eight were Democrats and twenty-two Republicans, while twenty-one Republicans, including Majority Leader Bob Dole, and eight Democrats voted against.

221. Twenty-three Republicans and forty-four Democrats voted in favor, and eight Democrats and fourteen Republicans opposed.

222. Quoted in David S. Cloud, "Senate Sends $27 Billion Bill Straight for a Veto," *CQ Weekly* 50 (October 10, 1992): 3133.

223. Gary Lee, "Darman Is Non-Committal on Bush Signing Tax Bill," *Washington Post*, October 5, 1992, A4.

224. Thus, the bill sat in a box on the Speaker's floor until October 23, ten business days until November 4.

225. "Read Bush's Veto Pen: No New Taxes," *CQWR* 50 (November 7, 1992): 3556.

226. Quoted in "The Democratic Platform," *New York Times*, July 15, 1992, A10.

227. Edward Walsh, "Clinton Economic Plan Targets Poor Families; Proposal Aims to Boost Savings, Communities," *Washington Post*, September 17, 1992.

228. Indeed, "new paradigm" advocates such as Pinkerton very much believed that Clinton had largely adopted its vision. James Pinkerton, interview by author, Washington, D.C., April 13, 2009.

229. Rubin is listed by the Heritage Foundation as one of a "list of experts and organizations that support tax based federal and state enterprise zone legislation." See Carl Horowitz, "New Life for Federal Enterprise Zone Legislation: Seven Lessons from the States," *The Heritage Foundation* (June 4, 1991). Her work on enterprise zones includes Marilyn Rubin and Regina Armstrong, "The New Jersey Enterprise Zone Program: An Evaluation," prepared for the New Jersey Department of Commerce, Energy and Economic Development, July 1989.

230. U.S. Congress, House Subcommittee on Economic Stabilization of the Committee on Banking, Finance, and Urban Affairs, *Enterprise Zones: Prospects for Economic Growth*, 102nd Cong., 2nd Sess., February 20, 1992, 86.

231. Michael Allan Wolf, "Enterprise Zones: A Decade of Diversity," *Economic Development Quarterly* 4 (1989): 3–14; Wolf, "Through the Legal Looking-Glass," 12.

232. U.S. Department of Housing and Urban Development, *State Designated Enterprise Zones: Ten Case Studies* (Washington, D.C.: Government Printing Office, 1986). Furthermore, as Rubin and Wilder point out, HUD's findings "must be qualified because it used interviews with zone officials who are potentially biased by a natural tendency to attribute any job growth within the zone exclusively to the enterprise zone's influence." See Barry Rubin and Margaret Wilder, "Rhetoric Versus Reality," *Journal of the American Planning Association* 62.4 (1992): 473–491.

233. Rodney A. Erickson and Susan W. Friedman, "Comparative Dimensions of State Enterprise Zones," in *Enterprise Zones: New Directions in Economic Development*, ed. Roy Green (Newbury Park, Calif.: Sage, 1991), 155–176.

234. Rubin and Wilder, "Urban Enterprise Zones."

235. Sar A. Levitan, *Enterprise Zones: A Promise Based on Rhetoric* (Washington, D.C.: Center for Social Policy Studies, George Washington University, 1992).

236. Ibid., 44.

237. Ibid., 47.

238. Dan Y. Dabney, "Do Enterprise Zone Incentives Affect Business Location Decisions?" *Economic Development Quarterly* 5.4 (November 1991): 1.

239. Robert Greenbaum and John Engberg, "An Evaluation of State Enterprise Zone Policies," *Review of Policy Research* 17.2–3 (2000): 30.

240. Alan H. Peters and Peter S. Fisher, *State Enterprise Zone Programs: Have They Worked?* (Kalamazoo, Mich.: W. E. Upjohn Institute for Employment Research, 2002), 226.

241. Ibid., 227.

242. Ibid., 10.

243. They are Pennsylvania, Connecticut, Illinois, Indiana, and New Jersey. Kemp, hearing, 1989, 72. This finding is slightly more critical than Mossberger's characterization of the evidence as "a mixed bag." See Mossberger, *The Politics of Ideas and the Spread of Enterprise Zones*, 70–74. Notably, Mossberger's work was published prior to that of Peters and Fisher. Suffice it to say, almost no scholars argue that the state zones were unambiguously successful.

244. Bendick has argued that although Democratic policy makers did support enterprise zones per se, they held hearings on them because they were seen as the "only game in town" and possibly "the only thing they could deliver to urban and poor constituents." Marc Bendick, interview by author, Washington, D.C., April 13, 2009.

245. Butler feels that "the most lasting benefit [of the enterprise debate] was to challenge the whole philosophy of redevelopment at that time. To challenge it head on! And I think we broadly won that argument . . . I think it helped change the direction about what constitutes an improvement and got much more down to a more empowerment vision and a less grand vision of development. And I think that's been a very lasting effect." Stuart Butler, interview by author, Heritage Foundation, Washington, D.C., February 3, 2009. For more on ideas as blueprints, see Blyth, *Great Transformations*.

Chapter 2

1. Margaret Thatcher was dubbed the "Iron Lady" by the Soviet Army newspaper, *Red Star*, on January 24, 1976.

2. Peter Jenkins, *Mrs. Thatcher's Revolution: The Ending of the Socialist Era* (Cambridge, Mass.: Harvard University Press, 1988); Prasad, *The Politics of Free Markets*; Pierson, *Dismantling the Welfare State?*; Gamble, *The Free Economy and the Strong State*; see, for example, Peter Kerr, *Postwar British Politics: From Conflict to Consensus* (London: Routledge, 2001).

3. Peter Jenkins argues that "settlement" is a far better descriptor than "consensus" given broad agreement on full employment and the welfare state but the many disagreements on monetary policy, the convertibility of sterling, state controls, and the distribution of wealth. See Jenkins, *Mrs. Thatcher's Revolution*. Peter Kerr is even more skeptical of the notion of consensus, arguing that the 1950s and 1960s were in fact rife with political conflict and, turning the prevailing wisdom on its head, that Thatcherism represented a consensus. See Kerr, *Postwar British Politics*.

4. See, for example, Joel Krieger, *Reagan, Thatcher, and the Politics of Decline* (New York: Oxford University Press, 1986); Jenkins, *Mrs. Thatcher's Revolution*; Nicholas Kaldor, *The Economic Consequences of Mrs Thatcher* (London: Duckworth, 1983).

5. Heffernan, *New Labour and Thatcherism*, 59.

6. Quoted in ibid.

7. Timothy J. Hatton and George R. Boyer, "Unemployment and the UK Labour Market Before, During and After the Golden Age," *European Review of Economic History* 9.1 (2005): 38.

8. Margaret Thatcher, Speech to Conservative Party Conference, October 10, 1980, Thatcher Archive, CCOPR 735/80.

9. In the election of February 1974, the results were Labour 301, Conservative 296, Liberal 14, and Others 24. Thus, Labour was the largest party but did not have an overall majority. They formed a minority government until the second election of that year in October, which delivered to Labour a majority of 3. The results were Labour 319, Conservative 276, Liberal 13, and Others 39.

10. The Social Contract was the basis of an agreement between the Trades Union Congress and the Labour Party under which the unions would comply with limits on wages in return for expansion of state benefits.

11. Harold Wilson resigned unexpectedly in April 1976.

12. Kerr, *Postwar British Politics*, 161.

13. Monetarism rests on the notion that inflation arises when the money supply in the economy increases at a faster rate than the supply of goods and services. Wages, as such, are said to have little influence. Therefore, in order to cut inflation, governments should reduce the money supply, often via raising interest rates. This is what U.S. Federal Reserve Chair Paul Volcker and British Chancellor Geoffrey Howe did between 1979 and 1985.

14. James Callaghan, Speech to the Labour Party Conference, December 28, 1976. The author of that section of the speech was Peter Jay, Callaghan's son-in-law and a committed monetarist. Jay wrote an influential column in *The Times*, which he used to argue for the abandonment of Keynesianism. Also important was Samuel Brittan, a journalist at the *Financial Times* whose columns heavily promoted monetarism.

15. Hall, "Policy Paradigms, Social Learning, and the State," 283–284.

16. These figures refer to estimates in the change in the Retail Price Index. Office of National Statistics, "Consumer Price Inflation 1947 to 2004," Office of National Statistics Online, http://www.statistics.gov.uk/statbase/TSDdownload1.asp.

17. Interestingly, one of the factors that persuaded Callaghan and Healey to request the International Monetary Fund loan were the pessimistic growth forecasts that turned out to be false. Had they followed Foreign Secretary Tony Crosland's advice and weathered the storm until the economy improved, Labour's monetarist turn might have been avoided. See Jones, *Masters of the Universe*, 245; also see William Keegan, *Mrs. Thatcher's Economic Experiment* (London: A. Lane, 1984), 33–34.

18. The results were Conservative 339, Labour 269, Liberal 11, and Others 16.

19. This is William Keegan's term for Keith Joseph, Margaret Thatcher, and the coalition of interests that supported monetarism with an almost religious zeal.

20. Keith Joseph was a member of Heath's cabinet from 1970 to 1974. His ideas would have a significant impact on Margaret Thatcher and many others within the party and beyond.

21. Quoted in E. H. H. Green, *Ideologies of Conservatism* (Oxford: Oxford University Press, 2002), 4. But as we will see, Joseph's brand of Conservatism was anything but conservative.

22. Their key works include Hayek, *The Road to Serfdom*; Friedrich A. von Hayek, *The Constitution of Liberty* (Chicago: University of Chicago Press, 1960); Milton Friedman, *Capitalism and Freedom* (Chicago: University of Chicago Press, 1962); Milton Friedman, *Monetarist Economics* (Oxford, U.K.: Blackwell, 1991); Milton Friedman, *Free to Choose: A Personal Statement* (New York: Harcourt Brace Jovanovich, 1980); Milton Friedman, *Inflation and Unemployment: The New Dimension of Politics* (London: Institute of Economic Affairs, 1977). Other central key influences were Karl Popper, Ludwig von Mises, and Enoch Powell, as was the Mont Pelerin Society.

23. See, for example, Jones, *Masters of the Universe.*

24. Daniel Yergin and Joseph Stainslaw, *The Commanding Heights: The Battle for the World Economy*, rev. and updated ed. (New York: Simon & Schuster, 2002), 89. Also see John Ranelagh, *Thatcher's People: An Insider's Account of the Politics, the Power and the Personalities* (London: HarperCollins, 1991), ix.

25. Friedrich von Hayek to Margaret Thatcher, May 5, 1979, Thatcher MSS, Churchill College Archive, Cambridge, THCR 2/4/1/8.

26. Margaret Thatcher to Friedrich von Hayek, May 18, 1979, Thatcher MSS, Churchill College Archive, Cambridge, THCR 2/4/1/8.

27. Willie Whitelaw was Margaret Thatcher's indubitably loyal deputy prime minister between May 1979 and January 1988. He also served as home secretary. Whitelaw's importance to Thatcher was reflected in her (in)famous remark, "every Prime Minister needs a Willie."

28. Keith Joseph to Willie Whitelaw, March 17, 1976, Thatcher MSS, Churchill College Archive, Cambridge, THCR 2/1/1/37.

29. Ibid.

30. Sir Geoffrey Howe to Keith Joseph, March 22, 1976, Thatcher MSS, Churchill College Archive, Cambridge, THCR 2/1/3/9.

31. Quoted in Yergin, *The Commanding Heights*, 80. Alfred Sherman, who was full-time director of the CPS, stated that "our object is to reshape the climate of opinion. The Centre proposes to fight vigorously on this front of the battle of ideas." Quoted in Keegan, *Mrs. Thatcher's Economic Experiment*, 47.

32. Ibid., 81. At that time, his "coterie" included Sir Geoffrey Howe. Continuing the religious metaphor, Howe notes that during 1974 and 1975, Joseph "embarked upon a series of fundamentalist speeches" attacking Keynesianism and promoting not just monetarism but a far broader ideologically informed program. See Geoffrey Howe, *Conflict of Loyalty* (London: Macmillan, 1994). Howe also notes that Hayek was one of Thatcher's "patron saints."

33. Robert Jacob Alexander Skidelsky, ed., *Thatcherism* (London: Chatto & Windus, 1988), 14.

34. Quoted in Jenkins, *Mrs. Thatcher's Revolution*, 62.

35. Ibid.

36. At Edgbaston on October 19, 1979, Joseph expressed concern that the increasing rate of pregnancy among single parents from "social classes 4 and 5" threatened to downgrade the quality of "human stock."

37. Howe, *Conflict of Loyalty*, 93.

38. Quoted in ibid., 94.

39. Jim Prior was shadow employment secretary; David Howell was shadow transport secretary. Both would serve in the Thatcher government.

40. "The Right Approach to the Economy," August 17, 1977, Thatcher MSS, Churchill College Archive, Cambridge, THCR 2/6/1/116.

41. Ibid., 31.

42. The French term often used to denote planned economies.

43. Margaret Thatcher, quoted in Heffernan, *New Labour and Thatcherism*, 35.

44. Hall, "Policy Paradigms, Social Learning, and the State."

45. Ibid., 284.

46. Howe, *Conflict of Loyalty*, 158–175.

47. Ibid., 265.

48. Kaldor, *The Economic Consequences of Mrs Thatcher*, 3.

49. Keegan, *Mrs. Thatcher's Economic Experiment*, 132. Kaldor's analysis also points to a central role for ideology, not least because many business groups opposed monetarism.

50. The Bow Group was founded in the 1950s as a counterweight to the Fabian Society. According to a Bow Group Publication, it "exists to provide a forum for the development of Conservative Party policy and thought; and to transmit the ideas of its members to a wider public." See Geoffrey Howe, *Enterprise Zones and the Enterprise Culture* (London: Bow Publications, 1988).

51. Geoffrey Howe, "Liberating Free Enterprise: A New Experiment," Speech to the Bow Group, London, June 26, 1978, reproduced in *Enterprise Zones and the Enterprise Culture* (London: Bow Publications, 1988), 7.

52. Ibid., 9.

53. Ibid.

54. Sir Geoffrey Howe, interview by author, House of Lords, London, July 7, 2009.

55. Geoffrey Howe, "Liberating Free Enterprise," 11.

56. Howe, *Enterprise Zones and the Enterprise Culture*, 23.

57. Ibid.

58. Sir Peter Hall, Speech, Thatcher MSS, Churchill College Archive, Cambridge, THCR 2/1/3/9.

59. Ibid., 9.

60. Sir Geoffrey Howe to Margaret Thatcher, July 20, 1978; Margaret Thatcher to Sir Geoffrey Howe, August 2, 1978, Thatcher MSS, Churchill College Archive, Cambridge, THCR 2/1/3/9. Thatcher's response appears to be more than mere politeness on her part since the Hall speech, which Howe sent to her, was littered with her underlinings.

61. Howe, *Conflict of Loyalty*, 174.

62. See Howe's 1980 Budget in Hansard, HC Deb, March 26, 1980, cc981–1439.

63. Department of the Environment, *Enterprise Zones* (London: HMSO, 1981).

64. Michael Heseltine, interview by author, London, July 7, 2009.

65. Michael Crick, *Michael Heseltine: A Biography* (London: Hamish Hamilton, 1997), 219.

66. Michael Heseltine, *Where There's a Will* (London: Hutchinson, 1987), 5.

67. Michael Heseltine, interview by author, London, July 7, 2009.

68. Michael Heseltine, *Life in the Jungle: My Autobiography* (London: Hodder & Stoughton, 2000), 215.

69. Local Government, Planning and Land Act 1980 (c.65), section 136.

70. Paul Lawless, *Britain's Inner Cities*, 2nd ed. (London: Paul Chapman, 1989), 82.

71. Local Government, Planning and Land Act 1980 (c.65), section 134. The "national interest" evokes the logic spelled out by Ted Gurr and Desmond King—that is, the state has an interest in urban areas, especially for the purposes of extraction. Thus, when a city's "use value" sharply differs from its "exchange value," the state steps in to revalorize urban areas.

72. Robert Imrie and Huw Thomas, eds., *British Urban Policy: An Evaluation of the Urban Development Corporations*, 2nd ed. (London: Sage, 1999), 3.

73. These were in Black Country, Cardiff Bay, Teeside, Trafford Park, Tyne and Wear, Bristol, Central Manchester, Leeds, Sheffield, Birmingham, and Plymouth.

74. Quoted in Imrie and Thomas, *British Urban Policy*, 7.

75. Brian Connell, "Ending the Blight of London Dockland," *The Times*, March 17, 1980, A11.

76. Lawless, *Britain's Inner Cities*, 82.

77. Ted Robert Gurr and Desmond S. King, *The State and the City* (Chicago: University of Chicago Press, 1987), 162. Also see Hatton and Boyer, "Unemployment and the UK Labour Market Before, During and After the Golden Age," 38.

78. See, for example, James Anderson, "The 'New Right,' Enterprise Zones and Urban Development Corporations," *International Journal of Urban and Regional Research* 14.3 (1990): 468–489; Rob Atkinson, *Urban Policy in Britain: The City, the State and the Market* (Baskingstoke, U.K.: Macmillan, 1994); Timothy Barnekov, Boyle Robin, and Daniel Rich, *Privatism and Urban Policy in Britain and the United States* (Oxford: Oxford University Press, 1989); Andrew Gamble, "Privatization, Thatcherism, and the British State," *Journal of Law and Society* 16.1 (1988): 1–20; Gurr and King, *The State and the City*; Doreen Massey, "Enterprise Zones: A Political Issue," *International Journal of Urban and Regional Research* 6.3 (1982): 429–434.

79. Harold Wolman, *Urban Politics and Policy: A Comparative Approach* (Oxford, U.K.: Blackwell, 1992), 219.

80. Crick, *Michael Heseltine*.

81. Harvey, *A Brief History of Neoliberalism*; Brenner and Theodore, *Spaces of Neoliberalism*, 3.

82. Barnekov, Robin, and Rich, *Privatism and Urban Policy*, 183; Michael Parkinson, "The Thatcher Government's Urban Policy, 1979–1989: A Review," *The Town Planning Review* 60.4 (October 1989): 421–440.

83. Barnekov, Robin, and Rich, *Privatism and Urban Policy*, 184.

84. Parkinson, "The Thatcher Government's Urban Policy," 434.

85. Quoted in Barnekov, Robin, and Rich, *Privatism and Urban Policy*, 182.

86. Crick, *Michael Heseltine*, 238–239.

87. Michael Heseltine, "Reviving the Inner Cities," *Conservative Political Centre* (1983).

88. Michael Heseltine, interview by author, London, July 7, 2009.

89. Ibid.

90. Harvey, *A Brief History of Neoliberalism*, 76–77.

91. Ibid., 70. This evidence largely supports Harvey's account but qualifies it in a number of respects. For as we have seen, environmental regulations were maintained in the EZs and the UDCs.

92. See, for example, Jordan, "Enterprise Zones in the UK and the US: Ideologically Acceptable Job Creation?"; Parkinson, "The Thatcher Government's Urban Policy, 1979–1989"; Barnekov, Robin, and Rich, *Privatism and Urban Policy*; Dilys M. Hill, *Urban Policy and Politics in Britain* (Basingstoke, U.K.: Macmillan, 1999); Jordan, "Enterprise Zones in the UK and the US."

93. Howe, *Enterprise Zones and the Enterprise Culture*, 19.

94. Ibid.

95. Ibid., 21.

96. Ibid., 24.

97. Department of the Environment, *Monitoring Enterprise Zones*, 1983; Department of the Environment, *Final Evaluation of Enterprise Zones* (London: HMSO, 1995). For an initial

assessment, see Roger Tym, *Monitoring Enterprise Zones* (London: Roger Tym Associates, 1984).

98. PA Cambridge Economic Consultants, *An Evaluation of the Enterprise Zone Experiment* (London: HMSO, 1987), 1. The report was based upon face-to-face interviews with 760 firms and postal questionnaires with over 1,200. This method is questionable since firms may locate in a given area for a range of reasons but have an interest in promoting the idea that tax incentives were decisive in their location decision since they benefit financially from the tax not due. .In this case, they would come to be the beneficiaries of tax giveaways. We can reasonably assume, therefore, that the report is very likely to *overestimate* the effect of the incentives on location and hiring decisions.

99. See table in ibid., 12.

100. Ibid., 53. Also see Peter Geoffrey Hall, "The British Enterprise Zones," in *Enterprise Zones: New Directions in Economic Development* (Newbury Park, Calif.: Sage, 1991), 187.

101. Hall, "The British Enterprise Zones," 189.

102. PA Cambridge Economic Consultants, *An Evaluation of the Enterprise Zone Experiment*. This study excludes the Isle of Dogs enterprise zone in London Docklands.

103. Ibid.

104. Ibid., 42.

105. Ibid., 44.

106. Ibid., 45.

107. See table in ibid., 47.

108. Barnekov, Robin, and Rich, *Privatism and Urban Policy*, 206.

109. Peter Geoffrey Hall, *Cities of Tomorrow: An Intellectual History of Urban Planning and Design in the Twentieth Century*, 3rd ed. (Oxford, U.K.: Blackwell, 2002), 388.

110. Butler, *Enterprise Zones*, 127.

111. Anderson, "The 'New Right,' Enterprise Zones and Urban Development Corporations."

112. Jordan, "Enterprise Zones in the UK and the US," 130.

113. Jenkins, *Mrs. Thatcher's Revolution*, 81. It is worth noting, however, that Jenkins does claim that Thatcher's government was transformative, hence the title of his book.

114. Gamble, *The Free Economy and the Strong State*, 94.

115. Gamble, "Privatization, Thatcherism, and the British State," 6.

116. Kerr, *Postwar British Politics*, 37.

117. David Marsh and R. A. W. Rhodes, "Evaluating Thatcherism: Over the Moon or as Sick as a Parrot?" *Politics* 15.1 (1995); Peter Riddell, *The Thatcher Era and its Legacy* (Oxford, U.K.: Blackwell, 1991). For an excellent review of the literature, see Colin Hay, "Whatever Happened to Thatcherism?" *Political Studies Review* 5.2 (May 2007): 183–201.

118. Pierson, *Dismantling the Welfare State?* 131.

119. Kerr, *Postwar British Politics*, 36.

120. See, for example, Prasad, *The Politics of Free Markets*; Pierson, *Dismantling the Welfare State?*

121. Office of National Statistics, "Consumer Price Inflation 1947 to 2004."

122. Norman Lamont, HC Deb, May 16, 1991, cc413.

123. Hall, *Cities of Tomorrow*.

124. Hood, *Explaining Economic Policy Reversals*.

125. Goldsmith, "Enterprise Zones," 441.

126. Quoted in Massey, "Enterprise Zones," 431.

127. G. B. Norcliffe and A. G. Hoare, "Enterprise Zone Policy for the Inner City: A Review and Preliminary Assessment," *Area* 14.4 (1982): 271.

128. John Elliot, "Beckett Call to Cut Costs for Industry," *Financial Times*, July 31, 1982, sec. 1, 24.

129. Bernard Tennant, "Development of Enterprise Zones," *The Times*, June 9, 1981, 18. Also see Alan C. Hollway, "Enterprise Zones," *The Times*, August 23, 1982. Mike Brookfield, "Enterprise Zones," *The Times*, September 7, 1982, 11.

130. Andrew Taylor, "Enterprise Zones Doubts Remain," *The Financial Times*, July 30, 1982, sec. 1.9.

131. Massey, "Enterprise Zones," 432.

132. Ibid., 431.

133. Duménil and Lévy, *Capital Resurgent*; Harvey, *A Brief History of Neoliberalism*; Doreen Massey, *World City*.

134. See, for example, Pierson, *Dismantling the Welfare State?*; Skocpol, *Protecting Soldiers and Mothers*; Gottschalk, *The Shadow Welfare State*.

135. Pierson, *Dismantling the Welfare State?* 47.

136. Ibid.

137. Barnekov, Robin, and Rich, *Privatism and Urban Policy*, 206.

138. However, it is worth noting that enterprise zone plans were reintroduced in 2010, as part of the first Conservative budget since 1996. Geoffrey Howe looked on approvingly from the Commons' gallery.

139. See Pierson and Skocpol, "Historical Institutionalism in Contemporary Political Science."

140. Weir, "Ideas and Politics."

141. Ibid., 62.

142. Ibid., 65.

143. Gottschalk, *The Prison and the Gallows*.

144. This is Gamble's central concern in his work on Thatcherism. See Gamble, *The Free Economy and the Strong State*. In a revision to this view, Loïc Wacquant argues that the strong carceral state necessarily follows from the effects of neoliberal economic policy. See Loïc J. D. Wacquant, *Punishing the Poor: The Neoliberal Government of Social Insecurity* (Durham, N.C.: Duke University Press, 2009).

145. Gottschalk, *The Prison and the Gallows*, 107.

146. Ibid.

147. Ibid.

148. Ibid., 109.

149. Howe, *Enterprise Zones and the Enterprise Culture*, 12.

150. In particular, Jordan notes that "the Department for the Environment argued to retain local authority involvement; the Department of Health and Social Security sought to maintain health protection; the Department for Employment did not agree to change employment legislation." See Jordan, "Enterprise Zones in the UK and the US," 131.

151. Ibid., 130.

152. Sir Geoffrey Howe, interview by author, House of Lords, London, July 7, 2009.

153. Draft memo from Nigel Dorling to Tom King, "Enterprise Zones: Designation and the Planning Regime," March 14, 1980, National Archives, File AT 81/67. Dorling was the head of the DOE's Inner Cities Directorate.

154. This is ironic due to the specious neoliberal claim that regulation undermines economic activity.

155. Gurr and King, *The State and the City*, 9.

156. Ibid. Emphasis theirs.

157. Ibid., 169.

158. Ibid., 170.

159. Lieberman, "Ideas and Institutions in Race Politics," 217.

160. Pierson, *Dismantling the Welfare State?*; King and Wood, "The Political Economy of Neoliberalism," 372.

161. Prasad, *The Politics of Free Markets*, 20.

162. Ibid.

163. Ibid., 21, also see 155.

164. It is not as if Thatcher had no economists who espoused neoliberal ideas. They included Professor Patrick Minford, Professor Brian Griffiths, Harold Rose of Barclays Bank, and Gordon Pepper of the stockbrokers W. Greenwell. See Keegan, *Mrs. Thatcher's Economic Experiment*, 125–126.

165. Blyth, *Great Transformations*. Also see Lieberman, "Ideas, Institutions, and Political Order."

166. Hall, "Policy Paradigms, Social Learning, and the State," 281, 284.

167. Ibid., 289.

168. Smith, "Which Comes First, the Ideas or the Institutions?" 111.

169. Ibid., 109.

170. In doing so, I follow Gamble, Heffernan, and Hay: Gamble, *The Free Economy and the Strong State*; Heffernan, *New Labour and Thatcherism*.

171. King and Wood, "The Political Economy of Neoliberalism," 372.

172. Gurr and King, *The State and the City*, 167.

173. Prasad, *The Politics of Free Markets*.

174. See, for example, Duménil and Lévy, *Capital Resurgent*; Hackworth, *The Neoliberal City*; Harvey, *A Brief History of Neoliberalism*; Peck, *Constructions of Neoliberal Reason*.

Chapter 3

1. Tony Blair, *A Journey* (London: Arrow, 2011), 116.

2. Skowronek, *The Politics Presidents Make*.

3. A third-way mantra used repeatedly by both Clinton and Blair.

4. Jamie Peck, *Workfare States* (New York: Guilford Press, 2001).

5. See, for example, Giddens, *The Third Way*; Hay, *The Political Economy of New Labour*; Heffernan, *New Labour and Thatcherism*; Peck, *Workfare States*; Stiglitz, *The Roaring Nineties*; Flavio Romano, *Clinton and Blair: The Political Economy of the Third Way* (London: Routledge, 2006).

6. Kenneth S. Baer, *Reinventing Democrats: The Politics of Liberalism from Reagan to Clinton* (Lawrence: University Press of Kansas, 2000); Jon F. Hale, "The Making of the New Democrats," *Political Science Quarterly* 110.2 (July 1995): 207–232.

7. Blyth, *Great Transformations*, 193. As Blyth puts it, "Hoover, it seemed, was running for the Democrats."

8. Hale, "The Making of the New Democrats," 215.

9. Ibid., 219.

10. Philip Klinkner, "Democratic Party Ideology in the 1990s: New Democrats or Modern Republicans?" in *The Politics of Ideas: Intellectual Challenges Facing the American Political Parties*, ed. John Kenneth White and John Clifford Green (Albany: State University of New York Press, 2001), 113–131.

11. William A. Galston and Elaine Kamarck, *The Politics of Evasion* (Washington, D.C.: Progressive Policy Institute, September 1989), 2.

12. Ibid.

13. Ibid., 17, 18–19.

14. Al From and Will Marshall, quoted in Baer, *Reinventing Democrats*, 134.

15. Ibid., 137.

16. Ibid., 195.

17. Robert Dreyfuss, "How the DLC Does It," *The American Prospect*, December 19, 2001.

18. Baer, *Reinventing Democrats*, 163.

19. Democratic Leadership Council, *The New Orleans Declaration: A Democratic Agenda for the 1990s* (Washington, D.C.: DLC, 1990).

20. Ibid.

21. Bill Clinton, "Keynote Address to DLC Convention" (Cleveland, Ohio, May 7, 1991).

22. Democratic Leadership Council, *The New American Choice Resolutions* (Washington, D.C.: DLC, 1991).

23. Ibid., 21.

24. Ibid., 22.

25. Baer, *Reinventing Democrats*, 199.

26. Skowronek, *The Politics Presidents Make*, 448.

27. Bill Clinton, "The New Covenant: Responsibility and Rebuilding the American Community," address at Georgetown University (Washington, D.C., October 23, 1991).

28. Bill Clinton, "A New Covenant for Economic Change," address at Georgetown University (Washington, D.C., November 20, 1991).

29. Ibid.

30. Ibid.

31. Ibid.

32. Bill Clinton, "The New Covenant: Responsibility and Rebuilding the American Community," address at Georgetown University (Washington, D.C., October 23, 1991).

33. Ibid.

34. By 1992, "30 percent of the Democratic House members and 57 percent of Democratic senators belonged" to the DLC. Stephen A. Borrelli, "Finding the Third Way: Bill Clinton, the DLC, and the Democratic Platform of 1992," *Journal of Policy History* 13.4 (2001): 440.

35. Borrelli, "Finding the Third Way."

36. Ibid., 436.

37. Ibid., 451.

38. Barbara Vobejda, "Leader of Mayors' Conference Calls Aid Plan 'Not Worthy of the Name': Hill Supporters Defend $ 5 Billion Plan for 50 Enterprise Zones," *Washington Post*, July 3, 1992, A4.

39. Borrelli, "Finding the Third Way," 452.

40. "The Democratic Platform," *New York Times*, July 15, 1992, A10.

41. Ibid.

42. James D. Savage, *Balanced Budgets & American Politics* (Ithaca, N.Y.: Cornell University Press, 1988).

43. For details, see Michael B. Katz, *In the Shadow of the Poorhouse: A Social History of Welfare in America* (New York: Basic Books, 1996), 262–282.

44. Blair described Gould as "the one with the divining rod." See Blair, *A Journey*, 22.

45. Philip Gould, *The Unfinished Revolution: How the Modernisers Saved the Labour Party* (London: Little, Brown, 1998), 174.

46. Matthias Matthijs, *Ideas and Economic Crises in Britain from Attlee to Blair (1945–2005)* (London: Routledge, 2011), 129.

47. Mark Wickham-Jones, "Signaling Credibility: Electoral Strategy and New Labour in Britain," *Political Science Quarterly* 120.4 (2005): 653–673.

48. Mark Wickham-Jones, *Economic Strategy and the Labour Party: Politics and Policy-Making, 1970–83* (Baskingstoke, U.K.: Macmillan, 1996); Hay, *The Political Economy of New Labour*; Richard Hill, *The Labour Party and Economic Strategy, 1979–1997: The Long Road Back* (Baskingstoke, U.K.: Palgrave, 2001); Heffernan, *New Labour and Thatcherism*.

49. Hill, *The Labour Party and Economic Strategy, 1979–1997*, 34.

50. Mark Bevir, "The Remaking of Labour, 1987–1997," *Observatoire de La Société Britannique. La Revue* 7 (March 2009): 351–366.

51. Ibid.

52. Hill, *The Labour Party and Economic Strategy, 1979–1997*, 73.

53. The Labour Party, *Time to Get Britain Working Again* (London: Labour Party, 1992).

54. Blair, *A Journey*, 231–232.

55. John Smith was Labour leader from 1992 until his untimely death in 1994, after which Tony Blair was elected leader. Smith has been described by many as the best prime minister Britain never had.

56. Blair, *A Journey*, 83.

57. Matthijs, *Ideas and Economic Crises in Britain from Attlee to Blair (1945–2005)*, 155.

58. Bevir, "The Remaking of Labour, 1987–1997."

59. For various descriptions, see Hay, *The Political Economy of New Labour*; Heffernan, *New Labour and Thatcherism*; Hill, *The Labour Party and Economic Strategy, 1979–1997*; Eric Shaw, *Losing Labour's Soul? New Labour and the Blair Government 1997–2007* (London: Routledge, 2007).

60. While Labour's economic policy was shaped by Gordon Brown, Blair's chancellor of the Exchequer (1997–2007) and later prime minister (2007–2010), who was considered to the left of Blair, Brown's refusal to raise the top rate of income tax, his commitment to Conservative spending plans for the first two years of the parliament, and giving independence to the Bank of England for the setting of interest rates were all consistent with neoliberalism. See William Keegan, *The Prudence of Mr Gordon Brown* (Chichester, U.K.: Wiley, 2003).

61. Matthijs, *Ideas and Economic Crises in Britain from Attlee to Blair (1945–2005)*, 160.

62. Tony Blair, "The Economic Framework for New Labour," in *Policy Makers on Policy: The Mais Lectures*, ed. Forrest Capie and Geoffrey Edward Wood, 2nd ed. (New York: Routledge, 2010).

63. Ibid., 172.

64. Ibid., 167.

65. Desmond S. King and Mark Wickham-Jones, "From Clinton to Blair: The Democratic (Party) Origins of Welfare to Work," *The Political Quarterly* 70.1 (1999): 72.

66. Nik Theodore, "New Labour at Work: Long-Term Unemployment and the Geography of Opportunity," *Cambridge Journal of Economics* 31.6 (2007): 929.

67. Quoted in ibid.

68. Blair, "The Economic Framework for New Labour," 178.

69. Bob Woodward, *The Agenda: Inside the Clinton White House* (New York: Pocket Books, 1995), 73.

70. Ibid., 161.

71. Taylor Branch, *The Clinton Tapes: Wrestling History with the President* (New York: Simon & Schuster, 2009), 66.

72. See Romano, *Clinton and Blair*, 39–42.

73. Stiglitz, *The Roaring Nineties*, xliv.

74. Paul Pierson, "The Deficit and the Politics of Domestic Reform," in *The Social Divide: Political Parties and the Future of Activist Government*, ed. Margaret Weir (Washington, D.C.: Brookings Institution Press, 1998), 140–141.

75. Stiglitz, *The Roaring Nineties*; Robert Pollin, *Contours of Descent: U.S. Economic Fractures and the Landscape of Global Austerity* (London: Verso, 2005).

76. Robert Pollin, *Contours of Descent: U.S. Economic Fractures and the Landscape of Global Austerity* (London: Verso, 2005), 24.

77. Ibid., 25.

78. Ibid., 29.

79. Ibid., 30.

80. See Michael B. Katz, *The Price of Citizenship: Redefining America's Welfare State* (New York: Henry Holt, 2001), 305.

81. Danilo Trisis and LaDonna Pavetti, *TANF Weakening as a Safety Net for Poor Families* (Washington, D.C.: Center on Budget and Policy Priorities, 2012).

82. Ibid.

83. However, according to Clinton aide George Stephanopoulos, Clinton told supporters from the financial community that he thought he raised taxes on the wealthy too much. Romano, *Clinton and Blair*, 56.

84. Pollin, *Contours of Descent*, 27.

85. Romano, *Clinton and Blair*, 89.

86. H. M. Treasury, *Public Expenditure: Statistical Analysis 2009* (London: H. M. Treasury, June 2009), 65.

87. Ibid.

88. Quoted in Romano, *Clinton and Blair*, 89.

89. Andrew Glyn and Stewart Wood, "Economic Policy Under New Labour: How Social Democratic Is the Blair Government?" *The Political Quarterly* 72.1 (2001): 50–66.

90. See Chapter 4 in Shaw, *Losing Labour's Soul?* There are clear parallels with the growth of private-public partnerships in the United States.

91. King and Wickham-Jones, "From Clinton to Blair"; Peck, *Workfare States.*

92. Glyn and Wood, "Economic Policy Under New Labour," 52–53.

93. The Labour Party, *Britain Will Be Better with New Labour*, Election manifesto (London: The Labour Party, 1997).

94. Shaw, *Losing Labour's Soul?* 50.

95. Glyn and Wood, "Economic Policy Under New Labour," 55–56.

96. Judd and Swanstrom, *City Politics*, 179.

97. Quoted in ibid., 183.

98. Harvey, "From Managerialism to Entrepreneurialism."

99. U.S. Department of Housing and Urban Development, *Urban Development Action Grant Program: Second Annual Report* (Washington, D.C.: Government Printing Office, November 1980), 1.

100. Logan and Molotch, *Urban Fortunes.*

101. It was the country's most costly example of civil disorder in terms of lives lost (53), injuries (2,383), and damage to property in the twentieth century. See Judd and Swanstrom, *City Politics*, 187.

102. Ibid.

103. In 1993, the legislature removed restrictions on the location of enterprise zones, extending the favorable tax treatment for business to the entire state.

104. Mollenkopf, "Urban Policy at the Crossroads," 473.

105. "The 1992 Campaign; Excerpts From Clinton's Speech on His Economic Proposals," *New York Times*, June 23, 1992.

106. Nicholas Lenmann, "The Myth of Community Development," *New York Times Magazine*, January 9, 1994, 27–31.

107. Quoted in Mollenkopf, "Urban Policy at the Crossroads," 473.

108. Vanessa Williams, "Staunchly Backing Urban Renewal Plan, Sen. Bill Bradley Helped Write the Empowerment Zone Legislation, the Difference, He Says, Is Grass-Roots Input," *Philadelphia Inquirer*, December 25, 1994.

109. William J. Clinton, Remarks on the Empowerment Zones and Enterprise Communities, January 17, 1994, http://www.presidency.ucsb.edu/ws/print.php?pid=50154.

110. Osborne and Gaebler, *Reinventing Government.*

111. Ibid., 15.

112. Ibid., 16.

113. Ibid., 17.

114. Ibid., 79.

115. Quoted in William A. Galston and Geoffrey L. Tibbetts, "Reinventing Federalism: The Clinton/Gore Program for a New Partnership Among the Federal, State, Local, and Tribal Governments," *Publius* 24.3 (July 1994): 25.

116. Draft memorandum to President Clinton, "An Economic Empowerment Strategy," Interagency Working Group on Community Development and Empowerment, April 2, 1993, Enterprise Zones [1], Box 108, Bruce Reed Collection, Digital Library, William J. Clinton Presidential Library, http://www.clintonlibrary.gov/assets/storage/Research%20-%20Digital%20Library/Reed-Subject/108/647386-enterprise-zones-1.pdf.

117. Ibid.

118. Memorandum to the National Economic Council, "OMB's Views on Enterprise Zones," March 31, 1993, Enterprise Zones [1], Box 108, Bruce Reed Collection, Digital

Library, William J. Clinton Presidential Library, http://www.clintonlibrary.gov/assets/storage/Research%20-%20Digital%20Library/Reed-Subject/108/647386-enterprise-zones-1.pdf.

119. Mossberger, "State-Federal Diffusion and Policy Learning," 44.

120. Mollenkopf, "Urban Policy at the Crossroads."

121. William Barnes, interview by author, National League of Cities, Washington, D.C., April 14, 2009.

122. Mossberger, "State-Federal Diffusion and Policy Learning," 49; also see Mossberger, *The Politics of Ideas and the Spread of Enterprise Zones.*

123. Sarah F. Liebschutz, "Empowerment Zones and Enterprise Communities: Reinventing Federalism for Distressed Communities," *Publius* 25.3 (July 1995): 125.

124. Ibid., 124.

125. Judd and Swanstrom, *City Politics*, 191.

126. Vice President Al Gore, "A National Commitment to Community Development," *Shelterforce Online*, March/April 1994, http://www.nhi.org/online/issues/74/gore.html.

127. Liebschutz, "Empowerment Zones and Enterprise Communities."

128. See, for example, M. Gittell, Empowerment Zones: An Opportunity Missed—A Six-City Comparative Study (New York: Howard Samuels State Management and Policy Center, The Graduate School and University Center of The City University of New York, 2001); Deirdre Oakley and Hui-Shien Tsao, "A New Way of Revitalizing Distressed Urban Communities? Assessing the Impact of the Empowerment Zone Program," *Journal of Urban Affairs* 28.5 (2006): 443–471; Noah Temaner Jenkins and Michael I. J. Bennett, "Toward an Empowerment Zone Evaluation," *Economic Development Quarterly* 13.23 (1999): 23–28; Government Accountability Office, *Empowerment Zone and Enterprise Community Program: Improvements Occurred in Communities, but the Effect of the Program Is Unclear*, GAO-06–727 (Washington, D.C.: Government Accountability Office, 2006); U.S. Department of Housing and Urban Development, *Empowerment Zones/Enterprise Communities, Annual Report: Philadelphia, Pennsylvania Annual Report*, 2004; Michael J. Rich and Robert P. Stoker, "Governance and Urban Revitalization: Lessons from the Urban Empowerment Zones Initiative," paper prepared for Conference on a Global Look at Urban and Regional Governance: The State-Market Civic-Nexus, January 2007.

129. Government Accountability Office, *Improvements Occurred in Communities, but the Effect of the Program Is Unclear* (Washington, D.C.: Government Accountability Office, 2006).

130. Ibid., 29.

131. Ibid., 44, 45.

132. Oakley and Tsao, "A New Way of Revitalizing Distressed Urban Communities?" 466.

133. Michael J. Rich and Robert P. Stoker, "Rethinking Empowerment: Evidence from Local Empowerment Zone Programs," *Urban Affairs Review* 45.6 (2010): 775–796. This study was funded in part by HUD.

134. Michael J. Rich and Robert P. Stoker, *Collaborative Governance for Urban Revitalization: Lessons from Empowerment Zones* (Ithaca, N.Y.: Cornell University Press, 2014).

135. Ibid., 124.

136. Mollenkopf, "Urban Policy at the Crossroads," 480.

137. Stuart Butler, interview by author, Heritage Foundation, Washington, D.C., February 3, 2009. Emphasis added.

138. Judd and Swanstrom, *City Politics*, 191.

139. Tony Blair, speech at the Alyesbury Estate, London, June 2, 1997.

140. Blair, *A Journey*, 26–27.

141. Hill, *Urban Policy and Politics in Britain*; Jessop, "Liberalism, Neoliberalism, and Urban Goveranance."

142. Craig Johnstone and Mark Whitehead, eds., *New Horizons in British Urban Policy: Perspectives on New Labour's Urban Renaissance* (Aldershot, U.K.: Ashgate, 2004), 8.

143. Phil Jones and James Evans, *Urban Regeneration in the UK* (London: Sage, 2008); also see Jones and Ward, "Excavating the Logic of British Urban Policy."

144. Department of the Environment, Transport and the Regions, *Towards an Urban Renaissance: Report of the Urban Task Force* (London: HMSO, 1999), 1.

145. Ibid., 42.

146. Lord (Richard) Rogers, telephone interview by author, September 9, 2010.

147. Department of the Environment, Transport and the Regions, *Towards an Urban Renaissance*, 7.

148. Ibid.

149. Ibid.

150. Smith, "New Globalism, New Urbanism"; also see Loretta Lees, "Visions of 'Urban Renaissance': The Urban Task Force Report and the Urban White Paper," in *Urban Renaissance? New Labour, Community and Urban Policy*, ed. Mike Raco and Robert Imrie (Bristol, U.K.: Policy Press, 2003), 61–82.

151. Smith, "New Globalism, New Urbanism," 94.

152. Department of the Environment, Transport and the Regions, *Our Towns and Cities—The Future: Delivering an Urban Renaissance* (London: HMSO, 2000), http://www .communities.gov.uk/documents/regeneration/pdf/131149.pdf.

153. Ibid., 77.

154. Office of the Deputy Prime Minister, *Urban Regeneration Companies: Guidance and Qualification Criteria—May 2004* (London: Office of the Deputy Prime Minister, 2004), 10, http://www.communities.gov.uk/documents/regeneration/pdf/131149.pdf.

155. Philip Booth, "Partnerships and Networks: The Governance of Urban Regeneration in Britain," *Journal of Housing and the Built Environment* 20.3 (2005): 257–269.

156. Annette Hastings, "Strategic, Multilevel Neighbourhood Regeneration: An Outward-Looking Approach at Last?" in *Urban Renaissance? New Labour, Community and Urban Policy*, ed. Mike Raco and Robert Imrie (Bristol, U.K.: Policy Press, 2003), 97.

157. Hazel Blears MP, interview by author, London, June 29, 2010.

158. Liz Troni and Tracy Komblatt, *City Markets: Business Location in Deprived Areas* (London: Center for Cities, 2006).

159. Gordon Brown MP, speech, October 2003.

160. Brownill, "London Docklands Revisited."

161. Michael Heseltine, interview by author, London, July 7, 2009.

162. Gerry Stoker, *Transforming Local Governance: From Thatcherism to New Labour* (New York: Palgrave Macmillan, 2003); also see Allan Cochrane, *Understanding Urban Policy: A Critical Approach* (Malden, Mass.: Blackwell, 2007).

163. Stuart Wilks-Heeg, "Economy, Equity or Empowerment? New Labour, Communities and Urban Policy Evaluation," in *Urban Renaissance? New Labour, Community and Urban Policy*, ed. Mike Raco and Robert Imrie (Bristol, U.K.: Policy Press, 2003), 210.

164. Department of the Environment, Transport and the Regions, *Regeneration Programmes—The Way Forward* (London: HMSO, 1997).

165. Department of the Environment, Transport and the Regions, *Towards an Urban Renaissance*, 49.

166. Social Exclusion Unit, *Bringing Britain Together: A National Strategy for Neighbourhood Renewal* (London: HMSO, 1998).

167. Hastings, "Strategic, Multilevel Neighbourhood Regeneration."

168. Mike Raco and Robert Imrie, eds., *Urban Renaissance? New Labour, Community and Urban Policy* (Bristol, U.K.: Policy Press, 2003), 27–29.

169. Jon Cruddas, interview by author, London, June 21, 2010.

170. Jessop, "Liberalism, Neoliberalism, and Urban Governance," 108.

171. Anthony Giddens, *The Third Way and Its Critics* (Cambridge, U.K.: Polity Press, 2000), 30.

172. Ibid., 35.

173. Ibid., 34.

174. Ibid., 52.

175. Ibid., 53.

176. Ibid., 100.

177. Michael Porter, "The Competitive Advantage of the Inner City," *Harvard Business Review* 73.3 (1995): 55–71.

178. Weir, "Political Parties and Social Policy Making."

179. Skowronek, *The Politics Presidents Make*, 455.

180. For a riveting, albeit journalistic, account see Woodward, *The Agenda*.

181. Hay, *The Political Economy of New Labour*; Heffernan, *New Labour and Thatcherism*; Shaw, *Losing Labour's Soul?*; Mark Wickham-Jones, "The Future of Socialism and New Labour: An Appraisal," *The Political Quarterly* 78.2 (2007): 224–240.

182. Peck and Tickell, "Neoliberalizing Space," 41.

183. Weir, "Political Parties and Social Policy Making"; Pierson and Skocpol, *The Transformation of American Politics*.

184. Skowronek, *The Politics Presidents Make*, 449.

185. Harvey, *A Brief History of Neoliberalism*, 19.

186. Wickham-Jones, "Signaling Credibility."

187. Hay, *The Political Economy of New Labour*; Heffernan, *New Labour and Thatcherism*.

188. Jessop, "Liberalism, Neoliberalism, and Urban Governance."

189. Matthijs, *Ideas and Economic Crises in Britain from Attlee to Blair (1945–2005)*, 161.

190. Blyth, *Great Transformations*, 201.

191. Blair, *A Journey*, xvi. "Liberal" here refers to classical liberalism, not the postwar American meaning of the word.

Chapter 4

1. U.S. Census Bureau, *Table DP-3 Profile of Selected Economic Characteristics: 2000, Philadelphia City, Pennsylvania, 2000* (Washington D.C.: U.S. Census Bureau).

2. The Brookings Institution Center of Urban and Metropolitan Policy, *Philadelphia in Focus: A Profile from Census 2000* (Washington, D.C.: Brookings Institution, 2003).

3. Kantor, *The Dependent City Revisited*, 3–4. This view is especially true of those working in the pluralist tradition such as Floyd Hunter, *Community Power Structure: A Study of*

Decision Makers (Garden City, N.Y.: Anchor Books, 1963), and Robert Alan Dahl, *Who Governs? Democracy and Power in an American City* (New Haven, Conn.: Yale University Press, 1961). In contrast, the following scholars are closely attuned to concerns about the effect of national-level forces on urban politics: Mollenkopf, *The Contested City*; Logan and Molotch, *Urban Fortunes*; Stone, *Regime Politics*; Savitch and Kantor, *Cities in the International Marketplace*; Dreier, Mollenkopf, and Swanstrom, *Place Matters*.

4. This view is informed by scholars within the subfields of historical institutionalism and American political development.

5. See, for example, Stein, *Pivotal Decade*; Judd and Swanstrom, *City Politics*; Guian A. McKee, *The Problem of Jobs: Liberalism, Race, and Deindustrialization in Philadelphia* (Chicago: University of Chicago Press, 2008).

6. O'Connor, "The Privatized City."

7. Peterson, *City Limits*; Fainstein et al., *Restructuring the City*.

8. Philadelphia prohibits mayors from governing for more than two consecutive terms. In 1979, Rizzo attempted to change the city charter in order to run again. He lost the referendum.

9. See various accounts in W. Wilson Goode, *In Goode Faith: Philadelphia's First Black Mayor Tells His Story* (Valley Forge, Pa.: Judson Press, 1992); Richard A. Keiser, "After the First Black Mayor: Fault Lines in Philadelphia's Biracial Coalition," in *Racial Politics in American Cities*, ed. Rufus P. Browning, Dale Rogers Marshall, and David H. Tabb, 2nd ed. (New York: Longman, 1997), 65–93.

10. Reed, *Stirrings in the Jug*, 99.

11. See Richard Gendron and G. William Domhoff, *The Leftmost City: Power and Progressive Politics in Santa Cruz* (Boulder, Colo.: Westview Press, 2009), and Pierre Clavel, *Activists in City Hall: The Progressive Response to the Reagan Era in Boston and Chicago* (Ithaca, N.Y.: Cornell University Press, 2010).

12. Peterson, *City Limits*.

13. Logan and Molotch, *Urban Fortunes*.

14. Harvey Molotch, "Urban Deals in Comparative Perspective," in *Beyond the City Limits: Urban Policy and Economic Restructuring in Comparative Perspective*, ed. John R. Logan and Todd Swanstrom (Philadelphia: Temple University Press, 1990), 17.

15. By "pro-growth," Logan and Molotch do not simply mean those policies that tend to favor growth but instead to denote a politics that promotes growth virtually at all costs. Logan and Molotch, *Urban Fortunes*.

16. Stone, *Regime Politics*.

17. See especially Stone, "Systemic Power in Community Decision Making."

18. See, for example, John R. Logan and Todd Swanstrom, eds., *Beyond the City Limits: Urban Policy and Economic Restructuring in Comparative Perspective* (Philadelphia: Temple University Press, 1990).

19. Rogers M. Smith, "Ideas and the Spiral of Politics: The Place of American Political Thought in American Political Development," *American Political Thought* 3.1 (2014): 126–136.

20. Hackworth, *The Neoliberal City*, 201.

21. Roger D. Simon, *Philadelphia: A Brief History* (University Park: Pennsylvania Historical Association, 2003), 57.

22. Jerome I. Hodos, *Second Cities: Globalization and Local Politics in Manchester and Philadelphia* (Philadelphia: Temple University Press, 2011).

23. Carolyn Teich Adams, David Bartlet, David Elesh, Ira Goldstein, Nancy Kleniewski, and William Yancy, *Philadelphia: Neighborhoods, Division, and Conflict in a Postindustrial City* (Philadelphia: Temple University Press, 1991), 14.

24. Ibid., 37.

25. U.S. Census Bureau, *Table DP-3 Profile of Selected Economic Characteristics: 2000, Philadelphia City, Pennsylvania, 2000.*

26. Thomas F. Luce and Anita A. Summers, *Local Fiscal Issues in the Philadelphia Metropolitan Area* (Philadelphia: University of Pennsylvania Press, 1987); Adams et al., *Philadelphia*. The "service sector" category includes business and legal services, education, health, and consulting.

27. Hodos, *Second Cities*.

28. Michael Peter Smith, *City, State, & Market* (Oxford, U.K.: Basil Blackwell, 1988).

29. Ibid.

30. Judd and Swanstrom, *City Politics*, 275.

31. Stephen Metraux, "Waiting for the Wrecking Ball: Skid Row in Postindustrial Philadelphia," *Journal of Policy History* 29.5 (1999): 691–716.

32. Ibid., 695.

33. Ibid., 696.

34. Kantor, *The Dependent City Revisited*, 144–145.

35. For details, see Martin Shefter, *Political Crisis, Fiscal Crisis: The Collapse and Revival of New York City* (New York: Basic Books, 1985).

36. This was the nickname given to the groups of Chilean economists who trained under Milton Friedman and returned to Chile to apply austerity measures and mass privatization following Pinochet's coup d'état of 1973. Inflation was tamed, and Chile became the fastest growing economy in South America. However, inequality soared and unemployment reached 30 percent.

37. For details, see R. Andrew Parker, "A Stealth Urban Policy in the US? Federal Spending in Five Large Metropolitan Regions, 1984–93," *Urban Studies* 34.11 (1997): 1831–1850.

38. Stein, *Pivotal Decade*.

39. Dilworth successfully ran as a reform candidate for district attorney in 1951 and served during Clark's term.

40. Lincoln Steffens, "Philadelphia: Corrupt and Contented" *McLures Magazine* (July 1903).

41. Adams et al., *Philadelphia*, 113.

42. McKee, *The Problem of Jobs*, 19–20.

43. James Wolfinger, *Philadelphia Divided: Race & Politics in the City of Brotherly Love* (Chapel Hill: University of North Carolina Press, 2007), 230–233.

44. McKee, *The Problem of Jobs*, 30. McKee points out that the key distinction between the New Deal coalition and the Clark-Dilworth alliance was the absence of an equivalent to the Southern Democrats. Also see Adams et al., *Philadelphia*, 125.

45. Wolfinger, *Philadelphia Divided*, 231.

46. McKee, *The Problem of Jobs*, 38. As scholars such as Mancur Olson have shown, for any societal group to achieve a given political outcome, coordination among the constituent

parts of a given group is a key challenge that must be overcome in order for cooperation around a shared goal to be achieved. This is often done through the creation of institutions—in Philadelphia, the Chamber of Commerce and the Greater Philadelphia Movement were such institutions.

47. See Matthew J. Countryman, *Up South: Civil Rights and Black Power in Philadelphia* (Philadelphia: University of Pennsylvania Press, 2006), chap. 4.

48. Adams et al., *Philadelphia*, 126–127; McKee, *The Problem of Jobs*, 72–73; Keiser, "After the First Black Mayor," 67–69.

49. Countryman, *Up South*, 153.

50. Keiser, "After the First Black Mayor," 69. Keiser notes that many of these jobs are menial, entry-level positions.

51. McKee, *The Problem of Jobs*, 73.

52. Keiser, "After the First Black Mayor," 70.

53. The candidates in the 1971 Democratic primary election were Frank Rizzo, Bill Green, and Anthony "Hardy" Williams.

54. Keiser, "After the First Black Mayor," 82.

55. Ibid., 71.

56. Mollenkopf, *The Contested City*; Judd and Swanstrom, *City Politics*.

57. Quoted in S. A. Paolantonio, *Frank Rizzo: The Last Big Man in Big City America* (Philadelphia: Camino Books, 1993), 146.

58. Ibid., 147.

59. Ibid., 251.

60. Ibid., 154.

61. Adams et al., *Philadelphia*, 141.

62. Ibid.

63. For details of white racial violence and extremism, see Wolfinger, *Philadelphia Divided*.

64. Countryman, *Up South*.

65. See McKee, *The Problem of Jobs*.

66. Stephen Samuel Smith, *Boom for Whom? Education, Desegregation, and Development in Charlotte* (Albany: State University of New York Press, 2004); Stone, *Regime Politics*.

67. Adams et al., *Philadelphia*, 141.

68. Keiser, "After the First Black Mayor," 73.

69. Ibid.

70. Ibid., 74.

71. Luce and Summers, *Local Fiscal Issues in the Philadelphia Metropolitan Area*, 217.

72. Roger D. Simon and Brian Alnutt, "Philadelphia, 1982–2007: Toward the Postindustrial City," *The Pennsylvania Magazine of History and Biography* 131.4 (October 2007): 396.

73. Keiser, "After the First Black Mayor," 74.

74. Paolantonio, *Frank Rizzo*, 254.

75. Ibid.

76. Judd and Swanstrom, *City Politics*, 224.

77. Timothy Barnekov and Douglas Hart, "The Changing Nature of US Urban Policy Evaluation: The Case of the Urban Development Action Grant," *Urban Studies* 30.9 (1993): 1469–1483.

78. Dreier, Mollenkopf, and Swanstrom, *Place Matters*, 138.

79. Robert P. Inman, "How to Have a Fiscal Crisis: Lessons from Philadelphia," *The American Economic Review* 85.2 (1995): 380.

80. Carolyn Teich Adams, "Philadelphia: The Slide Toward Municipal Bankruptcy," in *Big City Politics in Transition* (Newbury Park, Calif.: Sage, 1991), 38.

81. Judith Goode, "Polishing the Rustbelt: Immigrants Enter a Restructuring Philadelphia," in *Newcomers in the Workplace: Immigrants and the Restructuring of the U.S. Economy* (Philadelphia: Temple University Press, 1994), 201.

82. Inman notes that while Philadelphia continued to get its "fair share" of federal dollars (i.e., the same per capita as their national counterparts), Philadelphians only received $0.61 for every $1.00 of federal aid that went to Pennsylvanians. See Inman, "How to Have a Fiscal Crisis," 380.

83. Mossberger, *The Politics of Ideas and the Spread of Enterprise Zones*.

84. Press Release, Governor's Press Office, October 29, 1982, 1, Thornburgh Papers, available online at http://digital.library.pitt.edu/cgi-bin/t/text/text-idx?idno = AIS9830.11.02.0953;view = toc;c = thornnewsreleases.

85. Ibid., 2.

86. Ibid. As it turned out, of course, the federal zones were not created until Bill Clinton introduced the Empowerment Zones/Enterprise Community legislation in 1994.

87. Quoted in R. Duane Perry, *Enterprise Zones in Pennsylvania*, report for Mayor William Green (Philadelphia: Philadelphia City Planning Commission, July 1982).

88. Ibid., 1.

89. Ibid., 5.

90. Ibid., 40.

91. Perry, *Enterprise Zones in Pennsylvania*.

92. R. Duane Perry, interview by author, August 31, 2010.

93. Perry, *Enterprise Zones in Pennsylvania*, 6.

94. R. Duane Perry, interview by author, August 31, 2010.

95. Jan Schaffer, "City Selects 9 Areas for 'Enterprise,'" *Philadelphia Inquirer*, January 28, 1982.

96. Quoted in Jan Schaffer, "Enterprise-Zone Plan Is on the Table, and Skeptics Find Problems Aplenty," *Philadelphia Inquirer*, January 31, 1982.

97. Editorial, "Our Opinion: The Enterprise Zone Concept," *Philadelphia Tribune*, July 20, 1982.

98. Valeria M. Russ, "Executives Cool to Enterprise Zone Idea," *Philadelphia Daily News*, September 10, 1982.

99. Jim Davis, "Enterprise Zone Concept Urged for N. Phila.," *Philadelphia Tribune*, March 29, 1983.

100. Brian P. Sullivan, "Enterprise Zones Stir Little Interest Here, Poll Says," *Philadelphia Inquirer*, September 10, 1982.

101. Ibid.

102. Sherri Leronda Wallace, "A Case Study of the Enterprise Zone Program: 'EZ' Avenue to Minority Economic Development?," *Economic Development Quarterly* 13.3 (1999): 260.

103. The Philadelphia Enterprise Program, "Something Is Happening in Philadelphia: Philadelphia's Enterprise Zones" (Philadelphia: Philadelphia Enterprise Program, 1996).

104. Stephen Horton, interview by author, The Enterprise Center, Philadelphia, September 14, 2010.

105. Simon and Alnutt, "Philadelphia, 1982–2007," 405.

106. Jerome I. Hodos, "Globalization, Regionalism, and Urban Restructuring," *Urban Affairs Review* 37.3 (2002): 346.

107. Ibid., 364.

108. Adams et al., *Philadelphia*, 142.

109. John F. Bauman, "W. Wilson Goode: The Black Mayor as Urban Entrepreneur," *The Journal of Negro History* 77.3 (1992): 146; Albert K. Karnig and Susan Welch, eds., *Black Representation and Urban Policy* (Chicago: University of Chicago Press, 1980).

110. Richard A. Keiser, *Subordination or Empowerment? African-American Leadership and the Struggle for Urban Political Power* (New York: Oxford University Press, 1997), 99.

111. Ibid., 113.

112. Matthew J. Countryman, "'From Protest to Politics,'" *Journal of Urban History* 32.6 (2006): 813–861.

113. Ibid., 849.

114. Keiser, "After the First Black Mayor," 77. Also see Simon and Alnutt, "Philadelphia, 1982–2007"; Robert A. Beauregard, "Tenacious Inequalities," *Urban Affairs Review* 25.3 (1990): 420–434; Adams et al., *Philadelphia*.

115. Quoted in Keiser, *Subordination or Empowerment?* 114.

116. Adams et al., *Philadelphia*, 142; Bauman, "W. Wilson Goode," 149.

117. Countryman, "'From Protest to Politics,'" 849.

118. Simon and Alnutt, "Philadelphia, 1982–2007," 407; Bauman, "W. Wilson Goode," 149.

119. Russell Cooke, "Goode Looking for Unity with Council, Ex-Opponents," *Philadelphia Inquirer*, November 11, 1983. Also see Adams et al., *Philadelphia*, 142.

120. Russell Cooke and Roger Cohn, "Goode Fills Commerce Position," *Philadelphia Inquirer*, November 16, 1983.

121. Simon and Alnutt, "Philadelphia, 1982–2007," 416.

122. Ibid., 418. Also see David W. Bartlet, "Renewing Center City Philadelphia: Whose City? Which Public's Interests?" in *Unequal Partnerships: The Political Economy of Urban Redevelopment in Postwar America*, ed. Gregory D. Squires (New Brunswick, N.J.: Rutgers University Press, 1989), 80–102.

123. Simon and Alnutt, "Philadelphia, 1982–2007," 418.

124. Associated Press, "Lasers Etch Sky for New Skyscraper," *Philadelphia Daily News*, December 13, 1986.

125. Bartlet, "Renewing Center City Philadelphia," 97.

126. For the transatlantic comparison, see Harvey, "From Managerialism to Entrepreneurialism."

127. Beauregard, "Tenacious Inequalities," 426–427.

128. Keiser, "After the First Black Mayor," 81.

129. Adams et al., *Philadelphia*, 145.

130. Stone, *Regime Politics*.

131. See, for example, Kantor and Savitch, "Can Politicians Bargain with Business?"

132. Reed, *Stirrings in the Jug*, 107.

133. Ibid.

134. Peterson, *City Limits*.

135. For details see Michael Boyette, *"Let It Burn!" The Philadelphia Tragedy* (Chicago: Contemporary Books, 1989).

136. Simon and Alnutt, "Philadelphia, 1982–2007," 410.

137. Bauman, "W. Wilson Goode," 152–153.

138. Goode won 51.3 percent against Rizzo's 48.6 percent.

139. Keiser, *Subordination or Empowerment?* 123.

140. Ibid.

141. Keiser, "After the First Black Mayor," 79.

142. Huntly Collins, "For Him, Neighborhoods Are the Key," *Philadelphia Inquirer*, July 23, 1984.

143. Arthur Howe, "Revival City Agrees to Buy Site for Use as Industrial Park," *Philadelphia Inquirer*, June 1, 1985.

144. Peter Binzen, "Hope for the Other Philadelphia away from Center City, in Three Enterprise Zones, the City Is Trying to Encourage New Business and New Life," *Philadelphia Inquirer*, June 2, 1986.

145. Ibid.

146. Ibid.

147. John Claypool, interview by author, September 30, 2010.

148. "Prescription for Revival the American Street Enterprise Zone May Be Just the Cure for the City's Major Malady," *Philadelphia Inquirer*, October 3, 1989.

149. Leslie Scism, "The American S. Dream & Reality," *Philadelphia Daily News*, October 15, 1990.

150. Wallace, "A Case Study of the Enterprise Zone Program," 262.

151. "Jobs for the Ghetto Businesses Aren't Fond of Abandoned Areas, but Federal Tax Breaks Can Lure Them There," *Philadelphia Inquirer*, October 17, 1990.

152. Edward Rendell, U.S. House Hearings by the Subcommittee on Select Revenue Measures of the Ways and Means Committee Hearings, 102nd Cong., 1st Sess., July 11, 1991.

153. Ibid.

154. Peterson, *City Limits*.

Chapter 5

1. Peterson, *City Limits*, 12.

2. Ibid., 15.

3. Ibid., 28.

4. See these two edited volumes for the various critiques of the *City Limits* argument: Clarence N. Stone and Heywood T. Sanders, eds., *The Politics of Urban Development* (Lawrence: University Press of Kansas, 1987); Logan and Swanstrom, *Beyond the City Limits*.

5. Richard Edward DeLeon, *Left Coast City: Progressive Politics in San Francisco, 1975–1991* (Lawrence: University Press of Kansas, 1992); Clavel, *Activists in City Hall*.

6. Logan and Molotch, *Urban Fortunes*, 60.

7. Ibid., 62.

8. Ibid., 85. Emphasis added.

9. The Brookings Institution Center of Urban and Metropolitan Policy, *Philadelphia in Focus*.

10. See American Community Survey, 1-Year Estimates, 2010.

11. Inman, "How to Have a Fiscal Crisis," 378.

12. Ibid. In an attempt to ease the situation, Goode proposed an increase in the wage tax worth $65 million. However, these plans were rejected by the City Council.

13. Adams, "Philadelphia," 29.

14. Hackworth, *The Neoliberal City*, 22.

15. Robert P. Inman, "Philadelphia's Fiscal Management of Economic Transition," in *Local Fiscal Issues in the Philadelphia Metropolitan Area*, ed. Thomas F. Luce and Anita A. Summers (Philadelphia: University of Pennsylvania Press, 1987), 102.

16. Inman, "How to Have a Fiscal Crisis," 381.

17. The total number was 313,374. See U.S. Census, 1990.

18. See Marie McCullough, "City Fiscal Health Tied to State Aid," *Philadelphia Inquirer*, June 24, 1990.

19. Jospeh Gyourko and Anita A. Summers, "Philadelphia: Spatial Economic Disparities," in *Sunbelt/Frostbelt: Public Policies and Market Forces in Metropolitan Development*, ed. Janet Rothenberg Pack (Washington, D.C.: Brookings Institution Press, 2005), 110–139.

20. Despite Philadelphia's apparent financial stability, in 1978, the Pennsylvania Economy League urged the Philadelphia delegation to Harrisburg to introduce reforms to reduce state restrictions on the city's ability to raise revenue through taxes or borrowing. As Jenkins notes, Philadelphia's political leadership, which was sanguine about the city's financial state, failed to take up this opportunity even though it enjoyed significant political power in Harrisburg. Over time, the growth of the suburbs and shrinkage of the city's population would reduce the influence of the city's delegation. Therefore, the unintended consequence of this decision was to limit the options available to future administrations when the need to raise revenues arose. See Carol Jenkins, "The Miracle or Mirage of Local Governance? Mayor Rendell and the Philadelphia Fiscal Crisis" (Ph.D. diss., Temple University, 2001).

21. Inman, "How to Have a Fiscal Crisis," 383.

22. Neil Barsky, "Bootstrapping Mayor Raises Hope of Revival in, Yes, Philadelphia," *Wall Street Journal*, February 22, 1992.

23. See Inman, "Philadelphia's Fiscal Management of Economic Transition."

24. See Adams et al., *Philadelphia*; Keiser, *Subordination or Empowerment?* Street later went on to become president of the City Council (1992–1998) and mayor in 2000 until 2008.

25. Jenkins, "The Miracle or Mirage of Local Governance?" 96.

26. Gyourko and Summers, "Philadelphia," 110.

27. The members of the PICA board were Authority Chairman Bernard E. Anderson, an economist and management consultant; Executive Director Ronald G. Henry; Judith E. Harris; and Charles M. Andes. Only one was a politician—John Egan, the former Republican mayoral candidate.

28. It is instructive to note the similarities between the role of institutions such as PICA and those established by the International Monetary Fund and the World Bank. In both situations, funds are distributed to indebted governments on the condition that they agree to enact neoliberal reforms.

29. Marc Duvoisin, "PICA Rejects Draft of City Fiscal Plan. Goode Chides Members for Going Public," *Philadelphia Inquirer*, September 11, 1991.

30. Carolyn Teich Adams, David Bartlet, David Elesh, and Ira Goldstein, *Restructuring the Philadelphia Region: Metropolitan Divisions and Inequality* (Philadelphia: Temple University Press, 2008), 177.

31. Matthew Purdy, "Goode Plans for Layoffs New Draft Is Key to Pa. Board's Aid," *Philadelphia Inquirer*, October 6, 1991.

32. Editorial, "The Rescue Begins? The City Starts Its Crawl Back from the Brink," *Philadelphia Inquirer*, January 10, 1992.

33. In many respects, the urban politics literature, as with much of American political science more generally, pays too little attention to intraracial heterogeneity. Indeed, the assumption of racially induced preferences itself rests on racist ideology, as Reed points out. See Adolph L. Reed, *Class Notes: Posing as Politics and Other Thoughts on the American Scene* (New York: New Press, 2000).

34. Keiser, "After the First Black Mayor," 873.

35. Ibid., 87.

36. Edward Rendell, U.S. House Hearings by the Subcommittee on Select Revenue Measures of the Ways and Means Committee Hearings, 102nd Cong., 1st Sess., July 11, 1991.

37. Ibid.

38. Bill Clinton, speech, Los Angeles, September 16, 1992.

39. Edward Rendell, quoted in Marc Duvoisin, "Mayors Meet the Expansive Ed Rendell," *Philadelphia Inquirer*, January 24, 1992, A1.

40. Editorial, "Rendell's Priorities: Why He's Not Yearning for a Federal Bailout," *Philadelphia Inquirer*, January 26, 1992, C4.

41. Quoted in Anthony R. Wood, "Enterprise Zones Are Promoted Congress Gets a Rendell Plea," *Philadelphia Inquirer*, April 25, 1992, C10.

42. Donna Cooper, interview by author, June 24, 2011.

43. Vernon Loeb, "Rendell Plans a Push to Reap Funds from D.C. He Has an Ally in Clinton. He Says the City Could Get 'Substantial Aid' for Housing, Transit and the Poor," *Philadelphia Inquirer*, February 7, 1993, A1.

44. Donna Cooper, interview by author, June 24, 2011.

45. See Robert B. Reich, *Locked in the Cabinet* (New York: Knopf, 1997); Stiglitz, *The Roaring Nineties*.

46. Loeb, "Rendell Plans a Push to Reap Funds from D.C.," A1.

47. Nancy Haas, "Philadelphia Freedom: How Privatization Has Worked Wonders in the City of Brotherly Love and Beyond," *Financial World*, August 3, 1993; Stephen J. McGovern, "Mayoral Leadership and Economic Development Policy: The Case of Ed Rendell's Philadelphia," *Policy & Politics* 25.2 (1997): 154.

48. Quoted in Haas, "Philadelphia Freedom."

49. Osborne and Gaebler, *Reinventing Government*.

50. S. A. Paolantonio, "Rendell's Plan to Save Money Earns Him Unions' Wrath," *Philadelphia Inquirer*, February 21, 1991, B3.

51. S. A. Paolantonio, "Egan Starts with Jabs at Rendell," *Philadelphia Inquirer*, August 3, 1991, B1.

52. Lisa Ellis, "Key Committee of AFL-CIO Votes to Remain Neutral in Mayor's Race," *Philadelphia Inquirer*, August 28, 1991.

53. Keiser, *Subordination or Empowerment?* 124. Emphasis in original.

54. The results were Rendell, 146,373 (45.7 percent); Blackwell, 79,212 (24.7 percent); Burrell, 43,787 (13.7 percent); and Hearn, 26,353 (8.2 percent). See Committee of Seventy, "1991 Philadelphia Municipal Election Results," http://www.seventy.org/Elections_Past_Election_Results.aspx.

328 Notes to Pages 215–222

55. Simon and Alnutt, "Philadelphia, 1982–2007," 412.

56. There is some debate about the precise number. While Keiser suggests 50,000 voters switched parties, Jenkins suggests the number was closer to 40,000. See Keiser, "After the First Black Mayor"; Jenkins, "The Miracle or Mirage of Local Governance?"

57. There is some debate about this. While the black clergy insist this was Rendell's commitment, he denies it.

58. Paolantonio, *Frank Rizzo*, 359.

59. Keiser, "After the First Black Mayor," 88.

60. S. A. Paolantonio, "A Trip to City Hall for Rendell—in N.Y.," *Philadelphia Inquirer*, June 16, 1991.

61. S. A. Paolantonio, "Business Group Bucking History in Political Move," *Philadelphia Inquirer*, March 23, 1990. Other leading members of the Rubin Group include M. Walter D'Alessio, president of the mortgage and investment banking firm of Latimer & Buck, Inc.; Robert A. McClements Jr., chairman of Sun Co., Inc.; and Harold A. Sorgenti, president of Arco Chemical Co.

62. Doreen Carvajal and Marc Duvoisin, "For Most, a Contribution Is Like Money in the Bank," *Philadelphia Inquirer*, November 1, 1991.

63. S. A. Paolantonio, "Rendell Aims to Solidify His Political Foundation," *Philadelphia Inquirer*, November 10, 1991. Of the $50,000, the firm itself lent $40,000, while a partner in that firm, Robert J. F. Brobyn, lent $10,000.

64. The results were Rendell, 288,467 (59.5 percent), and Egan, 132,811 (27.4 percent). Three others won just under 20,000 votes. See Committee of Seventy, "1991 Philadelphia Municipal Election Results," http://www.seventy.org/Elections_Past_Election_Results.aspx.

65. Donna Cooper, interview by author, June 24, 2011. The Exxon Mobil executive was not a contributor to Rendell to Cooper's knowledge but did reflect the views of many in the corporate world who found Rendell's positions attractive.

66. Thomas Turcol, "Council, PICA Reach Accord on Labor Talks Members Also Approved the Transfer of the Port of History Museum," *Philadelphia Inquirer*, January 4, 1992.

67. See, for example, Jenkins, "The Miracle or Mirage of Local Governance?"

68. Dan Meyers, "City Didn't Expect Much from State, but Got Even Less," *Philadelphia Inquirer*, February 6, 1992.

69. Quoted in Jenkins, "The Miracle or Mirage of Local Governance?" 125.

70. See ibid.

71. Lisa Ellis, "Numbers Battle on Union Wages," *Philadelphia Inquirer*, March 8, 1992. One report was compiled by AFSCME and the other by the Washington consulting firm of Ruttenberg, Killgallon & Associates.

72. Ibid.

73. Imbroscio, *Urban America Reconsidered*.

74. H. G. Bissinger, *A Prayer for the City* (New York: Vintage, 1999), 106.

75. Lisa Ellis, "Labor's Love Lost over Five-Year Plan," *Philadelphia Inquirer*, March 5, 1992. The difference between the two figures rested on the definition of "management reforms." While the precise proportion of the total savings properly attributed to labor is controversial, it seems reasonable to suggest that the city's claim that workers would bear less than half of the burden is a significant underestimation since it fails to take into account the

cost of wages freezes and caps on overtime, both of which amount to approximately $300 million.

76. Marc Duvoisin and Dan Meyers, "Wall St. Warm to 5-Year Plan So Far So Good, Analysts Say. But Critics Call It Overly Optimistic on Federal and State Aid," *Philadelphia Inquirer*, February 22, 1992.

77. Jenkins, "The Miracle or Mirage of Local Governance?" 137–138.

78. Bissinger, *A Prayer for the City*, 112.

79. "Philadelphia (Horror) Story," *Wall Street Journal*, June 30, 1992.

80. "Philly Thinks Private," *Wall Street Journal*, June 30, 1992. It is worth noting how union members are differentiated from "taxpaying residents."

81. Bissinger, *A Prayer for the City*, 116.

82. Ibid.

83. Katz, *The Price of Citizenship*, 110; McGovern, "Mayoral Leadership and Economic Development Policy," 154.

84. Jenkins, "The Miracle or Mirage of Local Governance?"; Bissinger, *A Prayer for the City*.

85. Bissinger, *A Prayer for the City*, 151.

86. Neil Barsky, "Bootstrapping Mayor Raises Hope of Revival in, Yes, Philadelphia," *Wall Street Journal*, February 22, 1992.

87. Bissinger, *A Prayer for the City*, 279; Katz, *The Price of Citizenship*, 110. This moniker appears to have been picked up following a notable article by journalist Lisa DePaulo. See Lisa DePaulo, "How Many Ed Rendells Are There?" *Philadelphia Magazine*, April 1994.

88. Janet Ward, "Philadelphia Mayor Ed Rendell: 1996 Municipal Leader of the Year," *American City and Country*, November 1, 1996.

89. Hackworth, *The Neoliberal City*, 37.

90. See Clavel, *Activists in City Hall*.

91. See, for example, Imbroscio, *Urban America Reconsidered*.

92. Katz, *The Price of Citizenship*, 111.

93. Anthony R. Wood, "Enterprise Zones Are Promoted Congress Gets a Rendell Plea," *Philadelphia Inquirer*, April 25, 1992, C10.

94. Ibid.

95. Editorial, "An Urban Manifesto America Is Not Helpless to Deal with the Crises of Its Cities," *Philadelphia Inquirer*, May 6, 1992.

96. Ibid.

97. R. A. Zaldivar and Charles Green, *Philadelphia Inquirer*, May 10, 1992, C1.

98. Jeff Brown, "Urban Enterprise Zones: Examining the Record They Are Being Touted as the Cure for Inner-City Ills. Experts Say They Can Work, But . . .," *Philadelphia Inquirer*, May 31, 1992.

99. Ibid.

100. Sherri L. Wallace, personal email communication, June 6, 2010.

101. Bissinger, *A Prayer for the City*, 325.

102. While the EZ legislation was in conference committee, Senator Bill Bradley (D-NJ) inserted a requirement in the bill that one of the empowerment zones had to be bistate. See Vanessa Williams, "Staunchly Backing the Urban Renewal Plan, Sen. Bill Bradley Helped Write the Empowerment Zone Legislation," *Philadelphia Inquirer*, December 25, 1994.

103. Robert Nelson, interview by author, May 15, 2007.

104. Jeremy Nowak, telephone interview by author, March 28, 2007.

105. The other urban areas were Atlanta, Chicago, New York (Upper Manhattan), New York (Lower Bronx), Cleveland, Baltimore, Detroit, and Los Angeles.

106. Lori Montgomery, "Package Seen as a 'Mixed Bag' for Phila. and Many Other Cities There's New Money for Urban Empowerment Zones, but Block Grants and Public Housing Take Big Hits," *Philadelphia Inquirer*, February 8, 1994.

107. See Eric C. Twombly and Carol J. De Vita with Nadine Garrick, *Mapping Nonprofits in Philadelphia, Pennsylvania* (Washington, D.C.: The Urban Institute, October 2004), and Cities of Philadelphia and Camden, *Philadelphia and Camden Empowerment Zone Strategic Plan*, submitted to the Department of Housing and Urban Development, 1994.

108. Vanessa Williams, "Camden, Phila. Unite on Empowerment Zone After Weeks of Haggling," *Philadelphia Inquirer*, April 12, 1994.

109. Howard L. Nemon, "Challenges for Community Economic Development in Distressed Urban Neighborhoods: A Case Study of the Philadelphia Empowerment Zone" (PhD diss., University of Pennsylvania, 2002), 52.

110. Jeremy Nowak, interview by author, March 28, 2007.

111. Bissinger, *A Prayer for the City*, 289–290.

112. The geography of the zones is as follows: The North Philadelphia zone runs from 6th to 23rd and Poplar to Montgomery; the American Street zone includes an area that runs from Front to 6th and Girard to Lehigh; the West Philadelphia zone includes Parkside, Carroll Park, Cathedral Park, and Mill Creek. These areas compose a total of twelve census tracts, ten of which were situated within the boundaries of the Philadelphia part of the Model Cities Program of the 1960s. Moreover, some of the land within the American Street and West Philadelphia neighborhoods was also within a state enterprise zone.

113. Jeremy Nowak, telephone interview by author, March 28, 2007.

114. Philadelphia Empowerment Zone, *Momentum* (Philadelphia: Philadelphia Empowerment Zone, 2006), 18–19.

115. Ibid., 8, 19.

116. See, for example, M. Gittell, *Empowerment Zones: An Opportunity Missed—A Six-City Comparative Study* (New York: Howard Samuels State Management and Policy Center, The Graduate School and University Center of The City University of New York, 2001); Oakley and Tsao, "A New Way of Revitalizing Distressed Urban Communities?" 443–471; Temaner and Bennett, "Toward an Empowerment Zone Evaluation," 23–28; Government Accountability Office, *Empowerment Zone and Enterprise Community Program*; U.S. Department of Housing and Urban Development, *Empowerment Zones/Enterprise Communities, Annual Report*; Rich and Stoker, *Collaborative Governance for Urban Revitalization*.

117. Government Accountability Office, *Empowerment Zone and Enterprise Community Program*, 123.

118. Ibid., 122.

119. Ibid., 125.

120. Rojer Kern, interview by author, Philadelphia, April 4, 2007.

121. Ibid.

122. See Chapter 3.

123. Rich and Stoker, *Collaborative Governance for Urban Revitalization*, 121.

124. Donna Cooper, interview by author, Philadelphia, June 24, 2011.

125. These calculations are drawn from data from the 2000 Census and the 2007 American Community Survey using the Social Explorer application: http://www.socialexplorer.com/pub/home/home.aspx.

126. Nemon, "Challenges for Community Economic Development," 134.

127. Ibid., 134.

128. See Peter Nicholas, "HUD Audit Questions City on Spending," *Philadelphia Inquirer*, October 15, 1998.

129. Jim Smith, "Empowerment Zone Aide Jailed for Theft," *Philadelphia Inquirer*, October 9, 2002.

130. Paul Davies, "She Hasn't Delivered on Million $ Projects," *Philadelphia Daily News*, July 14, 1999.

131. Robert Nelson, interview by author, Philadelphia, May 15, 2007.

132. Ibid.

133. Rich and Stoker, *Collaborative Governance for Urban Revitalization*, 96.

134. Nathan Gorenstein, "Zone Lost 17 Pct. of People in a Decade," *Philadelphia Inquirer*, March 21, 2001.

135. McGovern, "Mayoral Leadership and Economic Development Policy."

136. Ibid., 158.

137. Ibid., 160.

138. Ibid., 165.

139. Hodos, "Globalization, Regionalism, and Urban Restructuring," 364. Emphasis in original.

140. Wolman, Hill, and Furdell, "Evaluating the Success of Urban Success Stories."

141. Ibid. "Experts" were members of the editorial boards of *Economic Development Quarterly*, *Housing Policy Debate*, the *Journal of Urban Affairs*, and the *Urban Affairs Review* and members of the executive boards of the International Economic Development Council and the Urban Land Institute.

142. It came 35th on income and education, 24th on jobs and population, 46th on poverty and unemployment, and 32nd on crime.

143. Philadelphia's composite score in 1990 was –2.95 and dropped to –4.23 in 2000.

144. Adams et al., *Restructuring the Philadelphia Region*, 62.

145. Carolyn Teich Adams, "The Meds and Eds in Urban Economic Development," *Journal of Urban Affairs* 25.5 (2003): 572.

146. Hackworth, *The Neoliberal City*, 37.

147. I borrow this term from Hodos, who uses it to describe the commitment to regionalism. See Hodos, "Globalization, Regionalism, and Urban Restructuring."

148. Adams et al., *Restructuring the Philadelphia Region*.

Chapter 6

1. Speech to the Bow Group entitled "Enterprise Zones and the Enterprise Zone Culture: Ten Years On," in Howe, *Enterprise Zones and the Enterprise Culture*, 24.

2. Janet Foster, *Docklands: Cultures in Conflict, Worlds in Collision* (London: UCL Press, 1999), 106.

3. A "ward" is the primary unit in the British electoral system. Each ward is usually represented by one councilor.

4. Brenner, Peck, and Theodore, "Variegated Neoliberalization."

5. See, for example, Gottschalk, *The Prison and the Gallows*; Pierson, *Dismantling the Welfare State?*; Prasad, *The Politics of Free Markets*.

6. See Gurr and King, *The State and the City*, 170–171.

7. Fainstein, *The City Builders*. Also see Duménil and Lévy, *Capital Resurgent*.

8. Massey, *World City*.

9. For a recent examination of the transformative role of ideas, see Béland and Cox, *Ideas and Politics in Social Science Research*.

10. Orren and Skowronek, *The Search for American Political Development*.

11. See, for example, Saskia Sassen, *The Global City: New York, London, Tokyo*, 2nd ed. (Princeton, N.J.: Princeton University Press, 2001); Massey, *World City*; Robert Imrie, Loretta Lees, and Mike Raco, eds., *Regenerating London: Governance, Sustainability and Community in a Global City* (London: Routledge, 2009). Also see Hamnett's work that suggests London's economic functions are primarily national rather than global in scope: Chris Hamnett, *Unequal City: London in the Global Arena* (London: Routledge, 2003).

12. Robert Imrie, Loretta Lees, and Mike Raco, "London's Regeneration," in *Regenerating London*, ed. Robert Imrie, Loretta Lees, and Mike Raco (London: Routledge, 2009), 3–23.

13. Foster, *Docklands*, 27.

14. Ibid., 39.

15. Dick Hobbs, *Doing the Business: Entrepreneurship, the Working Class, and Detectives in the East End of London* (Oxford: Clarendon Press, 1988), 128.

16. Foster, *Docklands*, 39.

17. Sue Brownill, *Developing London's Docklands: Another Great Planning Disaster?* (London: Paul Chapman Publishing Ltd, 1993), 21.

18. Andy Coupland, "Docklands: Dream or Disaster," in *The Crisis of London*, ed. Andy Thornley (London: Routledge, 1992), 149–162.

19. Brownill, *Developing London's Docklands*, 22.

20. Ibid.

21. For an in-depth description of the key groups involved, see Janet Foster's ethnographic study: Foster, *Docklands*.

22. Ibid., 49.

23. Quoted in ibid.

24. As Chapter 2 noted, Heath's government made its (in)famous U-turn when spiraling unemployment ended its brief neoliberal experiment.

25. Brownill, *Developing London's Docklands*, 22.

26. Initially, the forum had one member on the DJC. This was later increased to two.

27. Quoted in Brownill, *Developing London's Docklands*, 26.

28. See Coupland, "Docklands: Dream or Disaster," 152; Foster, *Docklands*, 51–52; Brownill, *Developing London's Docklands*, 27–29.

29. Howe, *Conflict of Loyalty*, 174.

30. Ibid., 110.

31. As mentioned in Chapter 2, the Bow Group was founded in the 1950s to counter the left-wing Fabian Society. Its raison d'être is "to provide a forum for the development of Conservative Party policy and to transmit the ideas of its members to the wider public."

32. Howe, *Conflict of Loyalty*, 10.

33. Geoffrey Howe, "Liberating Free Enterprise: A New Experiment," speech to the Bow Group, London, June 26, 1978, reproduced in Howe, *Enterprise Zones and the Enterprise Culture*, 7.

34. Ibid., 8.

35. Ibid., 8–9.

36. Ibid., 11.

37. Sir Geoffrey Howe, interview by author, House of Lords, London, July 7, 2009.

38. Howe, *Conflict of Loyalty*, 110.

39. Geoffrey Howe, "Enterprise Zones and the Enterprise Zone Culture: Ten Years On," speech to the Bow Group, South Quay, Isle of Dogs, June 26, 1988, reproduced in Howe, *Enterprise Zones and the Enterprise Culture*, 23.

40. Hansard, HC Deb., March 26, 1980, cc981–1439.

41. Fainstein, *The City Builders*, 182; Coupland, "Docklands: Dream or Disaster," 155.

42. See Mossberger, *The Politics of Ideas and the Spread of Enterprise Zones*, 18–23.

43. Butler, *Enterprise Zones*; Hall, "The British Enterprise Zones."

44. Foster, *Docklands*, 80.

45. Quoted in ibid., 81.

46. Coupland, "Docklands: Dream or Disaster," 155.

47. Department of the Environment, *Enterprise Zone Information: 1981–1994* (London: HMSO, 1995). All values are in 1994 prices.

48. Ibid., 9.

49. Ibid., 12.

50. Ibid., 30.

51. Department of the Environment, Transport and the Regions, *Regenerating London Docklands* (London: HMSO, 1998).

52. Fainstein, *The City Builders*, 181–185.

53. See Fainstein, *The City Builders*; Coupland, "Docklands: Dream or Disaster"; Brownill, *Developing London's Docklands*.

54. Fainstein, *The City Builders*, 183.

55. Eric Sorensen, interview by author, Guildhall, London, March 10, 2011.

56. Fainstein, *The City Builders*, 183.

57. Quoted in ibid., 187.

58. Foster, *Docklands*.

59. Brownill, *Developing London's Docklands*, 186.

60. Also see Anna Minton, *Ground Control: Fear and Happiness in the Twenty-First-Century City* (London: Penguin Books, 2009); Nick Buck, Ian Gordon, Peter Hall, Michael Harloe, and Mark Kleinman, *Working Capital: Life and Labour in Contemporary London* (London: Routledge, 2002); Hamnett, *Unequal City*; Sassen, *The Global City*.

61. Fainstein, *The City Builders*, 190.

62. Canary Wharf Group PLC, *2010 Report and Financial Statements* (London: Canary Wharf Group, 2010), 4.

63. John Barnes, Bob Colenutt, and Patrick Malone, "London: Docklands and the State," in *City, Capital, and Water*, ed. Patrick Malone (London: Routledge, 1996), 15.

64. Quoted in Brownill, *Developing London's Docklands*, 30.

65. Local Government, Planning and Land Act 1980 (c.65), section 136.

66. Lawless, *Britain's Inner Cities*, 82.

67. Heseltine, *Life in the Jungle*, 215.

68. Connell, "Ending the Blight of London Dockland," 11.

69. Lawless, *Britain's Inner Cities*, 82.

70. Quoted in Keith Shaw, "Doing Something About Those Inner Cities: Conservative Urban Policies in the 1980s," *Public Policy and Administration* 5.1 (1990): 65. Broackes was knighted for his services to Docklands in 1984.

71. Ibid.

72. Reg Ward quoted in Brownill, *Developing London's Docklands*, 52.

73. Quoted in Brian Edwards, *London Docklands: Urban Design in an Age of Deregulation* (Oxford, U.K.: Butterworth Architecture, 1992), 175.

74. Quoted in Foster, *Docklands*, 94.

75. Ibid., 94.

76. Nigel Broackes, quoted in ibid., 70.

77. Foster, *Docklands*, 70.

78. Fainstein, *The City Builders*, 178.

79. See Foster, *Docklands*, 123–129.

80. Department of the Environment, Transport and the Regions, *Regenerating London Docklands*.

81. Ibid.

82. Fainstein, *The City Builders*, 11.

83. Colin Hay, "Labour's Thatcherite Revisionism: Playing the Politics of Catch-up," *Political Studies* 42.4 (1994): 700–707; Hay, *The Political Economy of New Labour*.

84. Imbroscio, *Urban America Reconsidered*.

85. Shaw, "Doing Something About Those Inner Cities," 65.

86. Foster, *Docklands*, 105.

87. Ibid., 104.

88. Ibid., 95.

89. For example, the JDAG and Docklands Forum, Docklands Museum, Isle of Dogs.

90. See "London Docklands Study: Proposed Urban Development Corporation—Pressure Group Correspondence," National Archives, London, Box AT 41/325.

91. R. V. Colyer to Reverend Paul E. Regan, December 19, 1979, National Archives, London, Box AT 41/325.

92. Michael Heseltine to Kevin Halpin, May 2, 1980, National Archives, London, Box AT 41/325.

93. See "Petition Against an Urban Development Corporation for Docklands," July 25, 1980, in "London Docklands Study: Proposed Urban Development Corporation—Pressure Group Correspondence," National Archives, London, Box AT 41/325.

94. In the meantime, a shadow UDC was set up with an office in the Isle of Dogs in 1980.

95. House of Lords, *Report of House of Lords Select Committee on the London Docklands Development Corporation (Area and Constitution) Order* (London: HMSO, 1981).

96. Ibid., 9.

97. Ibid.

98. Ibid., 13.

99. Ibid., 14.

100. Ibid., 10.

101. For details of local opposition to the LDDC, see especially Brownill, *Developing London's Docklands*; Foster, *Docklands*.

102. Brownill, *Developing London's Docklands*, 127.

103. Roger Tym and Partners, "The Potential of Future Docks Use of the Royals," report for the Greater London Council (London: n.p., 1983).

104. Brownill, "London Docklands Revisited: The Dynamics of Waterfront Development."

105. Stephen Timms, interview by author, East Ham, London, August 28, 2008.

106. Local Docklands resident, quoted in Foster, *Docklands*, 106.

107. Johnstone and Whitehead, *New Horizons in British Urban Policy*.

108. Hill, *Urban Policy and Politics in Britain*.

109. Johnstone and Whitehead, *New Horizons in British Urban Policy*, 8.

110. Ibid.

111. In ibid., 144.

112. Quoted in Massey, *World City*, 93.

113. Raco and Imrie, *Urban Renaissance?*

114. Peck, *Workfare States*.

115. Blair, *A Journey*, 232.

116. Raco and Imrie, *Urban Renaissance?* 17.

117. Buck et al., *Working Capital*, 64.

118. Gareth Hoskins and Andrew Tallon, "Promoting the 'Urban Idyll': Policies for City Centre Living," in *New Horizons in British Urban Policy: Perspectives on New Labour's Urban Renaissance*, ed. Craig Johnstone and Mark Whitehead (Aldershot, U.K.: Ashgate, 2004), 25–40.

119. Hamnett, *Unequal City*, 15.

120. Ibid., 248.

121. Jim Fitzpatrick MP, interview by author, London, June 30, 2010.

122. London Borough of Tower Hamlets Corporate Research Unit, *Indices of Deprivation 2010*, June 2011, http://www.towerhamlets.gov.uk/lgsl/901-950/916_borough_statistics/research_and_briefings/income_and_poverty.aspx. These data suggest that Fainstein's conclusion that "Docklands development can be judged to have been be reasonably equitable" is unsustainable. See Susan S. Fainstein, *The Just City* (Ithaca, N.Y.: Cornell University Press, 2010), 124.

123. Hamnett, *Unequal City*, 149.

124. Audit Commission, *Tower Hamlets: Area Assessment* (London: Audit Commission, 2009).

125. Brownill, "London Docklands Revisited: The Dynamics of Waterfront Development"; Brownill, *Developing London's Docklands*.

126. Brownill, "London Docklands Revisited: The Dynamics of Waterfront Development," 129.

127. Ibid., 138.

128. Mike Raco, "Sustainable Development, Rolled-Out Neoliberalism and Sustainable Communities," *Antipode* 37.2 (2005): 324–347.

129. Quoted in ibid., 129.

130. Barnes, Colenutt, and Malone, "London: Docklands and the State," 130.

131. See Introduction.

132. Peck and Tickell, "Neoliberalizing Space."

133. Fainstein, *The City Builders*; Logan and Molotch, *Urban Fortunes*. It is worth noting that Fainstein's account is not purely materialistic. Her analysis ultimately sees developers not in a rationalistic mode but as being involved in subjective constructions of their interests. In this sense, she opens the door to the kind of ideational account I offer here. However, for her, property developers are the drivers, whereas for me, the Docklands' early development was politically led.

134. Harvey, *A Brief History of Neoliberalism*; Brenner and Theodore, *Spaces of Neoliberalism*, 3.

135. This is a reversal of Lieberman's formulation. See Lieberman, "Ideas and Institutions in Race Politics."

Conclusion

1. Jon Cruddas, interview by author, London, June 21, 2010.

2. Donna Cooper, interview by author, Philadelphia, June 24, 2011.

3. Orren and Skowronek, *The Search for American Political Development*.

4. See, for example, Hay, *The Political Economy of New Labour*; Hay, "Ideas, Interests and Institutions in the Comparative Political Economy of Great Transformations"; King and Wickham-Jones, "From Clinton to Blair"; Heffernan, *New Labour and Thatcherism*; Blyth, *Great Transformations*; Harvey, *A Brief History of Neoliberalism*; David Harvey, *The Enigma of Capital: And the Crises of Capitalism* (New York: Oxford University Press, 2010).

5. Pierson, *Dismantling the Welfare State?*; Pierson and Skocpol, *The Transformation of American Politics*.

6. Jacob S. Hacker and Paul Pierson, "Winner-Take-All Politics: Public Policy, Political Organization, and the Precipitous Rise of Top Incomes in the United States," *Politics & Society* 38.2 (2010): 152–204; Hacker and Pierson, *Winner-Take-All Politics*.

7. Peck, *Constructions of Neoliberal Reason*, 9.

8. Karl Marx, *The Communist Manifesto: A Modern Edition* (London; New York: Verso, 1998), 37. My thanks to David Bateman for reminding me of this quote.

9. Paul Krugman, *End This Depression Now!* (New York: Norton, 2012).

10. Jon Cruddas, interview by author, London, June 21, 2010.

11. See John Nichols, "Detroit Bankruptcy Bankrupts Democracy," *The Nation*, December 3, 2013, http://www.thenation.com/blog/177433/detroit-bankruptcy-bankrupts-democracy.

12. Donna Cooper, interview by author, Philadelphia, June 24, 2011.

13. Michael D. Shear, "Obama Announces 'Promise Zones' in 5 Poor Areas," *New York Times*, January 10, 2014, A12.

14. Richard Hall, "Osborne Hopes to Kick-start Economy with Enterprise Zones," *The Independent*, August 18, 2011, http://www.independent.co.uk/news/uk/politics/osborne-hopes-to-kickstart-economy-with-enterprise-zones-2339697.html.

15. House of Commons, "Enterprise Zones," *Commons Library Standard Note*, SN/EP/5942, August 13, 2014, 3, http://www.parliament.uk/business/publications/research/briefing-papers/SN05942/enterprise-zones.

16. Andrew Sissons with Chris Brown, "Do Enterprise Zones Work?" *The Work Foundation*, February 2011, 3.

17. House of Commons, "Enterprise Zones," 6.

18. Jim Pickard, "UK Chancellor's Enterprise Zones Slow to Take Off," *Financial Times*, April 2, 2014, http://www.ft.com/intl/cms/s/0/c01ddaa4-b5c1-11e3-81cb-00144feabdc0.html#axzz3LuJMFeCC.

19. On ideas and austerity economics, see Mark Blyth, *Austerity: The History of a Dangerous Idea* (Oxford: Oxford University Press, 2013).

20. Andy Bloxham, "Canary Wharf Takes Legal Action to Keep Out Potential Occupy London Protesters," *The Telegraph*, November 3, 2011.

Index

Hamnett, Chris, 272, 332 n.11, 333 n.60
Harrington, William, 195
Harvey, David, 17, 88, 90, 166, 275, 292 n.49, 293 n.66, 309 n.91, 312 n.174, 324 n.126, 336 n.4
Hastings, Annette, 150
Hattersley, Roy, 123
Hay, Colin, 156, 292 n.46, 310 n.117, 312 nn. 170, 5, 314 n.59, 336 n.4
Hayek, Friedrich/Hayekian neoliberalism, 12–13, 29, 34, 72, 77–79, 84–85, 95, 245, 275, 306 n.22, 307 n.32
Healey, Dennis, 76–77, 306 n.17
Hearn, Peter, 210, 215, 327 n.54
Heath, Ted, 75–80, 97, 104, 251, 306 n.20, 332 n.24
Heffernan, Richard, 156, 292 n.46, 307 n.43, 312 nn. 170, 5, 314 n.59, 336 n.4
Heritage Foundation, 30, 32–35, 37, 41, 44, 53, 63, 67, 115, 296 n.52, 302 n.198, 304 n.229
Heseltine, Michael, 88–90, 97, 134, 151, 154; and critique of enterprise zones, 86; and the LDDC, 261–62, 266; and promotion of UDCs, 85, 245, 247; and "Tory philosophy," 85–86
Hill, Dilys, 309 n.92
Hill, Richard, 125, 293 n.66, 314 n.59
historical institutionalism, 6–7, 10, 102, 289 n.9, 290 n.19, 320 n.4
Hobbs, Dick, 250
Hodos, Jerome, 168, 238, 331 n.147
Hood, Christopher, and role of interests, institutions and ideas, 98
Hoskins, Gareth, 272
Howe, Geoffrey, 7, 31, 80, 102, 106, 245, 259; and economic policy, 79–83, 89, 132, 306 n.13, 307 n.32, 311 n.138; on London Docklands, 243, 266. See also enterprise zones (U.K.), and role of Geoffrey Howe

ideas: as blueprints, 26, 56, 70–71, 244, 305n.245; and Conservative Party, 74, 78–80, 95, 307n.31, 308n.50, 332n.31; definition of, 5; and Democrats, 66; and enterprise zones, 3, 9, 72–74, 83–85, 95–97 100, 104–7, 112, 118, 253–54, 273, 275–81; and ideational political development, 4–7, 9; in London Docklands,

244–45, 248, 253, 263, 275–76; in Philadelphia's political development, 162–63, 165, 200, 212–13, 218–19, 241; and Reagan administration, 25, 27, 29; in relation to institutions and interests, 3–4, 18, 41, 73–74, 98–107; role of, 1–2, 8–9, 11, 14, 16, 278, 332n.9, 337n.19; skepticism about, 7–8, 14, 74, 283n.68, 312n164; and the third way, 110–16, 120–22, 151, 156, 278; and urban theory, 14–15, 166–67, 201
Imbroscio, David, 221, 265, 289 n.5, 291 n.25, 329 n.91
inequality, 2, 20–21, 63, 73, 145, 153, 157, 191, 242, 280, 282, 321 n.36
inflation, 8, 11, 28, 75–77, 79–82, 84, 97, 104–7, 110, 124, 126–27, 132–33, 172–73, 187–88, 205, 264, 306 nn. 13, 16, 321 n.36
Inman, Robert, 203–4, 206, 287, 323 n.82
Institute for Public Policy Research (IPPR), 124
Institute of Directors, 99
Institute of Economic Affairs (IEA), 78–80, 306 n.22
institutions: and the "three new institutionalisms," 5, 390 n.19; and contrast between U.K. and U.S., 275; role of, 245–46, 248, 265, 270. See also historical institutionalism; ideas, in relation to institutions and interests
International Monetary Fund (IMF), 76, 252, 306 n.17, 326 n.28

Jackson, Maynard, 192
Jacobs, Jane, 33–34, 296 n.42
James, Joseph, 194–95
Jenkins, Carol, 222, 326 n.20, 328 n.56
Jenkins, Peter, 95, 305 nn.3–4, 310 n.113
Jessop, Bob, 156
Johnson, Douglas, 47
Johnson, Lyndon Baines, 11, 46, 122, 188
Johnstone, Craig, 270–71
Joint Docklands Action Group (JDAG), 251
Jones, Martin, 271, 318 n.143
Jordan, Grant, 95, 102, 309 n.92, 311 n.150
Joseph, Keith, 77–81, 85, 89, 306 nn.19–21, 307 nn. 32, 36
Judd, Dennis, 36, 293 n.66, 295 nn. 13, 18, 316 n.101, 320 n.5

Acknowledgments

Though this book bears only my name, there are many others upon whom its completion depended. Space does not allow me to pay full tribute to those whose help has been indispensable, but I would like to take this opportunity to thank my colleagues, friends, and family, as well as those people who enriched this book through agreeing to be interviewed and enabling me to access the numerous archives that I consulted.

This book would not have been written without Adolph Reed Jr., who offered tremendous support and enthusiasm for this project. His sharp analysis of urban politics and political economy helped me refine many of the arguments developed here. Moreover, Rogers Smith, despite being in high demand, provided invaluable feedback, and Marie Gottschalk offered incredibly detailed and helpful advice. Michael Katz, before his sad and untimely passing, provided characteristically insightful thoughts on the central ideas developed within. Desmond King deserves my thanks for his close reading of an early version Chapter 2. Thanks are also due to Elaine Simon, Susan Seifert, Richardson Dilworth, and the anonymous reviewers of the manuscript, whose extensive analysis strengthened the book immensely. I would also like to thank my colleagues at the University of Louisville who have lent support and encouragement as this project reached completion, not least David Imbroscio. Finally, I would like to thank my editor at the University of Pennsylvania Press, Peter Agree. In addition, I am grateful to Amanda Ruffner and Erica Ginsburg at the press for making the publication process so smooth.

The most engaging element of my research has been the interviews I have conducted in the United States and United Kingdom. I would like to thank all those who so generously shared their time, experience, and ideas with me. They are William Barnes, Marc Bendick, Hazel Blears MP, Sue Brownill, Santiago Burgos, Stuart Butler, Mary Cannon, John Claypool,

Donna Cooper, John Cruddas MP, Jim Fitzpatrick MP, Mike Gapes MP, Eva Gladstein, Sir Peter Hall, Lord (Michael) Heseltine, Joe Houldin, Steve Horton, Lord (Geoffrey) Howe, Robert Inman, Rojer Kern, Marjorie Margolies, Jeremy Nowak, Duane Perry, James Pinkerton, Lord (Richard) Rogers, Lord (Clive) Soley, Eric Sorensen, Stephen Timms MP, Susan Wachter, and Sherri Wallace.

Some of the most original findings of this book have emerged from poring over documents in archives. I would like in particular to offer my warm thanks to Diane Barrie at the Ronald Reagan Presidential Library, Andrew Riley at the Margaret Thatcher archives at Churchill College, Cambridge, and Colin Harris and Sheridan Westlake at the Conservative Party Archives at the Bodleian Library at Oxford University. Moreover, I would like to thank the staff at the Neil Kinnock archives at Churchill College, the Peter Shaw archives at the London School of Economics, the Port of London Authority archives in Docklands, and the Jack Kemp archives at Pepperdine University.

But books are not written in an academic vacuum. To get to the end, one needs to draw on the love, support, and fellowship of friends and family. As this project was in its infancy, my friend Daniel Stedman Jones was an effervescent presence. His own project on the emergence of neoliberalism has been an inspiration, and our conversations about British politics always provide much fun as well as great intellectual succor. Daniel Amsterdam has also been a wonderful friend whose enthusiasm for this project helped spur me on. Stephan Stohler and David Bateman have been office mates, intellectual interlocutors, and, above all, fantastic friends. Outside of academia, but only just, is Pitou Devgon, someone with an indefatigable thirst for learning, debate, and having a good time.

No one has provided more love and support throughout this project than my best friend, partner, and love of my life, Joanna. She has helped me in ways that she will never fully know. As this book developed, our family expanded first with Benjamin and then Noah. They remind me just how crucial it is to construct an alternative to a world corroded and divided by neoliberal practices.

My brother, Michael, must also be thanked for being a source of unwavering support and light relief throughout this process. Time spent with him on my various trips back to Europe has given me some of my most cherished memories of the past few years. But, none of this, of course, would have been possible without my wonderful parents, Eileen and Bryan Weaver, who have encouraged and supported me throughout my life and at every stage of my academic career. The impact of their loving support has been so great that I cannot explain it in lines. It is to them that I dedicate this book.